Data Structures with STL

William H. Murray
Chris H. Pappas

PH PTR

Prentice Hall PTR
Upper Saddle River, NJ 07458
www.phptr.com

ISBN 0-13-028927-2

90000

9 780130 289278

Library of Congress Cataloging-in-Publication Data available

Editorial/Production Supervision: *MetroVoice Publishing Services*
Acquisitions Editor: *Jill Pisoni*
Editorial Assistant: *Justin Somma*
Marketing Manager: *Bryan Gambrel*
Cover Design: *Nina Scuderi*
Cover Design Direction: *Jerry Votta*
Manufacturing Manager: *Alexis R. Heydt*
Buyer: *Maura Zaldivar*

PH PTR

Prentice-Hall, Inc.
Upper Saddle River, NJ 07458

Prentice Hall books are widely used by corporations and government agencies for training, marketing, and resale.

The publisher offers discounts on this book when ordered in bulk quantities.
For more information, contact Corporate Sales Department, phone: 800-382-3419;
fax: 201-236-7141; e-mail: corpsales@prenhall.com
Or write: Prentice Hall PTR
Corporate Sales Department
One Lake Street
Upper Saddle River, NJ 07458

Printed in the United States of America
10 9 8 7 6 5 4 3 2

ISBN 0-13-028927-2

Prentice-Hall International (UK) Limited, **London**
Prentice-Hall of Australia Pty. Limited, **Sydney**
Prentice-Hall Canada Inc., **Toronto**
Prentice-Hall Hispanoamericana, S.A., **Mexico**
Prentice-Hall of India Private Limited, **New Delhi**
Prentice-Hall of Japan, Inc., **Tokyo**
Pearson Education Asia Pte. Ltd.
Editora Prentice-Hall do Brasil, Ltda., **Rio de Janeiro**

Dedicated to
Pastor Fahrion

Contents

Foreword

Data structures is a course taken by every programming student in every college in the United States. A knowledge of data structures has been a fundamental part of every Computer Science curriculum since the early days of PLI and Pascal. Of course, data structures in now taught using the C++ language. Actually, data structure concepts are language independent.

Currently, there is a shift in both text book and trade books to teach data structures with objects. With the latest standards from the ANSI/ISO committee, you will find that the Standard Template Library (STL) incorporates many of the components featured in traditional data structures courses.

Typically, you will find books on data structures or books on the STL. However, we have failed to identify or find books that carefully weave the concepts of both data structures and the STL together. In this text, we will go beyond an introductory works and integrate (side by side) many of the concepts taught in a data structures course with the newest STL techniques.

As such, this book is an intermediate level book for students and programmers who have mastered the fundamentals of the C++ language. However, even at the intermediate level, this book will have a broad appeal to all programmers interested in both data structures and the STL.

This book is not intended to replace college level data structures books. Instead, this text is intended to supplement them with the latest STL concepts. With complete code examples, you should find the solutions to many of the programming problems that plague both students and programmers alike.

If you are involved with data structures—you need this book.

CHAPTER 1

Easing into Standard Template Library (STL) Using Arrays—STL Vector

Congratulations! Yes, *you* deserve a word of praise. By picking up this book you have indirectly implied that you are serious about your understanding of C, C++, Object-Oriented Programming (OOP), and state-of-the-art programming with STL (ANSI/ISO C++ Standard Template Library). Kudos for your desire to learn the most exciting addition to ANSI/ISO C++ and the powerful programming solutions STL enables.

STL is as revolutionary to programming as is Object-Oriented Programming. But like OOP, STL has its own design roots, philosophies, and use. Understanding STL is like jumping into several hundred thousand lines of code, written by other programmers. Your task is to "jump onboard" with the logic, definitions, and syntax that make the whole package function.

What Do I Need to Know to Use This Book?

Simply, an understanding of C++ and familiarity with objects. Each chapter begins with a discussion of how a Data Structures concept is implemented using standard C++ syntax and then moves into the STL counterpart. The introductory section of each chapter reviews and bootstraps your understanding of the Data Structures concept and then rolls that understanding over into the STL equivalent.

Why Do I Need Calculus When I Can Buy a Calculator?

As a student, did you ever ask yourself the question: "Why do I need __________ - 101 (fill in the blank with any required course) when I can buy a piece of technology that does it all for me? The answer you may have been given by your advisor might have gone along the lines, “This course will give you the fundamentals necessary to skillfully employ said technological device.” You, on the other hand, may have heard them say: “Yada, yada, yada, just take it,” and it wasn’t until you obtained your degree and started working that you discovered just how important those fundamentals really are!

The Complexity of Multiplatform Target Environments

From a programming point-of-view, today’s development environment is a hundred times more complex than a decade ago. Instead of PC application development targeting a standalone DOS text-mode environment, it must now deal with hundreds of PC clones and other popular competing platforms.

These new architectures have their own evolving operating systems and multitasking, multimedia capabilities. Add to this the typical Internet presence. In other words, today’s programming environment, programmed by a single developer, was once the domain of systems, communications, security, networking, and utility specialists all working as a team to keep the “mother ship,” or mainframe, up and running!

Something had to come along to enable application developers to keep pace with this ever-increasing resource management nightmare. Voila, enter C and C++. These new languages incorporated brand new programming capabilities to melt through this hidden iceberg of programming demands.

Unintentional Misuse or Ignorance of C/C++ Features

The biggest stumbling block to accessing these incredibly powerful C/C++ features is ignorance of their existence. In the real world, most experienced FORTRAN, COBOL, Pascal, PL/I, and Assembly Language programmers, when asked by their bosses to use a new language, taught themselves the new language! Why? Because, of course, the company wouldn’t give them the time off. They diligently studied nights and weekends on their own, and mapped their understanding of whatever language they knew well to the new language’s syntax.

This approach worked for decades as long as a programmer went from one “older high-level language,” to the next. Unfortunately, when it comes to C/C++, this approach leaves the diligent, self-motivated, learn-on-their-own employee fired and wondering what went wrong *this time?*

Here’s a very small example to illustrate the point. In COBOL, for instance, to increment a variable by 1, you would write:

```
accumulator = accumulator + 1;
```

Then one day the boss says you need to write the program in FORTRAN. You learn FORTRAN and rewrite the statement:

```
accumulator = accumulator + 1;
```

No problem. Then your company migrates to Pascal and once again you teach yourself the new syntax:

```
accumulator := accumulator + 1;
```

Ta da! Now your boss says that your million dollar code needs to be ported over to Microsoft Windows in C/C++. After a divorce, heart attack, and alcohol addiction you emerge feeling you have mastered Microsoft Windows/C/C++ logic and syntax and finally rewrite the statement:

```
iaccumulator = iaccumulator + 1;   //i for integer in Hungarian notation
```

and you get fired! The senior programmer, hired from a local two-year college, looks at your code and scoffs at your inept translation. Oh, sure, you got the idea behind Hungarian Notation (a C/C++ naming convention that precedes every variable's name with an abbreviation of its data type), but you created a literal statement *translation* instead of incorporating the efficiency alternatives available in C/C++.

Your senior programmer, green, twenty years younger than you, only knowing Microsoft Windows, C and C++ syntax, knew the statement should have been written:

```
iaccumulator++;
```

This statement, using the C/C++ increment operator, efficiently instructs the compiler to delete the double fetch/decode of the incorrectly written *translation*, and to treat the variable *iaccumulator* as its name implies—as an accumulator within a register, a much more efficient machine language encoding.

This extremely simple code example is only the beginning of hundreds of C/C++ language features waiting, like quicksand, to catch the unwary programmer.

Data Structures—The Course to Separate Hackers from Pros!

In a programmer's formal educational path, there stands a course typically called Data Structures, which statistically has an attrition rate of 50%. Why? Because it deals with two extremely efficient concepts—pointers, and dynamic memory allocation/deallocation—which when combined generate a geometric complexity in program development and debugging requirements. These concepts typically present such a steep learning curve that many programmers either avoid the course altogether, or lop along getting by, and then *never* use the concepts in the real world.

This is unfortunate since pointers and dynamic memory allocation present some of the most powerful and efficient algorithms available to a programmer. Enter the Standard Template Library!

So, Just What Is the Standard Template Library?

In a nutshell, STL encapsulates the pure raw horsepower of the C/C++ languages plus the advanced efficient algorithms engendered within a good Data Structures course, all bundled into a simple-to-use form! It is similar in a way to having struggled with years of pre-Calc and Calculus courses, only to be given an advanced portable calculator that does all the work for you.

You may view the Standard Template Library as an extensible framework which contains components for language support, diagnostics, general utilities, strings, locales, standard template library (containers, iterators, algorithms, numerics), and input/output.

The Origins of STL

With the ever-increasing popularity of C/C++ and Microsoft Windows-controlled environments, many third-party vendors evolved into extremely profitable commodities by providing libraries of routines designed to handle the storage and processing of data. In an ever-ongoing attempt to maintain C/C++'s viability as a programming language of choice, and to keep the ball rolling by maintaining a strict control of the languages' formal definition, the ANSI/ISO C++ added a new approach to defining these libraries called the Standard Template Library.

STL, developed by Alexander Stepanov and Meng Lee of Hewlett Packard, is expected to become the standard approach to storing and processing data. Major compiler vendors are beginning to incorporate the STL into their products. The Standard Template Library is more than just a minor addition to the world's most popular programming language; it represents a revolutionary new capability. The STL brings a surprisingly mature set of generic containers and algorithms to the C++ programming language, adding a dimension to the language that simply did not exist before.

What Do I Need to Know to Take Advantage of STL?

You have all you need to know right now, simply by picking up this book. Unlike many other STL books which simply enumerate endless lists of STL template names, functions, constants, etc., this book will begin by first teaching you the advanced C/C++ language fundamentals that make the Standard Template Library syntactically possible.

Along the way, this instructional section will show you the syntax that allows an algorithm to be generic; in other words, how C/C++ syntactically separate *what* a program does from the *data type(s)* it uses. You will learn about generic `void *` pointer's strengths and weaknesses, the "better way" with generic types, the "even better way" using templates, and finally, the "best way" with cross-platform, portable, Standard Templates.

The section on template development begins with simple C/C++ structures used syntactically to create *objects* (yes, you can create an object with this keyword; however it is a very bad idea—you'll have to wait until the next chapter to see why)! The `struct` object definition is then evolved over, logically and syntactically, into the C++ `class`. Finally, the `class` object is mutated into a generic `template`. This progressive approach allows you to easily assimilate the new features of C/C++ and paves the way to technically correct use of the STL. With this under your belt, you will logically and syntactically understand how the STL works and begin to immediately incorporate this technology into your application development.

Generic programming is going to provide you with the power and expressiveness of languages like SmallTalk while retaining the efficiency and compatibility of C++. STL is guaranteed to increase the productivity of any programmer who uses it.

A High-Level View of STL

Although the STL is large and its syntax can be initially intimidating, it is actually quite easy to use once you understand how it is constructed and what elements it employs. At the core of the STL are three foundational items called *containers, algorithms*, and *iterators*. These libraries work together allowing you to generate, in a portable format, frequently employed algorithmic solutions, such as array creation, element insertion/deletion, sorting, and element output. But the STL goes even further by providing internally clean, seamless, and efficient integration of iostreams and exception handling.

Kudos to the ANSI/ISO C++ Committee

Multivendor implementations of C/C++ compilers would have long ago died on the vine were it not for the ANSI C/C++ Committees. They are responsible for giving us *portable* C and C++ code by filing in the missing details for the formal language descriptions of both C and C++ as presented by their authors, Dennis Ritchie and Bjarne Stroustrup, respectively. And to this day, it is the ANSI/ISO C++ Committee that continues to guarantee C++'s portability into the next millennium.

The ANSI/ISO C++ committee's current standards exceed their past recommendations which historically decided only to codify existing practice and resolve ambiguities and contradictions among existing translator implementations. The C++ committee's changes are innovations. In most cases, the changes implement features that committee members admired in other languages, features that they view as deficiencies in traditional C++, or simply features that they've always wanted in a programming language. A great deal of thought and discussion has been invested in each change and, consequently, the committee feels that the new C++ definition, along with the evolutionary definition of STL, is the best definition of C++ possible today.

Most of these recommended changes consist of language additions that should not affect existing code. Old programs should still compile with newer compilers as long as the old codes do not coincidentally use any of the new keywords as identifiers. However, even experienced C++ programmers may be surprised at how much C++ has evolved without even discussing STL; take for example, the use of namespaces, new-style type casting, and runtime type information (discussed in detail in Chapter 2).

STL's Tri-Component Nature

Conceptually, STL encompasses three separate algorithmic problem solvers. The three most important are containers, algorithms, and iterators. A *container* is a way that stored data is organized in memory; for example, an array, stack, queue, linked list, or binary tree. However, there are many other kinds of containers, and the STL includes the most useful. The STL containers are implemented by template classes so they can be easily customized to hold different data types.

All the containers have common management member functions defined in their template definitions: `insert()`, `erase()`, `begin()`, `end()`, `size()`, `capacity()`, and so on. Individual containers have member functions that support their unique requirements.

Algorithms are behaviors or functionality applied to containers to process their contents in various ways. For example, there are algorithms to sort, copy, search, and merge container contents. In the STL, algorithms are represented by template functions. These are not member functions of the container classes; they are stand-alone functions. Indeed, one of the surprising characteristics of the STL is that its algorithms are so general. You can use them not only on STL containers, but also on ordinary C++ arrays or any other application-specific container.

A standard suite of algorithms provides searching for, copying, reordering, transforming, and performing numeric operations on the objects in the containers. The same algorithm is used to perform a particular operation for all containers of all object types.

Once you have decided on a container type and data behaviors, the only thing left is to interact the two with *iterators*. You can think of an iterator as a generalized pointer that points to elements within a container. You can increment an iterator, as you can a pointer, so it points in turn to each successive element in the container. Iterators are a key part of the STL because they connect algorithms with containers.

Latest C++ ANSI/ISO Language Updates

While the ANSI/ISO committee was busy incorporating STL, they took the opportunity to introduce modifications to the C++ language definition. These modifications, in most cases, implement features that the committee members admired in other languages, features that they viewed as deficiencies in traditional C++. These new changes, which consist of language additions, should not affect any previously written code.

Using `namespace`

We'll look at the definition for *namespace* from a bottom-up point of view. Namespaces control scope or identifier (constants, variables, functions, classes, etc.) visibility. The tightest scope is local—those identifiers declared within a function. Also at this level would be member function or method declarations. Higher up on the scale would be class scope.

There are visibility issues associated with file scope, for example, when `1.cpp`, `2.cpp`, and `3.cpp` are combined to generate `123.exe`. Identifiers declared in `1.cpp` are not visible (by default) in `2.cpp` and `3.cpp`.

At the highest level is program or workspace scope. Historically, this worked fine until the advent of today's complex programming environment where source files are coming at you from all directions. Today's programs are a combination of source files you write, those supplied by the compiler(s), some from the operating system itself, and third-party vendors. Under these circumstances, program scope is not sufficient to prevent identifier collisions between categories. Namespaces allow you to lock down all program identifiers, successfully preventing these types of collisions.

Collisions usually fall under the category of external, global identifiers used throughout a program. They are visible to all object modules in the application program, in third-party class and function libraries, and in the compiler's system libraries. When two variables in global scope have the same identifier, the linker generates an error.

Many compiler manufacturers initially solved this problem by assigning unique identifiers to each variable. For example, under standard C, the compiler system prefixes its internal global identifiers with underscore characters, and programmers are told to avoid that usage to avoid conflicts.

Third-party vendors perpended unique mnemonic prefixes to global identifiers in an attempt to prevent collisions. This failed, however, whenever two developers chose the same prefix. The problem is that the language had no built-in mechanism with which a library publisher could stake out a so-called namespace of its own, one that would insulate its global identifiers from those of other libraries being linked into the same application.

Traditionally, a programmer had three choices to eliminate collisions: they could get the source code, modify it, and rebuild it; have the authors of the offending code change *their* declarations; or select an alternate code source containing the same functionality. Not a very pleasant set of alternatives!

The C++ `namespace` keyword limits an identifier's scope to the namespace identifier. All references from outside the block to the global identifiers declared in the block must, in one way or another, qualify the global idenfier's reference with the namespace identifier. In actuality, this is logically similar to perpending prefixes, however, namespace identifiers tend to be longer than the typical two- or three-character prefixes and stand a better chance of working.

`namespace` Syntax

To define a `namespace`, encapsulate your declarations within a `namespace` block, as in:

```
namespace your_namespace_name {
  int ivalue;
  class my_class {/*....*/};
  // more declarations;
}
```

In the above example, any code statements within `your_namespace_name` have direct access to the namespace's declarations. However, any code statements outside of `your_namespace_name` must use a qualifying syntax. For example, from the `main()` function, accessing `ivalue` would look like:

```
void main ( void )
{
  your_namespace_name::ivalue++;
}
```

The `using namespace` Statement

If you do not like the idea of always having to qualify an identifier with its namespace everytime you access it, you can employ the `using` statement, as in:

```
using namespace your_namespace_name;
void main ( void )
{
  ivalue++;
}
```

However, this approach can be like giving a hotel guest the key to the entire hotel instead of a single room. The `using namespace` syntax provides access to all of the namespace's declarations; proceed with care. Each application will benefit from the best selection of these two approaches.

The Selective `using` Statement

Somewhere between a fully qualified namespace identifier (`your_namespace_name::ivaluel++;`) and the `using namespace your_namespace_name` syntax, there's the simpler `using` statement. The `using` directive tells the compiler that you intend to use specific identifiers within a namespace. Using the previous examples, this would look like:

```
using your_namespace_name::ivalue;
void main ( void )
{
  ivalue++;
}
```

Just as a programmer would not choose to always use `for` loops when there are `while` and `do-while` alternatives, so too a programmer should carefully select the best, application-specific approach to namespace identifier access.

Renaming namespaces

Sometimes third-party `namespace` names can get in your way because of their length; for example, `your_namespace_name` is quite long. For this reason the `namespace` feature allows a programmer to associate a new name with the `namespace` identifier, as in:

```
namespace YNN = your_namespace_name;
void main ( void )
{
  YNN::ivalue++;
}
```

`static` File Scope vs. Unnamed namespaces

One way to enforce file scope is with the keyword `static`. For example, if `1.cpp`, `2.cpp`, and `3.cpp` all have the external variable declaration int `ivalue;`, and you do not want internal linkage (meaning all three identifiers *share* the same storage location), precede all three declarations with the keyword `static`:

```
// 1.cpp                 // 2.cpp                      // 3.cpp
static int ivalue;       static int ivalue;            static int ivalue;
void main ( void )       void some_funcs( void );      void more_funcs( void );
```

Unnamed namespaces provide the same capability, just a slightly different syntax:

```
// 1.cpp
namespace {
  int ivalue;
}
void main ( void )
{
  ivalue++;
}
```

To create an unnamed namespace, simply omit a namespace identifier. The compiler then generates an internal identifier that is unique throughout the program. All identifiers declared within an unnamed namespace are available only within the defining file. Functions in other files, within the program's workspace, cannot reference the declarations.

New Casting Operations

As traditional style casting proves to be unsafe, error-prone, and difficult to spot when reading programs, and even more challenging when searched for in large bodies of source code, the newer style cast is a huge improvement. There are four new types of casts. The general syntax looks like:

```
cast_operator <castType> (objectToCast)
```

Dynamic Casting

You use a `dynamic_cast` whenever you need to convert a base class pointer or reference to a derived class pointer or reference. The one restriction is that the base, parent, or root class must have at least one *virtual* function. The syntax for a `dynamic_cast` looks like:

```
dynamic_cast < castType > ( objectToCast );
```

This type of cast allows a program, at run time, to determine whether a base class pointer or reference points to an object of a specific derived class or to an object of a class derived from the specified class.

You can also use `dynamic_cast` to upcast a pointer or reference to a derived class to a pointer or reference to one of the base, parent, or root classes in the same hierarchy. Upcasting allows a program to determine, at run time, whether a pointer to a derived class really contains the address of an object of that class. At the same time, you want to force the address into a pointer of one of the object's ancestor classes.

Static Casting

A `static_cast` implicitly converts between types that are not in the same class hierarchy. The type-checking is static, where the compiler checks to ensure that the conversion is valid as opposed to the dynamic run-time type checking that is used with `dynamic_casts`. The syntax for a `static_cast` looks like:

```
static_cast < castType > ( objectToCast );
```

The `static_cast` operator can be used for operations such as converting a pointer to a base class to a pointer to a derived class. Such conversions are not always safe. For example:

```
class typeA { ... };

class typeB : public typeA { ... };

void someFunction(typeA* ptypeA, typeB* ptypeB)
{
    typeB* ptypeB2 = static_cast<typeB*>(ptypeA);  // not safe, ptypeB may
                                                   // point to just typeB

    typeA* ptypeA2 = static_cast<typeA*>(ptypeB);  // BETTER - this is a
                                                   // safe conversion
    ...
}
```

In this code segment the object pointed to by `ptypeA` may not be an object of `typeB`, in which case the use of `*ptypeB2` could be disastrous. For instance, calling a function that is a member of the `typeB` class, but not the `typeA` class, could result in an access violation.

Newer C-Type Cast

The `reinterpret_cast` operator replaces many of the older C-type casts except those removing an identifier `const` restriction. The `reinterpret_cast` is capable of converting one pointer type into another—numbers into pointers, and pointers into numbers. The syntax looks like:

```
reinterpret_cast < castType > ( objectToCast );
```

The `reinterpret_cast` operator can be used for conversions such as `char*` to `int*`, or `Base_class*` to `anyOtherNONrelated_class*`, which are inherently unsafe.

The result of a `reinterpret_cast` cannot safely be used for anything other than being cast back to its original type. Other uses are, at best, nonportable. The following code segment demonstrates a pointer type cast in C, C++, and C++ using the `reinterpret_cast` syntax:

```
void main ( void )
{
  int * pointer_to_int;
  /* in C */
  pointer_to_int = malloc(100); /* implicit void * cast to int *,
                                   with warning */
  pointer_to_int = (int *) new int[100]; // C++ required cast of void *
                                            to int *
  pointer_to_int = reinterpret_cast<int *>( new int[100]); // new style cast
}
```

Constant Cast

The `const_cast` operator can be used to remove the `const`, `volatile`, and `__unaligned` attribute(s) from a class. The general syntax looks like:

```
const_cast < castType > ( objectToCast )
```

With a `const_cast`, your program can cast a pointer to any object type or a pointer to a data member, to a type that is identical except for the `const`, `volatile`, and `__unaligned` qualifiers. For pointers and references, the result will refer to the original object. For pointers to data members, the result will refer to the same member as the original (uncast) pointer to data member.

Run-Time Type Information (RTTI)

The `typeid` operator, found in `<typeinfo>`, supports the new C++ run-time type information feature. The operator returns a reference to a system-maintained object of the type `type_info`, which identifies the type of the argument. RTTI was added to the C++ language because many vendors of class libraries were implementing this functionality themselves. This caused incompatibilities between libraries. Thus, it became obvious that support for run-time type information was needed at the language level.

The following code segment demonstrates their straightforward syntax and logical use:

```
#include <typeinfo>
#include <iostream>
using namespace std;
// ...
class someClassType { };
// ...
  someClassType sCTinstance;
  int ivalue;
  cout << "object type = " << typeid(sCTinstance).name(); // type's name
  if ( typeid ( ivalue ) == typeid ( sCTinstance ) ) // type comparisons
    cout << "I DON'T BELIEVE IT!";
```

If this code section defined and then dynamically created a plethora of object types and instances, knowing which dynamically allocated type was in use at any point within an algorithm would be an extremely useful piece of run-time logic control.

Introduction to the Standard C++ Library

No matter how sophisticated your procedural or object-oriented, stand-alone, or Windows application is, as a programmer you must invariably resort to tried and true Data Structures algorithms for creating linked-lists, stacks, queues, and binary trees. By necessity, you have again reinvented the wheel for each application's unique user-defined data types. Along with this application-specific proprietary code comes the developer's nightmare—design changes that are not easily added in such cases, and code maintenance.

Unlike many other object-oriented languages, such as SmallTalk, if these common programming components had been part of the C++ language, you could avoid re-inventing data-specific algorithms. In a nutshell, that is what STL is all about. Finally, the C++ language provides you with general purpose components for common programming tasks through the Standard C++ Library.

Some of the more interesting, reusable components of the Standard C++ Library include powerful and flexible containers and programmable algorithms. The facilities provided by the Standard C++ Library are as follows:

- **C++ Language Support**—includes common type definitions used throughout the library such as predefined types, C++ program start and termination function support, support for dynamic memory allocation, support for dynamic type identification, and support for exception processing.
- **Diagnostic Tools**—provides components for reporting several kinds of exceptional conditions, components for documenting program assertions, and a global variable for error number codes.
- **General C/C++ Utilities**—provides components used by other elements of the Standard C++ Library. This category also includes components used by the Standard Template Library (STL) and function objects, dynamic memory management utilities, and date/time utilities. These components may also be used by any C++ program. The general C/C++ utilities also include memory management components derived from the C library.
- **Strings—**includes components for manipulating sequences of characters, where characters may be of type `char`, `w_char` (used in UNICODE applications), or of a type defined in a C++ program. UNICODE uses a two-byte value to represent every known written language's symbol set versus the limiting one-byte ASCII code.
- **Cultural Formatting Support**—provides numeric, monetary, and date/time formatting and parsing and support for character classification and string collation.
- **STL (Standard Template Library)**—includes the most widely used algorithms and data structures in data-independent format. STL headers can be grouped into three major organizing concepts: containers, iterators, and algorithms. *Containers* are template classes that provide powerful and flexible ways to organize data; for example, vectors, lists, sets and maps. *Iterators* are the glue that paste together algorithms and containers.
- **Advanced Numerical Computation**—includes seminumerical operations and components for complex number types, numeric arrays, and generalized numeric algorithms.

- **Input/Output**—includes components for forward declarations of iostreams, predefined iostream objects, base iostream classes, stream buffering, stream formatting and manipulators, string streams, and file streams.
- The Standard C++ Library also incorporates the Standard C Library.

The Standard C++ Libraries

An application accesses Microsoft's Standard C++ Library facilities by using appropriate include files and associated static and dynamic libraries. Tables 1.1 and 1.2 list all the Standard C++ Library headers and the associated static and dynamic libraries provided by Visual C++.

Table 1.1 The Standard C++ Library Headers

algorithm	bitset	cassert	cctype	cerrno
cfloat	ciso646	climits	clocale	cmath
complex	csetjmp	csignal	cstdarg	cstddef
cstdio	cstdlib	cstring	ctime	cwchar
cwctype	deque	exception	fstream	functional
iomanip	ios	iosfwd	iostream	istream
iterator	limits	list	locale	map
memory	new	numeric	ostream	queue
set	sstream	stack	stdexcept	streambuf
string	strstream	utility	valarray	vector

Note

Remember, the Standard C++ Library headers have no .h file extension in accordance with the latest ANSI/ISO C++ standard.

Microsoft also provides the static and dynamic libraries as shown in Table 1.2.

Table 1.2 Static and Dynamic Libraries Included with Microsoft Visual C++

Library types	*C runtime library*	*Standard C++ Library*	*Old iostream library*
Single-Threaded	LIBC.LIB	LIBCP.LIB	LIBCI.LIB
Multithreaded	LIBCMT.LIB	LIBCPMT.LIB	LIBCIMT.LIB
Multithreaded DLL version	MSVCRT.LIB (uses MSVCRT.DLL)	MSVCPRT.LIB (uses MSVCRT.DLL)	MSVCIRT.LIB (uses MSVCIRT.DLL)
Debug Single-Threaded	LIBCD.LIB	LIBCPD.LIB	LIBCID.LIB
Debug Multithreaded	LIBCMTD.LIB	LIBCPMTD.LIB	LIBCIMTD.LIB
Debug Multithreaded	MSVCRTD.LIB (uses MSVCRT.DLL)	MSVCPRTD.LIB (uses MSVCRT.DLL)	MSVCIRTD.LIB (uses MSVCIRT.DLL)

Your First Standard C++ Library Application

To make you feel right at home, the following C++ program uses the Standard C++ Library `iostream` to print "Hello World!":

```
#include <iostream>
void main( void )
{
    cout << "Hello World!";
}
```

The code segment used the Standard C++ Library input/output component to print "Hello World!" by simply including the Standard C++ Library header `<iostream>`. It is important to remember that starting with Visual C++ 4.0, a C++ program, depending on the run-time library compiler option specified (/ML[d], /MT[d], or /MD[d]), will always link with one Basic C run-time library and, depending on headers included, will link with either a Standard C++ Library (as in the example program above) or the old `iostream` library (as in the following coded example):

```
#include <iostream.h>
void main( void )
{
  cout << "Hellow World!";
}
```

Implementing Your Own Template

Frequently, a C++ program uses common data structures such as stacks, queues, and linked-lists. Imagine a program that requires a queue of customers and a queue of messages. You could easily implement a queue of customers, and then take the existing code and implement a queue of messages.

If the program grows and there is a need for a queue of orders you could take the queue of messages and convert it to a queue of orders. But what if you need to make some changes to the queue implementation? This would not be a very easy task because the code has been duplicated in many places. Reinventing source code is not an intelligent approach in an object-oriented environment that encourages reusability. It seems to make more sense to implement a queue that can contain any arbitrary type rather than duplicating code. How does one do that? The answer is to use *type parameterization*, more commonly referred to as *templates.*

Templates are very useful when implementing generic constructs such as vectors, stacks, lists, and queues that can be used with any arbitrary type. C++ templates provide a way to reuse source code, as opposed to inheritance and composition, which provide a way to reuse object code.

C++ provides two types of templates: *class templates* and *function templates.* Use function templates to write generic functions; for example, searching and sorting routines that can be used with arbitrary types. The Standard Template Library generic algorithms have been implemented as function templates and the containers have been implemented as class templates.

Your First `class` Template

The good news is that a `class` template definition looks very similar to a regular `class` definition, except for the prefix keyword `template`. The following example defines a `stack class` template, independent from any stack element type definitions:

```
template <class T>

class genericStack
{
public:
        genericStack( sizeOfStack = 25);
        ~genericStack() { delete[] stackPtr; }
        int pushElement(const T&);
        int popElement(T&) ;
        int isStackEmpty()const { return stackTop == -1 ; }
        int isStackFull() const { return stackTop == sizeOfStack - 1 ; }
private:
        int sizeOfStack ;          // number of stack elements
        int stackTop ;
        T* stackPtr ;
} ;
```

T represents any data type. It is important to note that T does not have to be a class type as implied by the keyword class. T can be anything from a simple data type like int, to a complex data structure like pToArrayOfStructures *.

Function Templates Requirements

Implementing template member functions is somewhat different than implementing the regular class member functions. The declarations and definitions of the class-template member functions should all be in the same header file. Why do the declarations and definitions need to be in the same header file? Consider the following:

```
//sample.h
template <class t>
class sample
{
public:
    sample() ;
    ~sample() ;
} ;
```

```
//sample.cpp
#include "sample.h"
template <class t>
sample<t>::sample()
{
}
template <class t>
sample<t>::~sample()
{
}
```

```
//main.cpp
#include "sample.h"
void main( void )
{
    sample<int> si ;
    sample<float> sf ;
}
```

When compiling sample.cpp, the compiler has both the declarations and the definitions available. At this point, the compiler does not need to generate any definitions for template classes, since there are no instantiations. When the compiler compiles main.cpp, there are two instantiations: template classes sample<int> and sample<float>. At this point, the compiler has the declarations but no definitions!

Using a class Template

Using a class template is very easy. Create the required classes by plugging in the actual type for the type parameters. This process is commonly known as *instantiating* a class. Here is a sample class that uses the genericStack class template:

```
#include <iostream>
#include "stack.h"
using namespace std;
void main( void )
{
  typedef genericStack<float> floatStack;
  typedef genericStack<int> intStack;
  FloatStack actualFloatStackInstance( 10 );
```

In the above example we defined a class template, `genericStack`. In the program we instantiated a `genericStack` of `float` (`floatStack`) and a `genericStack` of `int` (`intStack`). Once the template classes are instantiated, you can instantiate objects of that type (for example, `actualFloatStackInstance`).

It is good programming practice to use `typedef` while instantiating template classes. Then, throughout the program, you can use the `typedef` name. There are two advantages to this method. First, `typedefs` are helpful when nesting template definitions. For example, when instantiating an `int` STL vector, you could use:

```
typedef vector<int, allocator<int> > intVECTOR ;
```

Secondly, should the template definition change, simply change the `typedef` definition. This practice is especially helpful when using STL components.

`class` Template Parameters

The `genericStack class` template, described in the previous section, used only type parameters in the template header. It is also possible to use nontype parameters. For example, the template header could be modified to take an `int number_of_elements` parameter as follows:

```
#define MAX_ELEMENTS 32
template <class T, int number_of_elements>
class genericStack ;
```

Then, a declaration such as:

```
genericStack<float, MAX_ELEMENTS> currentStackSize;
```

could instantiate (at compile time) a `MAX_ELEMENTS genericStack` template class named `currentStackSize` (of float values); this template class would be of type `genericStack<float, 32>`.

Default Template Parameters

Let's look at the `genericStack class` template again:

```
template <class T, int number_of_elements> genericStack { ....};
```

C++ allows you to specify a *default template parameter*, so the definition could now look like:

```
template <class T = float, int number_of_elements = 10> genericStack { ....};
```

Then a declaration such as:

```
genericStack<> defaultStackSize;
```

would instantiate (at compile time) a 10 element genericStack template class named defaultStackSize (of float values); this template class would be of type genericStack<float, 10>.

If you specify a default template parameter for any formal parameter, the rules are the same as for functions and default parameters. Once you begin supplying a default parameter, all subsequent parameters must have defaults.

The Standard Template Library

The Standard Template Library is part of the Standard C++ Library. Every C++ programmer at one time or another has implemented common data structures such as a vector, list, or queue, and common algorithms such as binary search, sort, and so on. Through STL, C++ gives programmers a set of carefully designed generic data structures and algorithms.

These generic data structures and algorithms are parameterized types (templates) that require only plugging in of actual types to be ready for use. Finally, STL brings to C++ the long promised goal of reusable software components. More importantly, the STL substructure generates extremely efficient code size and performance.

STL Components

- **Containers** are objects that store other objects.

  sequential containers include:

  ```
  vector
  list
  deque
  ```

  associative containers include:

  ```
  map
  multimap
  set
  multiset
  ```

- **Algorithms** include generic functions that handle common tasks such as searching, sorting, comparing, and editing.
- **Iterators** are generic pointers used to interface containers and algorithms. STL algorithms are written in terms of iterator parameters, and STL containers provide iterators that can be plugged into the algorithms. Iterators include:

`input`
`output`
`forward`
`bidirectional`
`random access`
`istream_iterator`
`ostream_iterator`

- **Function templates** are objects of any class or struct that overload the function call `operator()`. Most STL algorithms accept a function object as a parameter that can change the default behavior of the algorithm. Function template argument types include:

  `plus`
  `minus`
  `times`
  `divides`

  The unary, logical, bitwise, and comparison operator object types include:

  `modulus`
  `negate`
  `equal_to`
  `not_equal_to`
  `greater`
  `less`
  `greater_equal`
  `less_equal`
  `logical_and`
  `logical_or`
  `logical_not`

- **Adapters** modify the interface of other components. There are three kinds of STL adapters:

  Container Adapter: `stack`, `queue`, `priority_queue`

  Iterator Adapter: `reverse_bidirectional_iterator`, `back_insert_iterator`, `front_insert_iterator`, and `insert_iterator`

  Function Adapters: `not1`, `not2`, `bind1st`, and `bind2nd`

The individual STL libraries and glue components are designed to work together in useful ways to produce the kind of larger and more specialized algorithms needed in today's applications.

Rules for Using STL

The following sections highlight fundamental principles employed by the C++ compiler when using STL components. For example, when an object is used with an STL container, it is first copied with a call to the copy constructor, and the copy is what is actually inserted into the container. This means an object held by an STL container must have a copy constructor. If an application removes an STL container object, the object is destroyed with a call to the destructor. If the STL container is destroyed, it destroys all objects it currently holds.

Frequently, STL components use compare container objects with a complete set of logical tests such as <, <=, >, >=, ==, and `!=`. This means the comparison operators must be defined for objects used with an STL component. Of course, some STL components modify the value of an object. This is accomplished using the assignment operator. This means the assignment operator, =, must be defined for objects used with an STL component. Your application can use the `<utility>` definitions of the <=, >, >=, and != operators, which are all defined in terms of the < and ==.

The simplest way for you to guarantee that your objects will sucessfully interact with the STL containers is to make certain your objects contain:

1. A copy constructor
2. An assignment operator, =
3. An equality comparison operator, ==
4. A less than comparison operator, <

Function Objects

Function objects are relatively new to the C++ programming language. Their usage may seem odd at first glance, and the syntax may appear to be confusing. A function object is an object of a class or struct type that includes an `operator()` member function. An `operator()` member function allows the creation of an object that behaves like a function. For example, a two-dimensional `Array2D` class could overload `operator()` to access an element whose row and column index are specified as arguments to `operator()`.

```
class Array2D
{
  public:
    Array2D(int, int);
    int operator(int, int) const;
  private:
    Array<int> Array2Def;
    int rowOffset;
    int colOffset;
} ;
```

```
int Array2D::operator(int currentRow, int currentCol) const
{
  if ( currentRow > 0 && currentRow <= rowOffset && currentCol > 0 &&
currentCol <= colOffset)
    return Array2Def[currentRow, currentCol];
  else
    return (0);
}
Array2D intArray2D(10, 10);
int  intArray2D_element = intArray(5, 5);
```

It is important to note that function objects are objects that behave like functions, and, as such, they can be created and must always return a value.

STL Function Objects

The Standard Template Library provides function objects for standard math operations such as addition, subtraction, multiplication, and division. STL also provides function objects for unary operations, logical operations, bitwise operations, and comparison operations. Chapter 2 lists all the function objects defined in the STL header file `<functional>`.

The following example program demonstrates how these function objects can be used with STL algorithms to change their default behavior. The STL sort algorithm, by default, sorts in ascending order. However, by using the `greater(T)` function object, you can "trick" the sort algorithm to work in descending order:

```
#include <iostream>
#include <vector>
#include <functional>
#include <algorithm>
using namespace std;

void main( void )
{
  typedef vector<int, allocator<int> > iVECTOR;
  int iArray[5] = {10, 15, 22, 31, 18, 5};
  iVECTOR iVectorInstance(iArray, iArray + 5) ;

// default ascending sort
  copy(iVectorInstance.begin(), iVectorInstance.end(), out) ;
  sort(iVectorInstance.begin(), iVectorInstance.end()) ;
// use of function object to reverse sort to descinding

  copy(iVectorInstance.begin(), iVectorInstance.end(), out) ;
  sort(iVectorInstance.begin(), iVectorInstance.end(), greater<int>())
;
 }
```

Basically, it is the `greater<int>()` function object passed to `sort()` that inverts the comparison logic used by `sort()` thereby tricking it into a descending algorithm. You can also use STL function objects directly in a C++ program. The following two statements:

```
float floatCalculation = (times<float>())(1.1, 2.2);      // assigns 2.42
int intCalculation = (minus<int>())(15, 5);               // assigns 10
```

access the `times` and `minus` function objects directly.

STL Function Adapters

Function adapters help us construct a wider variety of function objects using existing function objects. Using function adapters is often easier than directly constructing a new function object type with a struct or class definition. STL provides three categories of function adapters: *binders*, *negators*, and *pointer-to-function adapters*.

Binders are function adapters that convert binary function objects into unary function objects by binding an argument to some particular value. STL provides two types of binder function objects: `binder1st<Operation>` and `binder2nd<Operation>`. A binder function object takes only a single argument. STL provides two template functions, `bind1st` and `bind2nd`, to create binder function objects.

The functions `bind1st` and `bind2nd` each take as arguments a binary function object *f* and a value *x*. `bind1st` returns a function object of type `binder1st<Operation>`, and `bind2nd` returns a function object of type `binder2nd<Operation>`. Here are the function prototypes for the `bind1st` and `bind2nd` functions:

```
template <class Operation, class T>
binder1st<Operation> bind1st(const Operation& f, const T& x) ;
template <class Operation, class T>
binder2nd<Operation> bind2nd(const Operation& f, const T& x) ;
```

Look at this first example:

```
int iGreater = (bind2nd(greater<int>(), 15))(actual_int_value)
```

If you assume `actual_int_value` is defined as type `int`, the above statement could have been rewritten as:

```
int iGreater = (greater<int>())(actual_int_value, 15)
```

Negators are the second type of function adaptors. Negators are used to return the complement of a result obtained by applying a provided unary or binary operation. STL provides two types of negator function objects: `unary_negate<Operation>` and `binary_negate<Operation>`. A negator function object takes only a single argument.

The two template functions, `not1` and `not2`, create negator function objects. The function `not1` takes a unary function object *f* as its argument and returns a function object of type `unary_negate<Operation>`. The function `not2` takes a binary function object *f* as its argument and returns a function object of type `binary_negate<Operation>`. Here are the function prototypes for the `not1` and `not2` functions:

```
template <class Operation>
unary_negate<Operation> not1(const Operation& f) ;
template <class Operation>
binary_negate<Operation> not2(const Operation& f) ;
```

The following code segment demonstrates `find_if()` used with the `not1` function used to locate the first element in the array that is not greater than 15:

```
int iArray[25] = {/* your initialization code here */};
int* offset = find_if(iArray, iArray+25,
not1(bind2nd(greater<int>(), 15)));
```

The function `bind2nd` creates a unary function object which returns the result of the comparison `int > 15`. The function `not1` takes the unary function object as an argument and creates another function object. This function object merely negates the results of the comparison `int > 15`. This next statement uses the `not2` function in a game playing match by causing the `greater` function object to trigger an ascending `sort` order:

```
sort(iVectorInstance.begin(), iVectorInstance.end(), not2(greater<int>())) ;
```

STL provides two types of *pointer-to-function objects*: `pointer_to_unary_function<Arg, Result>` and `pointer_to_binary_function<Arg1, Arg2, Result>`. An application can use adapters for pointers to functions to convert existing binary or unary functions to function objects. Adapters for pointers to functions allow the programmer to utilize the existing code to uniquely extend the library.

The `pointer_to_unary_function` function object takes one argument of type `Arg`, and `pointer_to_binary_function` takes two arguments of type `Arg1` and `Arg2`. STL provides two versions of the template function `ptr_fun` to create pointer-to-function function objects.

The first version of `ptr_fun` takes a unary function *f* as its argument and returns a function object of type `pointer_to_unary_function<Arg, Result>`. The second version of `ptr_fun` takes a binary function *f* as its argument and returns a function object of type `pointer_to_binary_function<Arg1, Arg2, Result>`. Here are the function prototypes for the `ptr_fun` functions:

```
template<class Arg, class Result>
    class pointer_to_unary_function
        : public unary_function<Arg, Result> {
public:
    explicit pointer_to_unary_function(Result (*pf)(Arg));
    Result operator()(const Arg x) const;
};
```

The template class stores a copy of `pf`. It defines its member function `operator()` as returning `(*pf)(x)`.

Standard Template Library Algorithms

This section serves to introduce the STL algorithm fundamentals and presents some examples. Remembering some basic rules will help you to understand the algorithms and how to use them. STL provides generic parameterized, iterator-based functions (a fancy description for template functions). These functions implement some common array-based utilities, including searching, sorting, comparing, and editing. The STL algorithms are user-programmable. What this means is that you can modify the default behavior of an algorithm to suit your needs, as in the example:

```
sort(first, last) ;          //sorts elements of a sequence
                             //in ascending order by default.
```

In this case, the STL algorithm assumes an operator `==` or operator `<` exists, and uses it to compare elements. The default behavior of the STL algorithms can be changed by specifying a predicate. The predicate function could be a C++ function. For example, `sort_descending` is a C++ function that compares two elements. In this case, the sort algorithm takes a function pointer, as follows:

```
sort(first, last, sort_descending);
```

Or, the predicate function could be a function object. Either define a function object, or use the function objects provided by STL. For example (as seen earlier):

```
sort(first, last, greater<int>());
```

Every algorithm operates on a range of sequence. A sequence is a range of elements in an array or container, or user-defined data structures delimited by a pair of iterators. The identifier first points to the first element in the sequence. The identifier points last to the one element beyond the end of the region you want the algorithm to process. A common notation used to represent the sequence is `[first, last)`. This is a notation for an open interval. The notation `[first, last)` implies that the sequence ranges from first to last, including first but not including last. The algorithm will increment an internal iterator with the `++` operator until it equals last. The element pointed to by last will not be processed by the algorithm.

STL algorithms do not perform range or validity checking on the iterator or pointer values. Many algorithms work with two sequences. For example, the copy algorithm takes three parameters, as follows:

```
copy(firstValue1, lastValue1, firstValue2);
```

If the second sequence is shorter than the first, `copy` will blindly continue writing into unconnected areas of memory. Some STL algorithms also creates an in-place version and a copying version. For example:

```
reverse(first, last);              // places results in original container
reverse_copy(firstValue1, lastValue1, firstValue1);  // results in
                                                      // duplicate location
```

The STL generic algorithms can be divided into the following four main categories: *Nonmutating*—sequence algorithms operate on containers without modifying the contents of the container. *Mutating*—sequence algorithms typically modify the containers on which they operate. *Sorting*—related algorithms include sorting and merging algorithms, binary searching algorithms, and set operations on sorted sequences. Finally, there is a small collection of *generalized* numeric algorithms defined in the files: `<algorithm>`, `<functional>`, `<numeric>`.

Standard C++ Library Language Support

The language support section of the Standard C++ Library provides common type definitions used throughout the library, characteristics of predefined types, functions supporting start and termination of C++ programs, support for dynamic memory allocation, support for dynamic type identification, support for exception processing, and other run-time support.

cstddef

This header file basically includes `stddef.h`. There are two macros, `NULL` and `offsetof`, and two types, `ptrdiff_t` and `size_t`, specifically listed in this section of the standard. To determine the distance (or the number of elements) between two elements you can use the `distance()` function. If you pass it, an iterator pointing to the first element and one pointing to the third element, it will return a 2. The distance function is in the utility header file; it takes two iterators as parameters and returns a number of type `difference_type`. `Difference_type` maps is an `int`.

Implementation Properties: limits, climits, cfloat

The `numeric_limits` component provides information about properties of fundamental types. Specializations are provided for each fundamental type such as `int`, `floating point`, and `bool`. The member, `is_specialized`, returns true for the specializations of `numeric_limits` for the fundamental types. The `numeric_limits` class is defined in the limits header file, as shown here:

```
template<class T>  class numeric_limits {
public:
static const bool has_denorm;
static const bool has_denorm_loss;
static const bool has_infinity;
static const bool has_quiet_NaN;
static const bool has_signaling_NaN;
static const bool is_bounded;
static const bool is_exact;
static const bool is_iec559;
static const bool is_integer;
static const bool is_modulo;
static const bool is_signed;
static const bool is_specialized;
static const bool tinyness_before;
static const bool traps;
static const float_round_style round_style;
static const int digits;
static const int digits10;
static const int max_exponent;
static const int max_exponent10;
static const int min_exponent;
static const int min_exponent10;
static const int radix;
static T denorm_min() throw();
static T epsilon() throw();
static T infinity() throw();
static T max() throw();
static T min() throw();
static T quiet_NaN() throw();
static T round_error() throw();
static T signaling_NaN() throw();
};
```

Exception Handling

The C++ Standard Library exception class defines the base class for the types of objects thrown as exceptions. The exception header file defines the exception class that is the base class for all exceptions thrown by the C++ Standard Library. The following code would catch any exception thrown by classes and functions in the Standard C++ Library:

```
try {
   // your code here
}
catch ( const exception &ex)
{
   cout << "exception: " << ex.what();
}
```

The exception class is defined in the header file exception, as follows:

```
class exception {
public:
    exception() throw();
    exception(const exception& rhs) throw();
    exception& operator=(const exception& rhs) throw();
    virtual ~exception() throw();
    virtual const char *what() const throw();
private:
// ...
};
```

Additional Support

Each of these headers files—`cstdarg`, `csetjmp`, `ctime`, `csignal`, and `cstdlib`—includes the corresponding C header file, `stdarg.h`, `setjmp.h`, `time.h`, `signal.h`, and `stdlib.h`. Macros, types, and functions for each of these in the Standard C++ Library are listed in Table 1.3.

Table 1.3 Macros, Types, and Functions

File	*Macros*	*Types*	*Functions*
cstdarg	va_arg, va_end,va_start	va_list	
csetjmp	Macro: setjmp	jmp_buf	longjmp
ctime	CLOCKS_PER_SEC	clock_t	clock
csignal	SIGABRT, SIGILL, SIGSEGV, SIG_DFL, SIG_IGN, SIGFPE, SIGINT, SIGTERM, SIG_ERR	sig_atomic_t	raise, signal
cstdlib	getenv, system		

STL Review

The following review is included to help you formalize the structural components of the Standard Template Library. You can logically divide the Standard Template Library into the following categories:

A) STL headers can be grouped into three major organizing concepts:

1) *Containers* are template classes that support common ways to organize data: <deque>, <list>, <map>, <multimap>, <queue>, <set>, <stack>, and <vector>
2) *Algorithms* are template functions for performing common operations on sequences of objects including: <algorithm>, <functional>, and <numeric>.
3) *Iterators* are the glue that pastes together algorithms and containers and include: <iterator>, <memory>, and <utility>

B) Input Output includes components for:

1) forward declarations of iostreams <iosfwd>
2) predefined iostreams objects <iostream>
3) base iostreams classes <ios>
4) stream buffering <streambuf>
5) stream formatting and manipulators: <iosmanip>, <istream>, and <ostream>
6) string streams <sstream>
7) file streams <fstream>

C) Other Standard C++ headers include:

1) Language Support
   a) components for common type definitions used throughout the library <cstddef>
   b) characteristics of the predefined types <limits>, <cfloat>, and <climits>
   c) functions supporting start and termination of a C++ program <cstdlib>
   d) support for dynamic memory management <new>
   e) support for dynamic type identification <typeinfo>
   f) support for exception processing <exception>
   g) other run-time support, <cstdarg>, <ctime>, <csetlmp>, and <csignal>
2) Diagnostics include components for:
   a) reporting several kinds of exceptional conditions <stdexcept>
   b) documenting program assertions <cassert>
   c) a global variable for error number codes <cerrno>
3) Strings include components for:
   a) string classes <string>

b) null-terminated sequence utilities: `<cctype>`, `<cwctype>`, and `<cwchar>`

4) Cultural Language components include:

a) internationalization support for character classification, string collation, numeric, monetary, and date/time formatting and parsing, and message retrieval using `<locale>` and `<clocale>`

Sample Code

The following four programs—`find.cpp`, `mdshfl.cpp`, `removif.cpp`, and `setunon.cpp`—demonstrate several of the `<algorithm>` template functions. These examples lay down the fundamental syntax requirements for using the `<algorithm>` template functions and STL iterators.

The `find.cpp` Application

The first example application, `find.cpp`, shows how the `find()` function template can be used to locate the first occurrence of a matching element within a sequence. The syntax for `find()` looks like:

```
template<class InIt, class T>
    InIt find(InIt first, InIt last, const T& val);
```

`find()` expects two input iterators (see Chapter 2) and the address of the comparison value, then returns an input iterator. The program looks like:

```
// find.cpp
// Testing <algorithm>
// find()
// Chris H. Pappas and William H. Murray, 1999

#include <iostream>
#include <algorithm>

using namespace std;

#define MAX_ELEMENTS 5

void main( void )
{
  // simple character array declaration and initialization
  char cArray[MAX_ELEMENTS] = { 'A', 'E', 'I', 'O', 'U' } ;

  char *pToMatchingChar, charToFind = 'I';
```

```
  // find() passed the array to search, length +1, and charToFind ptr
  pToMatchingChar = find(cArray, cArray + MAX_ELEMENTS, charToFind);

  if( pToMatchingChar!= cArray + MAX_ELEMENTS )
    cout << "The first occurrence of " << charToFind
         << " was at offset " << pToMatchingChar - cArray;
  else
    cout << "Match NOT found!";
};
```

Remember, all you need is the proper include statement to use any STL template function:

```
#include <algorithm>        // for this chapter
```

and the using statement:

```
using namespace std;
```

The program first defines the character array, `cArray`, and initializes it to uppercase vowels. The program then searches the array, using the `find()` function template, for the letter 'I', and reports its offset into the `cArray` if found. The output from the program looks like:

```
The first occurrence of I was at offset 2
```

The `rndshfl.cpp` Application

Randomization of data is an extremely important component to many applications, whether it's the random shuffle of a deck of electronic poker cards, to truly random test data. The following application uses the `random_shuffle()` template function to randomize the contents of an array of characters. This simple example can be easily modified to work on any container element type.

Note

Several of the applications use additional STL templates. Each chapter will emphasize, in the discussion, only those code segments relating to that chapter's STL template. Without this approach, each chapter would endlessly digress. With patience and practice you will soon understand how the support STL templates work together, in much the same way someone learning to speak a new language may know how to use a verb without really knowing the details of sentence construction.

The syntax for `random_shuffle()` looks like:

```
template<class RanIt>
    void random_shuffle(RanIt first, RanIt last);
```

`random_shuffle` requires two random access iterator formal arguments (discussed in the next chapter). The program looks like:

```
// rndshuf.cpp
// Testing <algorithm>
// random_shuffle()
// Chris H. Pappas and William H. Murray, 1999

#include <iostream>
#include <algorithm>
#include <vector>

using namespace std;

#define MAX_ELEMENTS 5

void main( void )
{
  // typedef for char vector class and iterator
  typedef vector<char> cVectorClass;
  typedef cVectorClass::iterator cVectorClassIt;

  //instantiation of character vector
  cVectorClass cVowels(MAX_ELEMENTS);

  // additional iterators
  cVectorClassIt start, end, pToCurrentcVowels;

  cVowels[0] = 'A';
  cVowels[1] = 'E';
  cVowels[2] = 'I';
  cVowels[3] = 'O';
  cVowels[4] = 'U';

  start = cVowels.begin();        // location of first cVowels
  end = cVowels.end();            // one past the last cVowels

  cout << "Original order looks like: ";
  cout << "{ ";
  for(pToCurrentcVowels = start; pToCurrentcVowels != end;
      pToCurrentcVowels++)
        cout << *pToCurrentcVowels << " ";
    cout << "}\n" << endl;
```

```
    random_shuffle(start, end);     // <algorithm> template function

    cout << "Shuffled order looks like: ";
    cout << "{ " ;
    for(pToCurrentcVowels = start; pToCurrentcVowels != end;
        pToCurrentcVowels++)
      cout << *pToCurrentcVowels << " ";
    cout << "}" << endl;
}
```

Notice the application incorporates to STL templates: `<vector>` and `<algorithm>`. The STL `<vector>` template provides the definitions necessary to create the character vector container, while `<algorithm>` defines the `random_shuffle()` template function. The application uses the `<vector>` templates `begin()` and `end()` to locate the front and back offset addresses into the `cVowles` container. These two parameters are then passed to the `random_shuffle()` template function so the algorithm knows where the container starts and ends in memory. The output from the program looks like:

```
Original order looks like: { A E I O U }

Shuffled order looks like: { U O A I E }
```

The `removif.cpp` Application

This next application uses the `remove_if()` template function along with the `<functional>` `less_equal()` template to remove any container elements matching the test value. The syntax for `remove_if()` looks like:

```
FwdIt remove_if(FwdIt first, FwdIt last, Pred pr);
template<class InIt, class OutIt, class T>
```

`remove_if()` is passed to two forward iterators (discussed in chapter 2) and a predicate telling `remove_if()` what comparison test to perform. The program looks like:

```
// removif.cpp
// Testing <algorithm>
// remove_if()
// Chris H. Pappas and William H. Murray, 1999

#include <iostream>
#include <algorithm>
#include <vector>
#include <functional>

using namespace std;
```

```
#define MAX_ELEMENTS 10

void main( void )
{
  typedef vector<int> cVectorClass ;
  typedef cVectorClass::iterator cVectorClassIt;

  cVectorClass iVector(MAX_ELEMENTS);

  cVectorClassIt start, end, pToCurrentint, last;

  start = iVector.begin();        // location of first iVector
  end = iVector.end();            // location of one past last iVector

  iVector[0] =  7;
  iVector[1] = 16;
  iVector[2] = 11;
  iVector[3] = 10;
  iVector[4] = 17;
  iVector[5] = 12;
  iVector[6] = 11;
  iVector[7] =  6;
  iVector[8] = 13;
  iVector[9] = 11;

  cout << "Original order: {";

  for(pToCurrentint = start; pToCurrentint != end;
      pToCurrentint++)
    cout << *pToCurrentint << " " ;
  cout << " }\n" << endl ;

  // call to remove all values less-than-or-equal to the value 11
  last = remove_if(start, end, bind2nd(less_equal<int>(), 11) ) ;

  cout << end-last << " elements were removed.\n" << endl;

  cout << "The " << MAX_ELEMENTS-(end-last)
       << " valid remaining elements are: { " ;
  for(pToCurrentint = start; pToCurrentint != last;
      pToCurrentint++)
    cout << *pToCurrentint << " " ;
    cout << " }\n" << endl ;

}
```

While many components of this application are similar to the two previous examples, this program uses the <functional> template function bind2nd(), along with the less_equal template class, as the second argument to remove_if(), to find all occurrences with values less than or equal to the integer value 11. The output from the program looks like:

```
Original order: { 7 16 11 10 17 12 11 6 13 11 }
6 elements were removed.
The 4 valid remaining elements are: { 16 17 12 13 }
```

Notice that the values 7, 11, 10, 11, 6, and 11, respectively, were removed.

The setunon.cpp Application

This last application uses the <algorithm> sort() and set_union() template functions. First, the program instantiates two integer vectors, iVector1 and iVector2, and a third, iUnionedVector, twice the length of the first two. Sorting is necessary for the set_union() template function to correctly locate and eliminate all duplicate values. The syntax for set_union() looks like:

```
template<class InIt1, class InIt2, class OutIt>
    OutIt set_union(InIt1 first1, InIt1 last1,
        InIt2 first2, InIt2 last2, OutIt x);
```

set_union() uses four input iterators and one output iterator to point to the comparison containers and output the results. The program looks like:

```
// setunon.cpp
// Testing <algorithm>
// set_union()
// Chris H. Pappas and William H. Murray, 1999

#include <iostream>
#include <algorithm>
#include <vector>
#include <functional>

using namespace std;

#define MAX_ELEMENTS 10

void main( void )
{
  typedef vector<int> cVectorClass ;
  typedef cVectorClass::iterator cVectorClassIt;
```

```
cVectorClass iVector1(MAX_ELEMENTS), iVector2(MAX_ELEMENTS),
             iUnionedVector(2 * MAX_ELEMENTS) ;

cVectorClassIt start1, end1,
               start2, end2,
                   pToCurrentint, unionStart;

start1 = iVector1.begin();       // location of first iVector1
end1 = iVector1.end();           // location of one past last iVector1

start2 = iVector2.begin();       // location of first iVector2
end2 = iVector2.end();           // location of one past last iVector2

// locating the first element address of result union container
unionStart = iUnionedVector.begin();

iVector1[0] =  7; iVector2[0] = 14;
iVector1[1] = 16; iVector2[1] = 11;
iVector1[2] = 11; iVector2[2] =  2;
iVector1[3] = 10; iVector2[3] = 19;
iVector1[4] = 17; iVector2[4] = 20;
iVector1[5] = 12; iVector2[5] =  7;
iVector1[6] = 11; iVector2[6] =  1;
iVector1[7] =  6; iVector2[7] =  0;
iVector1[8] = 13; iVector2[8] = 22;
iVector1[9] = 11; iVector2[9] = 18;

cout << "iVector1 as is : { ";

for(pToCurrentint = start1; pToCurrentint != end1;
    pToCurrentint++)
  cout << *pToCurrentint << " " ;
cout << "}\n" << endl ;

cout << "iVector2 as is : { ";

for(pToCurrentint = start2; pToCurrentint != end2;
    pToCurrentint++)
  cout << *pToCurrentint << " " ;
cout << "}\n" << endl ;

// sort of both containers necessary for correct union
sort(start1,end1);
sort(start2,end2);

cout << "\niVector1 sorted: { ";
```

```
  for(pToCurrentint = start1; pToCurrentint != end1;
      pToCurrentint++)
    cout << *pToCurrentint << " " ;
    cout << "}\n" << endl ;

  cout << "\niVector2 sorted: { ";

  for(pToCurrentint = start2; pToCurrentint != end2;
      pToCurrentint++)
    cout << *pToCurrentint << " " ;
    cout << "}\n" << endl;

  // call to set_union() with all necessary pointers
  set_union(start1,end1,start2,end2,unionStart);

  cout << "After calling set_union()\n" << endl ;

  cout << "iUnionedVector { " ;
  for(pToCurrentint = iUnionedVector.begin();
      pToCurrentint != iUnionedVector.end(); pToCurrentint++)
    cout << *pToCurrentint << " " ;
  cout << "}\n" << endl ;
}
```

The output from the program looks like:

```
iVector1 as is : { 7 16 11 10 17 12 11 6 13 11 }
iVector2 as is: { 14 11 2 19 20 7 1 0 22 18 }
iVector1 sorted: { 6 7 10 11 11 11 12 13 16 17 }
iVector2 sorted: { 0 1 2 7 11 14 18 19 20 22 }
After calling set_union():
iUnionedVector { 0 1 2 6 7 10 11 11 11 12 13 14 16 17 18 19 20 22 0 0 }
```

Notice that the union of `iVector1`'s and `iVector2`'s value of 11 removes their duplicate occurrences, explaining the last two `0`s in `iUnionedVector`, which indicate null elements.

Conclusion

In this chapter you explored several of the STL `<algorithm>` template functions as they relate to integer `<vector>` classes. The applications demonstrated how to find a container element, how to randomly shuffle container contents, how to scan a container for certain comparison conditions (less-than-or-equal-to), and how to perform a union.

CHAPTER 2

Lists—STL List

Computer science abounds with general purpose, intermediate-level data structures that are highly useful in constructing representations—strings, arrays, tables, lists, stacks, queues, trees, sets, and graphs. The notion of *abstract data types* (ADTs) refers to a way of packaging some intermediate-level data structures and their operations into a useful collection whose properties have been carefully studied.

These ADTs have clean, simple interfaces. They can be represented in many ways by lower-level representations (such as sequential or linked representations), but the several ways in which they can be represented have been hidden from view (through the use of information hiding), so that they can be used simply by knowing only their abstract interface properties. Moreover, they have precisely defined behaviors, permitting clear reasoning.

The programmers at Hewlett Packard have taken these lofty design goals and implemented them so successfully that the ANSI ISO C++ committee has put their universal stamp of approval on the code! STL, using standard C++ language features, implements all the best the ADT philosophy has touted for decades.

However, STL goes ADT one better. Yes, it does allow a programmer to use STL like a black box—data in, data out—but it also provides, via an open architecture, the code nuts 'n bolts should you need to *see how* the algorithms perform. This chapter concentrates on the ADT list.

No matter how you plan to implement a list, it must have two components: the *data* component being manipulated and the *algorithm* inserting, deleting, traversing, and sorting the data. In this chapter you will move quickly from the standard, internally inefficient introductory programming approach, using arrays-of-structures, onto the new STL vector and, finally, the more internally efficient STL list.

Lists Using Arrays

Introductory programming courses accomplish data storage using a standard C/C++ array-of-structures. Data insertion is accomplished with a simple increment of the next-available-position index into the array. Traversing the array list only requires incrementing the last legal offset address into the array-of-structures, and searching is accomplished with a slick call to the standard C/C++ `cstdlib qsort()` function (under the old style, ANSI/ISO C/C++ syntax `cstdlib` reverts to `stdlib.h`).

Array-of-structures deletions first search the array for a possible match and then, in a rather inefficient manner, copy each successive element over the preceding one, decrementing the total count of elements in the list (if in-orderness is to be maintained, otherwise, copying the last array element into the position being deleted is the preferred coding).

Constructing an Array of Structures

A structure can be thought of as a single card from a card file. The real power in using structures comes about when a collection of structures, called an *array of structures,* is used. An array of structures is similar to a whole card file containing a great number of individual cards. If you maintain an array of structures, a database of information can be manipulated for a wide range of items.

This array of structures might include information on all of the boats at a local marina. It would be practical for a boat dealer to maintain such a file and be able to pull out of a database all boats on the lot selling for less than $45,000, or all boats with a minimum of one stateroom.

The following example program, `ARRAYlst.cpp`, illustrates list creation using a procedural C++ array-of-structures:

```
// ARRAYlst.cpp
// A simple procedural C++ program creating
// a list of boat sales
// Chris H. Pappas and William H. Murray, 2000

#include <iostream>

using namespace std;

#define iSTRING15 15
#define iSTRING20 20
#define iNULL_CHAR 1
#define iMAX_BOATS 50

int iinstock;
```

```
struct stboat {
  char sztype [iSTRING15 + iNULL_CHAR];
  char szmodel[iSTRING15 + iNULL_CHAR];
  char sztitle[iSTRING20 + iNULL_CHAR];
  char szcomment[80];
  int iyear;
  long int lmotor_hours;
  float fretail;
  float fwholesale;
};

void vprint_data(stboat *stany_boatptr);

int main(void)
{
  int i;
  char newline;
  stboat astNineveh[iMAX_BOATS],*pastNineveh;
  pastNineveh=&astNineveh[0];

  cout << "How many boats in inventory? ";
  cin  >> iinstock;

  for (i=0; i<iinstock; i++) {
    cout << "\nPlease enter the make of the boat: ";
    cin  >> pastNineveh->sztype;

    cout << "\nPlease enter the model of the boat: ";
    cin  >> pastNineveh->szmodel;

    cout << "\nPlease enter the title number for the boat: ";
    cin  >> pastNineveh->sztitle;

    cout << "\nPlease enter the model year for the boat: ";
    cin  >> pastNineveh->iyear;

    cout << "\nPlease enter the current hours on "
         << "the motor for the boat: ";
    cin  >> pastNineveh->lmotor_hours;

    cout << "\nPlease enter the retail price of the boat: ";
    cin  >> pastNineveh->fretail;

    cout << "\nPlease enter the wholesale price of the boat: ";
    cin  >> pastNineveh->fwholesale;

    cout << "\nPlease enter a one line comment about the boat: ";
```

```
    cin.get(newline);              // process carriage return
    cin.get(pastNineveh->szcomment,80,'.');
    cin.get(newline);              // process carriage return

    pastNineveh++;
  }

  pastNineveh=&astNineveh[0];
  vprint_data(pastNineveh);

  return (0);
}

void vprint_data(stboat *stany_boatptr)
{
  int i;
  cout << "\n\n\n";
  for (i=0; i<iinstock; i++) {
    cout << "A " << stany_boatptr->iyear << " "
         << stany_boatptr->sztype << " "
         << stany_boatptr->szmodel << " beauty with "
         << stany_boatptr->lmotor_hours << " low hours.\n";
    cout << stany_boatptr->szcomment << endl;
    cout << "Grab the deal by asking your Nineveh "
         << "salesperson for #";
    cout << stany_boatptr->sztitle << "ONLY! $"
         << stany_boatptr->fretail << "\n\n";
    stany_boatptr++;
  }
}
```

While the example does use a nice mixture of array subscripting syntax, pointers, and pointer arithmetic, it is plagued by static definitions and run-time limitations.

Dynamic Memory Allocation—Linked Lists

Linked lists are often the best choice when trying to create memory-efficient algorithms. Traditional programs involving arrays of structures have all included definitions for the total number of structures used. For example, `MAX_BOATS` might be set to 25. This means that the program can accept data for a maximum of 25 boats. If 70 or 100 boats are brought into the marina, the program itself will have to be altered and recompiled to accommodate the increased number. This is because the structure allocation is *static* (do not confuse this with the storage class modifier—`static`). Static used in this sense means a variable that is created at load time. These types of variables exist for their normal scope and the programmer cannot create more of them, or destroy any of them, while the program is executing. The disadvantage of *static* allocation should be immediately clear.

One way around the problem is to set the number of structures higher than needed. If MAX_BOATS is set to 10000, not even Nineveh Boat Sales could have a marina that large. However, 10000 means that you are requiring the computer to set aside more than 400 times more memory than before. This is not a wise or efficient way to program.

A better approach is to set aside memory dynamically, as it is needed. You could think of this type of memory allocation as run-time allocation instead of a static variable's load-time allocation. With this approach, memory allocation for structures is requested as the inventory grows. Linked lists allow the use of dynamic memory allocation.

A linked list is a collection of structures. Each structure in the list contains an element or pointer that points to another structure in the list. Structures containing member pointers, defined as pointing to the same structure definition, are called *self-referential* structures. This is a syntactic requirement for creating linked lists. Self-referential structures are called *nodes* in linked-list terminology. This pointer serves as the link between structures. The concept is similar to an array, but enables the list to grow dynamically. The linked list for this example includes a pointer to the next boat in the inventory:

```
struct stboat {
  char sztype[15];
  char szmodel[15];
  char sztitle[20];
  char szcomment[80];
  int iyear;
  long int lmotor_hours;
  float fretail;
  float fwholesale;
  struct stboat *nextboat;
} Nineveh, *firstboat,*currentboat;
```

The user-defined structure type, stboat, is technically known as a self-referential structure because it contains a field that holds an address to another structure just like itself. The pointer, nextboat, contains the address of the next related structure. This allows the pointer, *nextboat, in the first structure to point to the second structure, and so on. This is the concept of a linked list of structures.

Considerations When Using Linked Lists

To allow your program to dynamically reflect the size of your data, you need a means for allocating memory as each new item is added to the list. In C, memory allocation is accomplished with the malloc() function, while in C++ new() is used. In the following section, the complete program allocates memory for the first structure with the code:

```
firstboat=new (struct stboat);
```

The following code segment demonstrates how you can use a similar statement to achieve subsequent memory allocation for each additional structure. The `while` loop continues the entire process while there is valid data to be processed:

```
while (datain(&Nineveh) == 0) {
  currentboat->nextboat = new (struct stboat);
  if (currentboat->nextboat == NULL) return(1);
  currentboat=currentboat->nextboat;
  *currentboat=Nineveh;
}
```

To give you some experience with passing structures, the `while` loop begins by sending `datain()`, the address of the `stboat` structure, `&Nineveh`. The function `datain()` takes care of filling the structure with valid data or returns a value of `1` if the user has entered the letter "Q," indicating that he or she wants to quit. If `datain()` does not return a `1`, the pointer, `currentboat->nextboat`, is assigned the address of a dynamically allocated `stboat` structure. The `if` statement checks to see if the function call to `new()` was successful or not (`new()` returns a `NULL` if unsuccessful).

Since the logical use for `currentboat` is to keep track of the address of the last valid `stboat` structure in the list, the statement after the `if` updates `currentboat` to the address of the new end of the list, namely, `currentboat`'s new `nextboat` address.

The last statement in the loop takes care of copying the contents of the `stboat` structure `Nineveh` into the new dynamically allocated structure pointed to by `*currentboat`. The last structure in the list will have its pointer set to `NULL`. Using `NULL` marks the end of a linked list. See if you can tell where this is done in the complete program that follows.

A Simple Procedural Linked List

The following program shows how to implement the Nineveh Boat Sales example using linked lists:

```
// dynamlst.cpp
// C++ program is an example of a simple linked list.
// Nineveh used boat inventory example.
// Chris H. Pappas and William H. Murray, 2000

#include <iostream>

using namespace std;

struct stboat {
  char sztype[15];
  char szmodel[15];
  char sztitle[20];
```

```
  char szcomment[80];
  int iyear;
  long int lmotor_hours;
  float fretail;
  float fwholesale;
  struct stboat *nextboat;
} Nineveh, *firstboat,*currentboat;

void boatlocation(struct stboat *node);
void output_data(struct stboat *boatptr);
int datain(struct stboat *Ninevehptr);

main( )
{
  firstboat=new (struct stboat);

  if (firstboat==NULL) exit(1);

  if (datain(&Nineveh) != 0) exit(1);

  *firstboat=Nineveh;
  currentboat=firstboat;

  while (datain(&Nineveh)==0) {
  currentboat->nextboat=
    new (struct stboat);
  if (currentboat->nextboat==NULL) return(1);
  currentboat=currentboat->nextboat;
  *currentboat=Nineveh;
  }

  currentboat->nextboat=NULL;            // signal end of list

  boatlocation(firstboat);

  return (0);
}


void boatlocation(struct stboat *node)
{
  do {
    output_data(node);
  } while ((node=node->nextboat) != NULL);
}
```

```
void output_data(struct stboat *boatptr)
{
  cout << "\n\n\n";
  cout << "A " << boatptr->iyear << " "
   << boatptr->sztype << boatptr->szmodel << " "
   << "beauty with " << boatptr->lmotor_hours << " "
   << "low miles.\n";
  cout << boatptr->szcomment << ".\n";
  cout << "Grab the deal by asking your Nineveh salesperson for";
  cout << " #" << boatptr->sztitle << " ONLY! $"
   << boatptr->fretail << ".\n";
}

int datain(struct stboat *Ninevehptr)
{
  char newline;

  cout << "\n[Enter new boat information - a Q quits]\n\n";
  cout << "Enter the make of the boat.\n";
  cin >> Ninevehptr->sztype;

  if (*(Ninevehptr->sztype) == 'Q') return(1);

  cout << "Enter the model of the boat.\n";
  cin >> Ninevehptr->szmodel;

  cout << "Enter the title number for the boat.\n";
  cin >> Ninevehptr->sztitle;

  cout << "Enter the model year for the boat.\n";
  cin >> Ninevehptr->iyear;

  cout << "Enter the number of hours on the boat motor.\n";
  cin >> Ninevehptr->lmotor_hours;

  cout << "Enter the retail price of the boat.\n";
  cin >> Ninevehptr->fretail;

  cout << "Enter the wholesale price of the boat.\n";
  cin >> Ninevehptr->fwholesale;

  cout << "Enter a one line comment about the boat.\n";
  cin.get(newline);              // process carriage return
  cin.get(Ninevehptr->szcomment,80,'.');

  cin.get(newline);              // process carriage return
  return(0);
}
```

Notice that the three functions are all passed pointers to a `stboat` structure:

```
int datain(struct stboat *Ninevehptr)
void boatlocation(struct stboat *node)
void output_data(struct stboat *boatptr)
```

The function `boatlocation()` checks the linked list for entries before calling the function `output_data()`. It does this with a `do...while` loop that is terminated whenever `node` pointer is assigned a `NULL` address. This is only true when you have tried to go beyond the last `stboat` structure in the list. The `output_data()` function formats the output from each linked list structure.

Note

As you test this application, don't forget to add a period (.) at the end of the comment regarding each boat. Failure to do this will cause the program to hang.

In most high-level languages, linked lists provide the most efficient use of memory, but are often the most difficult to debug.

An Object-Oriented Linked List in C++

In the previous section, a linked-list program was developed in C++ using a traditional procedural programming approach. When using the traditional approach, you learned that the linked-list program is difficult to alter and maintain. In this section, a linked-list program using objects is developed that will allow you to create a list of employee information. It will also be possible to add and delete employees from the list. To limit the size of the linked-list program, no user interface will be used for gathering employee data. Data for the linked list has been hardwired in the `main()` function. This program is slightly more difficult than the previous example. You will find that it includes, in addition to linked-list concepts, many standard object-oriented concepts such as parent/base/root or subclass definitions, `friend` classes, and `virtual` methods.

Creating a Parent Class

This program uses several child classes derived from a common parent class. The parent class for this linked-list example is named `P_and_M_Auto_Dealership`. The linked-list program is a database that will keep pertinent information and payroll data on company employees. The purpose of the parent class, `P_and_M_Auto_Dealership`, is to gather information common to all subsequent derived child classes. For this example, that common information includes an employee's last name, first name, occupation title, social security number, and number of years at the company.

The parent class, `P_and_M_Auto_Dealership`, has three levels of isolation: public, protected, and private. The protected section of this class shows the structure for gathering data common to each derived child class. The public section (member functions) shows how that information will be intercepted from the function `main()`.

```
// PARENT CLASS
class P_and_M_Auto_Dealership {

friend class employee_list;

protected:
  char lastname[20];
  char firstname[15];
  char occupation[30];
  char social_security[12];
  int years_employed;
  P_and_M_Auto_Dealership *pointer;
  P_and_M_Auto_Dealership *next_link;

public:
  P_and_M_Auto_Dealership(char *lname,char *fname,char *ssnum,
      char *occup,int c_years_employed)
  {
    strcpy(lastname,lname);
    strcpy(firstname,fname);
    strcpy(social_security,ssnum);
    strcpy(occupation,occup);
    years_employed=c_years_employed;
    next_link=0;
  }
      .
      .
      .
      .
```

The parent class and all derived child classes will use a friend class named `employee_list`. When you study the full program listing later in this chapter, notice that all derived child classes also share this common variable. (Remember how the terms "private" and "public" relate to encapsulation concepts used by object-oriented programmers.)

A Derived Child Class

This program uses four derived child classes. Each of these is derived from the parent class, `P_and_M_Auto_Dealership`, shown in the last section. This segment presents one child class, `salespersons`, which represents the points common to all four derived classes. A portion of this derived class is shown next. The derived child class satisfies the object-oriented concept of inheritance.

```
//SUB OR DERIVED CHILD CLASS
class salespersons:public P_and_M_Auto_Dealership {

friend class employee_list;

private:
  float unit_sales_average;
  int comm_rate;

public:
  salespersons(char *lname,char *fname,char *ssnum,
               char *occup,int c_years_employed,
               float w_avg,int c_rate):
               P_and_M_Auto_Dealership(lname,fname,ssnum,
               occup,c_years_employed)
  {
    unit_sales_average=w_avg;
    comm_rate=c_rate;
  }
      .
      .
      .
      .
```

In this case, the `salespersons` child class gathers information and adds it to the information already gathered by the parent class. This, in turn, forms a data structure composed of last name, first name, social security number, years worked, the total sales, and the appropriate commission rate.

Now take a look at the remainder of the child class description:

```
      .
      .
      .
      .

  void fill_average(float w_avg)
  {
    unit_sales_average=w_avg;
  }

  void fill_comm_rate(int c_rate)
  {
    comm_rate=c_rate;
  }
```

```
  void add_data()
  {
    pointer=this;
  }

  void send_info()
  {
    P_and_M_Auto_Dealership::send_info();
    cout << "\n Weekly Sales Average (units): " << unit_sales_average;
    cout << "\n Commission Rate: " << comm_rate << "%";
  }
};
```

Instead of `add_data()` setting aside memory for each additional linked-list node by using the `new` free store operator, the program uses each object's `this` pointer. The pointer is being assigned the address of a `P_and_M_Auto_Dealership` node.

Output information on a particular employee is constructed in a unique manner. In the case of the `salespersons` class, notice that `send_info()` makes a request to `P_and_M_Auto_Dealership`'s `send_info()` function. `P_and_M_Auto_Dealership`'s function prints the information common to each derived class; then the salespersons' `send_info()` function prints the information unique to the particular child class. For this example, this information includes the sales and the commission rate.

It would also have been possible to print the information about the salesperson completely from within the child class, but the method used allows another advantage of object-oriented programming to be illustrated—the use of virtual functions.

Using a Friend Class

The friend class, `employee_list`, contains the means for printing the linked list and for the insertion and deletion of employees from the list. Here is a small portion of this class:

```
//FRIEND CLASS
class employee_list {

private:
  P_and_M_Auto_Dealership *location;

public:
  employee_list()
  {
    location=0;
  }

  void print_employee_list();
```

```
  void insert_employee(P_and_M_Auto_Dealership *node);

  void remove_employee_id(char *social_security);

};
        .
        .
        .
        .
```

Notice that messages that are sent to the member functions—`print_employee_list()`, `insert_employee()`, and `remove_employee_Id()`—form the functional part of the linked-list program.

Consider the function, `print_employee_list()`, which begins by assigning the pointer to the list to the pointer variable present. While the pointer present is not zero, it will continue to point to employees in the linked list, direct them to `send_info()`, and update the pointer until all employees have been printed. The next section of code shows how this is achieved:

```
        .
        .
        .
        .
void employee_list::print_employee_list()
{
  P_and_M_Auto_Dealership *present=location;

  while(present!=0) {
    present->send_info();
    present=present->next_link;
  }
}
        .
        .
        .
```

You might recall from an earlier discussion that the variable pointer contains the memory address of nodes inserted via `add_data()`. This value is used by `insert_employee()` to form the link with the linked list. The insertion technique inserts data alphabetically by an employee's last name. Thus, the linked list is always ordered alphabetically by last name.

The program accomplishes a correct insertion by comparing the last name of a new employee with those already in the list. When a name (`node->lastname`), already in the list, is found that is greater than the `current_node->lastname`, the first `while` loop ends. This is a standard linked-list `insert` procedure that leaves the pointer variable, `previous_node`, pointing to the node behind where the new node is to be inserted and leaves current_node pointing to the node that will follow the insertion point for the new node.

When the insertion point is determined, the program creates a new link or node by calling node->add_data(). The current_node is linked to the new node's next_link. The last decision that must be made is whether or not the new node is to be placed at the front node in the list or between existing nodes. The program establishes this by examining the contents of the pointer variable previous_node. If the pointer variable is zero, it cannot be pointing to a valid previous node so location is updated to the address of the new node. If previous_node contains a nonzero value, it is assumed to be pointing to a valid previous node. In this case, previous_node->next_link is assigned the address of the new node's address, or node->pointer.

```
        .
        .
        .
        .
void employee_list::insert_employee(P_and_M_Auto_Dealership *node)
{
  P_and_M_Auto_Dealership *current_node=location;
  P_and_M_Auto_Dealership *previous_node=0;

  while (current_node != 0 &&
         strcmp(current_node->lastname,node->lastname) < 0) {
    previous_node=current_node;
    current_node=current_node->next_link;
  }
  node->add_data();
  node->pointer->next_link=current_node;
  if (previous_node==0)
    location=node->pointer;
  else
    previous_node->next_link=node->pointer;
}
        .
        .
        .
        .
```

The program can remove items from the linked list only by knowing the employee's social security number. This technique adds a level of protection against accidentally deleting an employee.

As you examine remove_employee_id(), shown in the next listing, note that the structure used for examining the nodes in the linked list is almost identical to that of insert_employee(). However, the first while loop leaves the current_node pointing to the node to be deleted, not the node after the one to be deleted.

```
    .
    .
    .
    .
void employee_list::remove_employee_id(char *social_security)
{
  P_and_M_Auto_Dealership *current_node=location;
  P_and_M_Auto_Dealership *previous_node=0;

  while(current_node != 0 &&
        strcmp(current_node->social_security,
        social_security) != 0) {
    previous_node=current_node;
    current_node=current_node->next_link;
  }

  if(current_node != 0 && previous_node == 0) {
    location=current_node->next_link;
    delete current_node;
  }
  else if(current_node != 0 && previous_node != 0) {
    previous_node->next_link=current_node->next_link;
    delete current_node;
  }
}
```

The first compound `if` statement takes care of deleting a node in the front of the list. The program accomplishes this by examining the contents of `previous_node` to see if it contains a zero. If it does, then the front of the list, location, needs to be updated to the node following the one to be deleted. This is achieved with the following line:

```
current_node->next_link
```

The second `if` statement takes care of deleting a node between two existing nodes. This requires the node behind to be assigned the address of the node after the one being deleted.

```
previous_node->next_link=current_node->next_link.
```

Now that the important pieces of the program have been examined, the next section puts them together to form a complete program.

Examining the Complete Program

The following listing is the complete operational C++ object-oriented linked-list program. The only thing it lacks is an interactive user interface. When the program is executed, it will add eight employees, with their different job titles, to the linked list and then print the list. Next, the program will delete three employees from the list. This is accomplished by supplying their social security numbers. The altered list is then printed. The `main()` function contains information on which employees are added and deleted.

```
// OOPlst.cpp
// C++ program illustrates object-oriented programming
// with a linked list. This program keeps track of
// employee data at the P_and_M_Auto_Dealership.
// Chris H. Pappas and William H. Murray, 2000

#include <iostream>
#include <string>

using namespace std;

// PARENT CLASS
class P_and_M_Auto_Dealership {

friend class employee_list;

protected:
  char lastname[20];
  char firstname[15];
  char occupation[30];
  char social_security[12];
  int years_employed;
  P_and_M_Auto_Dealership *pointer;
  P_and_M_Auto_Dealership *next_link;

public:
  P_and_M_Auto_Dealership(char *lname,char *fname,char *ssnum,
      char *occup,int c_years_employed)
  {
    strcpy(lastname,lname);
    strcpy(firstname,fname);
    strcpy(social_security,ssnum);
    strcpy(occupation,occup);
    years_employed=c_years_employed;
    next_link=0;
  }

  P_and_M_Auto_Dealership()
  {
    lastname[0]=NULL;
    firstname[0]=NULL;
    social_security[0]=NULL;
```

```
    occupation[0]=NULL;
    years_employed=0;
    next_link=0;
  }

  void fill_lastname(char *l_name)
  {
    strcpy(lastname,l_name);
  }

  void fill_firstname(char *f_name)
  {
    strcpy(firstname,f_name);
  }

  void fill_social_security(char *soc_sec)
  {
    strcpy(social_security,soc_sec);
  }

  void fill_occupation(char *o_name)
  {
    strcpy(occupation,o_name);
  }

  void fill_years_employed(int c_years_employed)
  {
    years_employed=c_years_employed;
  }

  virtual void add_data() {
  }
  virtual void send_info()
  {
    cout << "\n\n" << lastname << ", " << firstname
         << "\n Social Security: #" << social_security;
    cout << "\n Job Title: " << occupation;
    cout << "\n Years With Company: " << years_employed;
  }
};

//SUB OR DERIVED CHILD CLASS
class deal_closer:public P_and_M_Auto_Dealership {

friend class employee_list;

private:
  float yearly_salary;
```

```
public:
  deal_closer(char *lname,char *fname,char *ssnum,
              char *occup,int c_years_employed,
              float y_salary):
              P_and_M_Auto_Dealership(lname,fname,ssnum,
              occup,c_years_employed)
  {
    yearly_salary=y_salary;
  }

  deal_closer():P_and_M_Auto_Dealership()
  {
    yearly_salary=0.0;
  }

  void fill_yearly_salary(float salary)
  {
    yearly_salary=salary;
  }

  void add_data()
  {
    pointer=this;
  }

  void send_info()
  {
    P_and_M_Auto_Dealership::send_info();
    cout << "\n Yearly Salary: $" << yearly_salary;
  }
};


//SUB OR DERIVED CHILD CLASS
class salespersons:public P_and_M_Auto_Dealership {

friend class employee_list;

private:
  float unit_sales_average;
  int comm_rate;

public:
  salespersons(char *lname,char *fname,char *ssnum,
               char *occup,int c_years_employed,
               float w_avg,int c_rate):
               P_and_M_Auto_Dealership(lname,fname,ssnum,
               occup,c_years_employed)
```

```
  {
    unit_sales_average=w_avg;
    comm_rate=c_rate;
  }

  salespersons():P_and_M_Auto_Dealership()
  {
    unit_sales_average=0.0;
    comm_rate=0;
  }

  void fill_average(float w_avg)
  {
    unit_sales_average=w_avg;
  }

  void fill_comm_rate(int c_rate)
  {
    comm_rate=c_rate;
  }

  void add_data()
  {
    pointer=this;
  }

  void send_info()
  {
    P_and_M_Auto_Dealership::send_info();
    cout << "\n Weekly Sales Average (units): "
         << unit_sales_average;
    cout << "\n Commission Rate: " << comm_rate << "%";
  }
};

//SUB OR DERIVED CHILD CLASS
class mechanics:public P_and_M_Auto_Dealership {

friend class employee_list;

private:
  float hourly_salary;

public:
  mechanics(char *lname,char *fname,char *ssnum,char *occup,
        int c_years_employed,float h_salary):
        P_and_M_Auto_Dealership(lname,fname,ssnum,
        occup,c_years_employed)
```

```
  {
    hourly_salary=h_salary;
  }

  mechanics():P_and_M_Auto_Dealership()
  {
    hourly_salary=0.0;
  }

  void fill_hourly_salary(float h_salary)
  {
    hourly_salary=h_salary;
  }

  void add_data()
  {
    pointer=this;
  }

  void send_info()
  {
    P_and_M_Auto_Dealership::send_info();
    cout << "\n Hourly Salary: $" << hourly_salary;
  }
};

//SUB OR DERIVED CHILD CLASS
class parts:public P_and_M_Auto_Dealership {

friend class employee_list;

private:
  float hourly_salary;

public:
  parts(char *lname,char *fname,char *ssnum,char *occup,
           int c_years_employed,float h_salary):
           P_and_M_Auto_Dealership(lname,fname,ssnum,
           occup,c_years_employed)
  {
    hourly_salary=h_salary;
  }

  parts():P_and_M_Auto_Dealership()
  {
    hourly_salary=0.0;
  }
```

```
  void fill_hourly_salary(float h_salary)
  {
    hourly_salary=h_salary;
  }

  void add_data()
  {
    pointer=this;
  }

  void send_info()
  {
    P_and_M_Auto_Dealership::send_info();
    cout << "\n Hourly Salary: $" << hourly_salary;
  }

};

//FRIEND CLASS
class employee_list {

private:
  P_and_M_Auto_Dealership *location;

public:
  employee_list()
  {
    location=0;
  }

  void print_employee_list();

  void insert_employee(P_and_M_Auto_Dealership *node);

  void remove_employee_id(char *social_security);

};

void employee_list::print_employee_list()
{
  P_and_M_Auto_Dealership *present=location;

  while(present!=0) {
    present->send_info();
    present=present->next_link;
  }
}
```

```
void employee_list::insert_employee(P_and_M_Auto_Dealership \
                                    *node)
{
  P_and_M_Auto_Dealership *current_node=location;
  P_and_M_Auto_Dealership *previous_node=0;
  while (current_node != 0 &&
         strcmp(current_node->lastname,node->lastname) < 0) {
    previous_node=current_node;
    current_node=current_node->next_link;
  }
  node->add_data();
  node->pointer->next_link=current_node;
  if (previous_node==0)
    location=node->pointer;
  else
    previous_node->next_link=node->pointer;
}

void employee_list::remove_employee_id(char *social_security)
{
  P_and_M_Auto_Dealership *current_node=location;
  P_and_M_Auto_Dealership *previous_node=0;

  while(current_node != 0 &&
     strcmp(current_node->social_security,
            social_security) != 0) {
    previous_node=current_node;
    current_node=current_node->next_link;
  }

  if(current_node != 0 && previous_node == 0) {
    location=current_node->next_link;
    // delete current_node; needed if new() used in add_data()
  }
  else if(current_node != 0 && previous_node != 0) {
    previous_node->next_link=current_node->next_link;
    // delete current_node; needed if new() used in add_data()
  }
}

main()
{
  employee_list workers;

  cout.setf(ios::fixed);
  cout.precision(2);
```

```
  // static data to add to linked list
  salespersons salesperson1("Friendly","Fran","212-98-7654",
                            "Salesperson",1,7.5,4.00           );
  salespersons salesperson2("Pest","Perry","567-45-3412",
                            "Salesperson",2,2.0,2.20           );
  salespersons salesperson3("Yourfriend","Yancy","213-44-9873",
                            "Salesperson",1,10.6,5.70          );
  mechanics mechanicperson1("Hardwork","Harriet","076-45-3121",
                            "Mechanic",7,10.34                 );
  mechanics mechanicperson2("Lugwrench","Larry","886-43-1518",
                            "Mechanic",1,8.98                  );
  deal_closer closerperson ("Slick","Sally",
                            "111-22-4444","Closer",
                            10,40000.00                        );
  parts partperson1        ("Muffler","Mike","555-66-7891",
                            "Parts",4,7.34                     );
  parts partperson2        ("Horn","Hazel","345-77-7654",
                            "Parts",5,9.50                     );

  // add the eight workers to the linked list
  workers.insert_employee(&mechanicperson1);
  workers.insert_employee(&closerperson   );
  workers.insert_employee(&salesperson1   );
  workers.insert_employee(&partperson1    );
  workers.insert_employee(&partperson2    );
  workers.insert_employee(&salesperson2   );
  workers.insert_employee(&mechanicperson2);
  workers.insert_employee(&salesperson3   );

  // print the linked list
  workers.print_employee_list();

  // remove three workers from the linked list
  workers.remove_employee_id("555-66-7891");
  workers.remove_employee_id("111-22-4444");
  workers.remove_employee_id("213-44-3412");

  cout << "\n\n************************************";

  // print the revised linked list
  workers.print_employee_list();

  return (0);
}
```

Study the complete listing and see if you understand how employees are inserted and deleted from the list. If it is still a little confusing, go back and study each major section of code discussed earlier.

Linked-List Output

The linked-list program sends output to the monitor. The first section of the list contains the eight employee names that were used to create the original list. The last part shows the list after three employees are deleted. Here is a sample output sent to the screen:

```
Align, Alice
 Social Security: #174-43-6781
 Job Title: Technician
 Year Hired: 1989
 Hourly Salary: $12.55

Allpart, Albert
 Social Security: #443-89-3772
 Job Title: Supplies
 Year Hired: 1983
 Hourly Salary: $8.55

Flex, Frank
 Social Security: #663-65-2312
 Job Title: Salesperson
 Year Hired: 1985
 Sales (disks): 3
 Commission Rate: 3

Harddrive, Harriet
 Social Security: #313-56-7884
 Job Title: Salesperson
 Year Hired: 1985
 Sales (disks): 6.5
 Commission Rate: 7

Learnedmore, Lawrence
 Social Security: #987-99-9653
 Job Title: Vice President
 Year Hired: 1984
 Yearly Salary: $45000

Ordermore, Ozel
 Social Security: #111-44-5399
 Job Title: Supplies
 Year Hired: 1988
 Hourly Salary: $7.58

Ripoff, Randle
 Social Security: #512-34-7612
 Job Title: Salesperson
 Year Hired: 1987
```

```
 Sales (disks): 9.6
 Commission Rate: 6

Stuckup, Stewart
 Social Security: #238-18-1119
 Job Title: Vice President
 Year Hired: 1980
 Yearly Salary: $40000

Tightscrew, Tom
 Social Security: #682-67-5312
 Job Title: Technician
 Year Hired: 1992
 Hourly Salary: $10.34

***********************************

Align, Alice
 Social Security: #174-43-6781
 Job Title: Technician
 Year Hired: 1989
 Hourly Salary: $12.55

Allpart, Albert
 Social Security: #443-89-3772
 Job Title: Supplies
 Year Hired: 1983
 Hourly Salary: $8.55

Flex, Frank
 Social Security: #663-65-2312
 Job Title: Salesperson
 Year Hired: 1985
 Sales (disks): 3
 Commission Rate: 3

Harddrive, Harriet
 Social Security: #313-56-7884
 Job Title: Salesperson
 Year Hired: 1985
 Sales (disks): 6.5
 Commission Rate: 7

Learnedmore, Lawrence
 Social Security: #987-99-9653
 Job Title: Vice President
 Year Hired: 1984
 Yearly Salary: $45000
```

```
Ordermore, Ozel
 Social Security: #111-44-5399
 Job Title: Supplies
 Year Hired: 1988
 Hourly Salary: $7.58

Tightscrew, Tom
 Social Security: #682-67-5312
 Job Title: Technician
 Year Hired: 1992
 Hourly Salary: $10.34
```

Lists Using STL

As mentioned at the beginning of the chapter, all lists have a *data* component and an *algorithm* to manipulate the data. Under STL technology, the storage of your data is accomplished with an STL container. Data manipulation is via STL templetized functions and class methods.

As you saw in Chapter 1, vectors are the simplest STL container to use. They function most similarly to your standard C/C++ array with one exception—they grow and shrink dynamically. You can even syntactically address STL container elements using standard C/C++ subscripting, as in:

```
vector<int> iVector;
iVector[0]...
```

However, STL has an efficient, portable, and extensible design philosophy circumventing this old-style syntax. Using subscripting syntax forever forces your algorithm to be implemented as an STL vector container.

Vector

The following program recreates the previous object-oriented implementation of a linked-list using design philosophy specific to STL vector syntax. The original `OOPlst.cpp` algorithm is still in the code listing; however, the code segments that are no longer necessary for the STL vector implementation are commented out. This will allow you to easily see both the logical and syntactical changes necessary to roll over an OOP linked-list into STL vector technology:

```
// VECTRlst.cpp
// C++ program using STL vector to re-create
// the object-oriented program with a linked list.
// This program keeps track of employee data at the
// P_and_M_Auto_Dealership.
// Chris H. Pappas and William H. Murray, 2000

#include <iostream>
#include <string>
#include <vector>

using namespace std;

// PARENT CLASS
class P_and_M_Auto_Dealership {

// friend class employee_list replaced by the
// dynamic nature of the STL vector class
// friend class employee_list;

protected:
  char lastname[20];
  char firstname[15];
  char occupation[30];

  int years_employed;
//  Linking performed by dynamic STL vector
//  P_and_M_Auto_Dealership *pointer;
//  P_and_M_Auto_Dealership *next_link;

public:
  char social_security[12]; //made public for erase()
  P_and_M_Auto_Dealership(char *lname,char *fname,char *ssnum,
      char *occup,int c_years_employed)
  {
    strcpy(lastname,lname);
    strcpy(firstname,fname);
    strcpy(social_security,ssnum);
    strcpy(occupation,occup);
    years_employed=c_years_employed;
//  maintained by dynamic STL vector
//  next_link=0;
  }

  P_and_M_Auto_Dealership()
  {
    lastname[0]=NULL;
    firstname[0]=NULL;
```

```
    social_security[0]=NULL;
    occupation[0]=NULL;
    years_employed=0;
//  maintained by dynamic STL vector
//  next_link=0;
  }

  void fill_lastname(char *l_name)
  {
    strcpy(lastname,l_name);
  }

  void fill_firstname(char *f_name)
  {
    strcpy(firstname,f_name);
  }

  void fill_social_security(char *soc_sec)
  {
    strcpy(social_security,soc_sec);
  }

  void fill_occupation(char *o_name)
  {
    strcpy(occupation,o_name);
  }

  void fill_years_employed(int c_years_employed)
  {
    years_employed=c_years_employed;
  }

  virtual void add_data() {
  }
  virtual void send_info()
  {
    cout << "\n\n" << lastname << ", " << firstname
         << "\n Social Security: #" << social_security;
    cout << "\n Job Title: " << occupation;
    cout << "\n Years With Company: " << years_employed;
  }
};

//SUB OR DERIVED CHILD CLASS
class deal_closer:public P_and_M_Auto_Dealership {

// friend class replaced by dynamic STL vector
// friend class employee_list;
```

```
private:
  float yearly_salary;

public:
  deal_closer(char *lname,char *fname,char *ssnum,
              char *occup,int c_years_employed,
              float y_salary):
              P_and_M_Auto_Dealership(lname,fname,ssnum,
              occup,c_years_employed)
  {
    yearly_salary=y_salary;
  }

  deal_closer():P_and_M_Auto_Dealership()
  {
    yearly_salary=0.0;
  }

  void fill_yearly_salary(float salary)
  {
    yearly_salary=salary;
  }

// Maintained by dynamic STL vector
/* void add_data()
  {
    pointer=this;
  }
*/

  void send_info()
  {
    P_and_M_Auto_Dealership::send_info();
    cout << "\n Yearly Salary: $" << yearly_salary;
  }
};


//SUB OR DERIVED CHILD CLASS
class salespersons:public P_and_M_Auto_Dealership {

// friend class replaced by dynamic STL vector
// friend class employee_list;

private:
  float unit_sales_average;
  int comm_rate;
```

```
public:
  salespersons(char *lname,char *fname,char *ssnum,
               char *occup,int c_years_employed,
               float w_avg,int c_rate):
               P_and_M_Auto_Dealership(lname,fname,ssnum,
               occup,c_years_employed)
  {
    unit_sales_average=w_avg;
    comm_rate=c_rate;
  }

  salespersons():P_and_M_Auto_Dealership()
  {
    unit_sales_average=0.0;
    comm_rate=0;
  }

  void fill_average(float w_avg)
  {
    unit_sales_average=w_avg;
  }

  void fill_comm_rate(int c_rate)
  {
    comm_rate=c_rate;
  }

// Maintained by dynamic STL vector
/* void add_data()
  {
    pointer=this;
  }

  void send_info()
  {
    P_and_M_Auto_Dealership::send_info();
    cout << "\n Weekly Sales Average (units): "
         << unit_sales_average;
    cout << "\n Commission Rate: " << comm_rate << "%";
  }
*/
};


//SUB OR DERIVED CHILD CLASS
class mechanics:public P_and_M_Auto_Dealership {
```

```
// friend class replaced by dynamic STL vector
// friend class employee_list;

private:
  float hourly_salary;

public:
  mechanics(char *lname,char *fname,char *ssnum,char *occup,
         int c_years_employed,float h_salary):
         P_and_M_Auto_Dealership(lname,fname,ssnum,
         occup,c_years_employed)
  {
    hourly_salary=h_salary;
  }

  mechanics():P_and_M_Auto_Dealership()
  {
    hourly_salary=0.0;
  }

  void fill_hourly_salary(float h_salary)
  {
    hourly_salary=h_salary;
  }

// Maintained by dynamic STL vector
/*  void add_data()
  {
    pointer=this;
  }

  void send_info()
  {
    P_and_M_Auto_Dealership::send_info();
    cout << "\n Hourly Salary: $" << hourly_salary;
  }
*/
};


//SUB OR DERIVED CHILD CLASS
class parts:public P_and_M_Auto_Dealership {

// friend class replaced by dynamic STL vector
// friend class employee_list;

private:
  float hourly_salary;
```

```
public:
  parts(char *lname,char *fname,char *ssnum,char *occup,
          int c_years_employed,float h_salary):
          P_and_M_Auto_Dealership(lname,fname,ssnum,
          occup,c_years_employed)
  {
    hourly_salary=h_salary;
  }

  parts():P_and_M_Auto_Dealership()
  {
    hourly_salary=0.0;
  }

  void fill_hourly_salary(float h_salary)
  {
    hourly_salary=h_salary;
  }

// Maintained by dynamic STL vector
/* void add_data()
  {
    pointer=this;
  }

  void send_info()
  {
    P_and_M_Auto_Dealership::send_info();
    cout << "\n Hourly Salary: $" << hourly_salary;
  }
*/
};

/**************************************************************
Entire functionality of friend class employee_list
maintained by dynamic STL vector
//FRIEND CLASS
class employee_list {

private:
  P_and_M_Auto_Dealership *location;

public:
  employee_list()
  {
    location=0;
  }
```

```
  void print_employee_list();

  void insert_employee(P_and_M_Auto_Dealership *node);

  void remove_employee_id(char *social_security);

};

void employee_list::print_employee_list()
{
  P_and_M_Auto_Dealership *present=location;

  while(present!=0) {
    present->send_info();
    present=present->next_link;
  }
}

void employee_list::insert_employee(P_and_M_Auto_Dealership \
                                                   *node)
{
  P_and_M_Auto_Dealership *current_node=location;
  P_and_M_Auto_Dealership *previous_node=0;
  while (current_node != 0 &&
          strcmp(current_node->lastname,node->lastname) < 0) {
    previous_node=current_node;
    current_node=current_node->next_link;
  }
  node->add_data();
  node->pointer->next_link=current_node;
  if (previous_node==0)
    location=node->pointer;
  else
    previous_node->next_link=node->pointer;
}

void employee_list::remove_employee_id(char *social_security)
{
  P_and_M_Auto_Dealership *current_node=location;
  P_and_M_Auto_Dealership *previous_node=0;

  while(current_node != 0 &&
     strcmp(current_node->social_security,
            social_security) != 0) {
    previous_node=current_node;
    current_node=current_node->next_link;
  }
```

```
  if(current_node != 0 && previous_node == 0) {
    location=current_node->next_link;
    // delete current_node; needed if new() used in add_data()
  }
  else if(current_node != 0 && previous_node != 0) {
    previous_node->next_link=current_node->next_link;
    // delete current_node; needed if new() used in add_data()
  }
}
************************************************************/

void main( void )
{
  vector<P_and_M_Auto_Dealership> workers;

  cout.setf(ios::fixed);
  cout.precision(2);

  // instantiations done within STL vector push_back();
  // static data to add to linked list
  // salespersons salesperson1("Friendly","Fran","212-98-7654",
  //                           "Salesperson",1,7.5,4.00);
  // salespersons salesperson2("Pest","Perry","567-45-3412",
  //                           "Salesperson",2,2.0,2.20);
  // salespersons salesperson3("Yourfriend","Yancy","213-44-9873",
  //                           "Salesperson",1,10.6,5.70);
  // mechanics mechanicperson1("Hardwork","Harriet","076-45-3121",
  //                           "Mechanic",7,10.34);
  // mechanics mechanicperson2("Lugwrench","Larry","886-43-1518",
  //                           "Mechanic",1,8.98);
  // deal_closer closerperson ("Slick","Sally",
  //                           "111-22-4444","Closer",
  //                            10,40000.00);
  // parts partperson1        ("Muffler","Mike","555-66-7891",
  //                           "Parts",4,7.34);
  // parts partperson2        ("Horn","Hazel","345-77-7654",
  //                           "Parts",5,9.50);

  // add the eight workers to the linked list
  workers.push_back(mechanics    ("Hardwork","Harriet","076-45-3121",
                                  "Mechanic",7,10.34)            );
  workers.push_back(deal_closer  ("Slick","Sally",    "111-22-4444",
                                   "Closer",10,40000.00)         );
  workers.push_back(salespersons ("Friendly","Fran","212-98-7654",
                                  "Salesperson",1,7.5,4.00)      );
  workers.push_back(parts        ("Muffler","Mike","555-66-7891",
                                  "Parts",4,7.34)                );
```

```
    workers.push_back(parts          ("Horn","Hazel","345-77-7654",
                                      "Parts",5,9.50)                );
    workers.push_back(salespersons ("Pest","Perry","567-45-3412",
                                      "Salesperson",2,2.0,2.20)      );
    workers.push_back(mechanics      ("Lugwrench","Larry","886-43-1518",
                                      "Mechanic",1,8.98)              );
    workers.push_back(salespersons ("Yourfriend","Yancy","213-44-9873",
                                      "Salesperson",1,10.6,5.70)     );

    // print the linked list under OOP version
    // working workers.print_employee_list();

    // print the dynamic STL vector
    for( vector<P_and_M_Auto_Dealership>::iterator i = workers.begin();
         i != workers.end(); i++)
           i-> send_info();

    // remove three workers from the linked list
    // under OOP version
    // workers.remove_employee_id("555-66-7891");
    // workers.remove_employee_id("111-22-4444");
    // workers.remove_employee_id("213-44-3412");

    // example removing a worker from dynamic STL vector
    i = workers.begin();
    do
      if( strcmpi(i -> social_security, "555-66-7891") == 0)
        workers.erase(i);
    while( i++ != workers.end() );

    cout << "\n\n*************************************";

    // print the revised linked list under OOP version
    // workers.print_employee_list();

    // print the dynamic STL vector
    for( i = workers.begin(); i != workers.end(); i++)
      i->send_info();

}
```

Under STL technology, vector functions manipulate the container's contents; in this coded example it was the child or subclasses: `deal_closer`, `salespersons`, `mechanics`, and `parts`. For this reason, the symbiotic relationship between the `OOPlst.cpp friend` class `employee_list` (in fact, the entire `friend` class `employee_list`) is no longer needed. (Notice the volume and algorithm complexity eliminated by removing the `friend` class `employee_list`!) Keeping track of items in the list now becomes the responsibility of STL vector functions. This necessitated the removal of the parent class' P_and_M_Auto_Dealership members, pointer and next_link, commented out in the following code segment:

```
protected:
  char lastname[20];
  char firstname[15];
  char occupation[30];
  char social_security[12];
  int years_employed;
//  Linking performed by dynamic STL vector
//  P_and_M_Auto_Dealership *pointer;
//  P_and_M_Auto_Dealership *next_link;
```

Also, since the vector functions will maintain the list pointers, there is no need for any parent or subclass to make certain that the next_link pointer is initialized to 0 or NULL, so all references of this nature are now commented out, as in:

```
next_link=0;
```

In a logically related manner, all virtual subclass methods, such as add_data(), are commented out since the STL vector functions contain the list-insertion algorithms.

With all of the formal class/subclass and friend class definitions revamped for STL vector use, the main() program moves the instantiation of the eight instances into the STL vector push_back() function calls. These simple function calls invoke all of the STL vector code replacing the logically equivalent horsepower provided by the eliminated friend class employee_list.

Outputting the eight, freshly added employees is accomplished with an STL design-specific for loop:

```
// print the dynamic STL vector
  for( vector<P_and_M_Auto_Dealership>::iterator i = workers.begin();
       i != workers.end(); i++)
         i->send_info();
```

Remember, under STL, you find the beginning and ending addresses for any container by using container-specific functions begin() and end(). Also, the addresses returned by the STL functions must be assigned to container-specific iterators, as in:

```
vector<P_and_M_Auto_Dealership>::iterator i
```

To remove an element from the STL vector, first locate the address to the row containing the element being removed (in this example, accomplished with a call to strcmpi()) and then pass this address to the STL erase() function:

```
// example removing a worker from dynamic STL vector
  i = workers.begin();
  do
    if( strcmpi(i -> social_security, "555-66-7891") == 0)
      workers.erase(i);
  while( i++ != workers.end() );
```

In the original OOPlst.cpp algorithm, this functionality was provided by the friend class employee_list, whose job it was to maintain the *algorithm* component of the *data/algorithm* counterparts in any list.

List

With STL separating out *how* you store your data from *what* you want to do with your stored data, converting VECTRlst.cpp from an STL <vector> container over to an STL <list> container implementation is simple. To convert the algorithm, simply do a search-and-replace for "vector" and replace the string with "list." The following code segments show the needed changes:

First, the #include statement goes from:

```
#include <vector>
```

to

```
#include <list>
```

This pulls in the required STL dynamic linked-list definitions. The second change is the instantiation of workers, which goes from:

```
vector<P_and_M_Auto_Dealership> workers;
```

to

```
list<P_and_M_Auto_Dealership> workers;
```

The third change involves the typing for the for loop iterator used to traverse the list container. This statement goes from:

```
vector<P_and_M_Auto_Dealership>::iterator i = workers.begin();
```

to

```
list<P_and_M_Auto_Dealership>::iterator i = workers.begin();
```

As an alternative coding style, the delete portion of the algorithm was rewritten using the C/C++ break keyword and a do...while instead of while loop:

```
// example removing a worker from dynamic STL list
  i = workers.begin();
  while( i != workers.end() ) {
    if( strcmp(i -> social_security,"213-44-9873") == 0 )
      break;
     i++;
  }

  if( i != workers.end() )
    workers.erase(i);
```

What is so powerful about STL containers is that *how* your data component is stored (internally, as inefficient dynamic arrays or extremely efficient STL linked-lists) remains transparent from *what* you do with your data. Notice that all of the STL container functions, `push_back()`, `begin()`, `end()`, and `erase()`, perform flawlessly under both the vector and list implementations!

Once again, since most programmers learn best from coded examples, the completely rewritten program follows so that you can compare the logical and syntactical changes necessary to roll an algorithm over from OOP technology to STL list syntax:

```
// LISTlst.cpp
// C++ program using STL list to re-create
// the object-oriented program with a linked list.
// This program keeps track of employee data at the
// P_and_M_Auto_Dealership.
// Chris H. Pappas and William H. Murray, 2000

#include <iostream>
#include <string>
#include <list>

using namespace std;

// PARENT CLASS
class P_and_M_Auto_Dealership {

// friend class employee_list replaced by the
// dynamic nature of the STL list
// friend class employee_list;

protected:
  char lastname[20];
  char firstname[15];
  char occupation[30];
  int years_employed;
//  Linking performed by dynamic STL list
```

```
//  P_and_M_Auto_Dealership *pointer;
//  P_and_M_Auto_Dealership *next_link;

public:
  char social_security[12]; //made public for erase()
  P_and_M_Auto_Dealership(char *lname,char *fname,char *ssnum,
      char *occup,int c_years_employed)
  {
    strcpy(lastname,lname);
    strcpy(firstname,fname);
    strcpy(social_security,ssnum);
    strcpy(occupation,occup);
    years_employed=c_years_employed;
//  maintained by dynamic STL list
//  next_link=0;
  }

  P_and_M_Auto_Dealership()
  {
    lastname[0]=NULL;
    firstname[0]=NULL;
    social_security[0]=NULL;
    occupation[0]=NULL;
    years_employed=0;
//  maintained by dynamic STL list
//  next_link=0;
  }

  void fill_lastname(char *l_name)
  {
    strcpy(lastname,l_name);
  }

  void fill_firstname(char *f_name)
  {
    strcpy(firstname,f_name);
  }

  void fill_social_security(char *soc_sec)
  {
    strcpy(social_security,soc_sec);
  }

  void fill_occupation(char *o_name)
  {
    strcpy(occupation,o_name);
  }
```

```
  void fill_years_employed(int c_years_employed)
  {
    years_employed=c_years_employed;
  }

  virtual void add_data() {
  }
  virtual void send_info()
  {
    cout << "\n\n" << lastname << ", " << firstname
         << "\n Social Security: #" << social_security;
    cout << "\n Job Title: " << occupation;
    cout << "\n Years With Company: " << years_employed;
  }
};

//SUB OR DERIVED CHILD CLASS
class deal_closer:public P_and_M_Auto_Dealership {

// friend class replaced by dynamic STL list
// friend class employee_list;

private:
  float yearly_salary;

public:
  deal_closer(char *lname,char *fname,char *ssnum,
              char *occup,int c_years_employed,
              float y_salary):
              P_and_M_Auto_Dealership(lname,fname,ssnum,
              occup,c_years_employed)
  {
    yearly_salary=y_salary;
  }

  deal_closer():P_and_M_Auto_Dealership()
  {
    yearly_salary=0.0;
  }

  void fill_yearly_salary(float salary)
  {
    yearly_salary=salary;
  }

// Maintained by dynamic STL list
/* void add_data()
```

```
  {
    pointer=this;
  }
*/

  void send_info()
  {
    P_and_M_Auto_Dealership::send_info();
    cout << "\n Yearly Salary: $" << yearly_salary;
  }
};


//SUB OR DERIVED CHILD CLASS
class salespersons:public P_and_M_Auto_Dealership {

// friend class replaced by dynamic STL list
// friend class employee_list;

private:
  float unit_sales_average;
  int comm_rate;

public:
  salespersons(char *lname,char *fname,char *ssnum,
               char *occup,int c_years_employed,
               float w_avg,int c_rate):
               P_and_M_Auto_Dealership(lname,fname,ssnum,
               occup,c_years_employed)
  {
    unit_sales_average=w_avg;
    comm_rate=c_rate;
  }

  salespersons():P_and_M_Auto_Dealership()
  {
    unit_sales_average=0.0;
    comm_rate=0;
  }

  void fill_average(float w_avg)
  {
    unit_sales_average=w_avg;
  }

  void fill_comm_rate(int c_rate)
  {
```

```
    comm_rate=c_rate;
  }

// Maintained by dynamic STL list
/* void add_data()
  {
    pointer=this;
  }

  void send_info()
  {
    P_and_M_Auto_Dealership::send_info();
    cout << "\n Weekly Sales Average (units): "
         << unit_sales_average;
    cout << "\n Commission Rate: " << comm_rate << "%";
  }
*/
};


//SUB OR DERIVED CHILD CLASS
class mechanics:public P_and_M_Auto_Dealership {

// friend class replaced by dynamic STL list
// friend class employee_list;

private:
  float hourly_salary;

public:
  mechanics(char *lname,char *fname,char *ssnum,char *occup,
        int c_years_employed,float h_salary):
        P_and_M_Auto_Dealership(lname,fname,ssnum,
        occup,c_years_employed)
  {
    hourly_salary=h_salary;
  }

  mechanics():P_and_M_Auto_Dealership()
  {
    hourly_salary=0.0;
  }

  void fill_hourly_salary(float h_salary)
  {
    hourly_salary=h_salary;
  }
```

```
// Maintained by dynamic STL list
/*  void add_data()
   {
     pointer=this;
   }

   void send_info()
   {
     P_and_M_Auto_Dealership::send_info();
     cout << "\n Hourly Salary: $" << hourly_salary;
   }
*/
};


//SUB OR DERIVED CHILD CLASS
class parts:public P_and_M_Auto_Dealership {

// friend class replaced by dynamic STL list
// friend class employee_list;

private:
  float hourly_salary;

public:
  parts(char *lname,char *fname,char *ssnum,char *occup,
           int c_years_employed,float h_salary):
           P_and_M_Auto_Dealership(lname,fname,ssnum,
           occup,c_years_employed)
   {
     hourly_salary=h_salary;
   }

  parts():P_and_M_Auto_Dealership()
   {
     hourly_salary=0.0;
   }

  void fill_hourly_salary(float h_salary)
   {
     hourly_salary=h_salary;
   }

// Maintained by dynamic STL list
/* void add_data()
   {
     pointer=this;
   }
```

```
  void send_info()
  {
    P_and_M_Auto_Dealership::send_info();
    cout << "\n Hourly Salary: $" << hourly_salary;
  }
*/
};

/**********************************************************
Entire functionality of friend class employee_list
maintained by dynamic STL list
//FRIEND CLASS
class employee_list {

private:
  P_and_M_Auto_Dealership *location;

public:
  employee_list()
  {
    location=0;
  }

  void print_employee_list();

  void insert_employee(P_and_M_Auto_Dealership *node);

  void remove_employee_id(char *social_security);

};

void employee_list::print_employee_list()
{
  P_and_M_Auto_Dealership *present=location;

  while(present!=0) {
    present->send_info();
    present=present->next_link;
  }
}

void employee_list::insert_employee(P_and_M_Auto_Dealership \
                                    *node)
{
  P_and_M_Auto_Dealership *current_node=location;
  P_and_M_Auto_Dealership *previous_node=0;
  while (current_node != 0 &&
         strcmp(current_node->lastname,node->lastname) < 0) {
```

```
    previous_node=current_node;
    current_node=current_node->next_link;
  }
  node->add_data();
  node->pointer->next_link=current_node;
  if (previous_node==0)
    location=node->pointer;
  else
    previous_node->next_link=node->pointer;
}

void employee_list::remove_employee_id(char *social_security)
{
  P_and_M_Auto_Dealership *current_node=location;
  P_and_M_Auto_Dealership *previous_node=0;

  while(current_node != 0 &&
     strcmp(current_node->social_security,
            social_security) != 0) {
    previous_node=current_node;
    current_node=current_node->next_link;
  }

  if(current_node != 0 && previous_node == 0) {
    location=current_node->next_link;
    // delete current_node; needed if new() used in add_data()
  }
  else if(current_node != 0 && previous_node != 0) {
    previous_node->next_link=current_node->next_link;
    // delete current_node; needed if new() used in add_data()
  }
}
*************************************************************/

void main( void )
{
  list<P_and_M_Auto_Dealership> workers;

  cout.setf(ios::fixed);
  cout.precision(2);

  // instantiations done within STL list push_back();
  // static data to add to linked list
  // salespersons salesperson1("Friendly","Fran","212-98-7654",
  //                           "Salesperson",1,7.5,4.00);
  // salespersons salesperson2("Pest","Perry","567-45-3412",
  //                           "Salesperson",2,2.0,2.20);
```

```
// salespersons salesperson3("Yourfriend","Yancy","213-44-9873",
//                           "Salesperson",1,10.6,5.70);
// mechanics mechanicperson1("Hardwork","Harriet","076-45-3121",
//                           "Mechanic",7,10.34);
// mechanics mechanicperson2("Lugwrench","Larry","886-43-1518",
//                           "Mechanic",1,8.98);
// deal_closer closerperson ("Slick","Sally",
//                           "111-22-4444","Closer",
//                            10,40000.00);
// parts partperson1        ("Muffler","Mike","555-66-7891",
//                           "Parts",4,7.34);
// parts partperson2        ("Horn","Hazel","345-77-7654",
//                           "Parts",5,9.50);

// add the eight workers to the linked list
workers.push_back(mechanics    ("Hardwork","Harriet","076-45-3121",
                                "Mechanic",7,10.34)            );
workers.push_back(deal_closer  ("Slick","Sally",     "111-22-4444",
                                 "Closer",10,40000.00)          );
workers.push_back(salespersons ("Friendly","Fran","212-98-7654",
                                "Salesperson",1,7.5,4.00)      );
workers.push_back(parts        ("Muffler","Mike","555-66-7891",
                                "Parts",4,7.34)                );
workers.push_back(parts        ("Horn","Hazel","345-77-7654",
                                "Parts",5,9.50)                );
workers.push_back(salespersons ("Pest","Perry","567-45-3412",
                                "Salesperson",2,2.0,2.20)      );
workers.push_back(mechanics    ("Lugwrench","Larry","886-43-1518",
                                "Mechanic",1,8.98)             );
workers.push_back(salespersons ("Yourfriend","Yancy","213-44-9873",
                                "Salesperson",1,10.6,5.70)     );

// print the linked list under OOP version
// workers.print_employee_list();

// print the dynamic STL list
for( list<P_and_M_Auto_Dealership>::iterator i = workers.begin();
  i != workers.end(); i++)
    i -> send_info();

// remove three workers from the linked list
// under OOP version
// workers.remove_employee_id("555-66-7891");
// workers.remove_employee_id("111-22-4444");
// workers.remove_employee_id("213-44-3412");
```

```
  // example removing a worker from dynamic STL list
  i = workers.begin();
  while( i != workers.end() ) {
    if( strcmp(i -> social_security,"213-44-9873") == 0 )
      break;
    i++;
  }

  if( i != workers.end() )
    workers.erase(i);

  cout << "\n\n************************************";

  // print the revised linked list
  // workers.print_employee_list();

  // print the dynamic STL list
  for( i = workers.begin(); i != workers.end(); i++)
    i -> send_info();

}
```

STL Vector Versus List Efficiency

You may be asking yourself why, if STL vectors and lists are logical counterparts, STL supports the two container types. The answer involves efficiency, for example, inserting or erasing a vector element requires a block move of the array elements immediately following the insertion/erasure point. For this reason, the time expended performing this operation is proportional to the number of elements after the insertion/erasure point. STL lists, on the other hand, are internally represented as doubly-linked nodes, with each node having a reverse and forward pointer. This means list insertions and erasures in the middle of the container are much more efficient since they only require updating four or two (respectively) pointers.

Summary

In this chapter you progressively discovered how lists could be implemented, from the simple C++ procedural approach using arrays-of-structures, onto procedural linked-list syntax, then object-oriented linked-lists, and finally, the most up-to-date and portable ANSI ISO C++ STL vector and list technology. The concepts discussed in this chapter are expanded in following chapters, as you learn more about advanced methods for ordering, searching, and sorting your data with additional STL templates.

CHAPTER 3

Stacks and Queues—STL Adaptors

Any STL definition for a data structure that can hold information is called a container. Just about every program ever written stores data in some form of list. Regardless of how the internal coding implements this storage, additional functionality is always included to insert, delete, sort, and search data items and to find out if the list exists, and how many items the container holds. Moderations on this functionality include where the data items are inserted and removed and how efficiently internal container coding can retrieve information (remember the Big O function, or Order of Magnitude algorithm efficiency ratings).

This chapter introduces you to several of the most frequently used STL containers, namely vectors, stacks, and queues. Although, technically speaking, under STL, stacks and queues are not stand-alone container types. Stacks and queues under STL are a predefined set of operations, called adaptors, that you can apply to an STL vector. The STL list template also shares some of these capabilities. Since many stack and queue operations are identical to those used by simple vectors, this chapter begins with a detailed view of vector algorithms. This section of the chapter lays down many foundational logical and syntax rules necessary to correctly use STL technology.

Question: If `<vector>` containers are arrays, then are arrays `<vector>` containers? Answer: No! Ok, here's the good news. Using `<vector>` containers is logically and syntactically very similar to using simple C/C++ arrays. The great news is that unlike statically allocated arrays, `<vector>` containers are dynamic. Dynamic, in the sense of linked-list technology, meaning that the `<vector>` container can grow and shrink its size to maximize the use of RAM.

The `<stack>` and `<queue>` data types in the STL are interesting because they are not provided as true stand-alone data types, but rather are constructed as adaptors placed on top of other containers. The `<queue>` template, like the `<stack>` template, is implemented as an adaptor that wraps around an underlying container. As with the `<stack>`, the `<queue>` adaptor does not actually provide any new functionality, but simply modifies the interface. Operations are provided with their conventional queuelike names, but are actually performed using operations on the underlying containers.

Containers in the standard library that implement the necessary operations for the `<queue>` adaptor include the `<list>` and the `<deque>` data structure that we will introduce in the next chapter. Unlike the `<stack>` template, the `<queue>` class in STL provides the ability to access both the front and back elements of the queue, while the conventional description of the stack abstract data type (ADT) only permits access to the front.

Dynamic Arrays

The term *vector* is commonly used to mean an indexed collection of similarly typed values. In C++ we can represent this abstract concept as a one-dimensional array. Recall that an array is a fixed-size collection of values of homogeneous data types, indexed by integer keys. The number of elements held by the array is provided as part of the declaration. The following, for example, creates an array of ten float values:

```
float fArray[10];
```

Legal index values range from zero to one less than the size of the collection. Values are accessed using the subscript operator. A programmer can think of the elements of an array as being placed end to end in memory. The underlying C++ language provides only a primitive mechanism for the support of one-dimensional arrays, and this mechanism provides few safeguards. Most importantly, index values are *not* checked against declared bounds at run time.

The problem is compounded by the fact that there is no way to determine from the value of a simple C++ array the extent, or number of elements, it should contain. Furthermore, there are even fewer high-level operations defined for the array type than there are for character strings. By adding a new abstraction layer on top of the basic language framework, we can correct many of these deficiencies.

Making Vectors Data-Type Specific

A vector viewed as an abstract data type is different in one very important respect from the data types we have previously investigated. As an abstract concept, the idea of a vector describes an incomplete data type. The solution of any particular problem might require a vector of integers, a vector of floating-point values, or even a vector of strings. In order to abstract the concept of a vector out of these more concrete realizations, we need a facility to parameterize a type description with another type. That is, we need some way to describe the idea of a vector of type `T`, where `T` represents an unknown type.

Within a vector class description the unknown parameter type `T` can be used in any situation requiring the use of a type name. This allows you to declare an instance variable as a pointer to `T`, and we can declare an operator as returning a `T` reference. In the copy constructor, we need to refer to an object of the same type as the receiver. Although only the keyword vector is used, it is implicitly assumed to mean vector of `T`.

How To Instantiate a Vector

In order to use a template class as a type, you have to provide bindings for the unknown argument types. This is accomplished by providing the element type in a list, again surrounded by angle brackets. For example, the following declares a vector of five integer values, each entry initialized to 0; a vector consisting of 20 uninitialized, float-precision values; and a vector of ten strings, all initialized to the string "`abc`":

```
// overloaded <vector> constructors
vector<int> iVector(5,0);
vector<float> fVector(20);
vector<string> szVector(10,"abc");
```

An Example Using Vector Template Functions

The following template function, `max()`, which appears in the STL, is used to compute the maximum of two arguments. This functionality is parameterized using the template syntax:

```
template <class T> max(T a, T b)
{
  if( a < b )
    return b;
  return a:
}
```

The template function will work as long as the arguments are of a type that can be compared. Thus, the function will work with integers, floating-point precision, and strings. Many of the template functions used by the `<vector>` template library use this data-independent syntax.

Referencing Single Elements

Accessing an individual `<vector>` element is no more difficult than accessing a simple array element. The syntax looks identical:

```
standardArrayElementReference[ 1 ];
myVectorInstanceElementReference[ 1 ];
```

The syntax changes slightly when traversing an entire <vector> versus an array. Look at the two equivalent statements that follow:

```
// traversing a simple array
for( int offset = 0; offset < MAX_ELEMENTS; offset++)...
// traversing a <vector> instance
vector<int>::iterator iteratorOffset;
for( iteratorOffset = myVector.front(); iteratorOffset !=
myVector.end();
     iteratorOffset++)...
```

Similar to the `<string>` template, the `<vector>` template contains a type definition for the `name` iterator. This permits an iterator to be easily declared for any particular type of vector value. The template functions, `begin()` and `end()`, yield random access iterators for the vector. Again, note that the iterators yielded by these operations can become invalidated after insertions or removal of elements.

Adding and Deleting Elements

You use the `<vector>` template functions, `push_back()`, `insert()`, `pop_back()`, and `erase()`, to insert and remove `<vector>` elements. The template function, `push_back()`, takes a new value as argument and inserts the element at the end of the vector, increasing the size of the vector by one. The more general template function, `insert()`, takes as arguments an iterator and a value, and inserts the new element preceding the position specified by the iterator. Again, the size of the vector is increased by one.

The `<vector>` template function, `pop_back()`, removes the last element of the vector, reducing the size of the vector by one; the more general template function, `erase()`, is overloaded. In the easier form a single location is specified using an iterator, and the value denoted by the iterator is removed from the vector. Again, the size of the vector is then reduced by one. The more general form of `erase()` takes two iterator arguments, which specify a range of values within the vector. All elements within this range are removed regardless of the number of elements being removed.

The template function, `swap()`, takes as an argument another vector that holds the same type of elements. The values of the two vectors are then exchanged; after the operation all values from the argument will be held by the receiving vector, and all elements in the current vector will be held by the argument.

Determining the Size of a Vector Container

Unlike a standard C++ array, which has a fixed size determined by the declaring statement, `<vector>` vectors are dynamic in size, growing and shrinking as needed. However, vectors have two different sizes associated with them. The first is the number of elements currently in the vector, the second is the maximum size to which the vector can grow without actually allocating that new storage. The `<vector>` template function, `size()`, fulfills the first category, returning the actual number of vector elements, while `capacity()` returns your "wish list" for the total number of elements to be stored.

It therefore follows that inserting and deleting vector elements always changes the vector's size but may or may not change its capacity. An insertion that causes the size to exceed the capacity generally results in a new block of memory being allocated to hold the vector elements. Values are then copied into this new memory using the assignment operator appropriate to the element type, and the old memory is deleted. This can generate a *significant performance hit* on your algorithm should the vector be large in size!

The `<vector>` template function, `reserve()`, is a directive to the vector, indicating that the vector is expected to grow to at least the given size. If the argument used with `reserve()` is larger than the current capacity, then a reallocation occurs and the argument value becomes the new capacity. (If subsequent inserts cause the vector to grow even larger than this new value, the vector can grow even larger.) The reserved value is not a fixed delimiter, but an application's best guess at the maximum vector size. When the capacity is already in excess of the reserved size request, no reallocation takes place. Remember, calling `reserve()` does *not* change the actual size of the vector, nor the element values themselves.

Caution is the word when dealing with pointers to vectors, as a reallocation invalidates *all* references, pointers, and iterators denoting elements being held by a vector. This means that it is dangerous to lock onto an iterator's address thinking that the address associated with the pointer will *never* change:

```
vector<double>::iterator FrontOfVectorConstant;
FrontOfVectorConstant = myVector.begin();
// unstable code using FrontOfVectorConstant instead of myVector.begin()...
```

Using the `<algorithm>` Template with Vectors

While the `<vector>` template does not directly provide any template function that can be used to determine if a specific value is contained in the collection, the generic `<algorithm>` template functions, `find()` or `count()`, can be used for these purposes.

`<vector>` Example Programs

The following sample applications demonstrate many of the more frequently used `<vector>` template functions, overloaded operators, and areas of caution when using this template library.

The `ivector.cpp` Application

This first application demonstrates the dimensioning of vector containers, from the initial instantiation of the vector, to dynamically allocated "guess" length, to actually increasing the size of the container.

```
// ivector.cpp
// Testing <vector>
// push_back(), size(), capacity(), max_size(), reserve(), resize()
// Chris H. Pappas and William H. Murray, 2000


// When symbols are longer than 255 characters, the warning is
disabled.
#pragma warning(disable:4786)

#include <vector>
#include <iomanip>
#include <iostream>

using namespace std ;

typedef vector<int> iVector;

void main( void )
{
    // Instantiation of 0 element integer vector.
    iVector iVectorInstance;

    // Inserting a 5, at the end of the vector
    iVectorInstance.push_back(5);

    // Current vector statistics.
    cout << "Current statistics:" << endl;
    cout << "iVectorInstance's current size: "
         << setw(10) << iVectorInstance.size() << endl;
    cout << "iVectorInstance's maximum size: "
         << iVectorInstance.max_size() << endl;
    cout << "iVectorInstance's capacity     : "
         << setw(10) << iVectorInstance.capacity() << endl;

    // See if there is room for a total of 15 elements
    iVectorInstance.reserve(15);
    cout << "\nReserving storage for 15 elements:" << endl;
    cout << "iVectorInstance's size is      : "
         << setw(10) << iVectorInstance.size() << endl;
    cout << "iVectorInstance's maximum size: "
         << setw(10) << iVectorInstance.max_size() << endl;
```

```
    cout << "iVectorInstance's capacity is : "
         <<  setw(10) << iVectorInstance.capacity() << endl;

    // Demanding room for at least 25 elements.
    iVectorInstance.resize(25);
    cout << "\nAfter resizing storage for 25 elements:" << endl;
    cout << "iVectorInstance's size is          : "
         <<  setw(10) << iVectorInstance.size() << endl;
    cout << "iVectorInstance's maximum size: "
         <<  iVectorInstance.max_size() << endl;
    cout << "iVectorInstance's capacity is : "
         <<  setw(10) << iVectorInstance.capacity() << endl;
}
```

The program begins with the following `typedef`:

```
typedef vector<int> iVector;
```

that defines `iVector` as an integer vector type. Next, the `iVectorInstance` is instantiated:

```
iVector iVectorInstance;
```

Notice that the container does *not* specify any fixed length. The first action on the vector is to insert the integer value `5` into the container using the `push_back()` template function:

```
iVectorInstance.push_back(5);
```

The next series of statements output the container's `size()`, `max_size()`, and `capacity()`, all with template functions:

```
cout << "Current statistics:" << endl;
    cout << "iVectorInstance's current size: "
         <<  setw(10) << iVectorInstance.size() << endl;
    cout << "iVectorInstance's maximum size: "
         <<  iVectorInstance.max_size() << endl;
    cout << "iVectorInstance's capacity     : "
         <<  setw(10) << iVectorInstance.capacity() << endl;
```

This series of statements repeats the same statistics based on two container size-changing statements. The first looks like:

```
iVectorInstance.reserve(15);
```

Remember that `reserve()` only checks to see if the requested size could indeed fit in available RAM, but does *not* actually increase the actual size of the container. The second dimension change comes from the following statement:

```
iVectorInstance.resize(25);
```

Unlike `reserve()`, `resize()` physically increases the maximum number of elements. Look at the output from the program and notice the affect on the various container statistics:

```
Current statistics:
iVectorInstance's current size:          1
iVectorInstance's maximum size: 1073741823
iVectorInstance's capacity    :          1

Reserving storage for 15 elements:
iVectorInstance's size is     :          1
iVectorInstance's maximum size: 1073741823
iVectorInstance's capacity is :         15

After resizing storage for 25 elements:
iVectorInstance's size is     :         25
iVectorInstance's maximum size: 1073741823
iVectorInstance's capacity is :         25
```

Notice that the `reserve()` request did *not* change the number of elements from 1 to 15, but *did* change the capacity to 15. However, `resize()` changed both the *size* and *capacity*. Also, notice the `maximum_size()`, which returns the length of the longest sequence that the object can control, remains constant.

The `cvector.cpp` Application

This next example demonstrates how to access vector elements using iterators and various `insert()` and `erase()` operations. Pay particular attention to how you syntactically and logically access vector elements:

```
// cvector.cpp
// Testing <vector>
// push_back(), insert(), delete(), begin(), end()
// Chris H. Pappas and William H. Murray, 2000


// When symbols are longer than 255 characters, the warning is disabled.
#pragma warning(disable:4786)

#include <vector>
#include <iostream>

using namespace std ;

typedef vector<char> cVector;

void main( void )
{
```

```
    // Instantiation of 0 element integer vector.
    cVector cVectorInstance;

    // Inserting five vowels
    cVectorInstance.push_back('A');
    cVectorInstance.push_back('E');
    cVectorInstance.push_back('I');
    cVectorInstance.push_back('O');
    cVectorInstance.push_back('Y');

    // Accessing vector elements using array syntax - DANGEROUS
    for(int i = 0; i < 5; i++)
      cout << cVectorInstance[i];
    cout << endl;

    // Accessing vector elements using iterators - BEST APPROACH
    vector<char>::iterator p = cVectorInstance.begin();
    while(p != cVectorInstance.end()) {
      cout << *p;
      p++;
    }
    cout << endl;

    // Inserting a NEW fifth element extending the vector's size
    p = cVectorInstance.begin();
    p += 4; // moves pointer to fifth element's address
    cVectorInstance.insert(p,'U');

    // Accessing the NEW list
    p = cVectorInstance.begin();
    while(p != cVectorInstance.end()) {
      cout << *p;
      p++;
    }
    cout << endl;

    // Deleting the sixth element 'Y'
    p = cVectorInstance.end();
    cVectorInstance.erase(—p);

    // Printing the modified container
    p = cVectorInstance.begin();
    while(p != cVectorInstance.end()) {
      cout << *p;
      p++;
    }
}
```

Most of the initial program statements should now look familiar to you, so the discussion begins with the two methods for accessing container elements:

```
// Accessing vector elements using array syntax - DANGEROUS
for(int i = 0; i < 5; i++)
  cout << cVectorInstance[i];
cout << endl;
```

While this `for` loop works, it is not the most generalized approach and breaks many of the STL rules. In particular, it is hardwired to the element count. The better, standard STL approach below uses the `begin()` and `end()` template functions, along with the iterator `p`, to perform the task:

```
// Accessing vector elements using iterators - BEST APPROACH
vector<char>::iterator p = cVectorInstance.begin();
while(p != cVectorInstance.end()) {
  cout << *p;
  p++;
}
```

The next three statements insert a new fifth vowel into the container, preceding the current fifth element of `Y`:

```
p = cVectorInstance.begin();
p += 4;          // moves pointer to fifth element's address
cVectorInstance.insert(p,'U');
```

The reinitialization of `p` is necessary since the previous loop moved the pointer beyond the end of the vector container. Pointer arithmetic is next employed to move `p` to the address of the fifth element, followed by a call to the `insert()` template function. This function accepts an iterator, `p`, and valid element type, `U`.

In order to output the updated container, iterator `p` needs resetting:

```
p = cVectorInstance.begin();
while(p != cVectorInstance.end()) {
  cout << *p;
  p++;
}
```

The final two statements:

```
p = cVectorInstance.end();
cVectorInstance.erase(—p);
```

reset `p` one more time, only this time to the end of the container. Caution: The template function, `end()`, returns an interator *one beyond the end* of the container. This explains the prefix decrement of `p` in the template function call statement (`--p`). Lastly, the template function `erase()` removes the element at the specified location. The template function could have removed a range of values with just a slightly different syntax:

```
cVectorInstance.erase(initializedIterator, initializedIterator + n);
```

The output from the program looks like:

```
AEIOY
AEIOY
AEIOUY
AEIOU
```

Now that you have a thorough understanding of how STL vector logic and syntax operate, you are ready for the perfectly natural use of a one-dimensional array to implement a stack.

The ADT Stack

In general, a stack is used to reverse the order of data placed in it. Now, let's see how a stack works, beginning with a formal definition for a stack. A *stack* is a collection of data elements and related operations whereby all the insertions and deletions of elements to and from the stack are made at one end of the stack called the *top*. A stack operates on the *last-in-first-out*, or *LIFO*, principle.

To get the idea of a stack, think of a stack of wet, hot, cafeteria dishes sitting in a spring-loaded, stainless steel, dish holder. When you remove a dish from the container, you remove the just washed, wet, hot one, from the *top* of the stack of dishes in the container. You would prefer to grab the cool dry one at the bottom of the container, but it is inaccessible. As additional clean dishes are removed from the dishwasher and placed on the dish holder, they are added to the top of the stack, pushing all previously stored dishes down into the stainless steel container. Once again, it is the even wetter and hotter dishes that remain ready at the stack top.

All insertions and deletions of dishes to and from the stainless steel dish holder are made at the *top* of the stack. In other words, the last dish placed onto the stack will be the first dish removed from the stack. You can be thankful that many real world applications do *not* function the way a stack operates.

Take, for example, a bank teller line. If the line were operating on the LIFO principle, the last person in the line would be the first one processed. It might be quite some time until you were able to cash your paycheck, especially if other people kept entering the line. Wouldn't that make your day! To be fair, bank teller lines, grocery store checkout lines, and the like must operate on the *first-in-first-out,* or *FIFO,* principle. This principle is associated with queues and will be discussed later in the chapter.

Let's look at all the operations necessary to operate a stack implementation. Consider the cafeteria dish holder. What operations do you suppose could be performed on such a stack? Well, first of all, you can move an empty stainless steel dish holder into position in preparation for adding dishes to it. Then you can begin adding dishes to the container to form the initial stack of clean dishes. When a single dish is added to the stack, it can only be added at the *top* position and no other position. Adding an element to a stack is referred to as a *push* operation. You can remove a dish from the *top* of the stack; normally, you can't remove a dish from any position other than the top of the stack. Removing an element from a stack is called a `pop` operation.

You could also inspect the *top* dish, but no others. You could see if the stack of dishes were empty, but if not empty, you would not know how many dishes were in the stack. Given this situation, you are forced to access the dishes from the *top* of the stack. The stack of dishes provides a very good analogy to stacks in computer science, because the operations that can be performed on a stack of dishes form the basis for the stack ADT in computer science. Here is a summary of legal stack operations:

- `CreateStack`—Creates an empty stack.
- `Push`—Places an element on the top of a stack.
- `Pop`—Removes an element from the top of a stack.
- `TopElement`—Examines the top element of the stack, leaving the stack unchanged.
- `EmptyStack`—Reports if the stack is empty or not.

Creating a Stack Using an Array

To use an array stack implementation, you begin by creating an array of some arbitrary length and an integer variable called `Top` to keep track of the top element on the stack. Remember, you only need to keep track of the top element of the stack because, by definition, access to the stack elements must be through the top of the stack. To initialize the stack, you will set `Top` to the value `-1`, as seen in Figure 3.1 (note: Figure 3.1 numbers the indices bottom-up so that the value of `Top` looks like what it is; numbering the array indices top-down would make the stack look like it grows downward).

Notice the array is defined with indices ranging from `0` to `MaxElements-1`, and can hold a total of `MaxElements`. This array will be used to hold a stack so that the first stack element will be placed at position `[0]` in the array, the second stack element at position `[1]`, and so on. The integer variable called `Top` will point to the array index that locates the current top element in the stack. A value of `-1` indicates the stack is empty because there is no legal array index value of `-1`. Using this idea, all that is necessary to create a new empty stack is to define an array and set `Top` to the value `-1`. How do you know if the stack ever becomes empty when processing the stack data? The stack is empty if the value of `Top` becomes `-1`. The ADT algorithm required to create a stack looks like:

```
CreateStack() Algorithm
  BEGIN
    Set Top = -1.
  END.
```

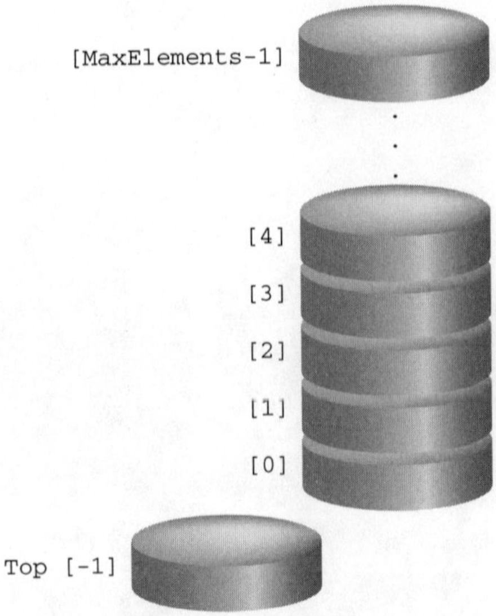

Figure 3.1
Initializing `Top` to empty or a value of –1.

Pushing Elements onto a Stack

With an array stack implementation, pushing the first element onto an empty stack is accomplished by incrementing `Top` to position `[0]` and inserting the value into the array. For example, if the array is storing the infix expression `A * B + C`, the first push operation would look like:

```
Push('A')
```

The push operation causes the value of `Top` to be incremented from `-1` to `0`, and then the letter 'A' is placed at position `[Top]`, or `[0]`, of the array. Next, suppose your program executes another push operation like:

```
Push('*')
```

The second call to `Push()` causes `Top` to be incremented from `0` to `1`, and then the symbol '`*`' is placed on the top of the stack, which is now array position `[1]`. The program completes by making three more calls to `push`, each first incrementing `Top` and then placing the next symbol on the stack top:

```
Push('B')
Push('+')
Push('C')
```

Figure 3.2 shows the successive changes made to the array and the variable `Top`.

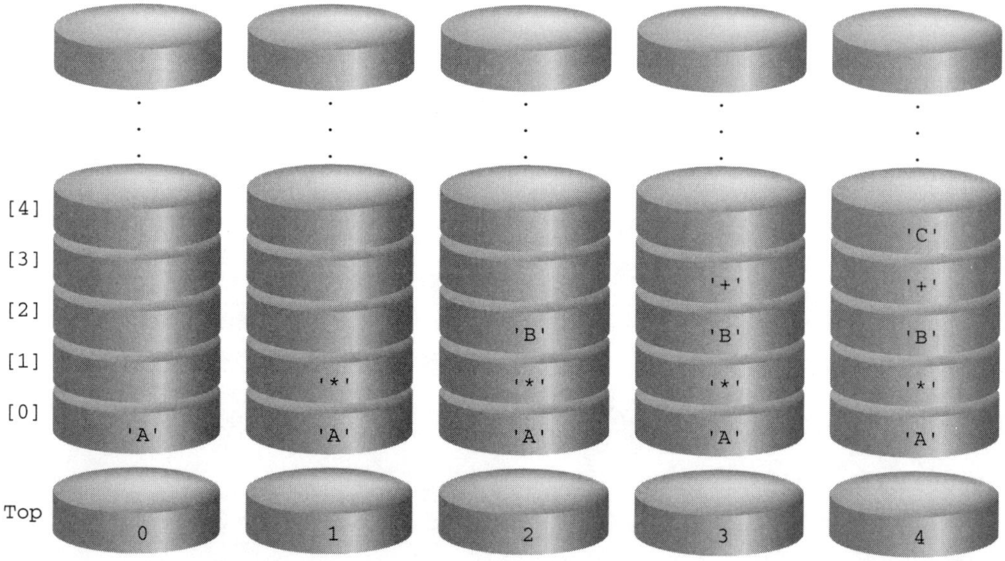

Figure 3.2 Displaying the five successive calls to `Push()`.

It is important to note that the value of `Top` must be incremented *prior* to placing the element on the stack. The algorithm for the operation `Push()` looks like:

```
Push() Algorithm
  BEGIN
    If the stack is not full
      Increment Top.
      Place element at array position [Top]
    Else
      Display full stack message.
  END.
```

Notice that a test is necessary to determine if the stack is full because you cannot push an element onto a full stack. When would the stack be full? When the variable `Top` equals `MaxElements`. Remember, the last legal offset into the array is when `Top` equals `MaxElements -1`! The first statement in `Push()` can be written as:

```
if( ++Top < MaxElements )
```

This statement first increments `Top` using the C/C++ prefix increment operator, and then checks to see if `Top`'s new value is beyond the legal range for the array. This one statement implements both the increment of `Top` and the test for stack not full.

Popping Elements from a Stack

Given the stack created in Figure 3.2, suppose the program executes a single `pop` operation:

```
Pop()
```

What happens to the stack? Well, `Top` is pointing to the *last* element placed on the stack (the letter 'C') so all that is necessary is to remove the element at array position `[Top]`, or `[4]`. However, once the element is removed, the value of `Top` must be decremented to locate the new top of the stack. Figure 3.3 illustrates the updated stack after this function call.

The letter 'C' at position `[4]` is removed, and the value of `Top` is decremented from `4` to `3` to locate array position `[3]`, which is now the new top of the stack. Three more calls to `Pop()`:

```
Pop() // removes '+', Top decremented to 2
Pop() // removes 'B', Top decremented to 1
Pop() // removes '*', Top decremented to 0
```

leaving `Top` with a value of `0`, and the top stack element, the letter 'A'. One more call to `Pop()` removes the letter 'A' from the stack and decrements `Top` to the value `-1`, indicating the stack is empty. Remember, the operation `Pop()` decrements `Top` after the element is removed from the stack. The `Pop()` algorithm looks like:

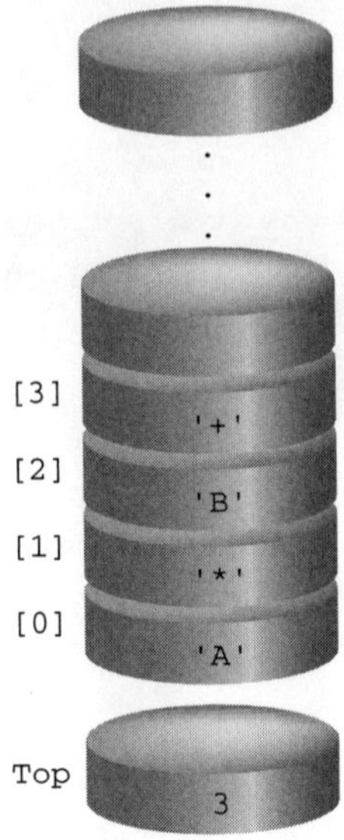

Figure 3.3
The results of executing one call to `Pop()`, removing 'C'.

```
Pop() Algorithm
  BEGIN
    If the stack is not empty
      Remove element at array position [Top].
      Decrement Top.
    Else
      Display empty stack message.
  END.
```

Notice that the algorithm first checks to see if the stack is empty because you cannot pop an element from an empty stack. How do you know when the stack is empty? Of course—when `Top` equals `-1`.

Viewing the Top Element of a Stack

`TopElement()` is the last operation for an ADT stack. This function simply examines the top element without removing it. Typically, `TopElement()` makes a copy of the stack top. Like the `Pop()` operation, the `TopElement()` operation reads the element at array position `[Top]`. However, unlike the `Pop()` operation, `TopElement()`, does not decrement the stack pointer `Top`. The algorithm for `TopElement()` looks like:

```
TopElement() Algorithm
  BEGIN
    If the stack is not empty
      Copy element at array position [Top].
    Else
      Display empty message.
  END.
```

A straightforward C++ stack class definition looks like:

```
//STACK CLASS DEFINITION
#ifndef STACK_H
#define STACK_H

const int MAXELEMENTS = 25

class Stack
{
  Stack(void);
  int EmptyStack(void);
  int FullStack(void);
  void Push(char Symbol);
  char Pop(void);
  char TopElement(void);
```

```
private:
  char symbolArray[MAXELEMENTS];
  int Top;
};
#endif
```

These same stack operations are automated for STL containers using the STL adaptors discussed in the following section.

The STL Stack

This section details the concepts of a stack as they apply to the STL `<stack>` template. The `<stack>` and `<queue>` abstract data types in the STL are interesting because they are not provided as true stand-alone data types, but rather are constructed as adaptors placed on top of other containers. This section illustrates the use of these abstractions in the solution of several programming problems.

Many everyday objects provide most people with a good intuitive understanding of the stack and queue abstract data types. An excellent example of a stack is a pile of papers on a desk (not segued); an even better example is a stack of dishes in a cupboard. The pivotal characteristic for both is that the item on the top is most easily accessed, with new items being added to the collection by placing them above all the current items in the stack. Items removed from a stack are those most recently added or last-in-first-out (LIFO).

Stacks are used by compilers (internal coding) and programmers to solve an array of problems. For example, compilers use stacks to allocate space for parameters and local variables. Each function call made by a program translates into machine code that increments a memory stack to create space for the parameters and local variables associated with the function. This use of a stack to perform memory allocation has many advantages. It allows recursive procedures that possess, in each iteration, a unique data area for local variables. The release of memory simply means decrementing the stack and invoking destructors for any values that define destructors. This construct allows the maximum use of memory, since no more memory is required for the stack than is absolutely necessary for the parameters and local variables in use at any one instance.

C++ uses a stack to implement the input stream mechanism. The stream data structure maintains two data areas. It must hold a pointer to the file from which the raw characters are obtained. It also maintains a stack of characters that have been pushed back into the input. This allows the method, `putback()`, to return a character to an input stream. A subsequent character read operation will first yield the pushed-back character before continuing with the remainder of input from the file.

STL Defines Stacks and Queues as Adaptors

STL implements both stacks and queues as adaptors. This means they do not directly implement the structures that hold the data values, but are instead built on top of other containers. In other words, they adapt the interface to these containers, providing names for the operations that make sense in the context of their use.

Any container that defines the internal type `T`, and that implements the operations `empty()`, `size()`, `back()`, `push_back()`, and `pop_back()`, can be used as a container for a stack. Both the `<vector>` and `<list>` templates support these operations, as well as the STL `<deque>`.

Care is needed when selecting the container type. Remember, vectors grow dynamically, but seldom shrink. On the other hand, space for a list both grows and shrinks as elements are added and removed from the collection. But, for a given size collection, a vector will use less overall memory space than will a list. For this reason, a vector, queue, or deque is a good candidate container if the size of the collection being maintained by a stack will remain relatively stable in size. You should select a list container when the collection will vary widely in size during program execution.

To appreciate these differences, consider the underlying container in response to the stack operations. The capacity of a vector is given by the largest number of elements it has been asked to hold up to a specific point in time, whereas the size of a vector represents the number of elements the vector currently holds. A `push_back()` will simply increase the size, unless the size reaches the capacity, in which case a memory reallocation is performed creating a larger buffer. However, in a list container, only the elements currently in the collection are maintained. Each `push()` operation causes a new memory allocation, and each `pop()` returns the memory location to the pool of available memory.

`<stack>` Template Syntax

The following listing gives the syntax for the <stack> template:

```
template<class T,
    class Cont = deque<T> >
    class stack {
public:
    typedef Cont::allocator_type allocator_type;
    typedef Cont::value_type value_type;
    typedef Cont::size_type size_type;
    explicit stack(const allocator_type& al = allocator_type()) const;
    bool empty() const;
    size_type size() const;
    allocator_type get_allocator() const;
    value_type& top();
    const value_type& top() const;
```

```
    void push(const value_type& x);
    void pop();
protected:
    Cont c;
    };
```

The `<stack>` template class describes an object that controls a varying-length sequence of elements. The object allocates and frees storage for the sequence it controls through a protected object named `c`, of class `Cont`. The type `T` of elements in the controlled sequence must match `value_type`. An object of class `Cont` must supply several public members defined the same as for `deque`, `list`, and `vector` (all of which are suitable candidates for class `Cont`). The required members are:

```
typedef T value_type;
typedef T0 size_type;
Cont(const allocator_type& al);
bool empty() const;
size_type size() const;
allocator_type get_allocator() const;
value_type& back();
const value_type& back() const;
void push_back(const value_type& x);
void pop_back();
```

<stack> Template Overloaded Operators

The <stack> template overloads the operators shown in Table 3.1.

Table 3.1 Overloaded Operators For <stack>

Overloaded Operators
bool **operator==**(const stack<T, Cont>& lhs, const stack<T, Cont>&);
bool **operator!=**(const stack<T, Cont>& lhs, const stack<T, Cont>&);
bool **operator<**(const stack<T, Cont>& lhs, const stack<T, Cont>&);
bool **"operator>**(const stack<T, Cont>& lhs, const stack<T, Cont>&);
bool **operator<=**(const stack<T, Cont>& lhs, const stack<T, Cont>&);
bool **="operator>=**(const stack<T, Cont>& lhs, const stack<T, Cont>&);

<stack> Template Methods

The <stack> template provides the methods shown in Table 3.2.

Table 3.2 <stack> Template Methods and Descriptions

Method	*Description*
`explicit stack(const allocator_type& al = allocator_type()) const;`	The constructor initializes the stored object with `c(al)` to specify an empty initial controlled sequence.
`bool empty() const;`	Returns true for an empty controlled sequence.
`size_type size() const;`	Returns the length of the controlled sequence.
`allocator_type get_allocator() const;`	Returns `c.get_allocator()`.
`value_type& top();` `const value_type& top() const;`	Returns a reference to the last element of the controlled sequence, which must be non-empty.
`void push(const value_type& x);`	Inserts an element with value x at the end of the controlled sequence.
`void pop();`	Removes the last element of the controlled sequence, which must be non-empty.

<stack> Example Program

The following example uses the `<stack>` STL template to convert an *infix* expression to *postfix*. Infix expressions are the way most people think of numeric calculations such as `4 * (16 + 2 * 8) + 22`. However, considering all of the arithmetic operators available in mathematics, writing a compiler to correctly translate an infinite combination would require a very inefficient, time consuming algorithm. Instead, compilers first take an infix expression, translate it into postfix, and then translate the postfix equation into machine code (postfix notation places the operators *after* the operands, for example, `A B +` instead of the infix `A + B`). What looks like unnecessary overprocessing on the surface ends up saving execution time. While the program that follows may initially look quite complicated, in essence it is a fraction of the code that would be necessary for a compiler to decipher an arithmetic equation using infix notation.

The `pushpop.cpp` Application

The following `<stack>` template application is based on a user defined, stack element type of *OPERATORS*. This enumerated type arranges the arithmetic operators from lowest precedence (ordinal value of 0) to highest (in this case `divideop` or 4):

```
// pushpop.cpp
// Testing <stack>
// push(), pop() top(), empty()
// Chris H. Pappas and William H. Murray, 2000

#pragma warning(disable:4786)
#include <stack>
#include <list>
#include <string>
#include <iostream>
#include <cctype>    // isdigit()

using namespace std ;

typedef enum tagOPERATORS { leftparenthesis, plusop,
                            minusop, multiplyop,
                            divideop } OPERATORS;

typedef stack<OPERATORS> CONVERSIONSTACK;


string ConvertOpToString(OPERATORS CurrentOperator);
void processOperator(OPERATORS currentOperator,
                     stack<OPERATORS>& ConversionStack,
                     string& result);

void main( void )
{
  CONVERSIONSTACK ConversionStack;

  string infix("4 * (16 + 2 * 8) + 22");
  string result("");
  int offset = 0;

  while(infix[offset] != '\0') {
    if(isdigit(infix[offset])) { // process values
      while(isdigit(infix[offset]))
        result += infix[offset++];
      result += " ";
    }
    else
```

```
      switch(infix[offset++]) {    // process non-values
      case '(': ConversionStack.push(leftparenthesis);
                break;
      case ')': while(ConversionStack.top() != leftparenthesis)
                {
                       result +=
ConvertOpToString(ConversionStack.top());
                         ConversionStack.pop();
                 }
                       ConversionStack.pop();
                         break;
      case '+': processOperator(plusop, ConversionStack, result);
                break;
      case '-': processOperator(minusop, ConversionStack, result);
                break;
      case '*': processOperator(multiplyop, ConversionStack, result);
                break;
      case '/': processOperator(divideop, ConversionStack, result);
                break;
      }
   }

   while(!ConversionStack.empty()) { // empty the stack
     result += ConvertOpToString(ConversionStack.top());
     ConversionStack.pop();
  }
  cout << result;
}

string ConvertOpToString(OPERATORS CurrentOperator)
{
  switch(CurrentOperator) {
    case plusop     : return " + ";
    case minusop    : return " - ";
    case multiplyop : return " * ";
    case divideop   : return " / ";
  }
}

void processOperator(OPERATORS currentOperator, stack<OPERATORS>&
ConversionStack,
               string& result)
{
  while( (!ConversionStack.empty()) && (currentOperator <
ConversionStack.top()) ) {
    result += ConvertOpToString(ConversionStack.top());
     ConversionStack.pop();
  }
  ConversionStack.push(currentOperator);
}
```

The program begins by defining the stack element type `OPERATORS`:

```
typedef enum tagOPERATORS { leftparenthesis, plusop,
                            minusop, multiplyop,
                            divideop } OPERATORS;
```

Next, using Microsoft styling conventions, a `typedef` creates the `CONVERSIONSTACK` type. Notice that the stack element type is `OPERATORS`:

```
typedef stack<OPERATORS> CONVERSIONSTACK;
```

The instantiation of `ConversionStack` takes the form (seen inside `main()`):

```
CONVERSIONSTACK ConversionStack;
```

For the sake of clarity, a sample infix expression is wired into the program avoiding superfluous I/O statements to interactively accept and verify any infix expression:

```
string infix("4 *  (16 + 2 * 8) + 22");
```

The algorithm parses the *infix* string, immediately appending numeric constants to the *result* string:

```
while(infix[offset] != '\0') {
    if(isdigit(infix[offset])) { // process values
      while(isdigit(infix[offset]))
        result += infix[offset++];
      result += " ";
    }
```

Operators, such as `+` and `*`, cannot be output until both their arguments have been processed. Therefore, they must be saved on the `ConversionStack`. If an operator being pushed onto the stack has a lower precedence level than the current top of the stack, then the top of the stack is popped and appended to `result`.

```
while( (!ConversionStack.empty()) && (currentOperator <
ConversionStack.top()) ) {
    result += ConvertOpToString(ConversionStack.top());
    ConversionStack.pop();
  }
  ConversionStack.push(currentOperator);
```

A left parenthesis is immediately pushed on the `ConversionStack`, regardless of the precedence of the current top of the stack.

```
case '(': ConversionStack.push(leftparenthesis);
```

A left parenthesis will be considered to have a precedence lower than any other symbol, and thus will never be popped off the stack. Instead, a right parenthesis will cause the stack to be popped and output until the corresponding left parenthesis is found. Notice the use of the template function, `top()`, to access the current stack top `OPERATOR`:

```
case ')': while(ConversionStack.top() != leftparenthesis)
           {
           result += ConvertOpToString(ConversionStack.top());
           ConversionStack.pop();
           }
         ConversionStack.pop();
```

The left parenthesis is popped but not appended to `result`. Finally, when the end of the *infix* expression is reached, the `ConversionStack` is popped until empty, appending symbols to the `result` string. The code segment uses the template function `empty()` to know when all `OPERATORS` have been processed:

```
while(!ConversionStack.empty()) { // empty the stack
     result += ConvertOpToString(ConversionStack.top());
     ConversionStack.pop();
  }
```

It is necessary to convert the enumerated representation of operators to strings that can be appended to `result` and explains the presence of `ConvertOpToString()`:

```
string ConvertOpToString(OPERATORS CurrentOperator)
{
  switch(CurrentOperator) {
    case plusop      : return " + ";
    case minusop     : return " - ";
    case multiplyop  : return " * ";
    case divideop    : return " / ";
  }
}
```

The output from the program looks like:

```
4 16 2 8  *  +  * 22  +
```

The ADT Queue

Another important abstract data type (ADT) is the queue. There are more examples of queues in the real world than stacks, because queues have the *first-in-first-out*, or *FIFO,* property. For instance, the bank teller line mentioned in the last section is an example of a queue. Aircraft in a holding pattern waiting to land at a busy airport represent a queuing operation. As aircraft approach the airport traffic area, they are placed in a holding pattern so that the first one in the pattern is the first one to land. We say that the aircraft are being queued into the pattern.

Recall that the LIFO property of stacks reverses the order of the stack elements from input to output. Queues, on the other hand, exhibit the FIFO property, which preserves the order of the elements from input to output.

Technically, a queue is defined as a collection of data elements in which all insertions of elements into the queue are made at one end of the queue, called the *rear* of the queue, and all deletions of elements from the queue are made at the other end of the queue, called the *front* of the queue. Here is a summary of legal queue operations:

- `CreateQ`—Creates an empty queue.
- `Insert`—Adds an element to the rear of a queue.
- `Remove`—Removes an element from the front of a queue.
- `FrontElement`—Copies the front element of a queue, leaving the queue unchanged.
- `EmptyQ`—Determines if the queue is empty.

Creating a Queue Using an Array

Like a stack, the queue ADT is not predefined in C++. In this section a standard array is modified to perform standard queue operations. The example uses a special array called a circular, or wraparound, array. Look at Figure 3.4 to see how to create a queue using a circular array.

To make an array hold a queue, you need to initialize two integer variables that locate the front and rear of the queue. In Figure 3.4, `Front` is initialized to `0`, and `Rear` is initialized

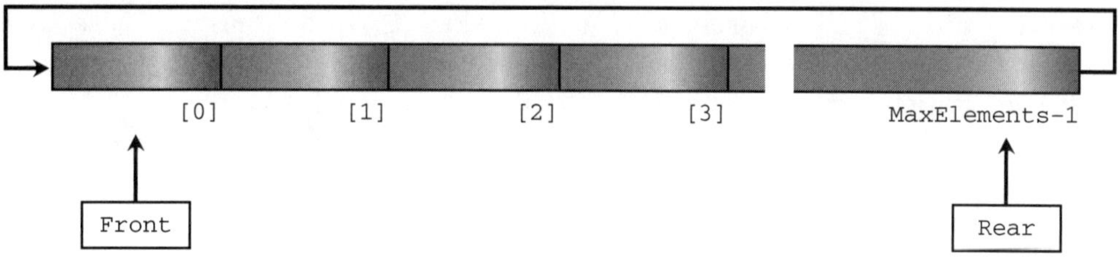

Figure 3.4 Using a circular array to implement a queue.

to `MaxElements-1` so that it locates the last array position. The algorithm for `CreateQ()` looks like:

```
CreateQ() Algorithm
  BEGIN
    Set Front = 0.
    Set Rear = MaxElements-1.
  END.
```

This is how the circular array works. When using an integer variable, such as `Front` or `Rear`, locate elements in the array by advancing the variable through the index range of the array, in the example, from `0` to `MaxElements-1`. If the variable needs to be advanced past the last array index, it is forced back to `0`—accomplished with a simple `if..else` statement:

```
If Rear == MaxElements-1
  Set Rear = 0.
Else
  Set Rear = Rear + 1.
```

Of course, the same operation is performed on `Front` to make it wrap around.

Inserting Elements into a Queue

To insert an element into the queue, first advance `Rear` and then place the element at array position `[Rear]`. Figure 3.5 shows the results of the following three calls to insert:

```
Insert("Jane")
Insert("John")
Insert("Mary")
```

First, the algorithm initializes the queue with a call to `CreateQ()`. Remember that this function initializes `Front` to `0` and `Rear` to `MaxElements-1`. When the first customer `Jane` is inserted into the queue, the value of `Rear` must be advanced prior to the name being placed into the queue. However, because `Rear` locates the last array index, `MaxElements-1`, the value of `Rear` is forced to `0` using the wraparound technique (see Figure 3.5). Once `Rear` is advanced to `0`, `Jane` is placed into the queue at position `[Rear]`. Notice that at the moment both `Front` and `Rear` point to `Jane`. This is always true when there is only one element in the queue.

Inserting `John` into the queue causes `Rear` to be advanced to locate the next array position. This time, however, the value of `Rear` does not equal `MaxElements-1`. Therefore, `Rear` is advanced to the value `1`, locating the next available queue position of `[1]`. The name `John` is now inserted into the queue.

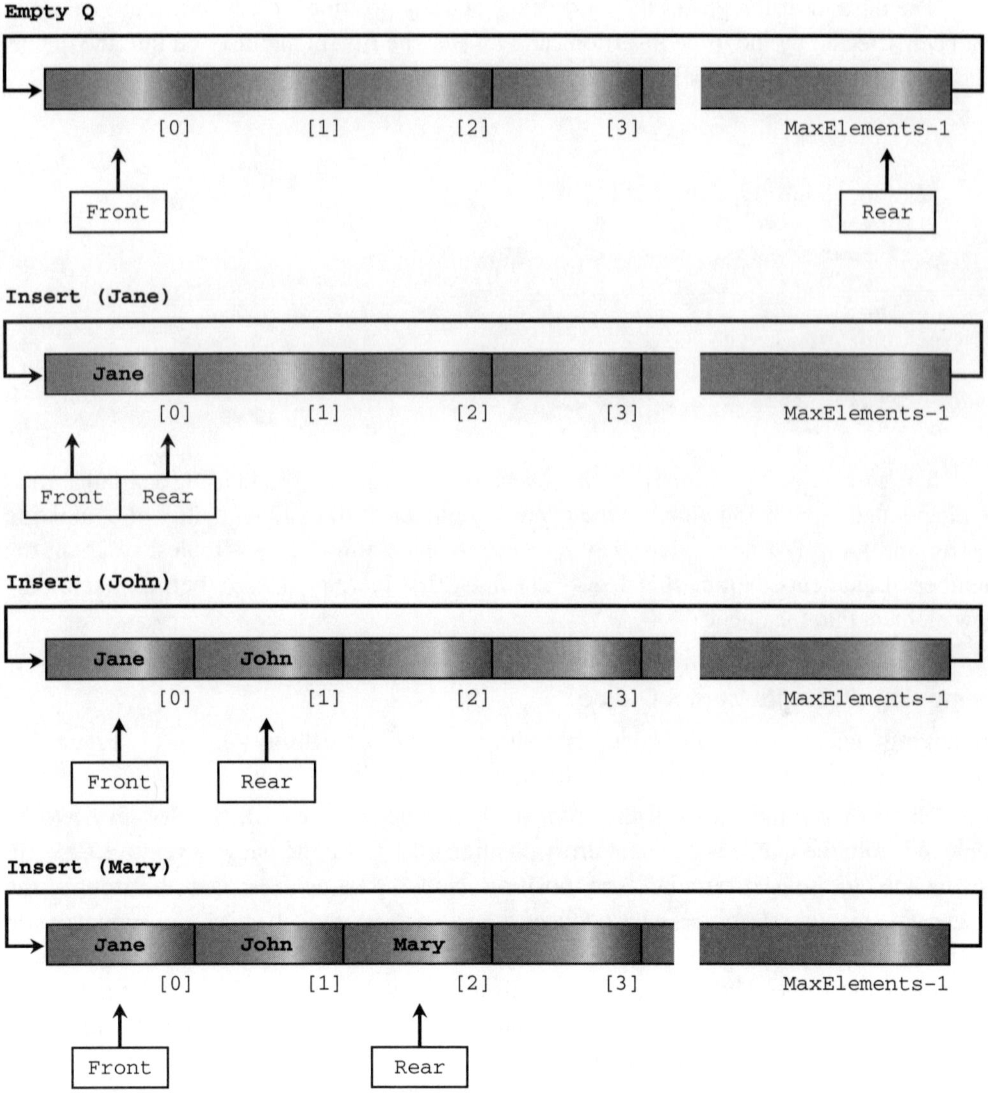

Figure 3.5 The results of calling `Insert()` three times: `Jane`, `John`, `Mary`.

The third insertion places the name `Mary` at array position `[2]`. Notice that `Front` has not been affected by the three insertions and locates the first name inserted into the queue. The algorithm for `Insert()` looks like:

```
Insert() Algorithm
  BEGIN
    If the queue is not full
      Increment count.
      If Rear == MaxElements-1
        Set Rear = 0.
      Else
        Set Rear = Rear + 1.
    Else
      Display full queue message.
  END.
```

The `Insert()` algorithm must first check for a full queue. When using a circular array implementation, knowing whether the queue is empty or full, is *not* a matter of comparing `Front` and `Rear`. With circular array queue implementations, it is simplest to count the number of elements. Notice that `Insert()` must first increment `Rear` before placing the new element into the queue.

Removing Elements from a Queue

Removing elements from the queue is a simple matter of calling `Remove()`. Figure 3.6 illustrates what happens to the queue with three calls to this function.

Names are removed from the front of the queue. As a result, the first name to be removed from the queue is `Jane`, at array position `[0]`. Once the name is removed, `Front` is advanced to the next circular array position. Now the name `John` is at the front of the queue. The second call to `Remove()` deletes the name `John` and advances `Front` to position `[2]`. Now the only remaining name is `Mary`. Notice that at this point both `Front` and `Rear` have the same value. The third and final call to `Remove()` deletes `Mary` and empties the queue. But `Front` and `Rear` are not in their original initialized positions. No problem. Remember, it does not matter where `Front` and `Rear` are located; whether the queue is empty or full is based on the value in the element counter. The algorithm for `Remove()` looks like:

```
Remove() Algorithm
  BEGIN
    If the queue is not empty
      Decrement element counter.
      Remove the element at array position [Front].
      If Front == MaxElements-1
        Set Front = 0.
```

```
    Else
      Set Front = Front + 1.
  Else
    Display empty queue message.
END.
```

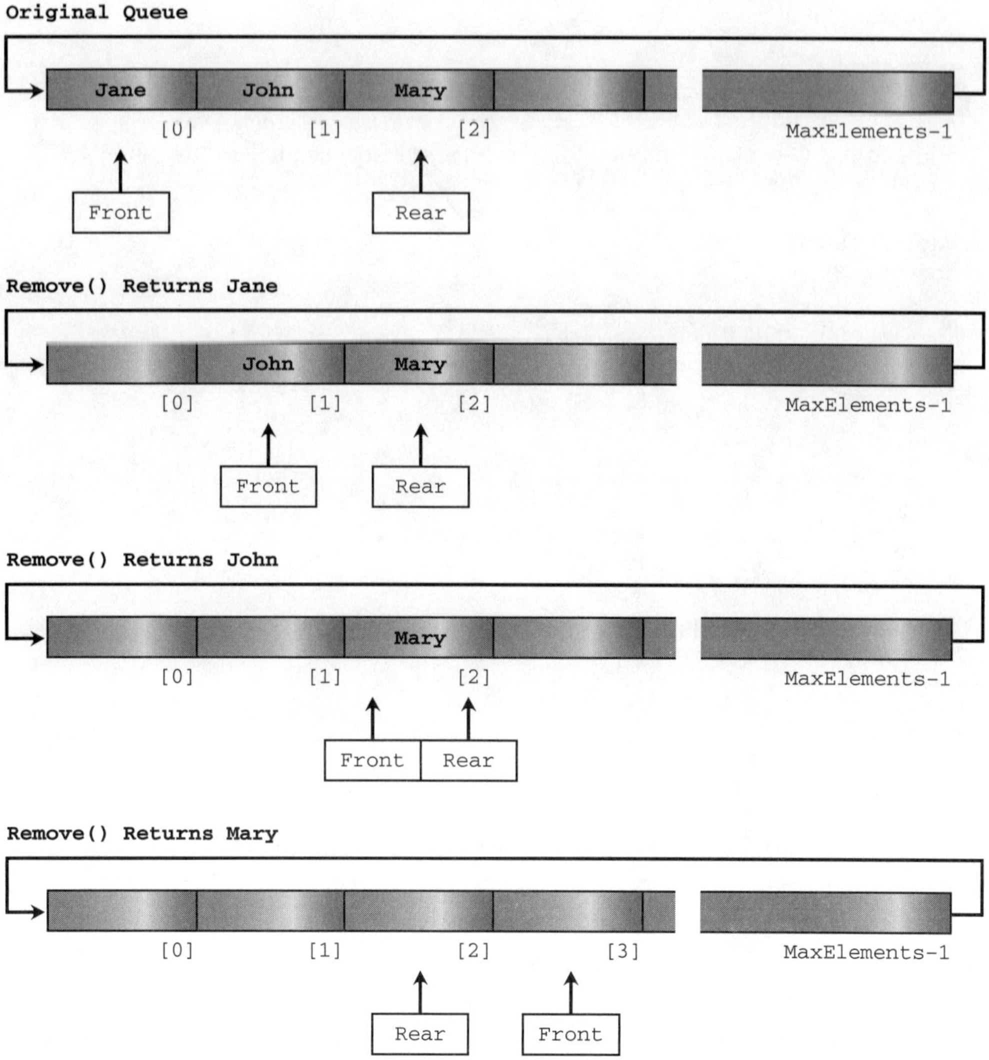

Figure 3.6 The results of removing three names from the queue.

Viewing the Front Element of a Queue

To view the front element of a queue, simply use the index `Front`, assuming the queue isn't empty. The straightforward algorithm for `FrontElement()` looks like:

```
FrontElement() Algorithm
  BEGIN
    If the queue is not empty
      Copy the element at array position [Front]
    Else
      Display a queue empty message
  END.
```

The formal C++ class definition for a circular array queue implementation looks like:

```
//QUEUE CLASS DEFINITION
#ifndef QUEUE_H
#define  QUEUE_H

const int MaxElements 25

class Queue
{
  public:
    Queue(void);
    int EmptyQ(void);
    int FullQ(void);
    void Insert(string  Name);
    string Remove(void);
    string FrontElement(void);

  private:
    string Q[MaxElements];
    int Front, Rear, ElementCount;
};
#endif
```

These same queue operations are automated for STL containers using the STL adaptors discussed in the following section.

The STL Queue

The `<queue>` template, like the `<stack>` template, is implemented as an adaptor that wraps around an underlying container. As with the `<stack>`, the `<queue>` adaptor does not actually provide any new functionality, but simply modifies the interface. Operations are provided with their conventional queuelike names, but are actually performed using operations on the underlying containers.

Containers in the standard library that implement the necessary operations for the `<queue>` adaptor include the `<list>` and the `<deque>` data structure which we will introduce in the next chapter. Unlike the `<stack>` template, the `<queue>` class in STL provides the ability to access both the front and back elements of the queue, while the conventional description of the stack abstract data type only permits access to the front.

<queue> Template Syntax

The following listing gives the syntax for the `<queue>` template:

```
template<class T,
    class Cont = deque<T> >
    class queue {
public:
    typedef Cont::allocator_type allocator_type;
    typedef Cont::value_type value_type;
    typedef Cont::size_type size_type;
    explicit queue(const allocator_type& al = allocator_type()) const;
    bool empty() const;
    size_type size() const;
    allocator_type get_allocator() const;
    value_type& top();
    const value_type& top() const;
    void push(const value_type& x);
    void pop();
protected:
    Cont c;
    };
```

The template class describes an object that controls a varying-length sequence of elements. The object allocates and frees storage for the sequence it controls through a protected object named `c`, of class `Cont`. The type `T` of elements in the controlled sequence must match `value_type`.

An object of class `Cont` must supply several public members defined the same as for `deque` and `list` (both of which are suitable candidates for class `Cont`). The required members are:

```
    typedef T value_type;
    typedef T0 size_type;
    Cont(const allocator_type& al);
    bool empty() const;
    size_type size() const;
    allocator_type get_allocator() const;
    value_type& front();
    const value_type& front() const;
```

```
value_type& back();
const value_type& back() const;
void push_back(const value_type& x);
void pop_front();
```

Here, `T0` is an unspecified type that meets the stated requirements.

<queue> Template Methods

The <queue> template provides the methods shown in Table 3.3.

Table 3.3 <queue> Template Methods and Descriptions

Method	*Description*
`explicit queue(const allocator_type& al = allocator_type());`	The constructor initializes the stored object with `c(al)`, to specify an empty initial controlled sequence.
`bool empty() const;`	The member function returns true for an empty controlled sequence.
`size_type size() const;`	The member function returns the length of the controlled sequence.
`allocator_type get_allocator() const;`	The member function returns `c.get_allocator()`.
`value_type& top();` `const value_type& top() const;`	The member function returns a reference to the first element of the controlled sequence, which must be non-empty.
`void push(const T& x);`	The member function inserts an element with value `x` at the end of the controlled sequence.
`void pop();`	The member function removes the last element of the controlled sequence, which must be non-empty.

<queue> Example Programs

The following sample applications illustrate various <queue> methods and areas of caution when using these templates.

The fifo.cpp Application

The following application illustrates the <queue> template's most frequently used methods, highlighting the actions of a logical queue's first-in-first-out (FIFO) algorithm. The <queue> is implemented as a <list> container. The fifo.cpp application instantiates both an integer and character queue for comparison purposes.

```
// fifo.cpp
// Testing <queue>
// push(), pop(), empty() ,back(), front(), size()
// Chris H. Pappas and William H. Murray, 2000


#include <list> // access to front() template function
#include <queue>
#include <iostream>

using namespace std ;

// queue implemented as <list> container
typedef list<int > INT_LIST_TYPE;
typedef queue<int>  INT_QUEUE_TYPE;
typedef queue<char*> CHAR_QUEUE_TYPE;

#define SPACER cout << "\n\n"

void main( void )
{
  int queueSize;

  INT_QUEUE_TYPE intQ;
  CHAR_QUEUE_TYPE charQ;

  // Pushing elements onto the queue
  intQ.push(1);
  intQ.push(2);
  intQ.push(3);
  intQ.push(4);
  intQ.push(5);
  intQ.push(6);
```

```
    // Verify queue size
    queueSize = intQ.size();
    cout << "The intQ contains " << queueSize << " elements\n\n";

    // Print queue elements in order
    // Elements accessed using front()
    // Elements removed using pop()
    while( !intQ.empty() )
    {
      cout << intQ.front() << endl;
      intQ.pop();

    }

    // Insert items in the queue(uses deque)
    charQ.push("First  in Q");
    charQ.push("Second in Q");
    charQ.push("Third  in Q");
    charQ.push("Fourth in Q");
    charQ.push("Fifth  in Q");

    SPACER;

    // Output the item inserted last using back()
    cout << "The last item inserted into charQ: "
         << "\"" << charQ.back() << "\"" << endl;

    // Output the size of queue
    queueSize = charQ.size();
    cout << "\nThe size of charQ is:" << queueSize << endl;

    SPACER;

    // Output items in queue using front()
    // and use pop() to get to next item until
    // queue is empty
    while (!charQ.empty())
    {
      cout << charQ.front() << endl;
      charQ.pop();

    }
}
```

Both `intQ` and `charQ` use the `push()` template function to add items to the back of their respective queues. Notice that the `size()` template function reports the actual number of elements contained within each queue.

The empty() template function provides an easy, reliable way to traverse queue list elements and drive the while loop test conditions:

```
while( !intQ.empty() )
  {
    cout << intQ.front() << endl;
    intQ.pop();

  }
```

The <list> template class provides the underlying front() template function required by the <queue> adaptor class, giving access to the container's front element. Note, however, that accessing the front element does not remove the element and explains the call to pop(), which officially deletes the front element after output.

The output from the program looks like:

```
The intQ contains 6 elements

1
2
3
4
5
6


The last item inserted into charQ: "Fifth  in Q"

The size of charQ is:5


First  in Q
Second in Q
Third  in Q
Fourth in Q
Fifth  in Q
```

Summary

In this chapter you were introduced to all of the necessary fundamentals for using a <vector> container. You learned about various dimension descriptors and template functions, how to traverse a vector container with iterators, the do's and don'ts of finding the beginning and ending address for a container via the template functions begin() and end(), how to insert and erase elements, and finally, that the end() template function does *not* return an iterator to the last element, but one beyond.

Next, you learned about the logical operations of a stack, last-in-first-out. You also discovered that the `<stack>` template does not directly implement its own data structures, but instead is considered one example of an adaptor class. Adaptors modify existing container functionality. The sample program demonstrated the most frequently used `<stack>` template functions—`empty()`, `push()`, `pop()`, and `top()`—to convert an arithmetic expression from infix to postfix form, most familiar to Hewlett Packard calculator users.

Finally, you explored both the `<queue>` and `<deque>` templates; both structures maintain collections of values in a linear sequence. In a queue, values are inserted at one end and removed from the other, unlike the `<stack>`, which inserts and removes elements from one end. You learned that while queues can be built on top of list structures, the advantage of a vector or deque implementation is improved performance, while the advantage of a list implementation is greater flexibility, because the number of elements need not be known in advance.

The deque, or double-ended queue (discussed in detail in the next chapter), is a data structure that provides a combination of features from both the vector and list types. Like a vector, a deque is a randomly accessible and indexed data structure. Like a list, elements can be efficiently inserted at either the front or the end of the structure. This actually provides a deque with both actions of either a stacklike or a queuelike behavior.

CHAPTER 4

Double-Ended Lists—STL Deque

This chapter introduces you to one of the most unique data structure in STL, the deque, pronounced DQ or deck. Of all the STL containers, the deque is the most unconventional representing a data type that is seldom considered to be one of the classic abstract data types (ADTs), as are vectors, lists, sets, or trees. Nevertheless, the deque is a powerful and versatile abstraction, solving unique programming problems.

Object-Oriented Deques

Arrays by definition are homogeneous data types stored in contiguous memory and are of a fixed number of elements. Vectors are identical except for the fact that they can grow and shrink dynamically. Deques improve upon vectors in that both ends of the container can grow and shrink dynamically. In a way, you can think of a deque as an array in the middle with vectors at each end. This subtlety is important when it comes to deque versus vector insertions and deletions. The good news is that the interface of vectors and deques is almost the same, so trying both is very easy when no special feature of a vector or a deque is necessary.

Deque Operations

Techniques for implementing vectors, lists, queues, trees, and so on are all well known. But there are many possible techniques that can be used to implement a deque, and the language definition does not constrain the software developer of the abstraction in any significant way. The basic approach is to internally represent a deque as a pair of connected vectors. While STL deques are similar to vectors, there are subtle differences, as listed here:

- Adding elements to the end of a vector is a very efficient process. Deques improve on this by providing fast insertions at both the front and end of the dynamic vector.
- However, unlike vectors, deques have one more indirection to access the elements, so element access and iterator movement of deques are usually slower than their vector counterpart.
- Because deque iterators must jump between different blocks they need to be smart pointers of a special type rather than ordinary vector pointers.
- Systems limiting memory block size could generate a larger internal deque size as a result of the increased number of memory blocks used to internally represent the deque.
- Inserting or deleting elements from the middle of a deque invalidates all pointers, references, and iterators. However, reallocation is typically more efficient than vectors since, according to their physical internal structure, deques do not have to copy all elements on reallocation. Insertions and deletions from the front and back of a deque retain all references and pointers to elements (except iterators).
- Deletions can also affect the size of the deque as entire memory blocks are freed when they are no longer used.
- Inserting and deleting elements from the middle of a deque can be a relatively slow process, as all elements up to either of both ends may be moved to accommodate the modifications.
- Deque iterators are random access iterators.
- Deques do not provide template functions to return the deques capacity, nor can a deque reserve memory as do vector containers.
- Deques do provide template functions to insert and delete front elements via `push_front()` and `pop_front()`.

To help you visualize how a deque functions, think of a train yard. Trains of up to one or two hundred cars are built from both ends. As cars are added to the end of the train, requiring more pulling power, engines are added to the front. The railroad track prevents any action in the middle of the train—exactly how a deque operates. However, here the STL diverges slightly since it does provide access to the deque middle.

The `<deque>` Template

Upon close examination you will discover that the operations provided by `<deque>` are a combination of those provided by the classes `<vector>` and `<list>`. For example, like a vector, the deque is randomly accessible. This means that instances of the class deque can be used in many of the same situations as a vector. Similarly, like a list, elements may be inserted into the middle of a deque, although such insertions are not as efficient as in the list equivalent.

Officially, deque stands for double-ended queue, and defines the structure as well. It manages its elements with a dynamic array, provides random access, and has almost the same interface as a vector. The deque is a combination of stack and queue, allowing elements to be inserted at either end. Whereas a vector allows efficient insertion only at one end, the deque can perform insertions in constant time at either the front or the back of the container. Like a vector, a deque is a very space-efficient structure, using far less memory for a given size collection than will a list, for example. However, as with a vector, insertions into the middle of the structure are permitted, but are not time-efficient. An insertion into a deque may require the movement of every element in the collection!

Typically, a deque is used as an underlying container for either a stack or a queue. The deque is the preferred container whenever the size of the collection remains relatively stable during the course of execution, although if the size varies widely, a list or vector is a better container choice. Ultimately, for time-critical applications, you will have to write the algorithm using the different forms and performing direct measurement of program size and run-time efficiency.

The <deque> Template Syntax

To use a deque, you must include the header file `<deque>`:

```
#include <deque>
```

There, the type is defined as a template class inside `namespace std`:

```
namespace std {
  template <class T,
    class Allocator = allocator<T> >
    class deque;
}
```

Like vectors, the type of elements is passed as the first template parameter and may be of any type that is assignable and copyable. Optionally, a second template argument defines the memory model, with allocator as the default. The following listing gives the syntax for the `<deque>` template:

```
template<class T, class A = allocator<T> >
    class deque {
public:
    typedef A allocator_type;
    typedef A::size_type size_type;
    typedef A::difference_type difference_type;
    typedef A::reference reference;
    typedef A::const_reference const_reference;
    typedef A::value_type value_type;
    typedef T0 iterator;
    typedef T1 const_iterator;
```

```
    typedef reverse_iterator<iterator, value_type,
        reference, A::pointer, difference_type>
            reverse_iterator;
    typedef reverse_iterator<const_iterator, value_type,
        const_reference, A::const_pointer, difference_type>
            const_reverse_iterator;
    explicit deque(const A& al = A());
    explicit deque(size_type n, const T& v = T(), const A& al = A());
    deque(const deque& x);
    deque(const_iterator first, const_iterator last,
        const A& al = A());
    iterator begin();
    const_iterator begin() const;
    iterator end();
    iterator end() const;
    reverse_iterator rbegin();
    const_reverse_iterator rbegin() const;
    reverse_iterator rend();
    const_reverse_iterator rend() const;
    void resize(size_type n, T x = T());
    size_type size() const;
    size_type max_size() const;
    bool empty() const;
    A get_allocator() const;
    reference at(size_type pos);
    const_reference at(size_type pos) const;
    reference operator[](size_type pos);
    const_reference operator[](size_type pos);
    reference front();
    const_reference front() const;
    reference back();
    const_reference back() const;
    void push_front(const T& x);
    void pop_front();
    void push_back(const T& x);
    void pop_back();
    void assign(const_iterator first, const_iterator last);
    void assign(size_type n, const T& x = T());
    iterator insert(iterator it, const T& x = T());
    void insert(iterator it, size_type n, const T& x);
    void insert(iterator it,
        const_iterator first, const_iterator last);
    iterator erase(iterator it);
    iterator erase(iterator first, iterator last);
    void clear();
    void swap(deque x);
protected:
    A allocator;
    };
```

The template class describes an object that controls a varying-length sequence of elements of type `T`. The sequence is represented in a way that permits insertion and removal of an element at either end with a single element copy (constant time). Such operations in the middle of the sequence require element copies and assignments proportional to the number of elements in the sequence (linear time).

The object allocates and frees storage for the sequence it controls through a protected object named `allocator`, of class `A`. Such an allocator object must have the same external interface as an object of template class `allocator`. Note that `allocator` is not copied when the object is assigned. Deque reallocation occurs when a member function must insert or erase elements of the controlled sequence.

<deque> Overloaded Operators

The `<deque>` template overloads the operators, as shown in Table 4.1.

Table 4.1 Overloaded Operators For <deque>

Overloaded Operators
`bool operator==( const deque <T, A>& lhs, const deque <T, A>& rhs);`
`bool operator!=( const deque <T, A>& lhs, const deque <T, A>& rhs);`
`bool operator<( const deque <T, A>& lhs, const deque <T, A>& rhs);`
`bool operator>( const deque <T, A>& lhs, const deque <T, A>& rhs);`
`bool operator<=( const deque <T, A>& lhs, const deque <T, A>& rhs);`
`bool operator>=( const deque <T, A>& lhs, const deque <T, A>& rhs);`

<deque> Template Methods

The <deque> template provides the methods, as shown in Table 4.2.

Table 4.2 <deque> Template Methods and Descriptions

Method	*Description*

`explicit deque(const A& al = A());`
`explicit deque(size_type n, const T& v = T(), const A& al = A());`
`deque(const deque& x);`
`deque(const_iterator first, const_iterator last, const A& al = A());`
	All constructors store the allocator object `al` (or, for the copy constructor, `x.get_allocator()`) in `allocator` and initialize the controlled sequence. The first constructor specifies an empty initial controlled sequence. The second constructor specifies a repetition of `n` elements of value `x`. The third constructor specifies a copy of the sequence controlled by `x`. The last constructor specifies the sequence (first, last).

Table 4.2 (continued)

Method	*Description*
`const_iterator begin() const;` `iterator begin();`	The member function returns a random-access iterator that points at the first element of the sequence (or just beyond the end of an empty sequence).
`const_iterator end() const;` `iterator end();`	The member function returns a random-access iterator that points just beyond the end of the sequence.
`const_reverse_iterator rbegin() const;` `reverse_iterator rbegin();`	The member function returns a reverse iterator that points just beyond the end of the controlled sequence. Hence, it designates the beginning of the reverse sequence.
`const_reverse_iterator rend() const;` `reverse_iterator rend();`	The member function returns a reverse iterator that points at the first element of the sequence (or just beyond the end of an empty sequence). Hence, it designates the end of the reverse sequence.
`void resize(size_type n, T x = T());`	The member function ensures that `size()` henceforth returns `n`. If it must lengthen the controlled sequence, it appends elements with value `x`.
`size_type size() const;`	The member function returns the length of the controlled sequence.
`size_type max_size() const;`	The member function returns the length of the longest sequence that the object can control.
`bool empty() const;`	The member function returns `true` for an empty controlled sequence. The member function returns `allocator`.
`const_reference at(size_type pos) const;` `reference at(size_type pos);`	The member function returns a reference to the element of the controlled sequence at position `pos`. If that position is invalid, the function throws an object of class `out_of_range`.
`const_reference operator[](size_type pos) const;` `reference operator[](size_type pos);`	The member function returns a reference to the element of the controlled sequence at position `pos`. If that position is invalid, the behavior is undefined.

Table 4.2 (continued)

Method	*Description*
`reference front();` `const_reference front() const;`	The member function returns a reference to the first element of the controlled sequence, which must be non-empty.
`reference back();` `const_reference back() const;`	The member function returns a reference to the last element of the controlled sequence, which must be non-empty.
`void push_front(const T& x);`	The member function inserts an element with value `x` at the beginning of the controlled sequence. Inserting the element invalidates all iterators, but no references, to existing elements.
`void pop_front();`	The member function removes the first element of the controlled sequence, which must be non-empty. Removing the element invalidates only iterators and references that designate the erased element.
`void push_back(const T& x);`	The member function inserts an element with value `x` at the end of the controlled sequence. Inserting the element invalidates all iterators, but no references, to existing elements.
`void pop_back();`	The member function removes the last element of the controlled sequence, which must be non-empty. Removing the element invalidates only iterators and references that designate the erased element.
`void assign(const_iterator first, const_iterator last);` `void assign(size_type n, const T& x = T());`	The first member function replaces the sequence controlled by `*this` with the sequence `(first, last)`. The second member function replaces the sequence controlled by `*this` with a repetition of `n` elements of value `x`.

Table 4.2 (continued)

Method	*Description*

`iterator insert(iterator it, const T& x = T());`
`void insert(iterator it, size_type n, const T& x);`
`void insert(iterator it, const_iterator first, const_iterator last);`
	Each of the member functions inserts, before the element pointed to by it in the controlled sequence, a sequence specified by the remaining operands. The first member function inserts a single element with value `x` and returns an iterator that points to the newly inserted element. The second member function inserts a repetition of `n` elements of value `x`. The last member function inserts the sequence `(first, last)`.

`iterator erase(iterator it);` `iterator erase(iterator first, iterator last);`	The first member function removes the element of the controlled sequence pointed to by it. The second member function removes the elements of the controlled sequence in the range `(first, last)`. Both return an iterator that designates the first element remaining beyond any elements removed, or `end()` if no such element exists. Removing `N` elements causes `N` destructor calls and an assignment for each of the elements between the insertion point and the nearer end of the sequence. Removing an element at either end invalidates only iterators and references that designate the erased elements. Otherwise, erasing an element invalidates all iterators and references.
`void clear() const;`	The member function calls `erase(begin(), end())`.
`void swap(deque& str);`	The member function swaps the controlled sequences between `*this` and `str`. If `allocator == str.allocator`, it does so in constant time. Otherwise, it performs a number of element assignments and constructor calls proportional to the number of elements in the two controlled sequences.

Sample Code

The following sample applications illustrate various `<deque>` methods and areas of caution when using the template. The first program, `arrayDQ.cpp`, implements a deque using a standard C++ class. The second program updates this algorithm using two STL vectors back to back. The third program rewrites the algorithm efficiently using the `<deque>` template.

The arrayDQ.cpp Application

The arrayDQ.cpp application begins with a formal class description, as follows:

```
class deque {
public:
    deque() {arrayOneIndex = arrayTwoIndex = -1;}
    void push_front(char cValue);
    void push_back(char cValue);
    void pop_front(void);
    void pop_back(void);
    bool empty(int arrayIndex);
    char front(void);
    char back(void);

protected:
    char arrayOne[SIZE/2];
    char arrayTwo[SIZE/2];
    int  arrayOneIndex;
    int  arrayTwoIndex;
};
```

All of the requisite deque functionality is implemented using C++ methods with deque data being stored in two back-to-back arrays, arrayOne and arrayTwo. Notice that the two arrays are dimensioned—each having half SIZE/2 the requested SIZE. arrayOneIndex is initialized to -1 by the constructor and increments from the middle of the imaginary deque to the left. arrayTwoIndex also starts at -1, however, it increments from the middle of the imaginary deque to the right. Logically, arrayOneIndex will always represent the front of the deque, with arrayTwoIndex representing the back.

The first method, push_front(), addresses the first limitation of an array implementation of the STL deque by having to first divide the desired deque dimensions by 2, since the total number of elements must be divided between two like-sized arrays. Next, the method has to see if the deque front is attempting to grow beyond its physical bounds.

```
void deque::push_front(char cValue)

{
    if( arrayOneIndex < SIZE/2-1 )
        arrayOne[++arrayOneIndex] = cValue;
    else cout << "\narray DQ front is full" << endl;
}
```

The prefix form of increment increases arrayOneIndex by one when it is within its legal subrange, adding the new cValue. Otherwise, the algorithm flags the user with a warning message that the array is full. The method, push_back(), doesn't actually look that different except for the fact it uses the arrayTwoIndex variable:

```
void deque::push_back(char cValue)
{
    if( arrayTwoIndex < SIZE/2-1)
        arrayTwo[++arrayTwoIndex] = cValue;
    else cout << "\narray DQ back is full" << endl;
}
```

Remember, the zero position of both indices logically represents the middle of the two joined arrays with each incrementing away from the center left and right, respectively.

The `pop_front()` method first checks to see if the `arrayOneIndex` is flagging an empty array front by comparing its contents with `-1` via a call to the method `empty()`. If this is not true, there must be elements in the front, and `arrayOneIndex` is decremented. Notice that this does not officially remove the data from the array but, instead, logically shrinks the front by one element.

```
void deque::pop_front(void)
{
    if( !empty(arrayOneIndex) )
        arrayOneIndex–;
}
```

The `pop_back()` method continues in a similar manner only using the second array's designated `arrayTwoIndex`:

```
void deque::pop_back(void)
{
    if( !empty(arrayTwoIndex) )
        arrayTwoIndex–;
}
```

The `empty()` method is used by both arrays to determine if they contain any elements by comparing their respective indices against a value of `-1`:

```
bool deque::empty(int arrayIndex)
{
    return arrayIndex == -1;
}
```

Initially, the `front()` method looks straightforward. Its job is to return the front element of the array flagged by the offset value stored in `arrayOneIndex`:

```
char deque::front(void)
{
    if( !empty(arrayOneIndex) )
        return arrayOne[arrayOneIndex];
    // else if( !empty(arrayTwoIndex) )
    //       return arrayTwo[0];
    else return 0;
}
```

However, if the front array is empty and the second array has data, then *front* is actually the zero position of the second array if it is full. Things get even worse if the user has not only popped all front array elements, but several from the second array, in which case, *front* would be somewhere in the *middle* of the second array.

A faithful array representation of a deque would necessitate four indices since the user could pop the second array into bit oblivion, with successive pops removing `arrayOne` elements starting at offset `0` and incrementing.

The reverse situation exists for `back()` when the user pops the back of the deque into bit oblivion, requiring a returned character value from the zero position of `arrayOne` and incrementing `arrayOneIndex`:

```
char deque::back(void)
{
    if (!empty(arrayTwoIndex) )
        return arrayTwo[arrayTwoIndex];
    // else if( !empty(arrayOneIndex) )
    //     return arrayOne[0];
    else return 0;
}
```

The `main()` function begins by instantiating the deque:

```
deque DQ;
```

The first three `push_front()` method calls insert the letters '`C`', '`B`', and '`A`,' leaving '`A`' at the front of `arrayOne` (`arrayOneIndex = 2`) with '`C`' at `arrayOneIndex = 0`, or the middle of the `DQ`. The fourth call to the method attempts to push a '`Z`' into a full `arrayOne`:

```
    DQ.push_front('C');
    DQ.push_front('B');
    DQ.push_front('A');
    DQ.push_front('Z');
```

The three calls to `push_back()` add the letters '`D`', '`E`', and '`F`' in left-to-right order in `arrayTwo` with '`D`' at `arrayTwoIndex = 0` and '`F`' at `arrayTwoIndex = 2`. Once again, the attempt to add '`Z`' exceeds `arrayTwo`'s dimensions:

```
    DQ.push_back ('D');
    DQ.push_back ('E');
    DQ.push_back ('F');
    DQ.push_back ('Z');
```

The program terminates by printing the `DQ.front()` or '`A`' and the `DQ.back()` or '`F`':

```
    cout << '\n' << DQ.front();
    cout << '\n' << DQ.back();
```

The complete `arrayDQ.cpp` program follows. You can compare this object-oriented C++ class implementation to the STL `vectorDQ.cpp` example described on page 139.

```
// arrayDQ.cpp
// C++ example implementing deque using two
// back-to-back arrays. The example program
// highlights the difficulties involved in
// implementing the deque abstract data type
// using static array logic and syntax.
// Chris H. Pappas and William H. Murray, 2000

#include <iostream>

#define SIZE 6

using namespace std;

class deque {
public:
    deque() {arrayOneIndex = arrayTwoIndex = -1;}
    void push_front(char cValue);
    void push_back(char cValue);
    void pop_front(void);
    void pop_back(void);
    bool empty(int arrayIndex);
    char front(void);
    char back(void);

protected:
    char arrayOne[SIZE/2];
    char arrayTwo[SIZE/2];
    int  arrayOneIndex;
    int  arrayTwoIndex;
};

void deque::push_front(char cValue)
{
    if( arrayOneIndex != SIZE/2-1 )
        arrayOne[++arrayOneIndex] = cValue;
    else cout << "\narray DQ front is full" << endl;
}

void deque::push_back(char cValue)
{
    if( arrayTwoIndex != SIZE/2-1)
        arrayTwo[++arrayTwoIndex] = cValue;
    else cout << "\narray DQ back is full" << endl;
}
```

```
void deque::pop_front(void)
{
    if( !empty(arrayOneIndex) )
        arrayOneIndex–;
}

void deque::pop_back(void)
{
    if( !empty(arrayTwoIndex) )
        arrayTwoIndex–;
}

bool deque::empty(int arrayIndex)
{
    return arrayIndex == -1;
}


char deque::front(void)
{
    if( !empty(arrayOneIndex) )
        return arrayOne[arrayOneIndex];
    // else if( !empty(arrayTwoIndex) )
    //      return arrayTwo[0];
    else return 0;
}

char deque::back(void)
{
    if (!empty(arrayTwoIndex) )
        return arrayTwo[arrayTwoIndex];
    // else if( !empty(arrayOneIndex) )
    //      return arrayOne[0];
    else return 0;
}

void main(void)
{
    deque DQ;

    DQ.push_front('C');
    DQ.push_front('B');
    DQ.push_front('A');
    DQ.push_front('Z');

    DQ.push_back ('D');
    DQ.push_back ('E');
```

```
    DQ.push_back ('F');
    DQ.push_back ('Z');

    cout << '\n' << DQ.front();
    cout << '\n' << DQ.back();
}
```

Before moving on to the vector implementation of a deque, remember that the logical complexity and failure of an array implementation involves the tracking of four indices into the two arrays, both of which are working like symbiotic circular queue arrays.

The `vectorDQ.cpp` Application

The STL vector implementation of a deque is the closest to a true deque in that the STL vector methods `begin()` and `end()` will function like the two indices necessary to track the front and back of our back-to-back arrays. This solves the weakness inherent in the previous array version.

The STL vector implementation begins with a modified formal class description seen here (commented out statements reflect the unnecessary array implementation coding):

```
class deque {
public:
    // deque() {arrayOneIndex = arrayTwoIndex = -1;}
    void my_push_front(char cValue);
    void my_push_back(char cValue);
    void pop_front(void);
    void pop_back(void);
    // bool empty(int vectorIndex); in STL vector
    char front(void);
    char back(void);
```

The STL vector implementation begins by eliminating the deque class constructor initializing the two array indices since the algorithm will locate the vector fronts and backs with calls to `begin()` and `end()`. Also, the method `empty()` is superfluous since STL vectors have their own method, `empty()`.

The two arrays, `arrayOne` and `arrayTwo`, are replaced with two vector instances, `vectorOne` and `vectorTwo`, which need no `SIZE` specification since they are dynamic:

```
protected:
    vector<char> vectorOne, vectorTwo;
    // not needed in with dynamic vectors
    // int  vectorOneIndex;
    // int  vectorTwoIndex;
};
```

The first method, `my_push_front()`, is renamed from the array version's `push_front()` so that it does not conflict with the STL vector's own definition:

```
void deque::my_push_front(char cValue)
{
    // if( vectorOneIndex < SIZE/2-1 )
    //    vectorOne[++vectorOneIndex] = cValue;
    // else cout << "\nvector DQ front is full" << endl;
    // becomes...
    vectorOne.push_back(cValue);
}
```

Notice how the method's body is dramatically streamlined with just a simple call to the STL vector call to `push_back()`. The new method, `my_push_back()`, takes advantage of a similar reduction in code size:

```
void deque::my_push_back(char cValue)
{
    // if( vectorTwoIndex < SIZE/2-1)
    //    vectorTwo[++vectorTwoIndex] = cValue;
    // else cout << "\nvector DQ back is full" << endl;
    // becomes...
    vectorTwo.push_back(cValue);
}
```

The only modifications necessary to `pop_front()` and `pop_back()` involve a simple reworking of a call to the array's `empty()` method call into the standard STL vector's `empty()`:

```
void deque::pop_front(void)
{
    // if( !empty(arrayOneIndex) )
    //      vectorOneIndex—;
    // becomes..
    if( !vectorOne.empty() )
        vectorOne.erase((vectorOne.end()-1));
}

void deque::pop_back(void)
{
    // if( vectorTwoIndex != -1 )
    //      vectorTwoIndex—;
    // becomes...
    if( !vectorTwo.empty() )
        vectorTwo.erase((vectorTwo.end()-1));
}
```

This completely eliminates the need for the array's `empty()` method which is commented out:

```
// empty is a standard STL vector function
// bool deque::empty(int vectorIndex)
// {
//      return vectorIndex == -1;
// }
```

The real advantage of the vector implementation of a deque over an array version is seen in the `front()` method, which returns an element from the vectorized deque. First, the method needs to define a `char` vector iterator.

```
char deque::front(void)
{
    vector<char>::iterator it;
    // if( !empty(vectorOneIndex) )
    //      return vectorOne[vectorOneIndex];
    // else if( !empty(vectorTwoIndex) )
    //      return vectorTwo[vectorTwoIndex];
    // else return 0;
    // becomes...
    if( !vectorOne.empty() )
        it = vectorOne.end()-1;
    else if( !vectorTwo.empty() )
        it = vectorTwo.begin();

    return *it;
}
```

The problem this method solves over its array counterpart is the ability to track the moving `vectorOne`'s back should the user deplete `vectorTwo`'s contents entirely, and vice versa when `vectorOne` is emptied, leaving `vectorTwo` holding the vectorized deque's front value! These missing array indices, which were left to the reader to implement in `arrayDQ.cpp`, are automated by calls to `vectorOne.end()` and `vectorTwo.begin()`, respectively.

Remember that a call to a vector's `end()` method returns a pointer one past the actual end of the vector and explains the `-1` after each call to `end()` which decrements the pointer to its vector's respective last value.

The `back()` method works identically to the `front()` method except that the `if..else` statement reverses the `vectorOne` and `vectorTwo` references:

```
char deque::back(void)
{
    vector<char>::iterator it;
    // if (!empty(vectorTwoIndex) )
    //      return vectorTwo[vectorTwoIndex];
    // // else if( !empty(vectorOneIndex) )
    // //       return vectorOne[vectorOneEndIndex];
    // else return 0;
    // becomes...
    if( !vectorTwo.empty() )
        it = vectorTwo.end()-1;
    else if( !vectorOne.empty() )
        it = vectorOne.begin();

    return *it;
}
```

The `main()` function highlights one additional advantage of the vector versus the array implementation: there is no `SIZE` limitation to the two back-to-back vectors explaining why the calls to `DQ.push_front('Z')` and `DQ.push_back ('Z')` are commented out. The complete `vectorDQ.cpp` program follows:

```
// vectorDQ.cpp
// STL example implementing deque using two
// back-to-back vectors.
// Chris H. Pappas and William H. Murray, 2000

#include <iostream>
#include <vector>

using namespace std;

// #define SIZE 6 not needed with dynamic vectors

class deque {
public:
    // deque() {arrayOneIndex = arrayTwoIndex = -1;}
    void my_push_front(char cValue);
    void my_push_back(char cValue);
    void pop_front(void);
    void pop_back(void);
    // bool empty(int vectorIndex); in STL vector
    char front(void);
    char back(void);
```

```
protected:
    vector<char> vectorOne, vectorTwo;
    // not needed in with dynamic vectors
    // int  vectorOneIndex;
    // int  vectorTwoIndex;
};

void deque::my_push_front(char cValue)
{
    // if( vectorOneIndex < SIZE/2-1 )
    //   vectorOne[++vectorOneIndex] = cValue;
    // else cout << "\nvector DQ front is full" << endl;
    // becomes...
    vectorOne.push_back(cValue);
}

void deque::my_push_back(char cValue)
{
    // if( vectorTwoIndex < SIZE/2-1)
    //   vectorTwo[++vectorTwoIndex] = cValue;
    // else cout << "\nvector DQ back is full" << endl;
    // becomes...
    vectorTwo.push_back(cValue);
}

void deque::pop_front(void)
{
    // if( !empty(arrayOneIndex) )
    //     vectorOneIndex—;
    // becomes..
    if( !vectorOne.empty() )
        vectorOne.erase((vectorOne.end()-1));
}

void deque::pop_back(void)
{
    // if( vectorTwoIndex != -1 )
    //     vectorTwoIndex—;
    // becomes...
    if( !vectorTwo.empty() )
        vectorTwo.erase((vectorTwo.end()-1));
}

// empty is a standard STL vector function
// bool deque::empty(int vectorIndex)
// {
//      return vectorIndex == -1;
// }
```

```
char deque::front(void)
{
    vector<char>::iterator it;
    // if( !empty(vectorOneIndex) )
    //      return vectorOne[vectorOneIndex];
    // else if( !empty(vectorTwoIndex) )
    //     return vectorTwo[vectorTwoIndex];
    // else return 0;
    // becomes...
    if( !vectorOne.empty() )
        it = vectorOne.end()-1;
    else if( !vectorTwo.empty() )
        it = vectorTwo.begin();

    return *it;
}

char deque::back(void)
{
    vector<char>::iterator it;
    // if (!empty(vectorTwoIndex) )
    //     return vectorTwo[vectorTwoIndex];
    // // else if( !empty(vectorOneIndex) )
    // //      return vectorOne[vectorOneEndIndex];
    // else return 0;
    // becomes...
    if( !vectorTwo.empty() )
        it = vectorTwo.end()-1;
    else if( !vectorOne.empty() )
        it = vectorOne.begin();

    return *it;
}

void main(void)
{

    deque DQ;
    DQ.my_push_front('C');
    DQ.my_push_front('B');
    DQ.my_push_front('A');
    // DQ.push_front('Z'); can't overfill vectorOne

    DQ.my_push_back ('D');
    DQ.my_push_back ('E');
    DQ.my_push_back ('F');
    // DQ.push_back ('Z'); can't overfill vectorTwo
```

```
    cout << '\n' << DQ.front();
    cout << '\n' << DQ.back();

    DQ.pop_back();
    DQ.pop_back();
    DQ.pop_back();
    cout << '\n' << DQ.back();
}
```

The end of the program trilogy terminates with the extremely efficient STL deque implementation in the next section.

The `dequeDQ.cpp` Application

An astonishing transformation occurs when the deque is implemented using only internally defined ANSI/ISO C++ standardized STL deque syntax, as shown here:

```
// dequeDQ.cpp
// STL example implementing deque
// using the <deque> template
// Chris H. Pappas and William H. Murray, 2000

#include <iostream>
#include <deque>

using namespace std;

void main(void)
{
    deque<char> DQ;

    DQ.push_front('C');
    DQ.push_front('B');
    DQ.push_front('A');

    DQ.push_back ('D');
    DQ.push_back ('E');
    DQ.push_back ('F');

    cout << '\n' << DQ.front();
    cout << '\n' << DQ.back();
}
```

This architecture-independent solution is portable, stable, and easily understood and modified. The next section will finalize your understanding of STL deque capabilities with example code that demonstrates overloaded deque operators.

The `deque.cpp` Application

For a slight change of pace the `intDQ.cpp` application illustrates several of the overloaded deque operators: `equality`, `less-than`, and `greater-than`. The application also uses the `assign()` template function to copy the contents of `intDQ2` to `intDQ1`.

```
// intDQ.cpp
// Testing <intDQ>
// Overloaded operators ==, >, <,
// push_front(), begin(), end(), and assign()
// Chris H. Pappas and William H. Murray, 2000

#include <deque>
#include <iostream>

using namespace std;

typedef deque<int>  INT_DEQUEUE_TYPE;
void printDequeue (INT_DEQUEUE_TYPE  intDQ, char*);

void main( void )
{
  // intDQ1 initialized with 4 1s
  INT_DEQUEUE_TYPE  intDQ1(4,1);

  // a 2 pushed to the front of intDQ1
  intDQ1.push_front(2);

  // intDQ2's initialized with 3 0s
  INT_DEQUEUE_TYPE  intDQ2(3,0);

  // print current container elements
    printDequeue (intDQ1,"intDQ1");
    printDequeue (intDQ2,"intDQ2");

  // check equality of intDQ1 and intDQ2
  if( intDQ1 == intDQ2 )
    cout <<"intDQ1 is equal to intDQ2"<<endl;
  else if( intDQ1 > intDQ2 )
      cout <<"intDQ1 is greater than intDQ2"<<endl;
    else
      cout <<"intDQ1 is less than intDQ2" <<endl;

  //assign the contents of intDQ2 to intDQ1
  intDQ1.assign(intDQ2.begin(),intDQ2.end());
  printDequeue (intDQ1,"intDQ1");
  printDequeue (intDQ2,"intDQ2");
```

```
  //compare intDQ1 and intDQ2 again
  if( intDQ1 == intDQ2 )
    cout <<"intDQ1 is equal to intDQ2"<<endl;
  else if( intDQ1 < intDQ2 )
      cout <<"intDQ1 is less than intDQ2"<<endl;
    else
      cout <<"intDQ1 is greater than intDQ2" <<endl;

}

void printDequeue (INT_DEQUEUE_TYPE  intDQ, char *name)
{
  INT_DEQUEUE_TYPE::iterator pintDQ;

  cout << name <<" contains these elements: ";
  for(pintDQ = intDQ.begin(); pintDQ != intDQ.end();
      pintDQ++) {
    cout << *pintDQ <<" " ;
  }
  cout<<endl;
}
```

The first overloaded operator (==) compares two objects of template class deque. The function returns: `intDQ1.size() == intDQ2.size()`. For equality, the number of elements must be equal in both deque objects.

The second overloaded operator (>) compares two objects of template class deque. The function returns: `lexicographical_compare(intDQ1.begin(), intDQ1.end(), intDQ2.begin(), intDQ2.end())`. Because a lexicographic (as in a dictionary) compare is used, the number of elements does not matter while using the overloaded operator >. For this reason, `intDQ1` is greater than `intDQ2`, *not* because it has more elements, but because `2` is greater than `0`.

The output from the program looks like:

```
intDQ1 contains these elements: 2 1 1 1 1
intDQ2 contains these elements: 0 0 0
intDQ1 is greater than intDQ2
intDQ1 contains these elements: 0 0 0
intDQ2 contains these elements: 0 0 0
intDQ1 is equal to intDQ2
```

Summary

In this chapter you learned that the deque, or double-ended queue, is a data structure that provides a combination of features from both the vector and list types. Like a vector, a deque is a randomly accessible, indexed data structure. Like a list, elements can be efficiently inserted at either the front or the end of the structure. This actually provides a deque with the actions of either a stacklike or a queuelike behavior.

Finally, this chapter explored the `<deque>` template, which maintains a collection of values in a linear sequence. In a queue, values are inserted at one end and removed from the other unlike the `<stack>`, which inserts and removes elements from one end. You also learned that while queues can be built on top of list structures, the advantage of a vector or deque implementation is improved performance, while the advantage of a list implementation is greater flexibility because the number of elements need not be known in advance.

CHAPTER 5

Sets—STL Sets and Multisets

Set theory is an important field in both mathematics and computer science. In fact, this area of study has formed the basis for the work we have done in earlier chapters on lists, stacks, and queues. A *set* can be defined, simply, as a collection of elements. The collection of elements might be as simple as a group of integer or character values, or as complex as student grades in a course or government tax records. Operations on sets often include determining if the set is empty, inserting elements, removing elements, finding the size of the set, and so on.

Boolean algebra allows operations such as *and*, *or*, *nand*, *nor*, *xor*, *xnor*, and *not* to be performed on binary data. These same bitwise operations can be applied to whole elementary sets. It is possible to produce differences, intersections, unions, and more on sets.

For example, if SetA is made up of the characters {a, b, c, d, e, f, g, h, i}, and SetB contains the characters {b, d, f, h}, then the *difference* formed by SetA and SetB will be those elements from SetA that do not appear in SetB, or {a, c, e, g, i}.

In another example, suppose SetA contains {a, b, c, d, e, f, g, h, i}, while SetC includes {b, d, f, g, j, k, l}. An *intersection* of SetC with SetA will yield {b, d, f, g}. Intersections are formed from elements contained in both SetA and in SetC. The *union* of SetA and SetC will contain all elements from SetC that are not already a part of SetA. Thus, the union of these two sets yields {a, b, c, d, e, f, g, h, i, j, k, l}.

Elements do not appear more than once in most abstractions of sets. The union of SetA and SetC, in the previous paragraph, illustrate this concept. However, multisets do permit elements to appear more than once within their structure.

Binary Sequences and the <bitset> Template

Sets composed of sequences of ones and zeros are called bit vectors. In STL, the <bitset> template class is used to describe objects that store sequences of bits (N). The bits can be set (1) or reset (0). An individual bit value can also be complimented or flipped.

The bit position (j) of an object class bitset <N> corresponds to a bit value of 1 << j when converting to an object of some integral type. In this case, an integral value that corresponds to multiple bits is the sum of their bit values.

<bitset> Template Syntax

The <bitset> template syntax is shown in the following listing:

```
template<size_t N>
  class bitset {
public:
  typedef bool element_type;
  class reference;
  bitset();
  bitset(unsigned long val);
  template<class E, class T, class A>
    explicit bitset(const string<E, T, A>&  str,
      string<E, T, A>size_type pos = 0,
      string<E, T, A>size_type n = string<E, T, A>::npos);
  bitset<N>& operator&=(const bitset<N>& rhs);
  bitset<N>& operator|=(const bitset<N>& rhs);
  bitset<N>& operator^=(const bitset<N>& rhs);
  bitset<N>& operator<<=(const bitset<N>& pos);
  bitset<N>& ="operator>>=(const bitset<N>& pos);
  bitset<N>& set();
  bitset<N>& set(size_t pos, bool val = true);
  bitset<N>& reset();
  bitset<N>& flip();
  bitset<N>& flip(size_t pos);
  reference operator[](size_t pos);
  bool operator[](size_t pos) const;
  reference at(size_t pos);
  bool at(size_t pos) const;
  unsigned long to_ulong() const;
  template<class E, class T, class A> string to_string() const;
  size_t count() const;
  size_t size() const;
  bool operator==(const bitset<N>& rhs) const;
  bool operator!=(const bitset<N>& rhs) const;
  bool test(size_t pos) const;
  bool any() const;
```

```
  bool none() const;
  bitset<N> operator<<(size_t pos) const;
  bitset<N> operator>>(size_t pos) const;
  bitset<N> operator~();
  static const size_t bitset_size = N;
  };
```

In this listing the `element_type` is a synonym for `bool`. The `const` static member, `bitset_size`, is initialized to the template parameter `N`.

The class reference has the following syntax:

```
class reference {
public:
    reference& operator=(bool b};
    reference& operator=(const reference& x);
    bool operator~() const;
    operator bool() const;
    reference& flip();
    };
```

The reference member class is used to describe an object that identifies a single bit in a sequence of bits. For example, assume `bvalue` is an object of type `bool` and `x` is an object of type `bitset<N>`. If `x[i] = bvalue`, then `bvalue` will be stored at bit position `i` in `x`. Likewise, if `bvalue = ~x[i]`, then `bvalue` holds the flipped value of the bit `x[i]`.

To flip a bit in `x`, use:

```
bvalue = ~x[i];
x[i] = bvalue;
```

Or, a better way is to use `flip()`:

```
x[i].flip();
```

You'll see how to use additional `<bitset>` methods in the sample code at the end of this section.

<bitset> Template Overloaded Operators

The <bitset> template overloads the operators, as shown in Table 5.1.

Table 5.1 Overloaded Operators For <bitset>

<table>
<tr><th>Overloaded Operators</th></tr>
<tr><td>bitset<N> operator~();</td></tr>
<tr><td>bitset<N> operator<<(size_t pos) const;</td></tr>
<tr><td>bitset<N> operator>>(size_t pos) const;</td></tr>
<tr><td>bitset<N>& operator&=(const bitset<N>& rhs);</td></tr>
<tr><td>bitset<N>& operator^=(const bitset<N>& rhs);</td></tr>
<tr><td>bitset<N>& operator|=(const bitset<N>& rhs);</td></tr>
<tr><td>bitset<N>& operator<<=(const bitset<N>& pos);</td></tr>
<tr><td>bitset<N>& operator>>=(const bitset<N>& pos);</td></tr>
<tr><td>bool operator!=(const bitset<N>& rhs) const;</td></tr>
<tr><td>bool operator[](size_t pos) const;</td></tr>
<tr><td>bool operator==(const bitset<N>& rhs) const;</td></tr>
<tr><td>reference operator[] (size_t pos);</td></tr>
</table>

An example using overloaded operators is included in the sample code section at the end of this section.

<bitset> Template Methods

The <bitset> template provides the methods, as shown in Table 5.2.

Table 5.2 Template Methods and Descriptions for <bitset>

Method	*Description*
bitset()	This constructor resets all bits in the sequence of bits.
bitset(unsigned long val)	This constructor sets just those bits at position j when val & 1 << j is nonzero.
template<class E, class T, class A> explicit bitset(const string<E, T, A>& str, string<E, T, A>size_type pos = 0, string<E, T, A>size_type n = string<E, T, A>::npos)	This template finds the initial bit values from elements of a string found in str. When str.size() < pos, an out_of_range is thrown. In all other cases, the string length, rlen, is selected to be smaller of n and str.size() - pos. An invalid_argument will be thrown when any rlen elements starting at position pos are other than 0 or 1. In all other cases, bits will be set at position j when the element at position pos + j is 1.

Table 5.2 continued

Method	*Description*
bitset<N>& set()	Resets all bits in the bit sequence. Returns *this.
bitset<N>& set(size_t pos, bool val = true)	Stores val in the bit at position pos, then returns *this. When size()<=pos, an out_of_range is thrown.
bitset<N>& reset()	Resets all bits in the bit sequence. Returns *this.
bitset<N>& reset(size_t pos)	Resets the bit at position pos, then returns *this. When size()<=pos, an out_of_range is thrown.
bitset<N>& flip()	Flips all bits in the bit sequence. Returns *this.
bitset<N>& flip(size_t pos)	Throws an out_of_range for cases where size() <= pos. In all other cases, it will flip the bit at position pos. Returns *this.
reference at(size_t pos) bool at(size_t pos) const	Returns an object of class reference. This object designates the bit at position pos when the object can be modified. For all other cases, it will return the value of the bit at position pos in the sequence of bits. When that bit position is invalid, it will throw an object of class out_of_range.
unsigned long to_ulong() const	Returns the sum of the bit values in the sequence of bits. It will throw an overflow_error if any bit in the sequence cannot be a type unsigned long.
template<class E, class T, class A> string to_string() const;	The template constructs str, which is an object of class string. The method appends a 1 if the bit is set in the bit sequence. Bit position zero is appended last. Returns str. If templates are not supported, the template is replaced with: string to_string() const;
size_t count() const	Returns the number of bits that are set in the sequence of bits.
size_t size() const	Returns the size N.

Table 5.2 continued

Method	*Description*
`bool test(size_t pos) const`	Returns true if the bit at position `pos` is set. Throws `out_of_range` when `size() <= pos`.
`bool any() const`	Returns true if any bit is set in the sequence of bits.
`bool none() const`	Returns true if none of the bits are set in the sequence of bits.

In the next section you'll learn how to apply many of these `<bitset>` methods in actual sample applications.

`<bitset>` Sample Code

This section provides five sample applications that illustrate various `<bitset>` methods, overloaded operators, and areas of caution when using this template.

The `bitset1.cpp` Application

The first example application, `bitset1.cpp`, shows how the `set()`, `reset()`, and `flip()` methods can be used to control all or individual bits.

```
// bitset1.cpp
// Testing <bitset>
// set(), reset() and flip()
// Chris H. Pappas and William H. Murray, 2000

#include <iostream>
#include <bitset>

using namespace std;

void main()
{
    bitset<8*sizeof(int)> x;
    int i;

    x = 0;

    // starting with bits set to 0
    for(i = 0; i <= 31; i++) {
      x.flip(i);
```

```
        cout << x  << " the bit flipped is " << i << "\n";
    }

    x.reset();
    cout << "\nnew reset value equals " << x << "\n";

    x.set();
    cout << "\nnew set value equals " << x << "\n\n";

    // starting with bits set to 1
    for(i = 0; i <=31 ; i++) {
        x.flip(i);
        cout << x << " the bit flipped is " << i  << "\n";
    }
}
```

The output from this application shows a series of bits as they are flipped from right to left.

```
00000000000000000000000000000001 the bit flipped is 0
00000000000000000000000000000011 the bit flipped is 1
00000000000000000000000000000111 the bit flipped is 2
00000000000000000000000000001111 the bit flipped is 3
00000000000000000000000000011111 the bit flipped is 4
00000000000000000000000000111111 the bit flipped is 5
00000000000000000000000001111111 the bit flipped is 6
00000000000000000000000011111111 the bit flipped is 7
00000000000000000000000111111111 the bit flipped is 8
00000000000000000000001111111111 the bit flipped is 9
00000000000000000000011111111111 the bit flipped is 10
00000000000000000000111111111111 the bit flipped is 11
00000000000000000001111111111111 the bit flipped is 12
00000000000000000011111111111111 the bit flipped is 13
00000000000000000111111111111111 the bit flipped is 14
00000000000000001111111111111111 the bit flipped is 15
00000000000000011111111111111111 the bit flipped is 16
00000000000000111111111111111111 the bit flipped is 17
00000000000001111111111111111111 the bit flipped is 18
00000000000011111111111111111111 the bit flipped is 19
00000000000111111111111111111111 the bit flipped is 20
00000000001111111111111111111111 the bit flipped is 21
00000000011111111111111111111111 the bit flipped is 22
00000000111111111111111111111111 the bit flipped is 23
00000001111111111111111111111111 the bit flipped is 24
00000011111111111111111111111111 the bit flipped is 25
00000111111111111111111111111111 the bit flipped is 26
00001111111111111111111111111111 the bit flipped is 27
```

```
00011111111111111111111111111111 the bit flipped is 28
00111111111111111111111111111111 the bit flipped is 29
01111111111111111111111111111111 the bit flipped is 30
11111111111111111111111111111111 the bit flipped is 31

new reset value equals 00000000000000000000000000000000

new set value equals 11111111111111111111111111111111

11111111111111111111111111111110 the bit flipped is 0
11111111111111111111111111111100 the bit flipped is 1
11111111111111111111111111111000 the bit flipped is 2
11111111111111111111111111110000 the bit flipped is 3
11111111111111111111111111100000 the bit flipped is 4
11111111111111111111111111000000 the bit flipped is 5
11111111111111111111111110000000 the bit flipped is 6
11111111111111111111111100000000 the bit flipped is 7
11111111111111111111111000000000 the bit flipped is 8
11111111111111111111110000000000 the bit flipped is 9
11111111111111111111100000000000 the bit flipped is 10
11111111111111111111000000000000 the bit flipped is 11
11111111111111111110000000000000 the bit flipped is 12
11111111111111111100000000000000 the bit flipped is 13
11111111111111111000000000000000 the bit flipped is 14
11111111111111110000000000000000 the bit flipped is 15
11111111111111100000000000000000 the bit flipped is 16
11111111111111000000000000000000 the bit flipped is 17
11111111111110000000000000000000 the bit flipped is 18
11111111111100000000000000000000 the bit flipped is 19
11111111111000000000000000000000 the bit flipped is 20
11111111110000000000000000000000 the bit flipped is 21
11111111100000000000000000000000 the bit flipped is 22
11111111000000000000000000000000 the bit flipped is 23
11111110000000000000000000000000 the bit flipped is 24
11111100000000000000000000000000 the bit flipped is 25
11111000000000000000000000000000 the bit flipped is 26
11110000000000000000000000000000 the bit flipped is 27
11100000000000000000000000000000 the bit flipped is 28
11000000000000000000000000000000 the bit flipped is 29
10000000000000000000000000000000 the bit flipped is 30
00000000000000000000000000000000 the bit flipped is 31
```

First, the number of bits is set in this example with:

```
bitset<8*sizeof(int)> x;
```

The `sizeof()` function returns 4 bytes for the size of an integer. The value returned is multiplied by 8 to obtain the number of bits. The value of all bits is set to 0 with:

```
x = 0;
```

Then, bits are flipped, starting with the LSB and moving toward the MSB using a simple `for` loop.

```
// starting with bits set to 0
for(i = 0; i <= 31; i++) {
  x.flip(i);
  cout << x  << " the bit flipped is " << i << "\n";
}
```

Since all of the bits were initially `0`, they will each become set to `1` when they are flipped. The bits could have all been reset to `0` by using the `reset()` method.

```
x.reset();
cout << "\nnew reset value equals " << x << "\n";
```

The `set()` method is used to initially set all of the bits to `1`; the remaining program code flips the individual bits back to a `0` value.

The `bitset2.cpp` *Application*

The second application, `bitset2.cpp`, shows how the `count()`, `size()`, `test()`, `any()`, and `none()` methods can be used.

```
// bitset2.cpp
// Testing <bitset>
// count(), size(), test(), any(), none()
// Chris H. Pappas and William H. Murray, 2000

#include <iostream>
#include <bitset>

using namespace std;

void main()
{
    bitset<8*sizeof(int)> x;

    x = 87654321;   // 5397FB1 hexadecimal
                    // 0101001110010111111110110001 binary

    cout << x.count() << " is the count of all set bits\n";

    cout << x.size() << " is the size (in bits)\n";

    cout << x.test(0) << " -> a 1 means the particular bit is set\n";

    cout << x.any() << " -> a 1 means at least one bit is set\n";

    cout << x.none() << " -> a 1 means no bits are set\n";
}
```

The output from this program shows the information returned by each of the five methods when applied to a value of 87654321. Since we are working with individual bits, a hexadecimal or binary representation would be more useful. The decimal number 87654321 is equivalent to 5397FB1 in hexadecimal, or 0101001110010111111110110001 in binary.

```
17 is the count of all set bits
32 is the size (in bits)
1 -> a 1 means the particular bit is set
1 -> a 1 means at least one bit is set
0 -> a 1 means no bits are set
```

The count() method returns a total of all bits set to one. In this example, count() returns a 17. The size() method returns the total size of the value, in bits. With these two methods and simple subtraction you could calculate the number of bits set to 0, if desired. The test() method can test any particular bit to see if it is set or reset. In this example, the first bit (position 0) is tested. The test() method returns a 1 if the bit is set and a 0 if the bit is reset. The any() method is useful if you want to check to see if any bits are set. The any() method will return a 1 if at least one bit in the sequence is 1 and a 0 otherwise. Likewise, the none() method can be used to check to see if none of the bits are set. The none() method will return a 1 if none of the bits are set and a 0 if at least one bit is set in the sequence.

The bitset3.cpp Application

The third application, bitset3.cpp, shows how the overloaded operators, ~ and ==, can be used with the <bitset> template.

```
// bitset3.cpp
// Testing <bitset>
// evaluating the ~ and == operators
// Chris H. Pappas and William H. Murray, 2000

#include <iostream>
#include <bitset>

using namespace std;

void main()
{
    bitset<8*sizeof(int)> x;
    x = 87654321;   // 5397FB1 hexadecimal
                    // 0101001110010111111110110001 binary

    cout << x << " -> represents the original bits.\n";
    cout << ~x << " -> represents the compliment of the bits.\n";
```

```
    if (x == ~x)
        cout << "The numbers are equal.\n";
    else
        cout << "The numbers are not equal.\n";
}
```

The output from this program shows the information returned by using the operators mentioned. The original sequence of bits is given by the decimal number 87654321. This, as you may recall, is equivalent to 5397FB1 in hexadecimal, or 0101001110010111111110110001 in binary.

```
00000101001110010111111110110001 -> represents the original bits.
11111010110001101000000001001110 -> represents the compliment of the bits.
The numbers are not equal.
```

The original number is printed first followed by the compliment of the number generated with the ~ operator.

A simple test for equality is then done on x and ~x. They are, of course, not equal. However, if the test for equality is done on x and x, the reported results will show that they are equal.

The bitset4.cpp Application

The fourth application, bitset4.cpp, shows how the to_long() method can be used to convert the sequence of bits to an unsigned long. You'll also see an interesting case of accidentally using a signed number where only an unsigned number should be supplied.

```
// bitset4.cpp
// Testing <bitset>
// signed and unsigned values
// Chris H. Pappas and William H. Murray, 2000

#include <iostream>
#include <bitset>

using namespace std;

void main()
{
    bitset<8*sizeof(char)> x;

    cout << "expected results using an unsigned number\n";
    x = 135;
    cout << x << " -> represents the original bits.\n";
    cout << x.to_ulong() << " -> bits represented as an unsigned long.\n";
```

```
    cout << "\nunexpected results using a signed number\n";
    x = -135;
    cout << x << " -> represents the original bits.\n";
    cout << x.to_ulong() << " -> bits represented as an unsigned long.\n";
}
```

The first three lines of output from this program correctly show the expected results. The second line of output shows the sequence of bits while the third line uses the `to_long()` method to correctly convert that sequence to an unsigned long.

In the second portion of code, there are attempts to duplicate the same feats using a negative number. Since an unsigned number is expected by `<bitset>`, you can anticipate unpredictable results.

```
expected results using an unsigned number
10000111 -> represents the original bits.
135 -> bits represented as an unsigned long.

unexpected results using a signed number
01111001 -> represents the original bits.
121 -> bits represented as an unsigned long.
```

You may be able to figure out what happened to each of the bits by using 1's and 2's compliment arithmetic. The secret is in the fact that even though you supplied a negative number, `<bitset>` treated the number as an unsigned sequence of bits.

The `bitset5.cpp` Application

The fifth application, `bitset5.cpp`, shows how the `and`, `or`, and `nand` logical operations can be performed on vector sets. This application uses the overloaded operators, `&`, `|`, and `~`.

```
// bitset5.cpp
// Testing <bitset>
// ANDing, ORing, and NANDing two vector sets
// Chris H. Pappas and William H. Murray, 2000

#include <iostream>
#include <bitset>

using namespace std;

void main()
{
    bitset<8*sizeof(int)> x;
    x = 87654321;   // 5397FB1 hexadecimal
                    // 0101001110010111111110110001 binary
```

```
    bitset<8*sizeof(int)> y;
    y = 63;            // 000003F hexadecimal
                       // 0000000000000000000000111111 binary

    cout << x << " -> represents the original x bits.\n";
    cout << y << " -> represents the original y bits.\n\n";
    cout << (x & y) << " -> ANDing x and y bits.\n";
    cout << (x | y) << " -> ORing x and y bits.\n";
    cout << ~(x & y) << " -> NANDing x and y bits.\n\n";
}
```

The output from this application takes on expected results.

```
00000101001110010111111110110001 -> represents the original x bits.
00000000000000000000000000111111 -> represents the original y bits.

00000000000000000000000000110001 -> ANDing x and y bits.
00000101001110010111111110111111 -> ORing x and y bits.
11111111111111111111111111001110 -> NANDing x and y bits.
```

Additional logical operations can be achieved, such as `nor`, `xor`, and `xnor` by combining `and`, `or`, and `compliment` operators.

Sets and Multisets Using the <set> and <multiset> Templates

The sets used with the `<bitset>` class, discussed in the previous section, were sets made up of groups of sequential ones and zeros. In this section, we'll investigate both the `<set>` and `<multiset>` templates and see how these data types allow working on sets that can store actual data values rather than just binary sequences.

The template classes describe the container template classes for `set` and `multiset`. The template classes show how an object can control a sequence of elements. The elements can vary in length but must be of type `const Key`. The sequence of elements allows lookup, insertion, and removal of an individual element since each element can function as a sort key and a value. Elements invalidate iterators that point at the removed elements but no invalidation occurs for element insertions.

The sequence is ordered with a call to a stored function object. This stored function must be of type `Pred` and is accessed by calling the `key_comp()` method. For any element `x` that precedes element `y` in the sequence, `key_comp()(y,x)` is false. With the template class `multiset` an object of the template class `set` insists that `key_comp()(y,x)` is true.

The protected object named `allocator`, of class A, is used to assign and free storage for the sequence. The allocator object and the object of template class `allocator` must have the same external interface.

The <set> and <multiset> Template Syntax

The following syntax is used to support both the `<set>` and `<multiset>` templates. The listing shows the template prototypes and the related template functions.

```
namespace std {
template<class Key, class Pred, class A>
  class set;
template<class Key, class Pred, class A>
  class multiset;
// Template Functions
template<class Key, class Pred, class A>
  bool operator==(
  const <Key, Pred, A>& lhs,
  const <Key, Pred, A>& rhs);
template<class Key, class Pred, class A>
  bool operator==(
  const multiset<Key, Pred, A>& lhs,
  const multiset<Key, Pred, A>& rhs);
template<class Key, class Pred, class A>
  bool operator!=(
  const <Key, Pred, A>& lhs,
  const <Key, Pred, A>& rhs);
template<class Key, class Pred, class A>
  bool operator!=(
  const multiset<Key, Pred, A>& lhs,
  const multiset<Key, Pred, A>& rhs);
template<class Key, class Pred, class A>
  bool operator<(
  const <Key, Pred, A>& lhs,
  const <Key, Pred, A>& rhs);
template<class Key, class Pred, class A>
  bool operator<(
  const multiset<Key, Pred, A>& lhs,
  const multiset<Key, Pred, A>& rhs);
template<class Key, class Pred, class A>
  bool "operator>(
  const <Key, Pred, A>& lhs,
  const <Key, Pred, A>& rhs);
template<class Key, class Pred, class A>
  bool "operator>(
  const multiset<Key, Pred, A>& lhs,
  const multiset<Key, Pred, A>& rhs);
template<class Key, class Pred, class A>
  bool operator<=(
  const <Key, Pred, A>& lhs,
  const <Key, Pred, A>& rhs);
```

```
template<class Key, class Pred, class A>
  bool operator<=(
  const multiset<Key, Pred, A>& lhs,
  const multiset<Key, Pred, A>& rhs);
template<class Key, class Pred, class A>
  bool ="operator>=(
  const <Key, Pred, A>& lhs,
  const <Key, Pred, A>& rhs);
template<class Key, class Pred, class A>
  bool ="operator>=(
  const multiset<Key, Pred, A>& lhs,
  const multiset<Key, Pred, A>& rhs);
template<class Key, class Pred, class A>
  void swap(
  const <Key, Pred, A>& lhs,
  const <Key, Pred, A>& rhs);
template<class Key, class Pred, class A>
  void swap(
  const multiset<Key, Pred, A>& lhs,
  const multiset<Key, Pred, A>& rhs),
  };
```

The following listing shows the syntax used to describe the `set` template class. Note: some long listing lines are wrapped due to page limitations.

```
template<class Key, class Pred = less<Key>,
         class A = allocator<Key> >
  class set {
public:
  typedef Key key_type;
  typedef Pred key_compare;
  typedef Key value_type;
  typedef Pred value_compare;
  typedef A allocator_type;
  typedef A::size_type size_type;
  typedef A::difference_type difference_type;
  typedef A::rebind<value_type>::other
                              ::const_reference reference;
  typedef A::rebind<value_type>::other
                              ::const_reference const_reference;
  typedef T0 iterator;
  typedef T1 const_iterator;
  typedef reverse_bidirectional_iterator<iterator, value_type,
                                         reference,
                                         A::pointer,
                                         difference_type>
                                         reverse_iterator;
```

```
  typedef reverse_bidirectional_iterator<const_iterator,
                                         value_type,
                                         const_reference,
                                         A::const_pointer,
                                         difference_type>
                                         const_reverse_iterator;
  explicit set(const Pred& comp = Pred(), const A& al = A());
  set(const set& x);
  set(const value_type *first, const value_type *last,
      const Pred& comp = Pred(), const A& al = A());
  const_iterator begin() const;
  iterator end() const;
  const_reverse_iterator rbegin() const;
  const_reverse_iterator rend() const;
  size_type size() const;
  size_type max_size() const;
  bool empty() const;
  A get_allocator() const;
  pair<iterator, bool> insert(const value_type& x);
  iterator insert(iterator it, const value_type& x);
  void insert(InIt first, InIt last);
  iterator erase(iterator it);
  iterator erase(iterator first, iterator last);
  size_type erase(const Key& key);
  void clear();
  void swap(set x);
  key_compare key_comp() const;
  value_compare value_comp() const;
  const_iterator find(const Key& key) const;
  size_type count(const Key& key) const;
  const_iterator lower_bound(const Key& key) const;
  const_iterator upper_bound(const Key& key) const;
  pair<const_iterator, const_iterator>
    equal_range(const Key& key) const;
protected:
  A allocator;
  };
```

The following listing is for the template class multiset. Again, some long listing lines are wrapped due to page limitations.

```
template<class Key, class Pred = less<Key>,
      class A = allocator<Key> >
  class multiset {
public: typedef Key key_type;
  typedef Pred key_compare;
  typedef Key value_type;
  typedef Pred value_compare;
  typedef A allocator_type;
```

```
typedef A::size_type size_type;
typedef A::difference_type difference_type;
typedef A::rebind<value_type>::other
                          ::const_reference reference;
typedef A::rebind<value_type>::other
                          ::const_reference const_reference;
typedef T0 iterator;
typedef T1 const_iterator;
typedef reverse_bidirectional_iterator<iterator,
  value_type,
  reference, A::const_pointer, difference_type>
 reverse_iterator;
typedef reverse_bidirectional_iterator<const_iterator,
  value_type,
  const_reference, A::pointer, difference_type>
const_reverse_iterator;
explicit multiset(const Pred& comp = Pred(),
const A& al = A());
multiset(const multiset& x);
multiset(const value_type *first,
  const value_type *last,
  const Pred& comp =  Pred(), const A& al = A());
const_iterator begin() const;
iterator end() const;
const_reverse_iterator rbegin() const;
const_reverse_iterator rend() const;
size_type size() const;
size_type max_size() const;
bool empty() const;
A get_allocator() const;
iterator insert(const value_type& x);
iterator insert(iterator it, const value_type& x);
void insert(const value_type *first,
  const value_type *last);
iterator erase(iterator it);
iterator erase(iterator first, iterator last);
size_type erase(const Key& key);
void clear();
void swap(multiset x);
key_compare key_comp() const;
value_compare value_comp() const;
const_iterator find(const Key& key) const;
size_type count(const Key& key) const;
const_iterator lower_bound(const Key& key) const;
const_iterator upper_bound(const Key& key) const;
pair<const_iterator, const_iterator>
  equal_range(const Key& key) const;
protected:
 A allocator;
 };
```

In the next sections you will learn the meaning of each `<set>` and `<multiset>` member function and template function.

The <set> and <multiset> Template Functions

The <set> and <multiset> template functions are shown in Table 5.3 along with a brief description of their purpose and return values.

Table 5.3 Template Functions For <set> and <multiset>

Template Function	*Description*
bool `operator!=`	Returns `!(lhs == rhs)`.
bool `operator==`	The <set> template uses this function and overloads the `operator==` and compares two objects of template class set. The <multiset> template uses this function and overloads the `operator==` and compares two objects of template class `multiset`. The template functions return `lhs.size() == rhs.size() && equal(lhs.begin(), lhs.end(), rhs.begin())`.
bool `operator<`	The <set> template uses this function and overloads the `operator<` and compares two objects of template class `set`. The <multiset> template uses this function and overloads the `operator<` and compares two objects of template class `multiset`. The template functions return lexicographical `compare(lhs.begin(), lhs.end(), rhs.begin(), rhs.end())`.
bool `operator<=`	Returns `!(rhs < lhs)`.
bool `operator>`	Returns `rhs < lhs`.
bool `operator>=`	Returns `!(lhs < rhs)`.
bool `swap`	This template function executes a `lhs.swap(rhs)`. Here, the `swap` member function switches between `*this` and `str`. When `allocator == str.allocator` the swapping occurs in constant time. For all other cases, `swap()` executes a number of element assignments and constructor calls. The number of executions is proportional to the number of elements in the controlled sequences.

An example that uses the `swap()` template function is included in the sample code section of this chapter.

The <set> Template Methods

The <set> and <multiset> templates provide the methods, as shown in Table 5.4. This table lists the template methods along with a short description of each method and returned values.

Table 5.4 The <set> and <multiset> Template Methods and Descriptions

Template Method	*Description*
`const_iterator begin() const`	Returns a `const_iterator` to the first object in the container. The `const_iterator` will equal the iterator returned by `end()` if the container is empty.
`iterator end() const`	Returns a `const` iterator. This iterator points beyond the last object in the container. The result is undefined when the container is empty.
`const_reverse_iterator rbegin() const`	Returns a `const_reverse_iterator`. This iterator points to the last location used in the container. `rbegin()` returns a value that must be stored in a `set&lT, A>::const_reverse_iterator`. A standard iterator should not be used.
`const_reverse_iterator rend() const`	Returns a `const_reverse_iterator`. This iterator points to a location just prior to the first element of the set container. `rend()` returns a value that must not be dereferenced.
`size_type size() const`	Returns the number of objects stored in the set container.
`size_type max_size() const`	Returns the maximum number of objects that can fit in the set container.
`bool empty() const`	Returns a true when the set container is empty. A false is returned for all other cases.
`A get_allocator() const`	Returns allocator.
`pair<iterator, bool> insert(const value_type& x)`	Inserts object `x` in the set if and only if `x` is not already present in the set and returns a pair. The bool value shows when the object is inserted in the set. (or)

Table 5.4 continued

Template Method	*Description*
`iterator insert(iterator it, const value_type& x)`	The iterator gives the object's position in the set when the object is inserted in the set. If the object is not inserted it gives the position of the element `x` that is present in the set. (or)
`void insert(InIt first, InIt last)`	Inserts the objects given in the range (first, last) in the set. The range must be valid and consist of elements of type `value_type`.
`iterator erase(iterator it)`	The element as position is removed from the set container. (or)
`iterator erase(iterator first, iterator last)`	The elements given in the range (first, last) are removed from the set container. Note: The iterators returned by the first two cases give the first element beyond the erased elements. If the element does not exist, `end()` is returned. (or)
`size_type erase(const Key& key)`	Removes the set elements that match the key. Returns the number of elements removed. Returns a `0` if no elements match the key.
`void clear()`	The elements of the set container are erased. This function calls `erase(begin(), end())`.
`void swap(set x)`	The elements of the set container are swapped with the elements of `x`.
`key_compare key_comp() const`	Returns the function object that set uses to order elements.
`value_compare value_comp() const`	Returns an object of type `value_compare`. This object is created from the function object used to order the elements of set.
`const_iterator find(const Key& key) const`	Returns a `const_iterator`. This iterator points to an element key if `key` is found in the set. If the element does not exist, an `end()` is returned.
`size_type count(const Key& key) const`	Returns the number of elements in the set which match key. If key is present, the function returns `1`, otherwise returns `0`.

Table 5.4 continued

Template Method	*Description*
`const_iterator lower_bound(const Key& key) const`	Returns a `const_iterator`. This iterator points to the first element that is not less than key. Returns `end()` if all of the elements in the set are less than `key`.
`const_iterator upper_bound(const Key& key) const`	Returns a `const_iterator`. The iterator is for the first element greater than `key`. Returns `end()` if no element is greater than `key`.
`pair<const_iterator, const_iterator> equal_range(const Key& key) const`	Returns a pair provided by: `pair(lower_bound(key), upper_bound(key))`.

In the next section, you'll learn how to apply many of these `<set>` and `<multiset>` methods in actual sample applications.

`<set>` and `<multiset>` Sample Code

The following sample applications illustrate various `<set>` and `<multiset>` methods. The first example illustrates the use of the `insert()`, `swap()`, `begin()`, and `end()` methods. The second example continues by illustrating the `size()`, `erase()`, and `clear()` methods. The remaining applications illustrate other features for sets and multisets.

The `set1.cpp` Application

The first example application, `set1.cpp`, shows how the `insert()`, `swap()`, `begin()`, and `end()` methods can be used to control elements in the sequence.

```
// set1.cpp
// Testing <set>
// insert(), swap(), begin() and end()
// Chris H. Pappas and William H. Murray, 2000

#include <set>
#include <iostream>
#pragma warning(disable:4786)

using namespace std ;

typedef set<char> SET_CHAR;
```

```
void main() {
  SET_CHAR set1;
  SET_CHAR set2;
  SET_CHAR::iterator it;

  // insert elements into first set
  cout << "insert a Z in set1" << endl;
  set1.insert(90);
  cout << "insert an A in set1" << endl;
  set1.insert(65);
  cout << "insert a F in set1" << endl;
  set1.insert(70);
  // set1 now holds Z, A and F

  // insert elements into second set
  cout << "insert a S in set2" << endl;
  set2.insert(83);
  cout << "insert a T in set2" << endl;
  set2.insert(84);
  cout << "insert a C in set2" << endl;
  set2.insert(67);
  // set2 now holds S, T and C

  // illustrate swap()
  cout << "swap set1 and set2" << endl;
  swap(set1, set2);

  // illustrates begin(), end() and results of
  // previous swap()
  // set1 now holds the ordered elements C, S, T
  for (it = set1.begin(); it != set1.end(); it++)
     cout << "set1 holds the following elements: "
        << *it << endl;

  // set2 now holds the ordered elements A, F, Z
  for (it = set2.begin(); it != set2.end(); it++)
     cout << "set2 holds the following elements: "
        << *it << endl;
}
```

The output from this program shows each element as it is added to the appropriate sequence, the swapping operation, and the elements as they are ordered in the swapped sequences.

```
insert a Z in set1
insert an A in set1
insert a F in set1
insert a S in set2
insert a T in set2
insert a C in set2
swap set1 and set2
set1 holds the following elements: C
set1 holds the following elements: S
set1 holds the following elements: T
set2 holds the following elements: A
set2 holds the following elements: F
set2 holds the following elements: Z
```

In this example the `swap()` function is used to swap the two sequences. The `begin()` function shows how to obtain an iterator that points to the first element in a sequence. The `end()` function shows how to obtain an iterator that points "just beyond" the last element in a sequence. Both `begin()` and `end()` return bidirectional iterators.

The `set2.cpp` Application

The second example application, `set2.cpp`, shows how the `size()`, `erase()`, and `clear()` methods can be used to control elements in the sequence.

```
// set2.cpp
// Testing <set>
// insert(), size(), clear(), erase(), begin() and end()
// Chris H. Pappas and William H. Murray, 2000

#pragma warning(disable:4786)
#include <set>
#include <iostream>

using namespace std ;

typedef set<int> SET_INT;

void main()
{
  SET_INT set1;
  SET_INT::iterator it;

  // insert elements into first set
  cout << "insert a 10 in set1" << endl;
  set1.insert(10);
  cout << "insert a 70 in set1" << endl;
  set1.insert(70);
```

```
   cout << "insert a 30 in set1" << endl;
   set1.insert(30);
   cout << "insert a 90 in set1" << endl;
   set1.insert(90);
   cout << "insert a 45 in set1" << endl;
   set1.insert(45);
   // set1 now holds 10, 70, 30, 90 and 45

   // illustrate size()
   cout << "\nThe size of the sequence: "
      << set1.size() << endl;
   // use begin() and end() to show current sequence
   for (it = set1.begin(); it != set1.end(); it++)
      cout << "set1 holds the following elements: "
         << *it << endl;

   // illustrate erase()
   set1.erase(45);  // erase any 45
   set1.erase(5);   // erase any 5
   set1.erase(70);  // erase any 70
   cout << "\nThe size of the sequence: "
      << set1.size() << endl;
   // use begin() and end() to show current sequence
   for (it = set1.begin(); it != set1.end(); it++)
      cout << "set1 holds the following elements: "
         << *it << endl;

   // illustrate clear()
   set1.clear();    // clear all elements
   cout << "\nThe size of the sequence: "
      << set1.size() << endl;
}
```

The output from this program shows each element as it is added to the appropriate sequence. The size of the sequence is checked and then elements are erased. Finally, the entire sequence is cleared.

```
insert a 10 in set1
insert a 70 in set1
insert a 30 in set1
insert a 90 in set1
insert a 45 in set1

The size of the sequence: 5
set1 holds the following elements: 10
set1 holds the following elements: 30
set1 holds the following elements: 45
```

```
set1 holds the following elements: 70
set1 holds the following elements: 90

The size of the sequence: 3
set1 holds the following elements: 10
set1 holds the following elements: 30
set1 holds the following elements: 90

The size of the sequence: 0
```

In this example the `size()` function is used to report the number of elements in the sequence. Initially, the sequence contains five elements. The `erase()` function is called three times to search the sequence for a 45, 5, and 70. The original sequence contains a 45 and 70, but not a 5. After eliminating the 45 and 70, the new sequence is printed. Finally, the entire sequence is cleared with a call to `clear()`. The sequence is now empty.

The set3.cpp Application

The third example application, `set3.cpp`, uses `insert()`, `begin()`, and `end()` as in the previous examples. However, this application also illustrates how the `unique_copy()` method can be used to help eliminate duplicate elements in a set.

```
// set3.cpp
// Testing <multiset>
// insert(), begin() and end()
// with additional unique features
// Chris H. Pappas and William H. Murray, 2000

#pragma warning(disable:4786)
#include <iostream>
#include <set>
#include <list>
#include <algorithm>

using namespace std ;

typedef set<int> SET_INT;

void main() {
  SET_INT set1;
  SET_INT::iterator it;

  // insert elements into set
  cout << "insert a 10 in set1" << endl;
  set1.insert(10);
  cout << "insert a 70 in set1" << endl;
  set1.insert(70);
```

```
  cout << "insert a 30 in set1" << endl;
  set1.insert(30);
  cout << "insert a 70 in set1" << endl;
  set1.insert(70);
  cout << "insert a 30 in set1" << endl;
  set1.insert(30);
  cout << "insert a 40 in set1" << endl;
  set1.insert(40);
  // set1 now holds 10, 70, 30, 70, 30 and 40

  // remove duplicates in set
  list<int> base;
  back_insert_iterator<list<int> > i(base);
  unique_copy(set1.begin(), set1.end(), i);

  for (it = set1.begin(); it != set1.end(); it++)
     cout << "set1 holds only unique elements: "
        << *it << endl;
}
```

The output from this program shows each element as it is added to the appropriate sequence. Next, duplicates are removed with a small portion of code:

```
list<int> base;
back_insert_iterator<list<int> > i(base);
unique_copy(set1.begin(), set1.end(), i);
```

The `<list>` template class is used to describe an object that controls a varying-length sequence of elements of type `T`. Just what we need! Recall that this sequence is stored as a bidirectional linked list of elements. Each element in the linked list contains a member of type `T`.

Next, the `back_insert_iterator` template class used to describe an output iterator object is used to insert elements into a container of type `Cont`. The container provides the member type, `value_type`, that is the type of element being used in the sequence. A member function `push_back(value_type c)` can be used to append a new element to the end of a sequence. It then returns `x`.

The `unique_copy()` function is used to remove duplicate elements. It removes from the sequence any duplicates without altering the relative order of remaining elements. It does this repeatedly and finally returns the iterator value that designates the end of the new sequence.

For this example, the output takes the following form:

```
insert a 10 in set1
insert a 70 in set1
insert a 30 in set1
insert a 70 in set1
```

```
insert a 30 in set1
insert a 40 in set1
set1 holds only unique elements: 10
set1 holds only unique elements: 30
set1 holds only unique elements: 40
set1 holds only unique elements: 70
```

Experiment with this application by inserting elements all with the same value. What happens then? Since this is a set, you should be able to predict the answer.

The set4.cpp Application

The fourth example application of this section , set4.cpp, uses insert(), begin(), and end() as in the previous examples. However, this application also illustrates how the set_union, set_difference, set_intersection, and set_symmetric_difference algorithms can be applied to sets.

```
// set4.cpp
// Testing <set>
// insert(), size(), clear(), erase(), begin() and end()
// set_union(), set_difference(), set_intersection and
// set_symmetric_difference.
// Chris H. Pappas and William H. Murray, 2000

#pragma warning(disable:4786)
#include <set>
#include <algorithm>
#include <iostream>

using namespace std ;

typedef set<int> SET_INT;

void main()
{
    SET_INT set1, set2, set3;
    SET_INT::iterator it;

    // insert elements into first set
    cout << "insert a 10 in set1" << endl;
    set1.insert(10);
    cout << "insert a 70 in set1" << endl;
    set1.insert(70);
    cout << "insert a 30 in set1" << endl;
    set1.insert(30);
    cout << "insert a 90 in set1" << endl;
    set1.insert(90);
```

```
cout << "insert a 45 in set1" << endl << endl;
set1.insert(45);
// set1 now holds 10, 70, 30, 90 and 45

// insert elements into second set
cout << "insert a 30 in set2" << endl;
set2.insert(30);
cout << "insert a 45 in set2" << endl;
set2.insert(45);
cout << "insert a 50 in set2" << endl;
set2.insert(50);
cout << "insert a 75 in set2" << endl;
set2.insert(75);
cout << "insert a 90 in set2" << endl;
set2.insert(90);
// set2 now holds 30, 45, 50, 75 and 90

// form union of set1 and set2
set_union (set1.begin(), set1.end(),
    set2.begin(), set2.end(),
    inserter(set3, set3.begin()));
// illustrate size()
cout << "\nThe size of the union sequence: "
     << set3.size() << endl;
// use begin() and end() to show current sequence
for (it = set3.begin(); it != set3.end(); it++)
   cout << "elements from set1 and set2: "
        << *it << endl;

// form difference of set1 and set2
set3.clear();
set_difference (set1.begin(), set1.end(),
    set2.begin(), set2.end(),
    inserter(set3, set3.begin()));
// illustrate size()
cout << "\nThe size of the difference sequence: "
     << set3.size() << endl;
// use begin() and end() to show current sequence
for (it = set3.begin(); it != set3.end(); it++)
   cout << "elements from set1 and set2: "
        << *it << endl;

// form intersection of set1 and set2
set3.clear();
set_intersection (set1.begin(), set1.end(),
    set2.begin(), set2.end(),
    inserter(set3, set3.begin()));
```

```
    // illustrate size()
    cout << "\nThe size of the intersection sequence: "
         << set3.size() << endl;
    // use begin() and end() to show current sequence
    for (it = set3.begin(); it != set3.end(); it++)
       cout << "elements from set1 and set2: "
            << *it << endl;

    // form symmetric difference of set1 and set2
    set3.clear();
    set_symmetric_difference (set1.begin(), set1.end(),
        set2.begin(), set2.end(),
        inserter(set3, set3.begin()));
    // illustrate size()
    cout << "\nThe size of the symmetric difference sequence: "
         << set3.size() << endl;
    // use begin() and end() to show current sequence
    for (it = set3.begin(); it != set3.end(); it++)
       cout << "elements from set1 and set2: "
            << *it << endl;
    cout << endl;
  }
```

The output from this application illustrates, in particular, the set formed with the use of `set_union()`, `set_difference()`, `set_intersection()`, and `set_symmetric_difference()`.

```
insert a 10 in set1
insert a 70 in set1
insert a 30 in set1
insert a 90 in set1
insert a 45 in set1

insert a 30 in set2
insert a 45 in set2
insert a 50 in set2
insert a 75 in set2
insert a 90 in set2

The size of the union sequence: 7
elements from set1 and set2: 10
elements from set1 and set2: 30
elements from set1 and set2: 45
elements from set1 and set2: 50
elements from set1 and set2: 70
elements from set1 and set2: 75
elements from set1 and set2: 90
```

```
The size of the difference sequence: 2
elements from set1 and set2: 10
elements from set1 and set2: 70

The size of the intersection sequence: 3
elements from set1 and set2: 30
elements from set1 and set2: 45
elements from set1 and set2: 90

The size of the symmetric difference sequence: 4
elements from set1 and set2: 10
elements from set1 and set2: 50
elements from set1 and set2: 70
elements from set1 and set2: 75
```

This would be a good place to test your own set theory and see if you agree with the results of this application.

The `multiset5.cpp` Application

The fifth example application of this section, `multiset5.cpp`, uses `insert()`, `begin()`, and `end()` as in the previous examples. However, this application also illustrates how the `set_union` algorithm can be applied to multisets.

```
// multiset5.cpp
// Testing <set>
// insert(), size(), clear(), erase(), begin() and end()
// set_union()
// Chris H. Pappas and William H. Murray, 2000

#pragma warning(disable:4786)
#include <set>
#include <algorithm>
#include <iostream>

using namespace std ;

typedef multiset<int> SET_INT;

void main()
{
    SET_INT multiset1, multiset2, multiset3;
    SET_INT::iterator it;

    // insert elements into first multiset
    cout << "insert a 10 in multiset1" << endl;
    multiset1.insert(10);
    cout << "insert a 70 in multiset1" << endl;
    multiset1.insert(70);
```

```
cout << "insert a 30 in multiset1" << endl;
multiset1.insert(30);
cout << "insert a 90 in multiset1" << endl;
multiset1.insert(90);
cout << "insert a 30 in multiset1" << endl;
multiset1.insert(30);
cout << "insert a 45 in multiset1" << endl;
multiset1.insert(45);
cout << "insert a 10 in multiset1" << endl << endl;
multiset1.insert(10);
// multiset1 now holds 10, 70, 30, 90, 30, 45 and 10

// insert elements into second multiset
cout << "insert a 30 in multiset2" << endl;
multiset2.insert(30);
cout << "insert a 45 in multiset2" << endl;
multiset2.insert(45);
cout << "insert a 50 in multiset2" << endl;
multiset2.insert(50);
cout << "insert a 75 in multiset2" << endl;
multiset2.insert(75);
cout << "insert a 90 in multiset2" << endl;
multiset2.insert(90);
cout << "insert a 30 in multiset2" << endl;
multiset2.insert(30);
cout << "insert a 30 in multiset2" << endl;
multiset2.insert(30);
// multiset2 now holds 30, 45, 50, 75, 90, 30 and 30

// form union of multiset1 and multiset2
set_union (multiset1.begin(), multiset1.end(),
    multiset2.begin(), multiset2.end(),
    inserter(multiset3, multiset3.begin()));
// illustrate size()
cout << "\nThe size of the union sequence: "
     << multiset3.size() << endl;
// use begin() and end() to show current sequence
for (it = multiset3.begin(); it != multiset3.end(); it++)
   cout << "elements from multiset1 and multiset2: "
        << *it << endl;
cout << endl;
```

The output from this example is shown next. Can you confirm that the results for the union of two multisets is correct?

```
insert a 10 in multiset1
insert a 70 in multiset1
insert a 30 in multiset1
insert a 90 in multiset1
insert a 30 in multiset1
insert a 45 in multiset1
insert a 10 in multiset1

insert a 30 in multiset2
insert a 45 in multiset2
insert a 50 in multiset2
insert a 75 in multiset2
insert a 90 in multiset2
insert a 30 in multiset2
insert a 30 in multiset2

The size of the union sequence: 10
elements from multiset1 and multiset2: 10
elements from multiset1 and multiset2: 10
elements from multiset1 and multiset2: 30
elements from multiset1 and multiset2: 30
elements from multiset1 and multiset2: 30
elements from multiset1 and multiset2: 45
elements from multiset1 and multiset2: 50
elements from multiset1 and multiset2: 70
elements from multiset1 and multiset2: 75
elements from multiset1 and multiset2: 90
```

Recall that multisets allow the same element to appear more than once, while sets require that an element appear just once.

Summary

The `<bitset>` template provides a number of useful overloaded operators and methods that allow control over individual bits in a sequence of bits. You may find this template useful when creating applications that encrypt or encode sequences of bits.

The `<set>` and `<multiset>` templates provides a number of useful template functions and methods that allow control over a sequence of elements. Now it is your turn to experiment with other methods such as `lower_bound()` and `upper_bound()`.

CHAPTER 6

Binary Trees

Dynamic Linked List Fundamentals

This chapter builds upon the syntax and concepts discussed in Chapter 2 where you learned that C/C++ arrays are inadequate for efficiently storing information because their dimension(s) must be set by the programmer at code time, not at run time.

STL vectors are an improvement in that they are dynamic, allowing them to grow and shrink as necessary at run time. Taking advantage of these run-time dimension changes required you to move away from array subscript syntax, for example:

```
for( offset = 0; offset < MAX_ELEMENTS; offset++ )
  std::cout << array[offset];
```

to the safer STL references to an array's front and end using STL-specific functions, as in:

```
for( it = vector.begin(); it < vector.end(); it++ )
  std:: cout << *it;
```

However, even though STL vectors are dynamic, linear lists of homogeneous data types have their (static-sized arrays or dynamically allocated vectors) own set of weaknesses, from the simplicity of the data elements referenced to run-time performance hits. Just as multiple C/C++ variables could not efficiently process the same information stored in an array or STL vector, STL vectors cannot compete with the sophisticated algorithmic solutions provided by the STL `<list>` template class.

You can conceptually think of an STL vector as a forward pointing linked list. STL `<list>` containers are implemented as forward *and* backward pointing linked lists. Before properly employing this advanced ADT, it is necessary to take a look at the STL `<list>` template.

The <list> Container

A <list> container is your best choice when the number of elements in a collection cannot be bounded or varies widely during the course of execution. Like a vector, a list maintains values of uniform type. Unlike a vector, a list can hold any number of values. Lists are not indexed. Instead, elements must be examined one by one in sequence. For this reason, the amount of time required to access an element in a list depends upon the position the element holds in the list.

Using an iterator to denote a given location, insertion into or deletion from a list can be performed in constant time. As with a vector, to determine whether or not a specific value occurs in a list requires a sequential search. While a list can be ordered, it is not possible to perform a binary search on a list, and therefore the sequential search time is generally the best that can be achieved.

<list> Template Syntax

The following listing gives the syntax for the <list> template:

```
template<class T, class A = allocator<T> >
    class list {
public:
    typedef A allocator_type;
    typedef A::size_type size_type;
    typedef A::difference_type difference_type;
    typedef A::reference reference;
    typedef A::const_reference const_reference;
    typedef A::value_type value_type;
    typedef T0 iterator;
    typedef T1 const_iterator;
    typedef reverse_bidirectional_iterator<iterator,
        value_type, reference, A::pointer,
            difference_type> reverse_iterator;
    typedef reverse_bidirectional_iterator<const_iterator,
        value_type, const_reference, A::const_pointer,
            difference_type> const_reverse_iterator;
    explicit list(const A& al = A());
    explicit list(size_type n, const T& v = T(), const A& al = A());
    list(const list& x);
    list(const_iterator first, const_iterator last,
        const A& al = A());
    iterator begin();
    const_iterator begin() const;
    iterator end();
    iterator end() const;
    reverse_iterator rbegin();
    const_reverse_iterator rbegin() const;
```

```
    reverse_iterator rend();
    const_reverse_iterator rend() const;
    void resize(size_type n, T x = T());
    size_type size() const;
    size_type max_size() const;
    bool empty() const;
    A get_allocator() const;
    reference front();
    const_reference front() const;
    reference back();
    const_reference back() const;
    void push_front(const T& x);
    void pop_front();
    void push_back(const T& x);
    void pop_back();
    void assign(const_iterator first, const_iterator last);
    void assign(size_type n, const T& x = T());
    iterator insert(iterator it, const T& x = T());
    void insert(iterator it, size_type n, const T& x);
    void insert(iterator it,
        const_iterator first, const_iterator last);
    void insert(iterator it,
        const T *first, const T *last);
    iterator erase(iterator it);
    iterator erase(iterator first, iterator last);
    void clear();
    void swap(list x);
    void splice(iterator it, list& x);
    void splice(iterator it, list& x, iterator first);
    void splice(iterator it, list& x, iterator first, iterator last);
    void remove(const T& x);
    void remove_if(binder2nd<not_equal_to<T> > pr);
    void unique();
    void unique(not_equal_to<T> pr);
    void merge(list& x);
    void merge(list& x, greater<T> pr);
    void sort();
    template<class Pred>
    void sort(greater<T> pr);
    void reverse();
protected:
    A allocator;
    };
```

The `<list>` template class describes an object that controls a varying-length sequence of elements of type `T`. The sequence is stored as a bidirectional linked list of elements, each containing a member of type `T`. The object allocates and frees storage for the sequence it controls through a protected object named `allocator`, of class `A`.

List reallocation occurs when a method must insert or erase elements within the container. In all such cases, only iterators or references that point at erased portions of the list become invalid.

The `<list>` template uses the following ten `typedef`s:

allocator_type

The `allocator_type` is a synonym for the template parameter `A` and has the following syntax:

```
typedef A allocator_type;
```

size_type

The `size_type` is defined as an unsigned integer that can represent the length of any list type. The syntax looks like:

```
typedef A::size_type size_type;
```

difference_type

The `difference_type` is defined as a signed integer that can represent the difference between the addresses of any two elements in a list. The syntax looks like:

```
typedef A::difference_type difference_type;
```

reference

The `reference` type describes an object that can serve as a reference to an element of the list. The syntax looks like:

```
typedef A::reference reference;
```

const_reference

The `const_reference` describes an object that can serve as a constant reference to an element of the list. The syntax looks like:

```
typedef A::const_reference const_reference;
```

value_type

The value_type is a synonym for the template parameter T. The syntax looks like:

```
typedef A::value_type value_type;
```

iterator

The iterator type describes an object that can serve as a bidirectional iterator for the list. It is described here as a synonym for the unspecified type T0. The syntax looks like:

```
typedef T0 iterator;
```

const_iterator

The const_iterator describes an object that can serve as a constant bidirectional iterator for the list. It is described here as a synonym for the unspecified type T1. The syntax looks like:

```
typedef T1 const_iterator;
```

reverse_iterator

The reverse_iterator defines an object that can serve as a reverse bidirectional iterator for the list. The syntax looks like:

```
typedef reverse_bidirectional_iterator<iterator,
    value_type, reference, A::pointer,
        difference_type> reverse_iterator;
```

const_reverse_iterator

The const_reverse_iterator describes an object that can serve as a constant reverse bidirectional iterator for the list. The syntax looks like:

```
typedef reverse_bidirectional_iterator<const_iterator,
    value_type, const_reference, A::const_pointer,
        difference_type> const_reverse_iterator;
```

<list> Template Methods

The <list> template provides the methods as shown in Table 6.1.

Table 6.1 <list> Template Methods and Descriptions

Method	*Description*

explicit list(const A& al = A());
explicit list(size_type n, const T& v = T(), const A& al = A());
list(const list& x);
list(const_iterator first, const_iterator last, const A& al = A());
	All constructors store the allocator object al (or, for the copy constructor, x. ()) in and initialize the list. The first constructor specifies an empty initial list. The second constructor specifies a repetition of n elements of value x. The third constructor specifies a copy of the sequence controlled by x. The last constructor specifies the sequence (first, last). None of the constructors perform any interim reallocations.

const_iterator begin() const; iterator begin();	The method returns a bidirectional iterator that points at the first element of the sequence (or just beyond the end of an empty sequence).
const_iterator end() const; iterator end();	The method returns a bidirectional iterator that points just beyond the end of the sequence.
const_reverse_iterator rbegin() const; reverse_iterator rbegin();	The method returns a reverse bidirectional iterator that points just beyond the end of the list.
const_reverse_iterator rend() const; reverse_iterator rend();	The method returns a reverse bidirectional iterator that points at the first element of the sequence (or just beyond the end of an empty sequence).
void resize(size_type n, T x = T());	The method ensures that () henceforth returns n. If it must make the list longer, it appends elements with value x.
size_type size() const;	The method returns the length of the list.
size_type max_size() const;	The method returns the length of the longest sequence that the object can control.
bool empty() const;	The method returns true for an empty list.
get_allocator() const;	The member function returns allocator.

Table 6.1 continued

Method	*Description*
`reference front();` `const_reference front() const;`	The method returns a reference to the first element of the list, which must be non-empty.
`reference back();` `const_reference back() const;`	The method returns a reference to the last element of the list, which must be non-empty.
`void push_front(const T& x);`	The method inserts an element with value `x` at the beginning of the list.
`void pop_front();`	The method removes the first element of the list, which must be non-empty.
`void push_back(const T& x);`	The method inserts an element with value `x` at the end of the list.
`void pop_back();`	The method removes the last element of the list, which must be non-empty.
`void assign(const_iterator first, const_iterator last);` `void assign(size_type n, const T& x = T());`	The first method replaces the sequence controlled by `*this` with the sequence `(first, last)`. The second method replaces the sequence controlled by `*this` with a repetition of `n` elements of value `x`.

`iterator insert(iterator it, const T& x = T());`
`void insert(iterator it,size_type n, const T& x);`
`void insert(iterator it, const_iterator first,`
`const_iterator last);`
	Each of the methods inserts, before the element pointed to by it in the list, a sequence specified by the remaining operands. The first method inserts a single element with value `x` and returns an iterator that points to the newly inserted element. The second method inserts a repetition of `n` elements of value `x`. The last method inserts the sequence `(first, last)`.

`iterator erase(iterator it);` `iterator erase(iterator first, iterator last);`	The first method removes the element of the list pointed to by it. The second method removes the elements of the list in the range `(first, last)`. Both return an iterator that designates the first element remaining beyond any elements removed. Erasing `N` elements causes `N` destructor calls. No reallocation occurs, so iterators and references become invalid only for the erased elements.

Table 6.1 continued

Method	*Description*
void clear() const;	The method calls erase(begin(),end()).
void swap(list& str);	The method swaps the lists between *this and str. If == str.allocator, it does so in constant time. Otherwise, it performs a number of element assignments and constructor calls proportional to the number of elements in the two lists.

void splice(iterator it, list& x);
void splice(iterator it, list& x, iterator first);
void splice(iterator it, list& x, iterator first, iterator last);
	The first method inserts the sequence controlled by x before the element in the list pointed to by it. It also removes all elements from x (&x must not equal this).
	The second method removes the element pointed to by first in the sequence controlled by x and inserts it before the element in the list pointed to by it. (If it == first || it == ++first, no change occurs.)
	The third method inserts the subrange designated by (first, last) from the sequence controlled by x before the element in the list pointed to by it. It also removes the original subrange from the sequence controlled by x. (If &x == this, the range (first, last) must not include the element pointed to by it.)

void remove(const T& x);	The method removes from the list all elements, designated by the iterator P, for which *P == x.
void remove_if(binder2nd<not_equal_to<T> > pr);	The method removes from the list all elements, designated by the iterator P, for which pr(*P) is true.
void unique(); void unique(not_equal_to<T> pr);	The first method removes from the list every element that compares equal to its preceding element. For the iterators Pi and Pj designating elements at positions i and j, the second method removes every element for which i + 1 == j && pr(*Pi, *Pj).

Table 6.1 continued

Method	*Description*
`void merge(list& x);` `void merge(list& x, greater<T> pr);`	Both methods remove all elements from the sequence controlled by `x` and insert them into the list. Both sequences must be ordered by the same predicate, described below. The resulting sequence is also ordered by that predicate. For the iterators `Pi` and `Pj` designating elements at positions `i` and `j`, the first method imposes the order `!(*Pj < *Pi)` whenever `i < j`. (The elements are sorted in ascending order.) The second method imposes the order `!pr(*Pj, *Pi)` whenever `i < j`.
`void sort();` `template<class Pred>` `void sort(greater<T> pr);`	Both methods order the elements in the list by a predicate, described below. For the iterators `Pi` and `Pj` designating elements at positions `i` and `j`, the first method imposes the order `!(*Pj < *Pi)` whenever `i < j`. (The elements are sorted in ascending order.) The member template function imposes the order `!pr(*Pj, *Pi)` whenever `i < j`. No pairs of elements in the original list are reversed in the resulting list.
`void reverse();`	The method reverses the order in which elements appear in the list.

In the next section, you'll learn how to apply many of these `<list>` methods in actual sample applications.

Sample Code

The following programs illustrate the logic and syntax used by STL lists. `list1.cpp` illustrates how to declare, join, and traverse STL lists. `list2.cpp` highlights how an STL list can mimic both stack and queue logic. The third program, `list3.cpp`, shows how to sort and reverse, how to splice list elements, and how to calculate a list's size.

The `list1.cpp` Application

The first example demonstrates the use of four `char` type lists. `ListA` and `ListB` are initialized when they are instantiated, while `ListC` and `ListD` are initialized at run time with the `insert()` method.

```
// list1.cpp
// Testing <list>
// insert(), begin(), end()
// Chris H. Pappas and William H. Murray, 2000

#include <list>
#include <iostream>

using namespace std ;

typedef list<char> CHAR_LIST_TYPE;

void main( void )
{
  char ListA[] = {'a','b','c'};
  char ListB[] = {'x','y','z','w'};

  CHAR_LIST_TYPE ListC;
  CHAR_LIST_TYPE ListD;
  CHAR_LIST_TYPE::iterator ListIterator;

  // After inserts ListC contains: m f q
  ListC.insert (ListC.begin(), 'f');
  ListC.insert (ListC.begin(), 'm');
  ListC.insert (ListC.end(), 'q');

  // Print m f q
  for (ListIterator = ListC.begin(); ListIterator != ListC.end();
       ++ListIterator)
    cout << *ListIterator << " ";
  cout << endl;

  // Insert 4 ks
  ListC.insert (ListC.end(), 4, 'k');

  // Print m f q k k k k
  for (ListIterator = ListC.begin(); ListIterator != ListC.end();
       ++ListIterator)
    cout << *ListIterator << " ";
  cout << endl;

  // Add a b c to ListC
  ListC.insert (ListC.end(), ListA, ListA + 3);
  // Print m f q k k k a b c
  for (ListIterator = ListC.begin(); ListIterator != ListC.end();
       ++ListIterator)
    cout << *ListIterator << " ";
  cout << endl;
```

```
  // ListD is appended with first two elements of ListB: x y
  ListD.insert (ListD.begin(), ListB, ListB+2);

  // ListC gets an entire copy of ListD from begin() to end()
  ListC.insert (ListC.end(), ListD.begin(), ListD.end());

  // Print ListC's copied contents of ListD
  for (ListIterator = ListC.begin(); ListIterator != ListC.end();
       ++ListIterator)
     cout << *ListIterator << " ";
  cout << endl;
}
```

The straightforward output from the program looks like:

```
m f q
m f q k k k k
m f q k k k k a b c
m f q k k k k a b c x y
```

The next application adds to your understanding of list manipulation by adding the methods `push_front()`, `push_back()`, `assign()`, and `erase()`.

The `list2.cpp` Application

The following program highlights the stack capabilities of a list with `push_front()`, and the queue logic of `push_back()` by adding an element at the end of a list. `ListB` sees a lot of action with initializations and multiple element reassignments with the use of the `assign()` method. Finally, `ListB` is deleted entirely with a call to the `erase()` method:

```
// list2.cpp
// Testing <list>
// push_front(), push_back(), assign(), begin(0, end(), erase()
// Chris H. Pappas and William H. Murray, 2000

#include <list>
#include <iostream>

using namespace std ;

typedef list<int> INT_LIST_TYPE;

void main( void )
{
  INT_LIST_TYPE ListA;
  INT_LIST_TYPE ListB;
  INT_LIST_TYPE::iterator ListIterator;
```

```
// Initialize ListA with 4 values: 11 12 40 44
ListA.push_front(12);
ListA.push_front(11);
ListA.push_back(40);
ListA.push_back(44);

cout << "ListA contains: ";
for (ListIterator = ListA.begin(); ListIterator != ListA.end();
     ++ListIterator)
  cout << *ListIterator << " ";
cout << endl;

// Initialize ListB with 5
ListB.push_front(5);

// Print ListB
cout << "ListB contains: ";
for (ListIterator = ListB.begin(); ListIterator != ListB.end();
     ++ListIterator)
  cout << *ListIterator << " ";
cout << endl;

// Reassing ListB to ListA's contents
ListB.assign(ListA.begin(), ListA.end());

// Reprint ListB
cout << "ListB now looks like ListA: ";
for (ListIterator = ListB.begin(); ListIterator != ListB.end();
     ++ListIterator)
  cout << *ListIterator << " ";
cout << endl;

ListB.assign(5,2);

// Reassign ListB to 5 2s
cout << "ListB reassigned 5 2s: ";
for (ListIterator = ListB.begin(); ListIterator != ListB.end();
     ++ListIterator)
  cout << *ListIterator << " ";
cout << endl;


// Erase the first element in ListB
ListB.erase(ListB.begin());

// Reprint ListB minus first 2
cout << "ListB minus the first element: ";
```

```
  for (ListIterator = ListB.begin(); ListIterator != ListB.end();
       ++ListIterator)
    cout << *ListIterator << " ";
  cout << endl;

  // Erase all of ListB and verify with if...empty()
  ListB.erase(ListB.begin(), ListB.end());
  if( ListB.empty() )
    cout << "ListB has been erased!";
}
```

Pay particular attention to the order in which `ListA` is initialized in the following four lines of source code:

```
ListA.push_front(12);
ListA.push_front(11);
ListA.push_back(40);
ListA.push_back(44);
```

The second call to `push_front()` inserts the `11` in front of the first value placed into the container, or `12`. The calls to `push_back()`, however, add list elements in the order you would expect. The output from the program looks like:

```
ListA contains: 11 12 40 44
ListB contains: 5
ListB now looks like ListA: 11 12 40 44
ListB reassigned 5 2s: 2 2 2 2 2
ListB minus the first element: 2 2 2 2
ListB has been erased!
```

The `list3.cpp` Application

This next application reverses `ListA`'s contents, displays the list's `size()` and `max_size()`, `sort()`s the list, and finally splices the middle of `ListB` after the first element in `ListA`:

```
// list3.cpp
// Testing <list>
// size(), max_size(), sort(), reverse(), splice(), begin(), end()
// Chris H. Pappas and William H. Murray, 2000

#include <list>
#include <iostream>

using namespace std ;

typedef list<int> INT_LIST_TYPE;
```

```
void main( void )
{
  INT_LIST_TYPE ListA;
  INT_LIST_TYPE ListB;
  INT_LIST_TYPE::iterator ListIterator;

  //Print size() and max_size() of ListA;
  cout << "ListA's size: " << ListA.size() << endl;
  cout << "ListA's max_size " << ListA.max_size() << endl;

  // Initialize ListA with 4 values: 10 11 12 13
  ListA.push_front(11);
  ListA.push_front(10);
  ListA.push_back(12);
  ListA.push_back(13);

  //Print size() and max_size() of ListA;
  cout << "ListA's size: " << ListA.size() << endl;
  cout << "ListA's max_size " << ListA.max_size() << endl;

  cout << "ListA contains: ";
  for (ListIterator = ListA.begin(); ListIterator != ListA.end();
       ++ListIterator)
    cout << *ListIterator << " ";
  cout << endl;

  // Reverse ListA
  ListA.reverse();

  // Reversed ListA
  cout << "ListA reversed: ";
  for (ListIterator = ListA.begin(); ListIterator != ListA.end();
       ++ListIterator)
    cout << *ListIterator << " ";
  cout << endl;

  // Sort ListA
  ListA.sort();

  // ListA after a call to the method sort()
  cout << "ListA sorted  : ";
  for (ListIterator = ListA.begin(); ListIterator != ListA.end();
       ++ListIterator)
    cout << *ListIterator << " ";
  cout << endl;
```

```
  // Initialize Listb
  ListB.insert(ListB.end(),1);
  ListB.insert(ListB.end(),2);
  ListB.insert(ListB.end(),3);
  ListB.insert(ListB.end(),4);
  ListB.insert(ListB.end(),5);

  // ListB after being initialized
  cout << "ListB contains: ";
  for (ListIterator = ListB.begin(); ListIterator != ListB.end();
       ++ListIterator)
    cout << *ListIterator << " ";
  cout << endl;

  // Splicing ListB's 2 3 4, after ListA's 10
  ListA.splice(++ListA.begin(),ListB, ++ListB.begin(), —ListB.end());

  // ListA after splicing with subrange of ListB
  cout << "ListA reversed: ";
  for (ListIterator = ListA.begin(); ListIterator != ListA.end();
       ++ListIterator)
    cout << *ListIterator << " ";
  cout << endl;

// ListB after the splice()
  cout << "ListB contains: ";
  for (ListIterator = ListB.begin(); ListIterator != ListB.end();
       ++ListIterator)
    cout << *ListIterator << " ";
  cout << endl;
}
```

Of the methods used in `list3.cpp`, the one needing additional explanation is `splice()`:

```
// Splicing ListB's 2 3 4, after ListA's 10
ListA.splice(++ListA.begin(),ListB, ++ListB.begin(), —ListB.end());
```

The `splice()` method has four arguments: the insertion point for the receiving list, the source list's location, where within the source list to begin transferring information, and where to end. These parameters are, in order: `++ListA.begin(),ListB`, `++ListB.begin()`, and `--ListB.end()`. Notice the use of the prefix increment `++` and decrement `--` operators to shift these default starting and ending points.

You will notice from the program's output, seen below, that `splice()` doesn't just copy the source's subrange, but transfers the elements as well.

```
ListA's size: 0
ListA's max_size 1073741823
ListA's size: 4
ListA's max_size 1073741823
ListA contains: 10 11 12 13
ListA reversed: 13 12 11 10
ListA sorted  : 10 11 12 13
ListB contains: 1 2 3 4 5
ListA reversed: 10 2 3 4 11 12 13
ListB contains: 1 5
```

Recursive Calls and the Call Stack

Many easily coded, but difficult to debug, binary tree algorithms take advantage of a C/C++ language feature known as *recursion*. The somewhat whimsical definition many computer science instructors use for recursion goes something like this: Definition for Recursion—see Recursion. And undoubtedly, the first time you encountered recursive algorithms in your formal training, you felt that definition perfectly matched your mental confusion. You thought, now really, a subroutine that calls itself? What possible use could there be for such a bizarre feature? Then you learned about binary trees, in-fix, pre-fix, and post-fix algorithms, and tree traversals.

While it is true that recursive algorithms are clean, tight, and fascinating code segments, tracing and debugging them requires a unique level of expertise and experience. Many C/C++ program development environments like the Microsoft Visual C++ Debugger's Call Stack window provide exactly what you need to detect errors in these clever code recyclers. This section uses the Microsoft Visual C++ Studio to visually illustrate just how recursive algorithms use compiler-generated stack algorithms to suspend and store recursive function parameters until the recursive algorithms reach their *limiting case* (the recursive subroutine's statement that finally stops the repetitive calls) and begin popping back calculated values.

Take, for example, the code segment that follows. At this point in your software engineering career, if you see one more "Hello World!" program or one more recursive Factorial example, you might well decide to become a travel agent! However, a recursive Factorial algorithm is, in all respects, a perfect starting point. The algorithm itself is straightforward. You simply multiply an initial value, say, for example, 4, by one less than 4, 3, then one less than 3, 2, and so on until you reach 1, as follows:

```
4 * 3 * 2 * 1
```

Hardwiring such an algorithm would necessarily be below a programmer's expertise:

```
iRecursiveCalculation = 4 * 3 * 2 * 1;
```

so naturally, you opt for a generic, recursive algorithm, something like the following application:

```
//
//BadRecursiveCallStack.cpp
//Program demonstrates recursive calls
//

int Factorial( int iCurrentValue );

void main ( void )
{
  int iRecursiveCalculation;

  iRecursiveCalculation = Factorial( 4 );
}

int Factorial( int iCurrentValue )
{
  if( iCurrentValue == 1 )
    return iCurrentValue;
  else
    return iCurrentValue *=
           Factorial( iCurrentValue– );
}
```

Proud as punch, you begin what you think will be a boring debugger trace, only to find out that your calculated `iRecursiveCalculation` value is el-wrongo! Fortunately, you know about the debugger's call stack window and begin a call-by-call examination. Figure 6.1 begins as you would expect.

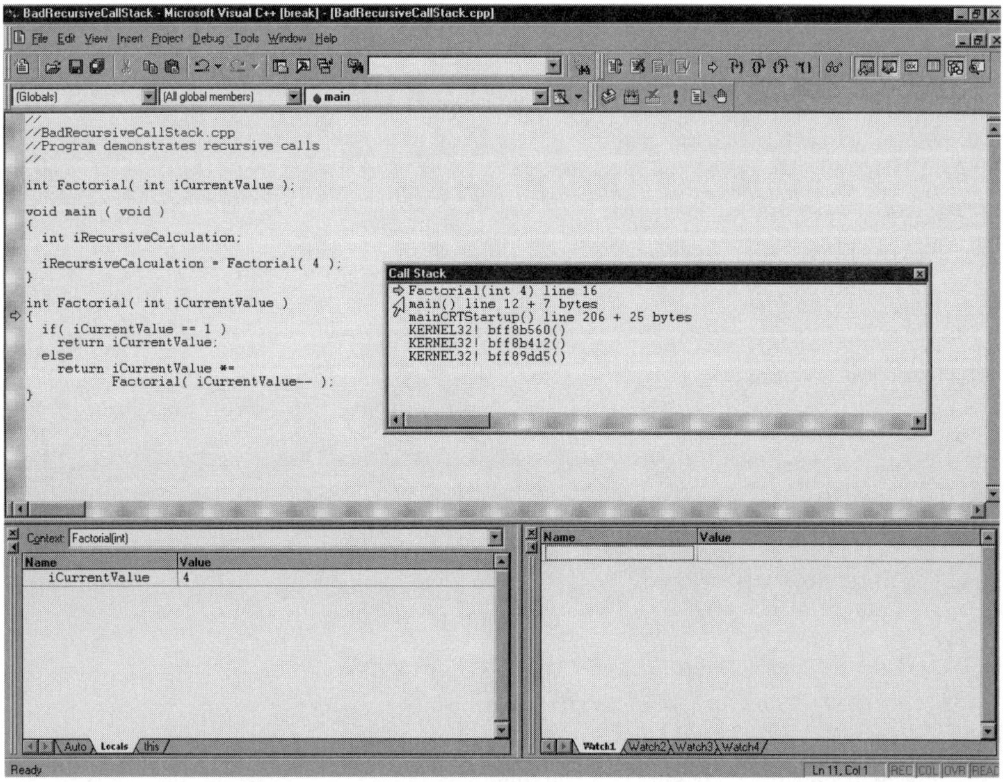

Figure 6.1 Initial recursive Factorial call showing the value 4 at the call stack top.

Even the second call to `Factorial()`, as seen in Figure 6.2, doesn't look too bad.

However, by the third trace into the function, you immediately recognize a serious miscalculation beginning to propagate (see Figure 6.3).

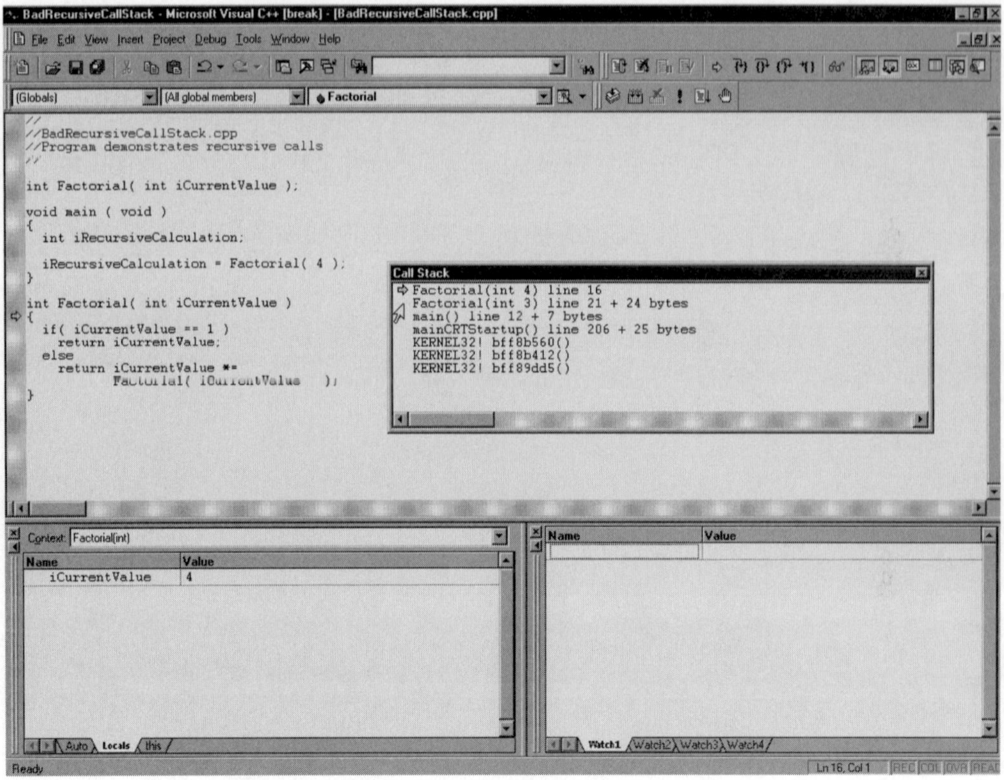

Figure 6.2 Second call to the recursive Factorial subroutine.

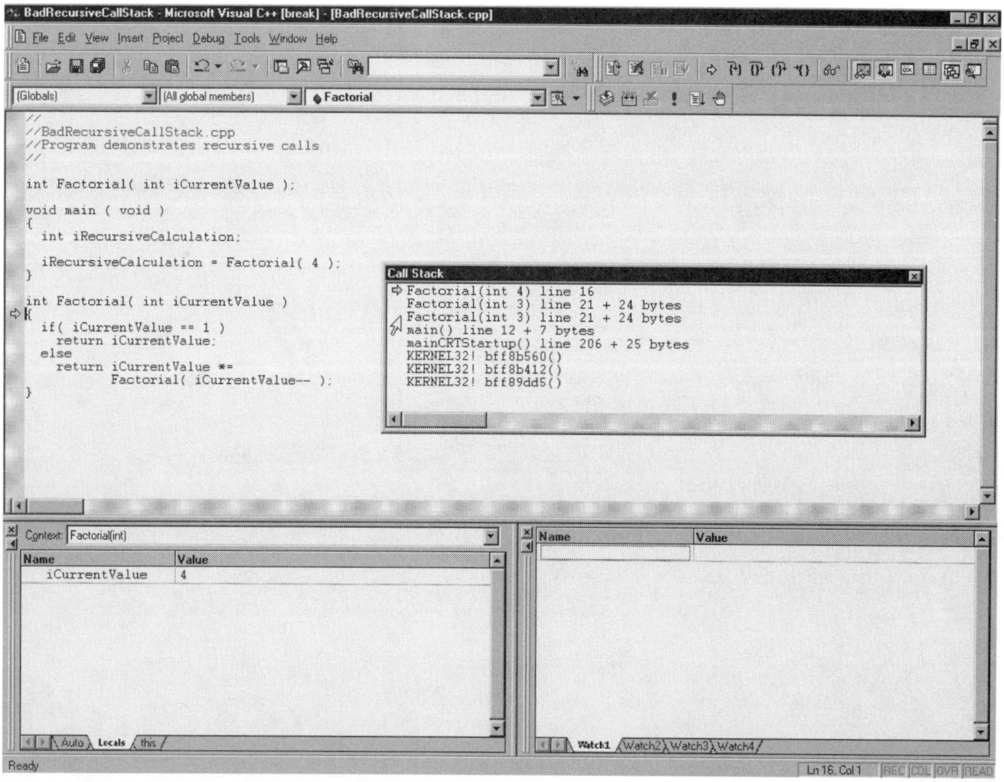

Figure 6.3 Recognizing the beginning of a `Factorial` miscalculation.

What you would expect to see, if the algorithm were functioning properly, is each call to the function `Factorial()` being passed to a value one less than the previous call. Clearly, the third trace, the call stack window, flags the error.

If you detected the error in `Factorial()`'s code right off the bat, you should go out and buy yourself something! However, without many years of C/C++ hard knocks, the code *should* still look okay.

The offending code statement generating the miscalculation involves `Factorial()`'s recursive call statement (highlighting and italics used for emphasis):

```
int Factorial( int iCurrentValue )
{
  if( iCurrentValue == 1 )
    return iCurrentValue;
  else
    return iCurrentValue *=
           Factorial( iCurrentValue-- );
```

When `Factorial()` is called from `main()`:

```
iRecursiveCalculation = Factorial( 4 );
```

there is no problem with the interpretation of the passed value, in this case `4`. However, when `Factorial()` is called from within `Factorial()`, the passed value is `iCurrentValue--`. Still confused?

At this point a programmer could *hack* a solution, or better still, use the Microsoft Visual C++ debugger's tools. The sophisticated approach to *intelligently* diagnosing and fixing `Factorial()`'s code problem now involves the debugger's ability to show you a source code segment's disassembly version.

View Disassembly Code

In the last section you used the debugger's call stack window to detect a calculation error residing within the `Factorial()` subroutine body. If you have been executing this chapter's programs, your monitor screen should still resemble that in Figure 6.3.

To activate the debugger's disassembly window, first click on the Visual C++'s view menu, debug windows option, then choose disassembly (Alt + 8). The disassembly window should autosynchronize the contents of the window to something similar to the disassembly code segment shown below:

```
14:
15:    int Factorial( int iCurrentValue )
16:    {
00401070   push        ebp
00401071   mov         ebp,esp
00401073   sub         esp,44h
00401076   push        ebx
00401077   push        esi
00401078   push        edi
00401079   lea         edi,[ebp-44h]
0040107C   mov         ecx,11h
00401081   mov         eax,0CCCCCCCCh
00401086   rep stos    dword ptr [edi]
17:      if( iCurrentValue == 1 )
00401088   cmp         dword ptr [ebp+8],1
0040108C   jne         Factorial+23h (00401093)
18:        return iCurrentValue;
0040108E   mov         eax,dword ptr [ebp+8]
00401091   jmp         Factorial+4Ah (004010ba)
19:      else
20:        return iCurrentValue *=
```

```
21:               Factorial( iCurrentValue– );
00401093   mov          eax,dword ptr [ebp+8]
00401096   mov          dword ptr [ebp-4],eax
00401099   mov          ecx,dword ptr [ebp-4]
0040109C   push         ecx
0040109D   mov          edx,dword ptr [ebp+8]
004010A0   sub          edx,1
004010A3   mov          dword ptr [ebp+8],edx
004010A6   call         @ILT+0(Factorial) (00401005)
004010AB   add          esp,4
004010AE   mov          ecx,dword ptr [ebp+8]
004010B1   imul         ecx,eax
004010B4   mov          dword ptr [ebp+8],ecx
004010B7   mov          eax,dword ptr [ebp+8]
22:    }
```

Once you have studied the disassembly window's contents, you will need to re-edit `Factorial()`'s offending statement from:

```
int Factorial( int iCurrentValue )
{
  if( iCurrentValue == 1 )
    return iCurrentValue;
  else
    return iCurrentValue *=
           Factorial( iCurrentValue– );
```

to:

```
int Factorial( int iCurrentValue )
{
  if( iCurrentValue == 1 )
    return iCurrentValue;
  else
    return iCurrentValue *=
           Factorial( iCurrentValue - 1 );
```

Now execute another build and begin a brand new trace, making certain you have called `Factorial()` at least three times. Your debugger window should now resemble Figure 6.4.

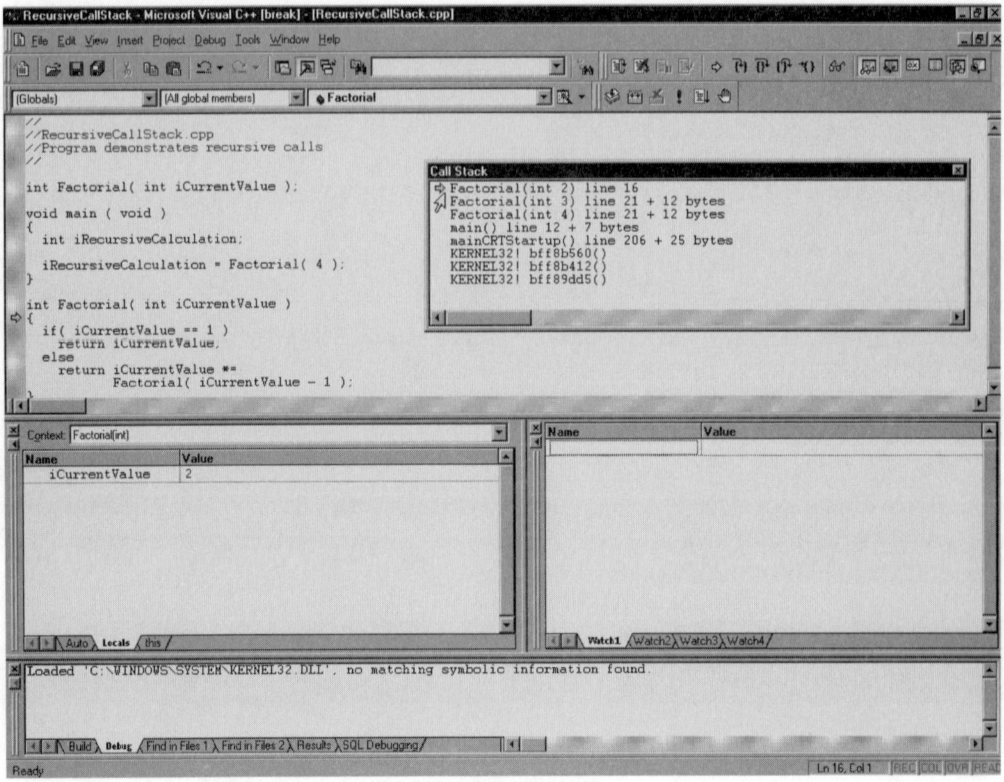

Figure 6.4 Showing corrected call stack values for `Factorial()`.

Now, open the disassembly window.

```
14:
15:    int Factorial( int iCurrentValue )
16:    {
00401070   push       ebp
00401071   mov        ebp,esp
00401073   sub        esp,40h
00401076   push       ebx
00401077   push       esi
00401078   push       edi
00401079   lea        edi,[ebp-40h]
0040107C   mov        ecx,10h
00401081   mov        eax,0CCCCCCCCh
00401086   rep stos   dword ptr [edi]
17:       if( iCurrentValue == 1 )
00401088   cmp        dword ptr [ebp+8],1
0040108C   jne        Factorial+23h (00401093)
```

```
18:         return iCurrentValue;
0040108E    mov          eax,dword ptr [ebp+8]
00401091    jmp          Factorial+3Eh (004010ae)
19:       else
20:         return iCurrentValue *=
21:                Factorial( iCurrentValue - 1 );
00401093    mov          eax,dword ptr [ebp+8]
00401096    sub          eax,1
00401099    push         eax
0040109A    call         @ILT+0(Factorial) (00401005)
0040109F    add          esp,4
004010A2    mov          ecx,dword ptr [ebp+8]
004010A5    imul         ecx,eax
004010A8    mov          dword ptr [ebp+8],ecx
004010AB    mov          eax,dword ptr [ebp+8]
22:    }
```

Table 6.2 compares the two most critical code segments. The column on the left shows the disassembly window's view of `iCurrentValue--`, while the column to the right highlights the translation of the rewritten formula, `iCurrentValue - 1`.

Table 6.2 Comparing the Two `iCurrentValue` Formula Disassembly Translations.

iCurrentValue--			iCurrentValue - 1		
21: Factorial(iCurrentValue–);			21: Factorial(iCurrentValue - 1);		
00401093	mov	eax,dword ptr [ebp+8]	00401093	mov	eax,dword ptr [ebp+8]
00401096	mov	dword ptr [ebp-4],eax	00401096	sub	eax,1
00401099	mov	ecx,dword ptr [ebp-4]	00401099	push	eax
0040109C	push	ecx	0040109A	call	@ILT+0(Factorial) (00401005)
0040109D	mov	edx,dword ptr [ebp+8]			
004010A0	sub	edx,1			
004010A3	mov	dword ptr [ebp+8],edx			
004010A6	call	@ILT+0(Factorial) (00401005)			

As you can plainly observe when debugging an application, the Variables window, with its autotracking of in-scope variables, is all you will need to detect an offending code statement. However, as your applications increase in complexity, from simple procedural, to recursive, to object-oriented, and on to full-fledged multithreaded Windows applications, the interaction between variables increases. Under these circumstances, you will need to use a combination of watches.

Before combining your in-depth understanding of recursive algorithms with what a binary tree is and how it works, you should learn *why* binary trees are worth using.

The "Big-O" Function

Before discussing the fundamentals of binary trees let's mention *why* they are so important in ADT—namely, efficiency. Locating information stored in a binary tree is one of the most efficient approaches to data retrieval. The "Big-O" function, or Order of Magnitude, is a way of expressing an algorithm's performance in a formal manner.

Typically, the Big-O function reports the upper bound of a function within a constant factor. Specifically, if `g(n)` is an upper bound of `f(n)`, then for some constant `c` it is possible to find a value of `n`, call it `n0`, for which any value of `n >= n0` will result in `f(n) <= cg(n)`.

Another way of looking at an algorithm's performance is through the amount of data it processes. For example, for some data of size `n`, the function's performance is reported as `f(n)`. However, while in many cases we can determine `f` exactly, usually it is not necessary to be this precise. Overall, you are interested only in the growth rate of `f`, which describes how quickly the algorithm's performance will degrade as the size of the data it processes becomes arbitrarily large. An algorithm's growth rate, or order of growth, is significant because ultimately it describes how efficient the algorithm is for arbitrary inputs.

A critical view of some function's `f(n)` in terms of growth rate reveals an unimportance in constant terms because their effect is minimized as they become larger and larger. For example, if `f(n) = n + 50` describes the running time of an algorithm, and `n`, the size of the data it processes, is only `1024`, the constant term in this expression already constitutes less than 5% of the running time.

Second, you can ignore constant multipliers of terms because they too will become insignificant as the value of `n` increases. Table 6.3 illustrates several algorithmic complexities and their Big-O rating:

Table 6.3 Big-O Efficiency Ratings for Common Algorithms

Big-O Rating	*Sample Algorithm*
$O(1)$	Retrieving the first element in a list.
$O(lg_2\ n)$	Splitting a list of data in half, then splitting the halves into halves, etc.
$O(n)$	Traversing a list.
$O(n\ lg_2\ n)$	Splitting a list of data in half repeatedly and traversing each half.
$O(n^2)$	Traversing a list of data once for each member of another set of equal size.
$O(n^n)$	Creating all possible subsets of data in a list.
$O(n!)$	Creating all possible permutations of data in a list.

Binary trees are efficient structures for searching because in the worst case you only end up searching the data in one branch, instead of having to search every piece of data. For this reason, searching becomes an `O(lg n)` operation, where `n` is the number of nodes in the tree, provided the tree is kept balanced.

Searching a binary tree for a value that matches a key value is also fast. If the tree is balanced, then each level contains about twice as many elements as the previous level. So a binary search tree with *n* elements would have a maximum of $\log_2 n$ levels, and thus a maximum of $\log_2 n$ comparisons would have to be made either to find a match or to determine that no match exists. This means, for example, that when searching a 100-element binary search tree, no more than 10 comparisons need to be made because $2^{10} > 1000$. When searching a 1,000,000-element binary search tree, no more than 20 comparisons need to be made because $2^{20} > 1,000,000$.

Binary Tree Fundamentals

Binary trees obtain their name from the binary number system that consists of *two* (*two* is the key here) symbols, `0` and `1`. Recall from earlier chapters that a *node* is defined as any structure that has a self-referential pointer as one of its members. Binary tree nodes add one additional self-referential pointer member to this node requirement. In other words, binary tree nodes have *two* pointers. These are typically referred to as *left child* and *right child* (or logical equivalents `previous`, `next`, `nodeBehind`, `nodeInFront`, and so on).

You can think of a binary tree like a family tree—only unlike a tree that has its roots in the ground and grows upwards, binary trees are typically represented with the *root node* or *parent node* at the top and the *child nodes* extending down—with every node having an information component, left child and right child pointer.

The topic of recursion was presented earlier in the chapter to prepare you for processing binary trees since a node can at one moment be a *child node*, and at the next moment operate as a *parent node*.

Additional family tree-related binary tree node definitions include *siblings, descendants,* and *ancestors*. As you might expect, the siblings of a node are the other children of its parent. The descendants of a node are all of the nodes branching out below it. The ancestors of a node are all the nodes along the path between it and the root. The performance associated with a tree is often discussed in terms of its *height*, the number of levels in which nodes reside.

Every node in a binary tree contains the three parts mentioned earlier: a data member and two pointers. Using this three-member structure, you form a binary tree by setting the left and right pointers of each node to point to its children. If a node does not have a child to its left or right, you set the appropriate pointer to NULL, a convenient sentinel value that marks the end of a branch. A *branch* is a series of nodes beginning at the root and ending at a *leaf* node. Leaf nodes are the nodes along the fringe of the tree that have no children.

STL Vector—Binary Tree

Because a binary tree possesses such a regular structure, the data values can easily be maintained in a vector. Just as the vector implementations of stacks and queues were more efficient than the linked list versions because they avoided the necessity of dynamic memory allocation, so too is the vector implementation of a tree very efficient. To represent a tree in a vector, you store the root of the tree in position `[0]`. The children of the node are located at position `[I]` and are stored in position `[2 * i + 1]` and `[2 * i + 2]`, respectively.

Referencing the parent is a straightforward process since the parent `[i]` is found at position `[(i-1)/2]`. For this reason, as the storage for pointers is not required in this representation, the operations used to move up and down the tree are simple arithmetic operations that can be performed very rapidly.

Unfortunately, this representation requires the binary tree to be *complete* where every level, except the leaf nodes, is filled from left to right. Representing an unbalanced tree would necessitate a large vector with many unused elements. Additionally, the algorithm would need to track which elements in the vector are valid, and which represent holes. Such a scheme is occasionally encountered. But in most cases where the complete binary tree structural property cannot be easily maintained, the more general dynamic memory implementation is used.

Templatized Class Binary Tree

The following program combines all you have learned so far in this chapter about binary trees and recursion using a C++ templatized binary tree class. The program, `btree.cpp`, begins by defining a proper binary tree node containing the required data, left child and right child member components:

```
template< class DATATYPE > class Btree;

template< class DATATYPE >
class BtreeNode {
  friend class Btree< DATATYPE >;
public:
  BtreeNode( const DATATYPE &d ):info(d), leftChild(0), rightChild(0) {
}
  DATATYPE getInfo() const { return info; }
private:
  DATATYPE info;
  BtreeNode< DATATYPE > *leftChild;
  BtreeNode< DATATYPE > *rightChild;
};
```

Because `BtreeNode` is templatized, it can be instantiated for any data type. The friend class `Btree` implements all of the binary tree insertion and traversal algorithms—separating *what* is stored in a binary tree node from what logical data manipulations are performed *on* the data.

The `BtreeNode` constructor is passed the data to be stored in the node with `leftChild` and `rightChild` initialized to `0`, meaning the two points do not point to any children. The `btree.h` header defines the C++ templatized class `Btree` which does all the work of creating, inserting, and recursively traversing the binary tree of `BtreeNodes`:

```
template< class DATATYPE >
class Btree {
public:
  Btree();
  void StartInsertNewNode( const DATATYPE & );
  void preOrderTraversal  (BtreeNode< DATATYPE > * ) const;
  void inOrderTraversal   (BtreeNode< DATATYPE > * ) const;
  void postOrderTraversal(BtreeNode< DATATYPE > * ) const;
  BtreeNode< DATATYPE > *root;
```

The public definitions of `Btree` define the constructor `Btree()`, a non-recursive `StartInsertNewNode()` method that initiates the process of adding a new node to the binary tree and the three recursive tree traversal methods, `preOrderTraversal()`, `inOrderTraversal()`, and `postOrderTraversal()`. The `public:` definitions also include a pointer root which streamlines the logic used in the three recursive methods. The formal declaration of `Btree` continues with a private definition for `recursiveInsertNode()`:

```
private:
  void recursiveInsertNode(BtreeNode< DATATYPE > **, const DATATYPE & );
};
```

This private definition in `Btree` contains the `recursiveInsertNode()` method which is called from the non-recursive public `StartInsertNewNode()` method.

The constructor for `Btree` automatically initializes the root node pointer to `NULL`, an ANSI C/C++ symbolic constant indicating that the root pointer officially points nowhere—meaning the tree is empty:

```
template< class DATATYPE >
Btree< DATATYPE >::Btree() { root = NULL; }
```

The `btree.cpp` program separates the process of inserting a new node into two separate methods. This approach provides the clean syntax seen in the `recursiveInsertNode()` method defined below:

```
template< class DATATYPE >
void Btree< DATATYPE >::StartInsertNewNode( const DATATYPE &value )
  { recursiveInsertNode( &root, value ); }

template< class DATATYPE >
void Btree< DATATYPE >::recursiveInsertNode(BtreeNode< DATATYPE >
**currentNode, const DATATYPE &value )
{
  if( *currentNode == 0 )
    *currentNode = new BtreeNode< DATATYPE >(value);
  else if( value < (*currentNode)->info )
      recursiveInsertNode( &( (*currentNode)->leftChild ), value );
    else if(value > (*currentNode)->info )
        recursiveInsertNode( &( (*currentNode)->rightChild ), value );
      else cout << "\nDuplicate value: " << value << endl;
}
```

As mentioned earlier in the chapter, any node can be seen logically, at one instance in time, as a child node, and at the next instance the same node can be viewed as a parent node.

`recursiveInsertNode()` is always passed a node pointer. The algorithm first sees if the node pointer's contents are `0` (`*currentNode == 0`). If this is true, the method knows that the current traversal path has reached the end of the tree. This is where the new node is inserted. This is also the *limiting case* for the recursive algorithm and stops the recursive tree traversal.

However, if `currentNode` is not equal to `0`, the algorithm realizes that it is pointing to a node already in the tree. At this point, `recursiveInsertNode()` needs to detect if the new value being inserted needs to be positioned into the left subtree or right subtree by comparing the current node's data value (`currentNode->info`) against the *value* to be inserted.

If the new *value* is less than the `currentNode`'s *info*, `recursiveInsertNode()` is passed the `currentNode`'s `leftChild` address. When this happens, the successive call to `recursiveInsertNode()` treats `currentNode->leftChild` as a parent node and starts the algorithm all over again.

The same scenario takes place if `value > currentNode->info`, except that the recursive call is passed `currentNode`'s `rightChild` pointer. Should `value` equal `currentNode`*'s* data value, the algorithm flags the user by displaying an appropriate message.

`recursiveInsertNode()` builds an `inorder` tree. This means that for every node, all of the node's left descendants contain data values that are less than the node's, and all of the node's right descendants contain data values that are greater than the node's. No duplicate values are present in the tree. This inorder-ness makes traversing the tree with the three infix, prefix, and postfix tree traversals a straightforward task.

Take, for example, the expression `A + B` stored in a node. `A` would be the left child's value, `B` the right child's, and the parent node would contain the operator `+`. An inorder tree traversal would visit the left child first, then the parent, then the right child abbreviated LPR. A preorder traversal would visit the parent node's value first, then the left child's, then the right child's abbreviated PLR. Finally, a postorder traversal would use the LRP approach.

The terms prefix, infix, and postfix lexically try to imply where the binary operator is in relation to its operands. Prefix has the operator *pre*ceding the operands. With infix, the operator is *in* between the operands. Postfix, like a p.s. in a letter, has the operator like a *post*script after the operands.

Notice how each of the following recursive methods all contain a limiting case—`currentNode != NULL`—to stop the recursive calls. The `preOrderTraversal()` method uses the PLR approach:

```
template< class DATATYPE >
void Btree< DATATYPE >::preOrderTraversal(BtreeNode< DATATYPE >
*currentNode ) const
{
  if( currentNode != NULL ) {
    cout << ' ' << currentNode->info;
    preOrderTraversal( currentNode->leftChild);
    preOrderTraversal( currentNode->rightChild);
  }
}
```

The `inOrderTraversal()` method uses the LPR logic:

```
template< class DATATYPE >
void Btree< DATATYPE >::inOrderTraversal(BtreeNode< DATATYPE >
*currentNode ) const
{
  if( currentNode != NULL) {
    inOrderTraversal(currentNode->leftChild);
    cout << ' ' << currentNode->info;
    inOrderTraversal(currentNode->rightChild);
  }
}
```

Finally, `postOrderTraversal()` traverses LRP:

```
template< class DATATYPE >
void Btree< DATATYPE >::postOrderTraversal(BtreeNode< DATATYPE >
*currentNode ) const
{
  if( currentNode != NULL ) {
    postOrderTraversal(currentNode->leftChild);
    postOrderTraversal(currentNode->rightChild);
    cout << ' ' << currentNode-> info;
  }
}
```

The main program in `btree.cpp` instantiates the C++ templatized class `Btree` for an `int` data type, followed by a declaration of an appropriate variable, `value`, to hold the integer values being inserted into the `tree`:

```
void main( void )
{
  Btree< int > Tree;
  int value;
```

The `for` loop prompts the user for the ten integer values being inserted:

```
  cout << "Input ten integer values: ";
  for(int i=0; i < 10; i++) {
    cin >> value;
    Tree.StartInsertNewNode(value);
  }
```

The program terminates with three calls to the recursive tree traversal methods:

```
  cout << "\nPreOrderTraversal : ";
  Tree.preOrderTraversal(Tree.root);

  cout << "\nInOrderTraversal  : ";
  Tree.inOrderTraversal(Tree.root);

  cout << "\nPostOrderTraversal: ";
  Tree.postOrderTraversal(Tree.root);
}
```

The complete executable program listing is included here to illustrate the relationship between the definitions and how to properly define and manage the multiple files. First, `btreenod.h`:

```
// btreenod.h
// Defines the binary tree node
// Chris H. Pappas and William H. Murray, 2000

template< class DATATYPE > class Btree;

template< class DATATYPE >
class BtreeNode {
  friend class Btree< DATATYPE >;
public:
  BtreeNode( const DATATYPE &d ):info(d), leftChild(0), rightChild(0) { }
  DATATYPE getInfo() const { return info; }
private:
  DATATYPE info;
  BtreeNode< DATATYPE > *leftChild;
  BtreeNode< DATATYPE > *rightChild;
};
```

The file `btree.h` defining the tree insertion and traversal methods:

```
// btree.h
// Defines the binary tree insert,
// InOrder,PreOrder, and PostOrder
// templatized methods.
// Chris H. Pappas and William H. Murray, 2000

#include <iostream>
#include "btreenod.h"

template< class DATATYPE >
class Btree {
public:
  Btree();
  void StartInsertNewNode( const DATATYPE & );
  void preOrderTraversal (BtreeNode< DATATYPE > * ) const;
  void inOrderTraversal  (BtreeNode< DATATYPE > * ) const;
  void postOrderTraversal(BtreeNode< DATATYPE > * ) const;
  BtreeNode< DATATYPE > *root;
private:
  void recursiveInsertNode(BtreeNode< DATATYPE > **, const DATATYPE & );
};

template< class DATATYPE >
Btree< DATATYPE >::Btree() { root = NULL; }

template< class DATATYPE >
void Btree< DATATYPE >::StartInsertNewNode( const DATATYPE &value )
  { recursiveInsertNode( &root, value ); }

template< class DATATYPE >
void Btree< DATATYPE >::recursiveInsertNode(BtreeNode< DATATYPE >
**currentNode, const DATATYPE &value )
{
  if( *currentNode == 0 )
    *currentNode = new BtreeNode< DATATYPE >(value);
  else if( value < (*currentNode)->info )
      recursiveInsertNode( &( (*currentNode)->leftChild ), value );
    else if(value > (*currentNode)->info )
        recursiveInsertNode( &( (*currentNode)->rightChild ), value );
      else cout << "\nDuplicate value: " << value << endl;
}

template< class DATATYPE >
void Btree< DATATYPE >::preOrderTraversal(BtreeNode< DATATYPE >
*currentNode ) const
```

```
{
  if( currentNode != NULL ) {
    cout << ' ' << currentNode->info;
    preOrderTraversal( currentNode->leftChild);
    preOrderTraversal( currentNode->rightChild);
  }
}

template< class DATATYPE >
void Btree< DATATYPE >::inOrderTraversal(BtreeNode< DATATYPE >
*currentNode ) const
{
  if( currentNode != NULL) {
    inOrderTraversal(currentNode->leftChild);
    cout << ' ' << currentNode->info;
    inOrderTraversal(currentNode->rightChild);
  }
}

template< class DATATYPE >
void Btree< DATATYPE >::postOrderTraversal(BtreeNode< DATATYPE >
*currentNode ) const
{
  if( currentNode != NULL ) {
    postOrderTraversal(currentNode->leftChild);
    postOrderTraversal(currentNode->rightChild);
    cout << ' ' << currentNode-> info;
  }
}
```

The `main()` function is defined by `btree.cpp`:

```
// btree.cpp
// Instantiates a binary tree of integers
// adding ten user-defined values,
// then traverses the binary tree using
// prefix,infix and postfix tree traversals.
// Chris H. Pappas and William H. Murray, 2000

#include <iostream>
#include "btree.h"

using namespace std;

void main( void )
{
  Btree< int > Tree;
  int value;
```

```
  cout << "Input ten integer values: ";
  for(int i=0; i < 10; i++) {
    cin >> value;
    Tree.StartInsertNewNode(value);
  }

  cout << "\nPreOrderTraversal : ";
  Tree.preOrderTraversal(Tree.root);

  cout << "\nInOrderTraversal  : ";
  Tree.inOrderTraversal(Tree.root);

  cout << "\nPostOrderTraversal: ";
  Tree.postOrderTraversal(Tree.root);
}
```

STL Stack—Binary Tree

This chapter concludes with an application that combines all you have learned with your understanding of STL stacks. The `bstack.cpp` program revisits the application discussed in Chapter 3, "Stacks and Queues," that converts infix expressions into postfix. However, unlike Chapter 3's version, `bstack.cpp` places the converted expression into a binary tree node!

For a quick test of your learning, the complete algorithm follows. Before discussing the details of the program, see if you can decipher the code statements:

```
// bstack.cpp
// Illustrates how to create a binary node
// using an STL stack
// Chris H. Pappas and William H. Murray, 2000

#pragma warning(disable:4786)
#include <stack>
#include <list>
#include <string>
#include <iostream>
#include <cctype>     // isalpha()

using namespace std ;

typedef enum tagOPERATORS { operand, leftparenthesis, plusop,
                            minusop, multiplyop,
                            divideop } OPERATORS;

class Operator_OR_Operand {
public:
  OPERATORS operatorValue;
  char      operandValue;
```

```
  Operator_OR_Operand(char n) : operatorValue(literal), operandValue(n) { }
  Operator_OR_Operand(OPERATORS anOperator) : operatorValue(anOperator) { }
};

template <class T>
class node {
public:
  node(T &eq): eqValue(eq) { }
  node(T &eq, node<T> *left, node<T> *right):
    eqValue(eq),leftChild(left),rightChild(right) { }
  T eqValue;
  node<T> * leftChild;
  node<T> * rightChild;
};

typedef stack<OPERATORS> OPERATORSTACK;
typedef stack<node<Operator_OR_Operand> *> OPERANDSTACK;

void GenerateBNode(OPERATORS currentOperator,
stack<node<Operator_OR_Operand> *> & OperandStack);
void processOperator(OPERATORS currentOperator,
  OPERATORSTACK & OperatorStack, OPERANDSTACK & OperandStack);

void main( void )
{
  OPERATORSTACK OperatorStack;
  OPERANDSTACK  OperandStack;

  string infix("A*(B+C*D)+E");
  int offset = 0;

  while(infix[offset] != '\0') {
    if(isalpha(infix[offset])) {
      node<Operator_OR_Operand> * newNode =
        new node<Operator_OR_Operand>
          (Operator_OR_Operand(infix[offset++]));
      OperandStack.push(newNode);
    }
    else
      switch(infix[offset++]) {
        case '(': OperatorStack.push(leftparenthesis);
                  break;
        case ')': while(OperatorStack.top() != leftparenthesis)
                  {
                        GenerateBNode(OperatorStack.top(), OperandStack);
                        OperatorStack.pop();
                    }
                        OperatorStack.pop();
                        break;
```

```
typedef enum tagOPERATORS { operand, leftparenthesis, plusop,
                            minusop, multiplyop,
                            divideop } OPERATORS;
```

The class `Operator_OR_Operand` is used to hold either an `operatorValue` or an `operandValue` with appropriately overloaded constructors:

```
class Operator_OR_Operand {
public:
  OPERATORS operatorValue;
  char      operandValue;

  Operator_OR_Operand(char n) : operatorValue(literal), operandValue(n) { }
  Operator_OR_Operand(OPERATORS anOperator) : operatorValue(anOperator) { }
};
```

Reviewing your understanding of templatized classes, class `node` does all the work of defining a generalized node with the requisite information component, i.e., `eqValue`, and two pointers, `leftChild` and `rightChild`:

```
template <class T>
class node {
public:
  node(T &eq): eqValue(eq) { }
  node(T &eq, node<T> *left, node<T> *right):
    eqValue(eq),leftChild(left),rightChild(right) { }
  T eqValue;
  node<T> * leftChild;
  node<T> * rightChild;
};
```

New to this chapter's version of the infix to postfix conversion algorithm is the `typdef` for `OPERANDSTACK`, which is a stack of pointers to `Operator_OR_Operand` instances:

```
typedef stack<OPERATORS> OPERATORSTACK;
typedef stack<node<Operator_OR_Operand> *> OPERANDSTACK;
```

The main function remains the same except for those code segments highlighted in bold:

```
void main( void )
{
  OPERATORSTACK OperatorStack;
  OPERANDSTACK  OperandStack;

  string infix("A*(B+C*D)+E");
  int offset = 0;
```

```
  while(infix[offset] != '\0') {
    if(isalpha(infix[offset])) {
      node<Operator_OR_Operand> * newNode =
        new node<Operator_OR_Operand>
          (Operator_OR_Operand(infix[offset++]));
      OperandStack.push(newNode);
    }
    else
      switch(infix[offset++]) {
        case '(': OperatorStack.push(leftparenthesis);
                  break;
      case ')': while(OperatorStack.top() != leftparenthesis)
                {
                        GenerateBNode(OperatorStack.top(), OperandStack);
                        OperatorStack.pop();
                   }
                  OperatorStack.pop();
                  break;
      case '+': processOperator(plusop, OperatorStack, OperandStack);
                break;
      case '-': processOperator(minusop, OperatorStack, OperandStack);
                break;
      case '*': processOperator(multiplyop, OperatorStack,
                                   OperandStack);
                break;
      case '/': processOperator(divideop, OperatorStack, OperandStack);
                break;
      }
  }

  while(!OperatorStack.empty()) { // empty the stack
    GenerateBNode(OperatorStack.top(), OperandStack);
    OperatorStack.pop();
  }
}
```

The main difference between Chapter 3's algorithm and the current implementation is that instead of the postfix expression being concatenated to a string variable when an operand is detected in the infix expression, an `Operator_OR_Operand` instance is created to hold the operand. This new instance is then pushed onto the `OperandStack`.

The processing of this new information is done by `processOperator()`. Once again, code variations between the two algorithms are highlighted in bold:

```
void processOperator(OPERATORS currentOperator,
OPERATORSTACK & OperatorStack, OPERANDSTACK & OperandStack)
{
  while( (!OperatorStack.empty()) && (currentOperator < OperatorStack.top())
) {
     GenerateBNode(OperatorStack.top(), OperandStack);
     OperatorStack.pop();
  }
  OperatorStack.push(currentOperator);
}
```

processOperator() takes care of popping any operator's right and left operand with the call to GenerateBNode() and then the removal of the instigating operator.

It is the totally new method, GenerateBNode(), that does all the work of generating the binary node representation of the final equation:

```
void GenerateBNode(OPERATORS currentOperator, OPERANDSTACK &
OperandStack)
{
  node<Operator_OR_Operand> * rightChild = OperandStack.top();
  OperandStack.pop();

  node<Operator_OR_Operand> * leftChild = OperandStack.top();
  OperandStack.pop();

  node<Operator_OR_Operand> * newNode =
    new node<Operator_OR_Operand>(Operator_OR_Operand(currentOperator),
             leftChild, rightChild);
      OperandStack.push(newNode);
}
```

GenerateBNode() does this by making each operator node point to its respective operands. First, an operator's right-side argument is popped from the OperandStack, then the operator's left-side argument, with the currentOperator, is assigned to the newNode. This newNode is then pushed onto the OperandStack. Remember, a postfix expression results from a postfix tree traversal of the information stored in the OperandStack, which technically stores the expression in order. As an exercise, try taking the algorithms presented in btree.h, btreenode.h, and btree.cpp and applying them to bstack.cpp!

Summary

In this chapter you examined the STL <list> template. A list is an unordered collection of values. Unlike a vector, a list has no fixed size, but instead grows or shrinks as elements are added or removed from the structure. In the basic list structure, elements can be added or removed only from the front or back of the list by means of iterators; elements can be added or removed from the middle of a list, as was the case with splice().

You also investigated, in depth, the concept and internal stack processes used by recursive subroutines. These short and sometimes difficult to trace algorithms provide the structural fundamentals used by many binary tree traversal routines. These recursive algorithms tap into a complete binary tree's ability to retrieve information using an efficient "Big-O" of $O(lg_2 n)$.

Next, you observed that while an STL vector can implement a binary tree algorithm, it has its own set of limitations, especially if the dimensions of the total tree are not known ahead of time and/or the tree is not complete. The C++ templatized binary tree algorithm improves upon the situation by dynamically allocating storage for new nodes as they are needed. Your understanding of binary tree nodes and the "Big-O" function are expanded in Chapter 7, "Searching and Sorting."

The chapter concluded with an STL application that created a binary tree representation of an infix expression. The modification combined all the best of C++ templates with the processing simplicity of STL.

CHAPTER 7

Searching and Sorting

Searching and sorting are common tasks for any type of collection of elements. Searching is performed to determine if a particular element is part of a collection, while sorting is used to order elements within a collection. Learning how efficiently these tasks are accomplished is a core component of any data structures course. In this chapter, the emphasis will not be on searching or sorting efficiencies, but rather on how traditional C++ coding can be migrated to the STL.

The example applications in this chapter are built using strings, arrays, and vectors. However, the STL examples can easily be extended to other collections of elements. Lists would be one such example.

Binary Search Using `bsearch()` to Search a String

A string can be searched for the occurrence of a substring with the use of the built-in `bsearch()` function. This binary search function requires that the elements be sorted in ascending order, and is thus often preceded with a call to the `qsort()` function which performs a quick sort on the elements.

The `stdlib.h` and `search.h` header files allow the use of the `qsort()` function that is required before using the `bsearch()` function. The `qsort()` function provides built-in quick sort capabilities and sorts in ascending order.

The function prototype for `qsort()` is described as follows:

```
void qsort(void *base, size_t num, size_t width, int (__cdecl *compare )(const
        void *elem1, const void *elem2 ));
```

The `qsort()` function returns no values. The `base` parameter represents the start of the target array. The `num` parameter equals the array size in elements. The `width` parameter identifies the element size in bytes. The `compare` parameter identifies the comparison function. The `elem1` parameter is a pointer to the search key, while the `elem2` parameter points to the array element to be compared with the key.

The `compare()` function will return a `<0` value if `elem1` is less than `elem2`. If `elem1` and `elem2` are equal, a `0` will be returned. If `elem1` is greater than `elem2`, a `>0` value will be returned. Normally, an ascending order sort is performed. To sort in the opposite order, the sense of "greater than" and "less than" must be reversed in the comparison function.

With `qsort()` completed, the elements are now sorted. There will be a further discussion of `qsort()` later in this chapter. A binary search is now possible with the built-in `bsearch()` function. As mentioned earlier, this function requires that the array first be sorted in ascending order.

The syntax for this function is:

```
void *bsearch(const void *key, const void *base, size_t num,
              size_t width, int (__cdecl *compare )
              (const void *elem1, const void *elem2 ));
```

The `key` parameter holds the search object. The `base` parameter points to the base of the search data. The `num` parameter holds the number of elements, while the `width` parameter holds the width of the elements. The `compare()` function will return a `<0` value if `elem1` is less than `elem2`. If `elem1` and `elem2` are equal, a `0` will be returned. If `elem1` is greater than `elem2`, a `>0` value will be returned. Normally, an ascending order sort is performed. To sort in the opposite order, the sense of "greater than" and "less than" must be reversed in the comparison function.

The `bsearch()` function returns a pointer to an occurrence of `key` in the array pointed to by `base`. If the `key` is not located, a `NULL` will be returned. Unpredictable results will occur if the array is not sorted in ascending order or if it contains duplicate records with identical keys.

The following C++ implementation allows the user to enter a string from the keyboard. A search is then performed for "binary." If the search is successful, the program will notify the user of success. Otherwise, an alternate message is printed.

```
// search1.cpp (traditional)
// performs a binary search of a sorted string
// uses qsort() to sort then bsearch() to find.
// Chris H. Pappas and William H. Murray, 2000


#include <search.h>
#include <string>
#include <iostream>

using namespace std;
```

```
int check(char **arg1, char **arg2);

void main(int argc, char **argv)
{
   char **check_information;
   char *search_string = "binary";

   // sort string before search
   qsort((void *)argv, (size_t)argc, sizeof(char *),
       (int (*)(const void*, const void*))check);

   // use binary search to find search_string
   check_information = (char **) bsearch((char *) &search_string,
                          (char *)argv, argc, sizeof(char *),
                          (int (*)(const void*, const void*))check);
   if(check_information)
      cout << "\nThe search string WAS found in the"
           << " original string.\n\n";
   else
      cout << "\nThe search string WAS NOT found in the"
           << " original string.\n\n";
}

int check(char **arg1, char **arg2)
{
   // check strings
   return _strcmpi(*arg1, *arg2);
}
```

The comparison function, `check()`, performs a string compare operation and returns the results to both the `qsort()` and `bsearch()` functions.

For example, if the user enters "This is a binary search," the search will be successful. However, if the user enters "This is a binarys search," the search will not be successful.

The `bsearch()` function performs searches in a quick and efficient manner. The only restriction is that the elements to be searched be sorted in ascending order.

The STL `basic_string` Class and Searches

As you'll see from the following listing, the STL `basic_string` class provides many member functions. Many of the functions you'll find in the `basic_string` class come in multiples in order to provide support for single characters, repeating characters with a repetition count, pointers to null-terminated character strings, and pointers to a character sequence with a sequence length provided, and so on.

```
template<class E,
    class T = char_traits<E>,
    class A = allocator<T> >
    class basic_string {
public:
    typedef T traits_type;
    typedef A allocator_type;
    typedef T::char_type char_type;
    typedef A::size_type size_type;
    typedef A::difference_type difference_type;
    typedef A::pointer pointer;
    typedef A::const_pointer const_pointer;
    typedef A::reference reference;
    typedef A::const_reference const_reference;
    typedef A::value_type value_type;
    typedef T0 iterator;
    typedef T1 const_iterator;
    typedef reverse_iterator<iterator, value_type,
        reference, pointer, difference_type>
            reverse_iterator;
    typedef reverse_iterator<const_iterator, value_type,
        const_reference, const_pointer, difference_type>
            const_reverse_iterator;
    static const size_type npos = -1;
    explicit basic_string(const A& al = A());
    basic_string(const basic_string& rhs);
    basic_string(const basic_string& rhs, size_type pos, size_type n,
        const A& al = A());
    basic_string(const E *s, size_type n, const A& al = A());
    basic_string(const E *s, const A& al = A());
    basic_string(size_type n, E c, const A& al = A());
    basic_string(const_iterator first, const_iterator last,
        const A& al = A());
    basic_string& operator=(const basic_string& rhs);
    basic_string& operator=(const E *s);
    basic_string& operator=(E c);
    iterator begin();
    const_iterator begin() const;
    iterator end();
    const_iterator end() const;
    reverse_iterator rbegin();
    const_reverse_iterator rbegin() const;
    reverse_iterator rend();
    const_reverse_iterator rend() const;
    const_reference at(size_type pos) const;
    reference at(size_type pos);
    const_reference operator[](size_type pos) const;
```

```
    reference operator[](size_type pos);
    const E *c_str() const;
    const E *data() const;
    size_type length() const;
    size_type size() const;
    size_type max_size() const;
    void resize(size_type n, E c = E());
    size_type capacity() const;
    void reserve(size_type n = 0);
    bool empty() const;
    basic_string& operator+=(const basic_string& rhs);
    basic_string& operator+=(const E *s);
    basic_string& operator+=(E c);
    basic_string& append(const basic_string& str);
    basic_string& append(const basic_string& str,
        size_type pos, size_type n);
    basic_string& append(const E *s, size_type n);
    basic_string& append(const E *s);
    basic_string& append(size_type n, E c);
    basic_string& append(const_iterator first, const_iterator last);
    basic_string& assign(const basic_string& str);
    basic_string& assign(const basic_string& str,
        size_type pos, size_type n);
    basic_string& assign(const E *s, size_type n);
    basic_string& assign(const E *s);
    basic_string& assign(size_type n, E c);
    basic_string& assign(const_iterator first, const_iterator last);
    basic_string& insert(size_type p0,
        const basic_string& str);
    basic_string& insert(size_type p0,
        const basic_string& str, size_type pos, size_type n);
    basic_string& insert(size_type p0,
        const E *s, size_type n);
    basic_string& insert(size_type p0, const E *s);
    basic_string& insert(size_type p0, size_type n, E c);
    iterator insert(iterator it, E c);
    void insert(iterator it, size_type n, E c);
    void insert(iterator it,
        const_iterator first, const_iterator last);
    basic_string& erase(size_type p0 = 0, size_type n = npos);
    iterator erase(iterator it);
    iterator erase(iterator first, iterator last);
    basic_string& replace(size_type p0, size_type n0,
        const basic_string& str);
    basic_string& replace(size_type p0, size_type n0,
        const basic_string& str, size_type pos, size_type n);
    basic_string& replace(size_type p0, size_type n0,
        const E *s, size_type n);
```

```
basic_string& replace(size_type p0, size_type n0,
    const E *s);
basic_string& replace(size_type p0, size_type n0,
    size_type n, E c);
basic_string& replace(iterator first0, iterator last0,
    const basic_string& str);
basic_string& replace(iterator first0, iterator last0,
    const E *s, size_type n);
basic_string& replace(iterator first0, iterator last0,
    const E *s);
basic_string& replace(iterator first0, iterator last0,
    size_type n, E c);
basic_string& replace(iterator first0, iterator last0,
    const_iterator first, const_iterator last);
size_type copy(E *s, size_type n, size_type pos = 0) const;
void swap(basic_string& str);
size_type find(const basic_string& str,
    size_type pos = 0) const;
size_type find(const E *s, size_type pos, size_type n) const;
size_type find(const E *s, size_type pos = 0) const;
size_type find(E c, size_type pos = 0) const;
size_type rfind(const basic_string& str,
    size_type pos = npos) const;
size_type rfind(const E *s, size_type pos,
    size_type n = npos) const;
size_type rfind(const E *s, size_type pos = npos) const;
size_type rfind(E c, size_type pos = npos) const;
size_type find_first_of(const basic_string& str,
    size_type pos = 0) const;
size_type find_first_of(const E *s, size_type pos,
    size_type n) const;
size_type find_first_of(const E *s, size_type pos = 0) const;
size_type find_first_of(E c, size_type pos = 0) const;
size_type find_last_of(const basic_string& str,
    size_type pos = npos) const;
size_type find_last_of(const E *s, size_type pos,
    size_type n = npos) con/t;
size_type find_last_of(const E *s, size_type pos = npos) const;
size_type find_last_of(E c, size_type pos = npos) const;
size_type find_first_not_of(const basic_string& str,
    size_type pos = 0) const;
size_type find_first_not_of(const E *s, size_type pos,
    size_type n) const;
size_type find_first_not_of(const E *s, size_type pos = 0) const;
size_type find_first_not_of(E c, size_type pos = 0) const;
size_type find_last_not_of(const basic_string& str,
    size_type pos = npos) const;
```

```
    size_type find_last_not_of(const E *s, size_type pos,
        size_type n) const;
    size_type find_last_not_of(const E *s,
        size_type pos = npos) const;
    size_type find_last_not_of(E c, size_type pos = npos) const;
    basic_string substr(size_type pos = 0, size_type n = npos) const;
    int compare(const basic_string& str) const;
    int compare(size_type p0, size_type n0,
        const basic_string& str);
    int compare(size_type p0, size_type n0,
        const basic_string& str, size_type pos, size_type n);
    int compare(const E *s) const;
    int compare(size_type p0, size_type n0,
        const E *s) const;
    int compare(size_type p0, size_type n0,
        const E *s, size_type pos) const;
    A get_allocator() const;
protected:
    A allocator;
    };
```

When you examine this listing you'll note that the template class provides a description of an object that controls a sequence of elements of type `E`. This sequence can vary in length. Support is provided by the Standard C++ library using string for elements of type `char`, and `wstring` for elements of type `wchar_t`. Elements of type `E` must be acceptable as parameters to `basic_istream` and `basic_ostream`.

Class `T` provides support for properties of the various `basic_string` elements. This class has the same external interface as an object of template class `char_traits`.

Class `A` provides a protected allocator object that allocates and frees storage for the sequence it controls. This class has the same external interface as an object of template class `allocator`.

The template class, `basic_string`, is used to control sequences referred to as strings. These objects are not the same as the frequently used null-terminate strings of C and C++. To operate on `basic_string` sequences, most `basic_string` member functions require the use of an operation sequence of elements of type `E`. Table 7.1 shows various operations sequences that you'll encounter.

Table 7.1 Operation Sequences for `basic_string` Member Functions

Sequence	*Description*
`c`	Represents a sequence with one element of value `c`.
`n, c`	Represents a repetition of `n` elements of value `c`.
`s`	Represents a null-terminated sequence that begins at `s` and terminates at an element whose value is `E(0)` and which is not part of the operand sequence. The null-terminated sequence can be a C string for an `E` of type char.
`s, n`	Represents a sequence of `n` elements that begins at `s`. This cannot be a null pointer.
`str`	Represents a sequence described with the `basic_string` object `str`.
`str, pos, n`	Represents a substring of the `basic_string` object `str`. The substring has a maximum of `n` elements and begins at position `pos`. If `pos` is beyond the number of elements in the sequence, an out-of-range error is reported.
`first, last`	Represents a sequence of elements that is delimited using the iterators `first` and `last` for the range.

The operation sequences are used by the member functions of `basic_string` to provide support for a wide variety of string manipulations. Table 7.2 provides a list of the member functions and a brief description of their use.

Table 7.2 Important `basic_string` Methods and Descriptions

Function	*Description*
`append`	Appends elements to the end of the string. Each function form allows alternate ways to specify the source of the elements to be appended. Returns a reference to the string where the elements were appended.
`assign`	Replaces the sequence controlled by `*this` with the operand sequence. Returns `*this`.
`at`	Returns a reference to the element of the controlled sequence at position `pos`, or reports an out-of-range error.
`begin`	Returns a random-access iterator pointing to the first element of the sequence. If the sequence is empty, it will point just beyond the sequence.
`c_str`	Returns a pointer to a C string constructed by adding a terminating null element (`E(0)`) to the controlled sequence. This C string is not modifiable. The pointer can be invalidated by calling any non-const member function for `*this`.
`capacity`	Returns the storage allocated to hold the controlled sequence. The minimum value will be equal to that of `size()`.

Table 7.2 continued

Function	*Description*
`compare`	Compares a maximum of `n0` elements of the controlled sequence starting at position `p0`. If these elements are not supplied to the argument, the entire controlled sequence will be compared. Returns a negative value when the first differing element in the controlled sequence compares to less than the corresponding element in the operand sequence (using `T::compare`), or when both have a common prefix but the operand sequence is longer. Returns a zero when the two compare equal element by element and are the same length. All other cases return a positive value.
`copy`	Copies up to `n` elements from the controlled sequence, starting at position `pos`, to the array of `E`, starting at `s`. Returns the number of elements copied.
`data`	Returns a pointer to the first element of the sequence. If the sequence is empty, a non-null pointer is returned. This pointer cannot be dereferenced.
`empty`	Returns true for an empty controlled sequence.
`end`	Returns a random-access iterator that points just beyond the end of the sequence.
`erase`	Depending on the invocation, the function can remove the elements of the controlled sequence in the range `[first, last)`, or remove the element of the controlled sequence pointed to by it. In these cases, an iterator is returned designating the first element remaining beyond the elements removed. If the element does not exist, `end()` is returned. Another invocation removes up to n elements of the controlled sequence starting at position `p0`. In this case, `*this` is returned.
`find`	Locates the first subsequence in the controlled sequence, starting at or after position `pos`, matching the operand sequence given by the remaining operands. Returns the position where the matching subsequence starts. If not found, returns `npos`.
`find_first_not_of`	Locates the first element of the controlled sequence, starting at or after position `pos`, matching none of the elements in the operand sequence given by the remaining operands. Returns the position where the matching subsequence starts. If not found, returns `npos`.
`find_first_of`	Locates the first element of the controlled sequence, starting at or after position `pos`, matching any of the elements in the operand sequence given by the remaining operands. Returns the position where the matching subsequence starts. If not found, returns `npos`.

Table 7.2 continued

Function	*Description*
`find_last_not_of`	Locates the last element of the controlled sequence, starting at or before position `pos`, matching none of the elements in the operand sequence given by the remaining operands. Returns the position where the matching subsequence starts. If not found, returns `npos`.
`find_last_of`	Locates the last element of the controlled sequence, starting at or before position `pos`, matching any of the elements in the operand sequence given by the remaining operands. Returns the position where the matching subsequence starts. If not found, returns `npos`.
`get_allocator`	Returns the allocator.
`insert`	Inserts the operand sequence given by the remaining operands prior to position `p0` or before the element pointed to by it in the controlled sequence. Returns `*this`.
`length`	Returns the length of the controlled sequence.
`max_size`	Returns the length of the longest sequence that the object can control.
`operator[]`	Returns a reference to the element of the controlled sequence at position `pos`. When that position is invalid, the behavior is not defined.
`rbegin`	Returns a reverse iterator pointing just beyond the end of the controlled sequence. This represents the start of the reverse sequence.
`rend`	Returns a reverse iterator pointing to the first element of the sequence. This represents the end of the reverse sequence.
`replace`	Used to replace a maximum of `n0` elements of the controlled sequence starting at `p0`, or the elements of the sequence starting at the one pointed to by first, up to but not including last. The replacement becomes the operand sequence given by the remaining operands. Returns `*this`.
`reserve`	Makes certain that `capacity()` will return at least `n`.
`resize`	Makes certain that `size()` will return `n`. When the control sequence is lengthened, it will append elements with value `c`.
`rfind`	Locates the last subsequence in the controlled sequence, starting at or before position `pos`, matching the operand sequence given by the remaining operands. Returns the position where the matching subsequence starts. If not found, returns `npos`.
`size`	Returns the length of the controlled sequence.
`substr`	Returns an object where the controlled sequence is a copy of a maximum of `n` elements of the controlled sequence starting at position `pos`.

If you are still wondering how to implement these methods, you'll find three of them illustrated with clear, straightforward code in the following examples of this section.

Using STL find_first_of() to Locate a Character

The sample program in this section shows how the basic_string::find_first_of can be used to find the first occurrence of a character in a string.

There are a variety of prototypes for this method:

```
size_type find_first_of(const basic_string& _X, size_type iPos = 0);
size_type find_first_of(const element_type *_S, size_type iPos, size_type
                        cElementsIn_S);
size_type find_first_of(const element_type *_S, size_type iPos = 0);
size_type find_first_of(element_type _C, size_type iPos = 0);
```

Note: Microsoft has modified the prototypes from those shown in the header files to improve readability.

Each method finds the first occurrence of an element (lowest position) of the controlled sequence, at or after position iPos, that matches any of the elements in the operand sequence given by the remaining operands. The position of the character will be returned if the search is successful. If the search is not successful, npos is returned. The position returned is 0-(zero) based. This is a special value used to indicate that none of the elements were found.

```
// search2.cpp (uses STL)
// uses find_first_of() to locate a character in a string.
// first charater of string at position 0.
// Chris H. Pappas and William H. Murray, 2000

#include <string>
#include <iostream>

using namespace std ;

void main()
{
    string string1("Is the character in this string?");
    int i = 0;

    i = string1.find_first_of('c', 0);

    cout << "Character found at an index position of " << i
         << " from the left." << endl << endl;
}
```

In this example, the string "Is the character in this string?" is searched for the first occurrence of the character "c". This character is in the string and the application will return the index position.

Using the STL `find_first_not_of()` to Locate a Character

The sample program in this section shows how the `basic_string::find_first_not_of()` can be used to find the first occurrence of a character not in a string.

Again, there are a variety of prototypes for this method:

```
size_type find_first_not_of(E c, size_type pos = 0) const;
size_type find_first_not_of(const E *s, size_type pos = 0) const;
size_type find_first_not_of(const E *s, size_type pos,
                            size_type n) const;
size_type find_first_not_of(const basic_string& str,
                            size_type pos = 0) const;
```

Here, each method locates the first element (lowest position) of the controlled sequence, occurring at or after `pos`, that does not match any of the elements in the operand sequence given by the remaining operands. If the method is successful, the position is returned. If the search is not successful, `npos` is returned. The position returned is `0`-(zero) based. This is a special value used to indicate that none of the elements were found.

```
// search3.cpp (uses STL)
// uses find_first_not_of() to locate a position of a
// character not contained in string2 in string1.
// first charater of string at position 0.
// Chris H. Pappas and William H. Murray, 2000

#include <string>
#include <iostream>

using namespace std ;

void main()
{
    string string1("locate the first character not in string2.");
    string string2("abcdefghijklmnopqrstuvwxyz");
    int i = 0;

    // locate first character in string2 not in string1
    i = string1.find_first_not_of(string2, 0);

    cout << "Character in string2 NOT in string1"
         << " found at position " << i << endl << endl;
}
```

In this example, each character in string1 is compared with those in string2. If a character occurs in string1 that is not in string2, the position of that character will be returned. When executed, this application returns a position of six (6). That is the position of the space character, with the "1" of the string, located at position zero (0).

Using the STL find() to Locate One String in Another

In this section you will learn how to use the basic_string::find() to locate one string within another.

Here are the prototypes for this method:

```
size_type find(E c, size_type pos = 0) const;
size_type find(const E *s, size_type pos = 0) const;
size_type find(const E *s, size_type pos, size_type n) const;
size_type find(const basic_string& str, size_type pos = 0) const;
```

The methods find the first subsequence (the lowest starting position) in the controlled sequence, starting on or after pos, that match the operand sequence given by the remaining operands. If the method is successful, the position is returned. If the search is not successful, npos is returned. The position returned is 0-(zero) based. This is a special value used to indicate that none of the elements were found.

```
// search4.cpp (uses STL)
// uses find() to locate the position of one
// string contained in another.
// first character of original string at position 0.
// Chris H. Pappas and William H. Murray, 2000

#include <string>
#include <iostream>

using namespace std ;

void main()
{
    string string1("Can we find a partial string within \
                    another string?");
    string string2("with");
    int i = 0;

    // locate string2 in string1
    i = string1.find(string2, 0);

    if (i >= 0)
      cout << "string2 FOUND in string1 "
```

```
            << "starting at position " << i << endl << endl;
    else
      cout << "string2 NOT FOUND in string1"
            << endl << endl;
}
```

This search will be successful. The index position returned is twenty-nine (29), which is the position of the "w" in the word "within."

A Bubble Sort Routine to Sort an Array of Integers (Ascending)

As you have already seen, many search algorithms require the set to be sorted; some require an ascending sort. There are literally dozens of sorting techniques that are studied in a data structures class. This group includes swap, bubble, insertion, enumeration, selection, and quick sorts—just to name a few. For each of these techniques there are again many coding variations for each implementation.

Of all of the sort techniques, the bubble sort is one of the most famous. The notoriety of this sort is not based on its efficiency, but on the ease in which it can be implemented with traditional C++ coding techniques.

The following C++ bubble sort will sort an array of integer values in ascending order within the original array, `iarray[]`.

```
// sort1.cpp (traditional)
// uses a simple bubble sort to sort an
// integer array in ascending order.
// Chris H. Pappas and William H. Murray, 2000

#include <iostream>

using namespace std ;

void exchange(int integer_array[], int, int);
void sort_routine(int integer_array[], int);

void main()
{
    int array_size = 14;
    int iarray[] = {99, 76, 43, 65, 84, 10, 43,
                    27, 12, 64, 73, 55, 65, 29};

    // print original array
    cout << "original integer array:" << endl;
    for (int i = 0; i < array_size; i++) {
        cout << iarray[i] << " ";
    }
    cout << endl  << endl;
```

```
    // call the sort routine
    sort_routine(iarray, array_size);

    // print the sorted array
    cout << "bubble sorted integer array:" << endl;
    for (i = 0; i < array_size; i++) {
        cout << iarray[i] << " ";
    }
    cout << endl  << endl;
}

void exchange(int integer_array[], int x, int y)
{
    int temp;
    temp = integer_array[x];
    integer_array[x] = integer_array[y];
    integer_array[y] = temp;
}

void sort_routine(int integer_array[], int a_size)
{
    for (int j = 0; j < a_size - 1; j++) {
        for (int k = a_size - 1; k > j; k–) {
            if (integer_array[k - 1] > integer_array[k])
                exchange(integer_array, k - 1, k);
        }
    }
```

Bubble sorts operate by comparing adjacent elements and swapping them if they are not in the proper order. An ascending order sort can start at the beginning or end of the array and move, or bubble, the smallest element to the top, one location at a time. This process is implemented by comparing adjacent elements and swapping values when needed.

For example, if the elements in the array are:

```
99 76 43 65
```

Then, starting at the left, the first swap would produce:

```
76 99 43 65
```

Pair comparison continues and the next swap yields:

```
76 43 99 65
```

Finally, the sort arrives at:

```
76 43 65 99
```

Now, the comparison process starts over at the start of the array, comparing 76 and 43 and yielding:

```
43 76 65 99
```

Subsequent swaps yield the following results:

```
43 76 65 99
43 65 76 99
```

The final array is sorted in ascending order. The order-of-magnitude analysis, or Big-O notation, used to measure the efficiency of a sort yields a measure of efficiency of $O(n^2)$ for the worse case and $O(n)$ for the best case for this sort.

In this implementation, the `sort_routine()` function performs the actual bubble sort by using two `for` loops. One `for` loop is used in the element pair comparisons, while the other `for` loop controls how many times the whole array is examined. When elements need to be exchanged, as determined by the `sort_routine()` function, the `exchange()` function is called to make the actual exchange.

The application returns the following information:

```
original integer array:
99 76 43 65 84 10 43 27 12 64 73 55 65 29

bubble sorted integer array:
10 12 27 29 43 43 55 64 65 65 73 76 84 99
```

If you have the time, it would be worth your effort to enter and execute this sort in the Visual C++ debugger. Then, step through the routine several times watching how the elements are moved into the final ascending sort.

A Quick Sort Routine to Sort an Array of Integers (Ascending)

The quick sort routine is perhaps the most favorite sort among programmers. This is interesting, because the quick sort is not as easy to implement as the bubble sort, nor does it yield significantly different sorting efficiencies. In the worst case scenario, the quick sort yields $O(n^2)$, just like the bubble sort. The average sort time for a quick sort is $O(n * \log n)$. Perhaps the quick sort's claim to fame is that it is usually the sort routine of choice when a language provides a built-in sorting function.

The following application implements a quick sort routine for an integer array using traditional C++ coding:

```
// sort2.cpp (traditional)
// uses a quick sort routine to sort an
// integer array in ascending order.
// Chris H. Pappas and William H. Murray, 2000

#include <iostream>

using namespace std ;

void exchange(int iarray[], int, int);
void quick_sort(int iarray[], int, int);
int partition(int iarray[], int, int);
void initialize_for_sort(int iarray[], int);

void main()
{
    int array_size = 12;
    int int_array[] = {99, 98, 43, 65, 84, 10,
                       27, 12, 64, 17, 55, 29};

    // print original array
    cout << "original integer array:" << endl;
    for (int i=0; i < array_size; i++) {
        cout << int_array[i] << " ";
    }
    cout << endl  << endl;

    // call the sort routine
    initialize_for_sort(int_array, array_size);

    // print the sorted array
    cout << "quick sorted integer array:" << endl;
    for (i = 0; i < array_size; i++) {
        cout << int_array[i] << " ";
    }
    cout << endl  << endl;
}

int partition(int iarray[], int s, int f)
{
    int pivot = iarray[s];  //pivot point
    int start = s;
    int finish = f;

    while (start < finish ) {
        if((iarray[finish] > pivot))
            finish—;
```

```
        if((iarray[start] < pivot))
            start++;

        exchange(iarray, start, finish);
    }
    return finish;
}

void exchange(int iarray[], int x, int y)
{
    int array_swap;
    array_swap = iarray[x];
    iarray[x] = iarray[y];
    iarray[y] = array_swap;
}

void quick_sort(int iarray[], int s, int f)
{
    int start = s;
    int finish = f;

    if ((finish - start) <= 0)
       return;

    int partition_point = partition(iarray, start, finish);

    quick_sort(iarray, start, partition_point - 1);
    quick_sort(iarray, partition_point + 1, finish);
}

void initialize_for_sort(int iarray[], int a_size)
{
    int begin = 0;
    int end = a_size - 1;
    quick_sort(iarray, begin, end);
}
```

The quick sort uses an interesting approach to sorting. While the bubble sort worked with the entire array of elements, the quick sort divides the array into partitions.

Note: The technique for correctly selecting the partition is the most problematic part of quick sort's implementation.

For the sake of space, let's use a group of five array elements:

```
321, 297, 113, 533, 415
 *                   ^
```

The selection of the partition's location can be anywhere, but for this example we'll choose `321`, or `int_array[0]`. Two pointers are used: `start` and `finish`. Initially, the start pointer (illustrated with the * symbol) will point to `321` (`int_array[0]`), and the `finish` pointer (illustrated with the ^ symbol) to `415` (`int_array[4]`).

Now, the value pointed to by the `finish` pointer (`415`) is compared to the partition value (`321`). If the `finish` value is greater than the partition value (in this case it is), the `finish` pointer will be moved to the left until it encounters a value less than the partition value. If the value pointed to by the `finish` pointer is not greater than the partition value, the pointer will not be changed.

```
321, 297, 113, 533, 415
 *         ^
```

Next, the value pointed to by the `start` pointer (`321`) is compared to the partition value (`321`). The `start` pointer will be moved to the right until it is pointing to an element equal to or greater than the partition value. In this case, (`321`) = (`321`), so the `start` pointer is not moved.

Next, if the `start` pointer is to the left of the `finish` pointer, the values pointed to by the pointer will be exchanged. As a result, the array now appears as:

```
113, 297, 321, 533, 415
 *         ^
```

The process now starts again, with the `start` pointer pointing to (`113`) and the `finish` pointer pointing to (`321`). The value pointed to by the `finish` pointer (`321`) is compared to the partition value (`321`). If the finish value is greater than the partition value (in this case it is not), the `finish` pointer will be moved to the left until it encounters a value less than the partition value. If it is not greater, it will not be moved. So the pointers remain in the previous position.

```
113, 297, 321, 533, 415
 *         ^
```

Next, the value pointed to by the `start` pointer (`113`) is compared to the partition value (`321`). The `start` pointer will be moved to the right until it is pointing to an element equal to or greater than the partition value. In this case, (`321`) = (`321`).

```
113, 297, 321, 533, 415
          *^
```

Once the `start` and `finish` pointer meet or cross, the elements to the left of the pointers are smaller than the partition value. The values to the right are larger than the partition value.

Once these conditions are met, the `quick_sort()` function is called recursively to sort the two arrays.

Quick Sort Using `qsort()` to Sort an Array of Integers (Ascending)

In the following example we'll take a quick look at the quick sort function provided by C++ for performing sorts on array elements. By default, the sort will be performed in ascending order.

```
// sort3.cpp (traditional)
// uses the qsort() function provided in
// search.h to sort an integer array in
// ascending order.
// Chris H. Pappas and William H. Murray, 2000

#include <search.h>
#include <iostream>

using namespace std;

int icompare_funct(const void *, const void *);
int (*ifunct_ptr)(const void *, const void *);

void main()
{
    int array_size = 12;
    int int_array[] = {99, 98, 43, 65, 84, 10,
                       27, 12, 64, 17, 55, 29};

    // print original array
    cout << "original integer array:" << endl;
    for (int i = 0; i < array_size; i++) {
        cout << int_array[i] << " ";
    }
    cout << endl  << endl;

    // call the qsort() function
    ifunct_ptr = icompare_funct;
    qsort(int_array, array_size, sizeof(int), ifunct_ptr);

    // print the sorted array
    cout << "quick sorted integer array:" << endl;
    for (i = 0; i < array_size; i++) {
        cout << int_array[i] << " ";
    }
```

```
    cout << endl  << endl;
}

int icompare_funct(const void *iresult_a,
                   const void *iresult_b)
{
    return((*(int *)iresult_a) - (*(int *)iresult_b));
}
```

Return to the section in this chapter describing the `bsearch()` function for a more detailed description of the `qsort()` function. Recall that `bsearch()` requires that the elements be sorted before performing the search.

This application returns the following information:

```
original integer array:
99 98 43 65 84 10 27 12 64 17 55 29

quick sorted integer array:
10 12 17 27 29 43 55 64 65 84 98 99
```

Because the `qsort()` function is so easy to use, a quick sort has become the defacto standard for sorting array elements in C++.

Sorting under STL

The `<vector>` template does not directly provide any template function that can be used to determine if a specific value is contained in a collection. However, there are a group of `<algorithm>` template functions ideal for `<vector>` related operations. Table 7.3 lists several functions that can be used with vectors.

Table 7.3 `<algorithm>` Related `<vector>` Template Functions

`<algorithm>` *Template Functions For Use with Vectors*	*Description*
`fill()`	Fills a vector with a given initial value.
`copy()`	Copies one sequence into another.
`max_element()`	Finds the largest value in a collection.
`min_element()`	Finds the smallest value in a collection.
`reverse()`	Reverses the container's elements.
`count()`	Counts the elements that match a target value, incrementing a counter.
`count_if()`	Counts elements that satisfy the unary template function passed to it, incrementing a counter.

Table 7.3 continued

<algorithm> *Template Functions For Use with Vectors*	*Description*
`transform()`	Transforms elements using the unary template function passed to it, from source container to destination container.
`find()`	Finds a value for which the template function passed to it returns true, returning an iterator for the matching element's location.
`find_if()`	Finds a value in the container, returning an iterator to the matching element.
`replace()`	Replaces the target element with new value.
`replace_if()`	Replaces elements for which unary template function passed to it returns true, with replacement value.
`sort()`	Places elements into ascending order.
`for_each()`	Executes template function passed to it, on each container element.
`iter_swap()`	Swaps the values specified by two iterators.

Of even more interest to us are several `<algorithm>` template functions that can be used with `sort()`, as shown in Table 7.4.

Table 7.4 `<algorithm>` Template Functions Used with `sort()`

<algorithm> *Template Functions That Can be Used with* `sort()`	*Description*
`merge()`	Merges two sorted collections into a third container.
`inplace_merge()`	Merges two adjacent sorted sequences into one.
`binary_search()`	Searches for elements within a container; returns true or false.
`lower_bound()`	Finds first element larger than or equal to the specified value; returns an iterator pointing to the match.
`upper_bound()`	Finds first element greater than the value specified; returns an iterator pointing to the match.

The `sort()` template function uses the following syntax:

```
template<class RanIt>
    void sort(RanIt first, RanIt last);
template<class RanIt, class Pred>
    void sort(RanIt first, RanIt last, Pred pr);
```

The first template function reorders the sequence designated by iterators in the range `[first, last)` to form a sequence ordered by operator `<(X, Y)`. The elements are sorted in ascending order by default. The ordering predicate, `X < Y`, is evaluated by the function no more than `ceil((last - first) * log(last - first))` times.

The second template function version operates in a manner similar to the first, except that `operator<(X, Y)` is replaced with the predicate, `pr(X, Y)`.

You'll see several examples of the `sort()` template function through the remainder of this chapter.

Using the STL `sort()` to Sort a `<vector>` of Integers (Ascending)

In the following example, application `sort4.cpp` uses `sort()` to sort a vector of integers in the default ascending order.

```
// sort4.cpp (using STL)
// uses sort(), provided by <algorithm>, to
// sort a vector of integers in
// ascending order.
// Chris H. Pappas and William H. Murray, 2000

#include <vector>
#include <algorithm>
#include <iostream>

using namespace std ;

void main()
{
    vector<int> vec;
    vector <int>::iterator it1;

    // initialize values in vector
    vec.push_back(99);
    vec.push_back(98);
    vec.push_back(43);
    vec.push_back(65);
    vec.push_back(84);
    vec.push_back(10);
    vec.push_back(27);
```

```
    vec.push_back(12);
    vec.push_back(64);
    vec.push_back(17);
    vec.push_back(55);
    vec.push_back(29);

    // print original vector
    cout << "original integer array:" << endl;
    for (it1 = vec.begin(); it1 != vec.end(); it1++) {
        cout << *it1 << " ";
    }
    cout << endl  << endl;

    // perform sort on vector
    sort(vec.begin(), vec.end());

    // print the sorted vector
    cout << "original integer array:" << endl;
    for (it1 = vec.begin(); it1 != vec.end(); it1++) {
        cout << *it1 << " ";
    }
    cout << endl  << endl;
}
```

The application code uses the `vector::push_back`, provided by `<vector>` to initialize the empty vector with twelve integer values.

The `vector::push_back` uses the following syntax:

```
template<class _TYPE, class _A>
  void vector::push_back(const _TYPE& X);
```

Microsoft has modified the class/parameter names in the prototype to improve readability.

The elements in the original unsorted vector are printed out with the use of a standard `for` loop. However, you will note that the loop's start and ending values are provided by `vector::begin` and `vector::end`.

Here is the syntax for these member functions:

```
const_iterator begin() const;
iterator begin();

const_iterator end() const;
iterator end();
```

Here the `vector::begin` member function returns a random-access iterator pointing at the first element of the sequence. This element is just beyond the end of an empty sequence.

The `vector::end` member function returns a random-access iterator pointing just beyond the end of the sequence.

Sorting the whole vector is just a matter of using the following code:

```
// perform sort on vector
sort(vec.begin(), vec.end());
```

The vector is sorted in a flash, then the sorted vector is printed to the screen. The default sorting order is an ascending sort.

Using the STL `sort()` to Sort a `<vector>` of Integers (Descending)

This example is a slight modification of the previous example. Instead of sorting a vector in the default ascending order, this example will sort the vector in descending order. Examine the following listing and note the changes in the code over the previous example.

```
// sort5.cpp (using STL)
// uses sort(), provided by <algorithm>, to
// sort a vector of integers in
// decending order.
// Chris H. Pappas and William H. Murray, 2000

#include <vector>
#include <algorithm>
#include <iostream>

using namespace std ;

bool descending_order(int x, int y)
{
    return x > y;
}

void main()
{
    vector<int> vec;
    vector <int>::iterator it1;

    // initialize values in vector
    vec.push_back(99);
    vec.push_back(98);
    vec.push_back(43);
    vec.push_back(65);
    vec.push_back(84);
    vec.push_back(10);
    vec.push_back(27);
```

```
    vec.push_back(12);
    vec.push_back(64);
    vec.push_back(17);
    vec.push_back(55);
    vec.push_back(29);

    // print original vector
    cout << "original integer array:" << endl;
    for (it1 = vec.begin(); it1 != vec.end(); it1++) {
        cout << *it1 << " ";
    }
    cout << endl  << endl;

    // perform sort on vector
    sort(vec.begin(), vec.end(), descending_order);

    // print the sorted vector
    cout << "descending integer array:" << endl;
    for (it1 = vec.begin(); it1 != vec.end(); it1++) {
        cout << *it1 << " ";
    }
    cout << endl  << endl;
}
```

As you can see, an alternate form of `sort()` is being used. In this example, the `descending_order()` method is used to specify the sort order.

```
bool descending_order(int x, int y)
{
    return x > y;
}
```

Other than this simple alteration, the two examples are identical. Now you know how to sort integers in both ascending and descending order.

Using the STL `sort()` to Sort a `<vector>` of Strings (Ascending)

The previous `vector::sort` examples can be modified to sort a vector of strings. Examine the following application:

```
// sort6.cpp (with STL)
// uses the sort() function provided by
// <algorithm> to sort a vector of strings in
// ascending order.
// Chris H. Pappas and William H. Murray, 2000

#pragma warning(disable: 4786)
```

```
#include <vector>
#include <functional>
#include <algorithm>
#include <string>
#include <iostream>

using namespace std ;

void main()
{
    const int V_SIZE = 8;
    typedef vector<string> StringVector;
    typedef StringVector::iterator StringVectorIt;

    StringVector data_vec(V_SIZE);
    StringVectorIt it1;

    // initialize values in vector
    data_vec[0] = "found";
    data_vec[1] = "boy";
    data_vec[2] = "a";
    data_vec[3] = "nine";
    data_vec[4] = "rings";
    data_vec[5] = "the";
    data_vec[6] = "since";
    data_vec[7] = "uprising";

    // print original strings
    cout << "original strings:" << endl;
    for (it1 = data_vec.begin(); it1 != data_vec.end(); it1++) {
        cout << *it1 << " ";
    }
    cout << endl  << endl;

    // perform sort on strings
    sort(data_vec.begin(), data_vec.end());

    // print the sorted strings
    cout << "sorted strings:" << endl;
    for (it1 = data_vec.begin(); it1 != data_vec.end(); it1++) {
        cout << *it1 << " ";
    }
    cout << endl  << endl;
}
```

The approach is very similar to the earlier examples. However, in this example the vector is initialized with eight strings. Again, `sort()` is called to sort the whole vector by using `vector::begin` and `vector::end`. As you might have guessed, the sort will be performed in ascending order.

Here are the results of the sort: "a boy found nine rings since the uprising." Has sorting ever been easier? Do you think you can sort these in descending order?

Using `merge()` to Merge Two Vectors Containing Ordered Elements

The STL provides a `merge()` template function that can be used to merge two ordered lists of elements, either a list or vector, for example. The function is described using the following syntax:

```
template<class InIt1, class InIt2, class OutIt>
    OutIt merge(InIt1 first1, InIt1 last1,
                InIt2 first2, InIt2 last2, OutIt x);

template<class InIt1, class InIt2, class OutIt, class Pred>
    OutIt merge(InIt1 first1, InIt1 last1,
                InIt2 first2, InIt2 last2, OutIt x, Pred pr);
```

The first variation of `merge()` determines the number of elements to copy, `K`, as the `(last1 - first1) + (last2 - first2)`. Next, the function copies two sequences, alternately. The sequences are specified by iterators in the range `[first1, last1)` and `[first2, last2)`. Here, each sequence is ordered by `operator<`, forming a merged sequence whose length is K. The merged sequence, starting at `x`, is also ordered by `operator<`. The function returns `x + K`. Merging takes place without the relative order of the elements, of either sequence, being altered.

The second variation of `merge()` behaves in a similar manner with the only change being that `operator<(X, Y)` is replaced with the predicate, `pr(X, Y)`.

The following example illustrates how two vectors can be merged. Note that the vectors are first sorted with a call to `sort()`.

```
// merge1.cpp (using STL)
// uses merge(), provided by <algorithm>, to
// merge two sorted sequences.
// Chris H. Pappas and William H. Murray, 2000

#include <vector>
#include <algorithm>
#include <iostream>
#include <deque>

using namespace std ;
```

```
void main()
{
    const int VEC1_ELEMENTS = 12;
    const int VEC2_ELEMENTS = 5;

    // template classes of vectors and deque
    typedef vector<int> iVector1, iVector2;
    typedef deque<int> iDeque3;

    iVector1 vec1(VEC1_ELEMENTS);
    iVector2 vec2(VEC2_ELEMENTS);
    iDeque3 deq3(VEC1_ELEMENTS + VEC2_ELEMENTS);

    // iterators
    typedef iVector1::iterator it1, it2;
    typedef iDeque3::iterator it3;

    it1 itv1;
    it2 itv2;
    it3 itd3;

    // initialize values in vec1
    vec1[0] = 99;
    vec1[1] = 98;
    vec1[2] = 43;
    vec1[3] = 65;
    vec1[4] = 84;
    vec1[5] = 10;
    vec1[6] = 27;
    vec1[7] = 12;
    vec1[8] = 64;
    vec1[9] = 17;
    vec1[10] = 55;
    vec1[11] = 29;

    // initialize values in vec2
    vec2[0] = 109;
    vec2[1] = 93;
    vec2[2] = 74;
    vec2[3] = 2;
    vec2[4] = 35;

    // print original vec1
    cout << "vec1 integer elements before sorting:" << endl;
    for (itv1 = vec1.begin(); itv1 != vec1.end(); itv1++) {
        cout << *itv1 << " ";
    }
    cout << endl  << endl;
```

```
    // perform sort on vector vec1
    sort(vec1.begin(), vec1.end());

    // print original vec2
    cout << "vec2 integer elements before sorting:" << endl;
    for (itv2 = vec2.begin(); itv2 != vec2.end(); itv2++) {
        cout << *itv2 << " ";
    }
    cout << endl  << endl;

    // perform sort on vector vec2
    sort(vec2.begin(), vec2.end());

    // call merge() to merge vec1 and vec2
    merge(vec1.begin(), vec1.end(), vec2.begin(), vec2.end(),
          deq3.begin());

    // print the merged and sorted elements
    cout << "merged and sorted integer elements:" << endl;
    for (itd3 = deq3.begin(); itd3 != deq3.end(); itd3++) {
        cout << *itd3 << " ";
    }
    cout << endl  << endl;
}
```

The magic in this application occurs when `merge()` is actually used. You have already learned how to initialize and sort elements in a vector in previous examples. Examine the following portion of code:

```
// call merge() to merge vec1 and vec2
merge(vec1.begin(), vec1.end(), vec2.begin(), vec2.end(),
      deq3.begin());
```

Here, `vec1.begin()` and `vec1.end()` indicate the entire vector, `vec1`, will be merged with the entire `vec2`. In this case, the `vec2.begin()` and `vec2.end()` denote the entire `vec2` vector. The results of the ordered merge will be saved in the deque, `deq3`.

Observe the results of executing this code:

```
vec1 integer elements before sorting:
99 98 43 65 84 10 27 12 64 17 55 29

vec2 integer elements before sorting:
109 93 74 2 35

merged and sorted integer elements:
2 10 12 17 27 29 35 43 55 64 65 74 84 93 98 99 109
```

Summary

In this chapter you have learned several important search and sort techniques. Several traditional C++ coding examples have been included along with STL coding techniques. The STL examples in this chapter can be extended to include not only vectors but other collections of elements such as, lists, queues, and so on.

CHAPTER 8

Priority Queues

This chapter is an extension of what you learned in Chapter 3, "Stacks and Queues." Stacks and queues embody two commonly used scheduling disciplines: LIFO and FIFO, respectively. Either LIFO or FIFO, scheduling directly supports many kinds of processing.

LIFO is used for nested suspend-and-resume processing, as in subroutine calls. FIFO is used to manage first-come first-serve ordering, such as printer queues. FIFO can also be used for suspend-and-resume scheduling: the current process is suspended and put back *at the end* of the queue. This supports processor sharing, in which each task is allowed to use a certain amount of resources before being suspended in favor of the next one waiting.

However, there are times when a more sophisticated scheduling discipline is required. *Priority queues* ADTs are a generalization of stacks and queues that support arbitrary schedule regimes, or what might be called best-next processing.

FIFO with Priorities

As you have already discovered, stacks and queues store their task descriptions in an order reflecting the way in which the information they store will be processed. Priority queues can also do that by inserting each new task in its proper place relative to the other items currently stored. Alternately, they can store the tasks in arbitrary order, and a `RemoveItem()` method can search for the best one each time it is invoked. The latter approach is necessary if the evaluation is dependent on time or changing conditions. The former approach is appropriate when evaluations of queued tasks do *not* change, in which case the evaluations can be included in the task description. Either way, a priority queue orders its tasks according to some kind of priority.

Large corporate computer systems use priority queues in allocating shared resources among multiple users. Batch processing systems might use a priority queue to manage job requests. Time-shared systems usually have printer queues to manage output requests. For either example, a request's priority might be calculated as a function of the size of the task to be performed, the privileges of the requester, and the amount of time the request has been waiting in the queue.

How Priority Queues Differ from Queues

The logic used by priority queues is similar to that of a stack or a queue. The main difference is in either `AddItem()` or `RemoveItem()`, according to whether or not tasks are stored in order. If stored in order, then `RemoveItem()` is unaffected, but `AddItem()` must evaluate the new item and successive old items until the new item's place in the ordering is determined, and then insert the new task at that location. With an array-based representation, insertion requires moving subsequent tasks down in the array. One modification of the array-based implementation is to have an array-of-queues, each of which represent (by array-index-position) their respective priorities.

When tasks are not stored in order, then `AddItem()` is unaffected, but `RemoveItem()` must evaluate all the tasks to select the one with the highest priority. With an array-based representation, deletion of items can be managed either by marking the entry free (assuming entries are pointers, by setting the value to `NULL`), or by moving subsequent entries up. The latter wastes a little time shuffling items in `RemoveItem()`, whereas the former wastes a little time in each `AddItem()` looking for an empty array position. If this inefficiency becomes significant, a more sophisticated implementation like a linked list is required.

One ADT solution to priority queue algorithms combines the idea of a queue with that of a priority queue, useful when there are a small number of possible priority values. An array-of-queues can be maintained, each corresponding to a particular priority value. When a task is added, it is simply added to the end of the queue corresponding to the task's priority value. To find and remove the next task to be processed, the queue with the highest priority is examined: if not empty, its first task is selected. Should that queue be empty, the one with the next highest priority is examined.

Priority Queue Operations

Priority queues are a finite collection of items with the following five primary operations:

1. Initializing the priority queue to be the empty priority queue.
2. Determining whether or not the priority queue is empty.
3. Determining whether or not the priority queue is full (for array-based implementations).
4. Inserting new item into the priority queue.
5. When the priority queue is not empty, remove from the priority queue an item of highest priority.

At this point in your reading you are very familiar with C++ classes, templatized classes, STL fundamentals, and hands-on coded examples. The next section takes these general priority queue operations and shows how the programmers at Hewlett-Packard have implemented the algorithms. The listing is from Microsoft's Visual C++ `<queue>` header (found in the Microsoft Visual C++ "include" subdirectory).

STL <queue> Standard Header

Hewlett-Packard, author of STL logic and syntax, have licensed many C++ compiler manufacturers to use their formal definitions. The following listing takes their formal description of STL queues and priority queues and intersperses them with a layman's coded interpretation for comparison. Notice that STL priority queues are a superset of definitions provided by the STL `<queue>` template:

```
// queue standard header

#if     _MSC_VER > 1000
#pragma once
#endif

#ifndef _QUEUE_
#define _QUEUE_
#include <algorithm>
#include <deque>
#include <vector>
#include <functional>

#ifdef  _MSC_VER
#pragma pack(push,8)
#endif  /* _MSC_VER */
_STD_BEGIN
      // TEMPLATE CLASS queue
template<class _Ty, class _C = deque<_Ty> >
    class queue {
public:
    typedef _C::allocator_type allocator_type;
    typedef _C::value_type value_type;
    typedef _C::size_type size_type;
    explicit queue(const allocator_type& _Al = allocator_type())
      : c(_Al) {}
    allocator_type get_allocator() const
      {return (c.get_allocator()); }
    bool empty() const
      {return (c.empty()); }
    size_type size() const
      {return (c.size()); }
```

```
    value_type& front()
      {return (c.front()); }
    const value_type& front() const
      {return (c.front()); }
    value_type& back()
      {return (c.back()); }
    const value_type& back() const
      {return (c.back()); }
    void push(const value_type& _X)
      {c.push_back(_X); }
    void pop()
      {c.pop_front(); }
    bool operator==(const queue<_Ty, _C>& _X) const
      {return (c == _X.c); }
    bool operator!=(const queue<_Ty, _C>& _X) const
      {return (!(*this == _X)); }
    bool operator<(const queue<_Ty, _C>& _X) const
      {return (c < _X.c); }
    bool operator>(const queue<_Ty, _C>& _X) const
      {return (_X < *this); }
    bool operator<=(const queue<_Ty, _C>& _X) const
      {return (!(_X < *this)); }
    bool operator>=(const queue<_Ty, _C>& _X) const
      {return (!(*this < _X)); }
protected:
    _C c;
    };
      // TEMPLATE CLASS priority_queue
template<class _Ty, class _C = vector<_Ty>,
    class _Pr = less<_C::value_type> >
    class priority_queue {
public:
    typedef _C::allocator_type allocator_type;
    typedef _C::value_type value_type;
    typedef _C::size_type size_type;
    explicit priority_queue(const _Pr& _X = _Pr(),
      const allocator_type& _Al = allocator_type())
      : c(_Al), comp(_X) {}
    typedef const value_type *_It;
    priority_queue(_It _F, _It _L, const _Pr& _X = _Pr(),
      const allocator_type& _Al = allocator_type())
      : c(_Al), comp(_X)
      {for (; _F != _L; ++_F)
            push(*_F); }
    allocator_type get_allocator() const
      {return (c.get_allocator()); }
    bool empty() const
      {return (c.empty()); }
```

```
    size_type size() const
      {return (c.size()); }
    value_type& top()
      {return (c.front()); }
    const value_type& top() const
      {return (c.front()); }
    void push(const value_type& _X)
      {c.push_back(_X);
      push_heap(c.begin(), c.end(), comp); }
    void pop()
      {pop_heap(c.begin(), c.end(), comp);
      c.pop_back(); }
protected:
    _C c;
    _Pr comp;
    };
_STD_END
#ifdef  _MSC_VER
#pragma pack(pop)
#endif  /* _MSC_VER */

#endif /* _QUEUE_ */

/*
 * Copyright (c) 1995 by P.J. Plauger.  ALL RIGHTS RESERVED.
 * Consult your license regarding permissions and restrictions.
 */

/*
 * This file is derived from software bearing the following
 * restrictions:
 *
 * Copyright (c) 1994
 * Hewlett-Packard Company
 *
 * Permission to use, copy, modify, distribute and sell this
 * software and its documentation for any purpose is hereby
 * granted without fee, provided that the above copyright notice
 * appear in all copies and that both that copyright notice and
 * this permission notice appear in supporting documentation.
 * Hewlett-Packard Company makes no representations about the
 * suitability of this software for any purpose. It is provided
 * "as is" without express or implied warranty.
 */
```

If you or I were to begin writing our own priority queue class, it might look like the more familiar version that follows. Notice how even this implementation takes advantage of STL template methods such as `size()` and `empty()`:

```
template <class Container>
class priority_queue {
public:
  typedef typename Container::value_type value_type;

  bool empty() {return c.empty();}
  int size() {return c.size();}
  value_type & top() {return c.front;}
  void push(value_type & newElement) {c.push_back(c.begin(),c.end());}
  void pop(){pop_heap(c.begin(),e.end());c.pop_back();}
protected:
  Container c;
};
```

As you can see, the priority queue uses the STL's heap algorithms. These algorithms include `push_heap()`, `pop_heap()`, `make_heap()`, and `sort_heap()`:

```
// TEMPLATE FUNCTION push_heap
template<class _RI> inline
     void push_heap(_RI _F, _RI _L)
     {_Push_heap_0(_F, _L, _Dist_type(_F), _Val_type(_F)); }
template<class _RI, class _Pd, class _Ty> inline
     void _Push_heap_0(_RI _F, _RI _L, _Pd *, _Ty *)
     {_Push_heap(_F, _Pd(_L - _F - 1), _Pd(0), _Ty(*(_L - 1))); }
template<class _RI, class _Pd, class _Ty> inline
     void _Push_heap(_RI _F, _Pd _H, _Pd _J, _Ty _V)
     {for (_Pd _I = (_H - 1) / 2; _J < _H && *(_F + _I) < _V;
        _I = (_H - 1) / 2)
        *(_F + _H) = *(_F + _I), _H = _I;
     *(_F + _H) = _V; }
```

When translated into programmer's English, `push_heap()` looks like:

```
template <class PQ>
void push_heap(PQ start,PQ stop)
{
  unsigned int position = (stop-start)-1;
  unsigned int parent = (position-1)/2;

  while((position > 0) && (start[position] < start[parent])) {
    swap(start[position],start[parent]);
    position = parent;
    parent = (position-1)/2;
  }
}
```

The formal STL `pop_heap()` is defined as:

```
        // TEMPLATE FUNCTION pop_heap
template<class _RI> inline
    void pop_heap(_RI _F, _RI _L)
    {_Pop_heap_0(_F, _L, _Val_type(_F)); }
template<class _RI, class _Ty> inline
    void _Pop_heap_0(_RI _F, _RI _L, _Ty *)
    {_Pop_heap(_F, _L - 1, _L - 1, _Ty(*(_L - 1)),
      _Dist_type(_F)); }
template<class _RI, class _Pd, class _Ty> inline
    void _Pop_heap(_RI _F, _RI _L, _RI _X, _Ty _V, _Pd *)
    {*_X = *_F;
    _Adjust_heap(_F, _Pd(0), _Pd(_L - _F), _V); }
template<class _RI, class _Pd, class _Ty> inline
    void _Adjust_heap(_RI _F, _Pd _H, _Pd _N, _Ty _V)
    {_Pd _J = _H;
    _Pd _K = 2 * _H + 2;
    for (; _K < _N; _K = 2 * _K + 2)
      {if (*(_F + _K) < *(_F + (_K - 1)))
            —_K;
      *(_F + _H) = *(_F + _K), _H = _K; }
    if (_K == _N)
      *(_F + _H) = *(_F + (_K - 1)), _H = _K - 1;
    _Push_heap(_F, _H, _J, _V); }
```

The logic for `pop_heap()` in a more readable style looks like:

```
template <class PQ>
void pop_heap(PQ start, PQ stop)
{
  unsigned int lastPosition = (stop-start) -1;

  swap(start[0],start[lastPosition]);
  adjust_heap(start,lastPosition,0);
}
```

The STL `make_heap()` template is defined next:

```
        // TEMPLATE FUNCTION make_heap
template<class _RI> inline
    void make_heap(_RI _F, _RI _L)
    {if (2 <= _L - _F)
      _Make_heap(_F, _L, _Dist_type(_F), _Val_type(_F)); }
template<class _RI, class _Pd, class _Ty> inline
    void _Make_heap(_RI _F, _RI _L, _Pd *, _Ty *)
    {_Pd _N = _L - _F;
    for (_Pd _H = _N / 2; 0 < _H; )
      —_H, _Adjust_heap(_F, _H, _N, _Ty(*(_F + _H))); }
```

```
        // TEMPLATE FUNCTION sort_heap
template<class _RI> inline
     void sort_heap(_RI _F, _RI _L)
     {for (; 1 < _L - _F; —_L)
       pop_heap(_F, _L); }
```

Once again, when translated into programmer's English, `make_heap()` is easily translated into the form:

```
template <class PQ>
void make_heap(PQ start, PQ stop)
{
  unsigned int heapSize = stop-start;

  for(int i = heapSize/2; i>= 0; i—)
    adjust_heap(start,heapSize,i);
}
```

Notice that `make_heap()` makes a call to the method `adjust_heap()` which uses the following algorithm:

```
template <class PQ>
void adjust_heap(PQ start,unsigned heapSize,unsigned position)
{
  while(position < heapSize) {
    unsigned int childpos = position * 2 + 1;
    if(childpos < heapSize) {
      if((childpos+1 < heapSize) && start[childpos+1] >
start[childpos])
        childpos++;
      if(start[position] >start[childpos])
        return;
      else
        swap(start[position],start[childpos]);
      }
  position = childpos;
  }
}
```

The formal STL <queue> template definition ends with the template for `sort_heap()`:

```
// TEMPLATE FUNCTION sort_heap
template<class _RI> inline
     void sort_heap(_RI _F, _RI _L)
     {for (; 1 < _L - _F; —_L)
       pop_heap(_F, _L); }
```

When translated, `sort_heap()` resembles the straightforward algorithm seen here:

```
template <class PQ>
void sort_heap(PQ start, PQ stop)
{
  unsigned int lastPosition = stop-start-1;

  while(lastPosition >0) {
    swap(start[0],start[lastPosition]);
    adjust_heap(start,lastPosition,0);
    lastPosition—;
  }
}
```

Type Definitions

The `<queue>` template has the straightforward interface typical of all STL container adaptors.

value_type

```
typedef Container::value_type value_type
```

This is one of two (excluding the required `STL _type`) `typedefs` defined for `<queue>`. It defines `value_type` as identical to the `value_type` definition for the container. For example, if you declare your `priority_queue` as `priority_queue<int>`, `value_type` is int.

size_type

```
typedef Container::size_type size_type
```

This second `typedef`, `size_type`, is defined in the container by the allocator class. Under most standard memory models, `size_type` equals `size_t`, the ANSI C type definition.

Container

```
_C c
```

This data member defines the container that holds the `priority_queue`. It is of the type specified in the class definition, and will usually be a `deque<T>` or `vector<T>`. This protected data member of the queue encapsulates the container. This means your interface to this container will be restricted to the templatized member functions of `<queue>`. The container `c` is coerced into being a heap at the time it is first constructed. From that point on, it remains a heap. The only time this has to be dealt with is when an object is either added to or removed from the container. The adaptor manages this transparently.

Constructors

The first priority_queue constructor:

```
explicit priority_queue(const _Pr& _X = _Pr(),
     const allocator_type& _Al = allocator_type())
     : c(_Al), comp(_X) {}
```

creates an empty `priority_queue`. Note that you have the option to provide a constructed comparison object for the class to use, `comp(_X)`. Under most circumstances, there is no reason to use anything other than the default comparison object, particularly if you're using the function objects provided with STL. With STL function objects, one instance is identical to any other, so there is no reason to construct unique objects.

The second overloaded `priority_queue` constructor:

```
priority_queue(_It _F, _It _L, const _Pr& _X = _Pr(),
   const allocator_type& _Al = allocator_type())
   : c(_Al), comp(_X)
   {for (; _F != _L; ++_F)
          push(*_F); }
```

initializes the `priority_queue` with an existing list of objects. All objects in the range of first, `_F`, to last, `_L` (remember last is one past the end of the list so `_L-1` is the true last element), are copied into container `c`. This presents a small problem because, after the objects have been copied, the container won't necessarily be a valid heap. The source code for the class definition shows how the constructor deals with this problem by making a call to `push()`. This method then calls the method `push_heap()`, an STL function that sorts the elements of the container into heap order. Once that is done, the first element of the heap is the greatest element, at least by the standards of the comparison object, and future additions or removals can be handled in order.

Other Operations

The four major operations of the STL `priority_queue`—`empty()`, `size()`, `push()`, and `pop()`—are described next.

bool empty() const

The method `empty()` is a boolean public member function that returns the value given from evaluating `{return (c.empty());}`. Under the definitions for the two sequential STL classes that can be used here, `empty()` is true when the container holds zero objects.

size_type size() const

The method `size()` returns `c.size()`. The container classes normally define this member function to return the number of objects held in the container `c`.

value_type& top() and *const value_type& top() const*

The method `top()` returns a reference to the top element in the container `c` with a call to `c.front()`. The top element is the next element to come off the heap when a call to `pop()` is made. Since the class does not guarantee there is in fact a top element in the container `c`, it is up to you to make certain the call is not made for an empty `priority_queue`.

void push(const value_type& _X)

The method `push()` places a copy of the argument `_X` into the container `c`. Since the container is being maintained as a heap, the insertion requires two steps: first the call to `c.push_back(_X` then a call to `push_heap(c.begin(), c.end(), comp)`. The first step adds the object to the end of the heap. This adds the item to the end of the container, but does not adjust the heap. The second method call within `pop()` takes the new last element and properly incorporates it into the heap. At this point the container is once again a valid heap.

void pop()

The last method, `pop()`, removes the highest priority element from the top of the container. Since `c` is maintained internally as a valid heap, the first element is always the highest priority item. Previously discussed containers and adaptors implement `pop_front()` by a straightforward process. They destroy the first element in the container then adjust internal pointers or data members to free up the memory that was occupied by the front element.

Unfortunately, the `priority_queue pop()` requires a more sophisticated approach. First, it calls an STL method `pop_heap(c.begin(), c.end(), comp)`. This method is the converse of `push_heap()`. It takes element `0` and moves it to the end of the container. The remaining elements are shuffled until what remains is once again a valid heap starting at location `0`. With this accomplished, the call to `c.pop_back()` destroys the last element in the container.

The Underlying Heap

You will need an understanding of heaps since STL `priority_queues` are represented internally as binary tree heaps. Frequently, sorting data is one approach to the problem of quickly locating the largest, smallest, or in the case of priority queues, highest priority element, from a set that is undergoing frequent insertions and deletions. Sorted data provides the maximum or minimum element at the beginning of the set. However, sorting a set over and over again is inefficient. In addition, because it is not the goal to keep every element in order, you could end up doing more work than is really needed. To efficiently determine only the largest or highest priority element, all you need to know is *where* to find it. Heaps and priority queues are the efficient solution.

A *heap* by definition is a binary tree organized so that you can quickly determine the node with the largest value. The cost to preserve this property is much less than that of sorting the entire set. *Priority queues* are a natural extension to heaps since data is organized in a heap so that you can quickly determine the node with the next highest priority. This is usually accomplished with a heapsort algorithm. In heapsort, the data to be sorted begins in a heap. Nodes are extracted from the heap one at a time and placed at the end of a sorted set. As each node is extracted, the next node for the sorted set percolates to the top of the heap. Heapsort has the same run-time complexity as quicksort, but a good implementation of quicksort usually beats it by a small constant factor.

A binary tree heap always has each child node containing a smaller or lower priority element than its parent. Thus, the root node is the highest priority node in the tree. A heap in which each child is smaller than its parent is called top heavy. Heaps are also left-balanced, so as nodes are added the tree grows level by level from left to right. A particularly good way to represent left-balanced binary trees, and therefore heaps, is to store nodes contiguously in an array in the order we would encounter them in a level traversal. Assuming a zero-indexed array, this means that the parent of each node at some position i in the array is located at position $(i-1)/2$. The left and right children of a node are located at positions $2i+1$ and $2i+2$. This organization is especially important for heaps because it allows us to locate a heap's last node quickly—the last node is the right-most node at the deepest level.

C++ Object Examples

In this section you will explore four sample programs beginning with the simplest non-STL approach, arrays-of-queues, then moving on to a more sophisticated non-STL linked list approach to priority queues, and ending with two STL implementations. The first STL algorithm combines simple arrays with the STL `<queue>` template. The last STL example is the simplest to use, yet the most sophisticated under the hood, since it employs the full `<queue>` template `priority_queue` definitions.

arrayPQ.cpp

The following program, `arrayPQ.cpp`, illustrates how to define a priority queue by creating an array-of-queues. `MAX_PRIORITIES` defines the number of priority levels used by the algorithm and simultaneously dimensions the array-of-queues. As both the array-of-queues and the individual queues use static (as opposed to dynamic linked lists) array definitions, `MAX_ELEMENTS` delimits the number of elements in each queue:

```
#define MAX_PRIORITIES 5
#define MAX_ELEMENTS   4
```

Each individual queue is based upon the previously discussed `Queue` class that implements a queue as a circular list (see Chapter 3).

```
class Queue
{
  public:
    Queue(void);
    void QInsert(int NewValue);
    int  QEmptyQ(void);
    void QRemove(void);
    int  QFrontElement(void);
    int  Q[MAX_ELEMENTS];
    int  Front, Rear, ElementCount;
    int  QFullQ(void);
};

Queue::Queue(void)
{
  Front = 0;
  Rear = MAX_ELEMENTS-1;
  ElementCount = 0;
}

int Queue::QEmptyQ(void)
{
  return( ElementCount == 0 );
}

int Queue::QFullQ(void)
{
  return( ElementCount == MAX_ELEMENTS );
}

void Queue::QInsert(int NewValue)
{
  if(!QFullQ()) {
    ElementCount++;
    if( Rear == MAX_ELEMENTS - 1 )
      Rear = 0;
    else
      Rear++;
    Q[Rear] = NewValue;
    }
  else
    cout << "Queue is Full";
}

void Queue::QRemove(void)
{
  if(!QEmptyQ()) {
    ElementCount—;
```

```
    if( Front == MAX_ELEMENTS - 1 )
      Front = 0;
    else
      Front = Front + 1;
  }
  else
    cout << "Queue is Empty";
}

int Queue::QFrontElement(void)
{
  if(!QEmptyQ())
    return( Q[Front] );
  else {
    cout << "Queue is Empty";
    return( 0 );
  }
}
```

It is the `PriorityQueue` class defined below that actually performs the work of instantiating the array-of-`Queue` objects, `PQ`:

```
class PriorityQueue
{
public:
  Queue PQ[MAX_PRIORITIES];
  void Insert(int Priority, int NewValue);
  int  NotEmpty(void);
  void Remove(void);
  int  FrontElement(void);
};
```

Notice there is no `PriorityQueue` constructor. This is unnecessary since each `PQ` array element is in itself an instantiation of the `Queue` class, which does have a constructor to initialize all noteworthy `Queue` instance variables.

The `PriorityQueue::Insert()` method becomes the driver for each array-of-queue instance which calls the `Queue`'s `QInsert()` method. When `Insert()` is called it is passed the `Priority` of the `NewValue`. This `Priority` is used as an array-of-`Queues` row selector. Since there are `MAX_PRIORITIES` rows, legal offsets into the array-of-`Queues` become `Priority-1`:

```
void PriorityQueue::Insert(int Priority, int NewValue)
{
  PQ[Priority-1].QInsert(NewValue);
}
```

To keep the `Queue` class definitions as close to their previously discussed counterparts, no additional variables were added to their formal class definition. For this reason, the `PriorityQueue` method `NotEmpty()` must traverse the entire array-of-`Queues`, totaling each individual `Queue`'s `ElementCount` to determine if `PQ` is actually empty:

```
int PriorityQueue::NotEmpty(void)
{
  int tempTotal = 0;
  for(int Priority = 0; Priority < MAX_PRIORITIES; Priority++)
    tempTotal += PQ[Priority].ElementCount;
  return( tempTotal );
}
```

The `PriorityQueue` `Remove()` method begins at the highest array-of-`Queues` offset, `MAX_PRIORITIES-1`, looking for any `Queue` that is not empty and then calling its respective `Queue` class method, `QRemove()`, to eliminate the element:

```
void PriorityQueue::Remove(void)
{
  for(int Priority = MAX_PRIORITIES 1; Priority >= 0; Priority )
    if(!PQ[Priority].QEmptyQ()) {
      PQ[Priority].QRemove();
      break;
    }
}
```

The `PriorityQueue` method, `FrontElement()`, progresses in a similar fashion to `Remove()`, only upon locating a `Queue` containing an element, it simply returns a copy:

```
int PriorityQueue::FrontElement(void)
{
  for(int Priority = MAX_PRIORITIES-1;
          Priority >= 0; Priority—)
    if(!PQ[Priority].QEmptyQ())
      return(PQ[Priority].QFrontElement());
}
```

The `main()` function inserts into the `pq` priority queue from lowest-to-highest priority, illustrating how the first argument to `Insert()` determines which `Queue` is being addressed, with each `Queue`-element insertion containing two consecutive values:

```
void main(void)
{
  PriorityQueue pq;

  pq.Insert(1,11);
  pq.Insert(1,10);
  pq.Insert(2,22);
  pq.Insert(2,20);
  pq.Insert(3,33);
  pq.Insert(3,30);
  pq.Insert(4,44);
  pq.Insert(4,40);
  pq.Insert(5,55);
  pq.Insert(5,50);
  pq.Insert(5,55);

  while(pq.NotEmpty()) {
    cout << pq.FrontElement() << endl;
    pq.Remove();
  }
}
```

The complete program follows:

```
// arrayPQ.cpp
// A simple C++ program illustrating how
// a priority queue may be constructed
// using a prioritized array-of-queues.
// Chris H. Pappas and William H. Murray, 2000

#include <iostream>

using namespace std;

#define MAX_PRIORITIES 5
#define MAX_ELEMENTS   4

class Queue
{
  public:
    Queue(void);
    void QInsert(int NewValue);
    int  QEmptyQ(void);
    void QRemove(void);
    int  QFrontElement(void);
    int  Q[MAX_ELEMENTS];
    int  Front, Rear, ElementCount;
    int  QFullQ(void);
};
```

```
Queue::Queue(void)
{
  Front = 0;
  Rear = MAX_ELEMENTS-1;
  ElementCount = 0;
}

int Queue::QEmptyQ(void)
{
  return( ElementCount == 0 );
}

int Queue::QFullQ(void)
{
  return( ElementCount == MAX_ELEMENTS );
}

void Queue::QInsert(int NewValue)
{
  if(!QFullQ()) {
    ElementCount++;
    if( Rear == MAX_ELEMENTS - 1 )
      Rear = 0;
    else
      Rear++;
    Q[Rear] = NewValue;
    }
  else
    cout << "Queue is Full";
}

void Queue::QRemove(void)
{
  if(!QEmptyQ()) {
    ElementCount—;
    if( Front == MAX_ELEMENTS - 1 )
      Front = 0;
    else
      Front = Front + 1;
  }
  else
    cout << "Queue is Empty";
}

int Queue::QFrontElement(void)
{
  if(!QEmptyQ())
```

```
    return( Q[Front] );
  else {
    cout << "Queue is Empty";
    return( 0 );
  }
}

class PriorityQueue
{
public:
  Queue PQ[MAX_PRIORITIES];
  void Insert(int Priority, int NewValue);
  int  NotEmpty(void);
  void Remove(void);
  int  FrontElement(void);
};

void PriorityQueue::Insert(int Priority, int NewValue)
{
  PQ[Priority-1].QInsert(NewValue);
}

int PriorityQueue::NotEmpty(void)
{
  int tempTotal = 0;
  for(int Priority = 0; Priority < MAX_PRIORITIES; Priority++)
    tempTotal += PQ[Priority].ElementCount;
  return( tempTotal );
}

void PriorityQueue::Remove(void)
{
  for(int Priority = MAX_PRIORITIES-1; Priority >= 0; Priority—)
    if(!PQ[Priority].QEmptyQ()) {
      PQ[Priority].QRemove();
      break;
    }
}

int PriorityQueue::FrontElement(void)
{
  for(int Priority = MAX_PRIORITIES-1;
          Priority >= 0; Priority—)
    if(!PQ[Priority].QEmptyQ())
      return(PQ[Priority].QFrontElement());
}
```

```
void main(void)
{
  PriorityQueue pq;

  pq.Insert(5,55);
  pq.Insert(5,50);
  pq.Insert(4,44);
  pq.Insert(4,40);
  pq.Insert(3,33);
  pq.Insert(3,30);
  pq.Insert(2,22);
  pq.Insert(2,20);
  pq.Insert(1,11);
  pq.Insert(1,10);

  while(pq.NotEmpty()) {
    cout << pq.FrontElement() << endl;
    pq.Remove();
  }
}
```

dListPQ.cpp

The next algorithm, `dListPQ.cpp`, implements a priority queue using a sorted linked list technology. To keep this algorithm analogous to the previously discussed program, `MAXCOUNT` is set equal to `20`, or `MAX_PRIORITIES * MAX_ELEMENTS`. The `typedef` for `DATA` allows the priority queue to hold any element type with a quick redefinition when desired:

```
#define MAXCOUNT 20

typedef int DATA;
```

Each node in the linked list will contain three members: a node `Priority`, the `Data` being stored, and a `NextNode` pointer.

```
typedef struct pqnode{
  int Priority;
  DATA Data;
  pqnode *NextNode;
}PQNODE;
```

The class `pq` takes care of defining the data and function members necessary to manipulate the linked list as a priority queue. `Count` maintains an accurate measure of the number of elements in the priority queue at any instance in time. However, with a linked-list implementation of a priority queue, in theory, as long as there is enough memory, there is no limit to the priority queue's size.

The pointer `PQList` is responsible for maintaining the address to the front of the priority queue:

```
class pq {

private:
  int Count;
  PQNODE *PQList;
```

The methods for class `pq` look very similar to the array-of-`Queues` implementation, at least in function, although they use linked-list technology:

```
  int Full(void);
  PQNODE *RecursiveInsert(int NewNodePriority, DATA NewData, PQNODE
*CurrentNode);

public:
  pq();
  void Insert(int NewNodePriority,int NewData);
  int Remove(void);
  int Empty(void);
};
```

The `pq` constructor takes care of initializing the `Count` to `0` and the pointer to the front of the priority queue, `PQList` to `NULL`, or empty:

```
pq::pq(void)
{
  Count = 0;
  PQList = NULL;
}
```

The `Empty()` method returns a `1` or logical true if the `Count` equals `0`, otherwise it returns `0` or a logical false:

```
int pq::Empty(void)
{
  return(Count == 0);
}
```

The `Full()` method performs a similar test only using `MAXCOUNT` for its extent:

```
int pq::Full(void)
{
  return(Count == MAXCOUNT);
}
```

The pq method Insert() invokes a RecursiveInsert() in order to place the NewData in priority order (highest to lowest priority) with an efficient recursive algorithm:

```
void pq::Insert(int NewNodePriority, DATA NewData)
{
  if(!Full()) {
    Count++;
    PQList = RecursiveInsert(NewNodePriority, NewData, PQList);
  }
}
```

RecursiveInsert() takes care of the necessary node instantiation and initialization. It also takes care of traversing any existing list to find the appropriate location for an inorder, or sorted, link-up to the new data:

```
PQNODE *pq::RecursiveInsert(int NewNodePriority, DATA NewData,
            PQNODE *CurrentNode)
{
  PQNODE *NewNode;

  if((CurrentNode == NULL) ||
     (NewNodePriority >= CurrentNode->Priority)) {
    NewNode = (PQNODE *) new PQNODE;
    NewNode->Priority = NewNodePriority;
    NewNode->Data = NewData;
    NewNode->NextNode = CurrentNode;
    return(NewNode);
  }
  else {
    CurrentNode->NextNode = RecursiveInsert(NewNodePriority, NewData,
                                            CurrentNode->NextNode);
    return(CurrentNode);
  }
}
```

The Remove() method employs a straightforward removal of the existing list's front node, since it is this node that contains the Data with the highest priority:

```
DATA pq::Remove(void)
{
  DATA temp;

  if(!Empty()) {
    temp = PQList->Data;
    PQList = PQList->NextNode;
    Count—;
    return(temp);
  }
  return (0);
}
```

The `main()` function instantiates `PQ` and exercises a few `Insert()` and `Remove()` method calls before printing out the entire priority queue:

```
void main(void)
{
  pq PQ;

  PQ.Insert(1,11);
  PQ.Insert(3,33);
  PQ.Insert(2,22);
  PQ.Insert(5,55);

  cout << PQ.Remove() << endl;

  PQ.Insert(4,44);

  while(!PQ.Empty())
    cout << PQ.Remove() << endl;
}
```

The complete program follows:

```
// dListPQ.cpp
// A C++ program demonstrating how to
// implement a priority queue using
// a dynamic linked list.
// Chris H. Pappas and William H. Murray, 2000

#include <iostream>

using namespace std;

#define MAXCOUNT 10

typedef int DATA;

typedef struct pqnode{
  int Priority;
  DATA Data;
  pqnode *NextNode;
}PQNODE;

class pq {

private:
  int Count;
  PQNODE *PQList;
```

```
  int Full(void);
  PQNODE *RecursiveInsert(int NewNodePriority, DATA NewData, PQNODE
*CurrentNode);

public:
  pq();
  void Insert(int NewNodePriority,int NewData);
  int Remove(void);
  int Empty(void);
};

pq::pq(void)
{
  Count = 0;
  PQList = NULL;
}

int pq::Empty(void)
{
  return(Count == 0);
}

int pq::Full(void)
{
  return(Count == MAXCOUNT);
}


void pq::Insert(int NewNodePriority, DATA NewData)
{
  if(!Full()) {
    Count++;
    PQList = RecursiveInsert(NewNodePriority, NewData, PQList);
  }
}

PQNODE *pq::RecursiveInsert(int NewNodePriority, DATA NewData,
            PQNODE *CurrentNode)
{
  PQNODE *NewNode;

  if((CurrentNode == NULL) ||
     (NewNodePriority >= CurrentNode->Priority)) {
    NewNode = (PQNODE *) new PQNODE;
    NewNode->Priority = NewNodePriority;
    NewNode->Data = NewData;
    NewNode->NextNode = CurrentNode;
    return(NewNode);
  }
```

```
  else {
    CurrentNode->NextNode = RecursiveInsert(NewNodePriority, NewData,
                                  CurrentNode->NextNode);

    return(CurrentNode);
  }
}

DATA pq::Remove(void)
{
  DATA temp;

  if(!Empty()) {
    temp = PQList->Data;
    PQList = PQList->NextNode;
    Count--;
    return(temp);
  }
  return (0);
}

void main(void)
{
  pq PQ;

  PQ.Insert(1,11);
  PQ.Insert(3,33);
  PQ.Insert(2,22);
  PQ.Insert(5,55);

  cout << PQ.Remove() << endl;

  PQ.Insert(4,44);

  while(!PQ.Empty())
    cout << PQ.Remove() << endl;
}
```

STL Priority Queue Examples

Now that you have seen the under-the-hood logic and code necessary to brute-force a priority queue class definition (inefficiently with arrays-of-`Queues` and efficiently with linked-list technology) it's time to examine the brief coding requirements of an STL equivalent.

If the programs look short, *they should*! Remember, STL is designed to be inherently efficient, easy to understand and use, and portable across all architectures. The first program, `STL_PQ1.cpp`, wades into STL syntax by taking your understanding of arrays-of-

Queues (non-STL object-oriented design) and permuting the algorithm to arrays-of-<queues> (non-STL + STL design).

STL_PQ1.cpp

The STL STL_PQ1.cpp algorithm presents some interesting similarities and differences to its array-of-Queue counterpart. The first requirement is to include the STL definitions for the <queue> template class. MAX_PRIORITIES functions as in previous examples, however, the FIX_OFFSET definition is new. This symbolic constant is used to correct the difference between the chosen priority level and its associated array-offset-position, which is one less. For example, a priority level of 5 is at offset 4:

```
#include <queue>

#define MAX_PRIORITIES 5
#define FIX_OFFSET 1
```

The typedef for priority_queue streamlines the later definition of the pq array and instantiates the priority_queue data type as integer:

```
typedef priority_queue<int> INT_QUEUE_TYPE;
```

The main() function merely defines the array-of-INT_QUEUE_TYPE, pq, and accesses STL-supplied <queue> methods push(), empty(), top(), and pop() to insert, query for existence, see the highest priority element, and remove elements. Notice that the for loop begins processing the pq array-of-INT_QUEUE_TYPE from logical highest priority, or MAX_PRIORITIES - 1, to lowest:

```
void main(void)
{
  INT_QUEUE_TYPE pq[MAX_PRIORITIES];

  pq[1 - FIX_OFFSET].push(11);
  pq[2 - FIX_OFFSET].push(22);
  pq[3 - FIX_OFFSET].push(33);
  pq[4 - FIX_OFFSET].push(44);
  pq[5 - FIX_OFFSET].push(55);

  for(int i = MAX_PRIORITIES - 1; i >= 0; i—)
    while(!pq[i].empty()) {
      cout << pq[i].top() << endl;
      pq[i].pop();
  }
}
```

The complete algorithm follows:

```
// STL_PQ1.cpp
// An STL implementation of priority queues
// using an array-of-<queue>s
// Chris H. Pappas and William H. Murray, 2000

#include <iostream>

using namespace std;

#include <queue>

#define MAX_PRIORITIES 5
#define FIX_OFFSET 1

typedef priority_queue<int> INT_QUEUE_TYPE;

void main(void)
{
  INT_QUEUE_TYPE pq[MAX_PRIORITIES];

  pq[1 - FIX_OFFSET].push(11);
  pq[2 - FIX_OFFSET].push(22);
  pq[3 - FIX_OFFSET].push(33);
  pq[4 - FIX_OFFSET].push(44);
  pq[5 - FIX_OFFSET].push(55);

  for(int i = MAX_PRIORITIES - 1; i >= 0; i–)
    while(!pq[i].empty()) {
      cout << pq[i].top() << endl;
      pq[i].pop();
  }
}
```

And finally, what you have been waiting for, the example program using the STL superset definition to <queue>, namely, `priority_queue`.

STL_PQ2.cpp

Once again, this full powered STL example highlights the programmer-friendly simplicity embodied by STL technology. The program begins as before by including the STL <queue> class template definitions. Note: STL priority queues do *not* have their own unique header file definitions:

```
#include <queue>

typedef priority_queue<int> INT_QUEUE_TYPE;
```

Notice how in this example there is no visible declaration for an instance variable to hold the priority queue that either resembles an array-of-*anything*, or even a linked list. STL `priority_queues` are implemented as binary tree heaps!

```
void main(void)
{
  INT_QUEUE_TYPE pq;

  pq.push(11);
  pq.push(22);
  pq.push(33);
  pq.push(44);
  pq.push(55);

  while(!pq.empty()) {
    cout << pq.top() << endl;
    pq.pop();
  }
}
```

The very brief but complete program follows:

```
// STL_PQ2.cpp
// A complete and straightforward
// implementation of STL priority_queues.
// Chris H. Pappas and William H. Murray, 2000

#include <iostream>

using namespace std;

#include <queue>

typedef priority_queue<int> INT_QUEUE_TYPE;

void main(void)
{
  INT_QUEUE_TYPE pq;

  pq.push(11);
  pq.push(22);
  pq.push(33);
  pq.push(44);
  pq.push(55);

  while(!pq.empty()) {
    cout << pq.top();
    pq.pop();
  }
}
```

Summary

In this chapter you have covered a lot of territory. Much of that material was necessary for you to fully appreciate and understand just how a priority queue functions, how STL implements the abstract data type, and finally, how simple STL `priority_queue`s are to use.

In bootstrapping your logical understanding of priority queues, you first examined an application employing an array-of-`Queues`. This straightforward algorithm "worked," however, it was not very efficient. The object-oriented linked-list approach lent itself more closely to how STL actually implements priority queues. However, you also learned what a heap is and how STL `priority_queues` more efficiently apply this algorithmic adaptor to binary trees.

CHAPTER 9

The STL <map> and <multimap> Templates

In this chapter, as in Chapter 5, we'll depart from our study of data structures to examine another important STL concept—maps and multimaps. You'll find many parallels between this chapter and Chapter 5.

Many languages support the concept of a map, sometimes referred to as a table, dictionary, associative array, or vector, meaning an indexed collection of data. However, unlike a vector with integer indices, maps may be keyed on different data types. You can think of a map as a collection of associations of key and value pairs. Certainly a phone book meets this definition, with the phone number being the key and the associated value being the person's name.

Many of the concepts presented in this chapter will be used in later chapters dealing with data structures.

Maps and Containers

The following `Cont` template shows those characteristics common to all STL containers:

```
namespace std {
template<class T, class A>
    class Cont;
//    TEMPLATE FUNCTIONS
template<class T, class A>
    bool operator==(
        const Cont<T, A>& lhs,
        const Cont<T, A>& rhs);
```

```
template<class T, class A>
    bool operator!=(
        const Cont<T, A>& lhs,
        const Cont<T, A>& rhs);
template<class T, class A>
    bool operator<(
        const Cont<T, A>& lhs,
        const Cont<T, A>& rhs);
template<class T, class A>
    bool "operator>(
        const Cont<T, A>& lhs,
        const Cont<T, A>& rhs);
template<class T, class A>
    bool operator<=(
        const Cont<T, A>& lhs,
        const Cont<T, A>& rhs);
template<class T, class A>
    bool ="operator>=(
        const Cont<T, A>& lhs,
        const Cont<T, A>& rhs);
template<class T, class A>
    void swap(
        const Cont<T, A>& lhs,
        const Cont<T, A>& rhs);
    };
```

A container is an STL template class that manages a sequence of elements. These elements can be of any object type that supplies a default constructor, a destructor, and an assignment operator. Also, particular container template classes can have additional template parameters and additional methods. The STL template container classes are: `deque`, `list`, `map`, `multimap`, `multiset`, `set`, and `vector`. Even the Standard C++ library template class `string` meets the requirements for a template container class.

<map> and <multimap> Template Syntax

The following listing gives the syntax for the STL <map> template:

```
template<class Key, class T, class Pred = less<Key>, class A = allocator<T> >
    class map {
public:
    typedef Key key_type;
    typedef T referent_type;
    typedef Pred key_compare;
    typedef A allocator_type;
    typedef pair<const Key, T> value_type;
    class value_compare;
```

```
typedef A::size_type size_type;
typedef A::difference_type difference_type;
typedef A::rebind<value_type>::other::reference reference;
typedef A::rebind<value_type>::other::const_reference const_reference;
typedef T0 iterator;
typedef T1 const_iterator;
typedef reverse_bidirectional_iterator<iterator,
    value_type, reference, A::pointer,
        difference_type> reverse_iterator;
typedef reverse_bidirectional_iterator<const_iterator,
    value_type, const_reference, A::const_pointer,
        difference_type> const_reverse_iterator;
explicit map(const Pred& comp = Pred(), const A& al = A());
map(const map& x);
map(const value_type *first, const value_type *last,
    const Pred& comp = Pred(),
        const A& al = A());
iterator begin();
const_iterator begin() const;
iterator end();
iterator end() const;
reverse_iterator rbegin();
const_reverse_iterator rbegin() const;
reverse_iterator rend();
const_reverse_iterator rend() const;
size_type size() const;
size_type max_size() const;
bool empty() const;
A get_allocator() const;
A::reference operator[](const Key& key);
pair<iterator, bool> insert(const value_type& x);
iterator insert(iterator it, const value_type& x);
void insert(const value_type *first, const value_type *last);
iterator erase(iterator it);
iterator erase(iterator first, iterator last);
size_type erase(const Key& key);
void clear();
void swap(map x);
key_compare key_comp() const;
value_compare value_comp() const;
iterator find(const Key& key);
const_iterator find(const Key& key) const;
size_type count(const Key& key) const;
iterator lower_bound(const Key& key);
const_iterator lower_bound(const Key& key) const;
iterator upper_bound(const Key& key);
const_iterator upper_bound(const Key& key) const;
```

```
    pair<iterator, iterator> equal_range(const Key& key);
    pair<const_iterator, const_iterator>
        equal_range(const Key& key) const;
protected:
    A allocator;
    };
```

You'll see that the <multimap> template syntax is very similar to that for <map> when you examine the following listing.

```
template<class Key, class T, class Pred = less<Key>, class A =
allocator<T> >
    class multimapap {
public:
    typedef Key key_type;
    typedef T referent_type;
    typedef Pred key_compare;
    typedef A allocator_type;
    typedef pair<const Key, T> value_type;
    class value_compare;
    typedef A::size_type size_type;
    typedef A::difference_type difference_type;
    typedef A::rebind<value_type>::other::reference reference;
    typedef A::rebind<value_type>::other::const_reference const_reference;
    typedef T0 iterator;
    typedef T1 const_iterator;
    typedef reverse_bidirectional_iterator<iterator,
        value_type, reference, A::pointer,
            difference_type> reverse_iterator;
    typedef reverse_bidirectional_iterator<const_iterator,
        value_type, const_reference, A::const_pointer,
            difference_type> const_reverse_iterator;
    explicit multimap (const Pred& comp = Pred(), const A& al = A());
    multimap (const multimap& x);
    multimap (const value_type *first, const value_type *last,
        const Pred& comp = Pred(), const A& al = A());
    iterator begin();
    const_iterator begin() const;
    iterator end();
    iterator end() const;
    reverse_iterator rbegin();
    const_reverse_iterator rbegin() const;
    reverse_iterator rend();
    const_reverse_iterator rend() const;
    size_type size() const;
    size_type max_size() const;
    bool empty() const;
    A get_allocator() const;
    iterator insert(const value_type& x);
```

```
    iterator insert(iterator it, const value_type& x);
    void insert(const value_type *first, const value_type *last);
    iterator erase(iterator it);
    iterator erase(iterator first, iterator last);
    size_type erase(const Key& key);
    void clear();
    void swap(multimap x);
    key_compare key_comp() const;
    value_compare value_comp() const;
    iterator find(const Key& key);
    const_iterator find(const Key& key) const;
    size_type count(const Key& key) const;
    iterator lower_bound(const Key& key);
    const_iterator lower_bound(const Key& key) const;
    iterator upper_bound(const Key& key);
    const_iterator upper_bound(const Key& key) const;
    pair<iterator, iterator> equal_range(const Key& key);
    pair<const_iterator, const_iterator>
        equal_range(const Key& key) const;
protected:
    A allocator;
    };
```

This template class defines a container that controls a varying-length sequence of elements of pair (see `typedef` below). The first element of each pair is the sort key and the second is its associated value. A map container allows the operations of lookup, insertion, and removal of an arbitrary element with a number of operations proportional to the logarithm of the number of elements in the sequence. Multimaps can contain equal keys.

<map> and <multimap> Template Methods

The <map> template provides the methods as shown in Table 9.1.

Table 9.1 <map> Template Methods and Descriptions

Method	*Description*

`explicit map(const Pred& comp = Pred(), const A& al = A());`
`map(const map& x);`
`map(const value_type *first, const value_type *last, const Pred& comp = Pred(), const A& al = A());`
	The constructors with an argument named comp store the function object so that it can be later returned by calling `key_comp()`. All constructors also store the allocator object `al` (or, for the copy constructor, `x.get_allocator()`) in allocator and initialize the controlled container. The first constructor defines an empty initial controlled container. The second constructor defines a copy of the container controlled by `x`. The last constructor defines the container of element values `[first, last)`.

Table 9.1 continued

Method	*Description*
`const_iterator begin() const;` `iterator begin();`	The method returns a bidirectional iterator that points at the first element of the container (or just beyond the end of an empty container).
`const_iterator end() const;` `iterator end();`	The method returns a bidirectional iterator that points just beyond the end of the container.
`const_reverse_iterator rbegin() const;` `reverse_iterator rbegin();`	The method returns a reverse bidirectional iterator that points just beyond the end of the container. Therefore, it identifies the beginning of the reverse container.
`const_reverse_iterator rend() const;` `reverse_iterator rend();`	The method returns a reverse bidirectional iterator that points at the first element of the container (or just beyond the end of an empty container). Therefore, it identifies the end of the reverse container.
`size_type size() const;`	The method returns the length of the container.
`size_type max_size() const;`	The method returns the length of the longest container that the object can control.
`bool empty() const;`	The method returns true for an empty container.
`A get_allocator() const;`	The method returns allocator.
`A::reference operator[](const Key& key);`	The method determines the iterator `it` as the return value of `insert(value_type(key, T())`. (It inserts an element with the specified key if no such element exists.) It then returns a reference to `(*it). second`.

`pair<iterator, bool> insert(const value_type& x);`
`iterator insert(iterator it, const value_type& x);`
`void insert(const value_type *first, const value_type *last);`
	The first method determines whether an element `y` exists in the container whose key matches that of `x`. (The keys match if `!key_comp()(x. first, y.first) && !key_comp()(y.first, x.first)`.) If not, it creates such an element `y` and initializes it with `x`. The function then determines the iterator `it` that identifies `y`. If an insertion occurred, the function returns `pair(it, true)`. Otherwise, it returns `pair(it, false)`.

Table 9.1 continued

Method	*Description*
	The second method returns `insert(x)`, using it as a starting place within the container to search for the insertion point. (Insertion can occur in amortized constant time, instead of logarithmic time, if the insertion point immediately follows `it`.) The third method inserts the container of element values in the range `[first, last)`.
`iterator erase(iterator it);` `iterator erase(iterator first, iterator last);` `size_type erase(const Key& key);`	The first method removes the element of the container pointed to by `it`. The second method removes the elements in the interval `[first, last)`. Both return an iterator that identifies the first element remaining beyond any elements removed, or `end()` if no such element exists. The third method removes the elements with sort keys in the range `(lower_bound(key), upper_bound(key))`. It returns the number of elements removed.
`void clear() const;`	The method calls `erase(begin(), end())`.
`void swap(map& str);`	The method swaps the containers between `*this` and `str`. If `allocator == str.allocator`, it does so in constant time. Otherwise, it performs a number of element assignments and constructor calls proportional to the number of elements in the two containers.
`key_compare key_comp() const;`	The method returns the stored function object that determines the order of elements in the container.
`value_compare value_comp() const;`	The method returns a function object that determines the order of elements in the container.
`iterator find(const Key& key);` `const_iterator find(const Key& key) const;`	The method returns an iterator that identifies the earliest element in the container whose sort key equals `key`. If no such element exists, the iterator equals `end()`.
`size_type count(const Key& key) const;`	The method returns the number of elements `x` in the range `[lower_bound(key), upper_bound(key))`.

Table 9.1 continued

Method	Description
`iterator lower_bound(const Key& key);` `const_iterator lower_bound(const Key& key) const;`	The method returns an iterator that identifies the earliest element `x` in the container for which `key_comp()(x. first, key)` is false, otherwise the function returns `end()`.
`iterator upper_bound(const Key& key);` `const_iterator upper_bound(const Key& key) const;`	The method returns an iterator that identifies the earliest element `x` in the container for which `key_comp()(key, x.first)` is true, otherwise, the function returns `end()`.
`pair<iterator, iterator> equal_range(const Key& key);` `pair<const_iterator, const_iterator> equal_range(const Key& key) const;`	The method returns a pair of iterators `x` such that `x.first == lower_bound(key)` and `x.second == upper_bound(key)`.

Sample Code

The declaration of a map follows the pattern we have seen repeatedly throughout the use of other Standard Template Libraries. A `map` is a template data structure, specialized by the type of the key elements and the type of the associated values. There is an optional third template argument that defines the function to be used in comparing key values. Like dynamic `<vector>` containers, a `map` initially contains no elements. Some example definitions look like:

```
map<double, string> a_string_map;
map<int, float> a_float_map;
map<int, int> an_int_map;
```

The STL `<map>` also defines several container-specific type definitions. These are most commonly used in declaration statements. For example, an iterator for a map of integers to floats can be defined as:

```
map<int, float>::iterator it;
```

In addition to the iterator, two other types are defined: `key_type`, the type associated with the keys used to index the map, and `value_type`, the type of the pair used to store entries in the map. The constructor for this type is used to create new container entries.

You insert entries into a map using the `insert()` method. Notice that the actual arguments must be a key-value pair. This pair is easily generated using the constructor for the value_type specification, as in:

```
a_float_map.insert(a_float_map::value_type(1, 1.1));
```

Of course, values can be removed from a map by providing the `key_value`. The following example erases element 4:

```
an_int_map.erase(4);
```

Also, elements being removed can be referenced by means of an iterator, as, for example, the iterator yielded by a `find()` operation. The following two statements first locate the value 4, then delete the container entry:

```
an_int_map::iterator it = an_int_map.find(4);
an_int_map.erase(it);
```

Entire subranges of container elements are removed by making a call to `erase()`. The next example erases all values between 4 and 9:

```
an_int_map::iterator start = an_int_map.find(4);
an_int_map::iterator end = an_int_map.find(9);
an_int_map.erase(start, end);
```

Remember from previous chapters that the methods `begin()` and `end()` represent bidirectional `map` iterators. Dereferencing a map iterator yields a map element pair of key and value. You can use the types `first_type` and `second_type` (seen below) to reference these values individually. The `first_type` is a constant that cannot be modified. the `second_type` field however, can be used to change the value being held in association with a given key, and will modify the value being maintained in the container. Elements will be generated in the container based on the ordering of the key fields. The iterators generated by calls to `rbegin()` and `rend()` allow you to access container elements in reverse.

```
pair
template<class T, class U>
    struct pair {
    typedef T first_type;
    typedef U second_type
    T first;
    U second;
    pair();
    pair(const T& x, const U& y);
    template<class V, class W>
        pair(const pair<V, W>& pr);
    };
```

To traverse or count map elements you use the `find()`, `empty()`, and `size()` methods. The method `size()` returns the number of elements held by the container, while `empty()` returns a Boolean true if the container is empty. This is faster than testing the value returned by `size()` with zero. The method `find()` takes a `key_type` argument, and returns an iterator denoting the associated key and value pair.

Advanced container element searches are possible with the methods `lower_bound()` and `upper_bound()`. The `lower_bound()` method yields the first entry that matches the argument key, while the method `upper_bound()` returns the first value past the last entry matching the argument. The method `equal_range()` returns a pair of iterators, holding both the lower and upper bounds. The `count()` method returns the number of elements that match the key value supplied as the argument.

A <map> Application

Much of the code in the following example is built upon the code developed in earlier chapters. You should notice, for example, that the use of iterators is now a concrete commonplace STL regular.

Let's take a look at the completed <map> application named `map.cpp`:

```
// map.cpp
// Testing <map>
// insert(), begin(), end(), size(), erase(),
// upper_bound(), lower_bound(), find(),
// rbegin(), rend(), empty(), count(), equal_range()
// Chris H. Pappas and William H. Murray, 2000

#pragma warning(disable:4786)
// "Microsoft has confirmed this to be a bug in the Microsoft
// products listed at the beginning of this article. We are
// researching this bug and will post new information here in
// the Microsoft Knowledge Base as it becomes available."

#include <map>
#include <string>
#include <iostream>

using namespace std;

typedef map<string, string, less<string> > STR2STR;
typedef pair<STR2STR::iterator,STR2STR::iterator> STR2STRPAIR;

void main( void )
{
  STR2STR phoneBook;
  STR2STR::iterator it, upperBound, lowerBound;
```

```
// Inserting five pairs
phoneBook.insert(STR2STR::value_type("111-111-1111",
                                     "Adam Smith"));
phoneBook.insert(STR2STR::value_type("555-555-5555",
                                     "Tina Smith"));
phoneBook.insert(STR2STR::value_type("222-222-2222",
                                     "Fred Smith"));
phoneBook.insert(STR2STR::value_type("444-444-4444",
                                     "John Smith"));
phoneBook.insert(STR2STR::value_type("333-333-3333",
                                     "Jane Smith"));

// Print phoneBook
cout << "phoneBook now contains:\n";
for(it = phoneBook.begin(); it != phoneBook.end(); it++)
  cout << it->first << " " << it->second << endl;

// Print phoneBook's size
cout << "\n\nphoneBook size = " << phoneBook.size();

// Print phoneBook in reverse
cout << "\n\nphoneBook in reverse order:\n";

STR2STR::reverse_iterator rit;
for(rit = phoneBook.rbegin(); rit != phoneBook.rend(); rit++)
  cout << rit->first << " " << rit->second << endl;

// Find key value "333-333-3333"
cout << "\n\nName for phone number 333-333-3333 = ";
it = phoneBook.find("333-333-3333");
cout << it->second << endl;

// Find subrange of key_values
cout << "\n\nPairs between 222-222-222 and 444-444-444:\n";
lowerBound = phoneBook.lower_bound("222-222-2222");
upperBound = phoneBook.upper_bound("444-444-4444");
for(it = lowerBound; it!= upperBound; it++)
  cout << it->first << it->second << endl;

// Declare iterator pair
STR2STRPAIR itPair;
itPair = phoneBook.equal_range("444-444-4444");

// Print one equal_range() value
cout << "\n\nequal_range() = ";
for(it = itPair.first; it != itPair.second; it++)
  cout << it->first << endl;
```

```
  // Find key value "333-333-3333" again
  it = phoneBook.find("333-333-3333");
  it->second = "New Name";
  cout << "\n\n333-333-3333 with new paired name: ";
  cout << it->second << endl;


  // Counting key values matching "555-555-5555"
  cout << "\n\nNumber of 555-555-5555s = "
       << phoneBook.count("555-555-5555");

  // Erasing key value pair "111-111-1111"
  cout << "\n\nphoneBook minus 111-111-1111:\n";
  phoneBook.erase("111-111-1111");
  for(it = phoneBook.begin(); it != phoneBook.end(); it++)
    cout << it->first << " " << it->second << endl;

  // Erasing entire phoneBook
  phoneBook.erase(phoneBook.begin(),phoneBook.end());
  if(phoneBook.empty())
    cout << "\n\nThe phoneBook is empty!";
}
```

Understanding the `map.cpp` application starts with knowing why the Microsoft-specific `#pragma` pre-processor directive is used to eliminate several screen's worth of warning messages.

Note: Microsoft is working on this "bug" and therefore the statement may not be needed in the Microsoft Visual C++ studio you are using:

```
#pragma warning(disable:4786)
```

The program code continues with an STL style of declaring appropriate types needed by `map.cpp`:

```
typedef map<string, string, less<string> > STR2STR;
typedef pair<STR2STR::iterator,STR2STR::iterator> STR2STRPAIR;
```

Remember that `<map>` by definition creates a container of paired elements. The identifier, `STR2STR`, represents a map container keyed on strings and containing string elements. This is ideal for our `phoneBook`, with the key being the phone number in string format, and the `value_type` being a string representing the name associated with the phone number.

Later on in the program a call is made to `equal_range()`. This method returns a pair of iterators and therefore explains the need for the `STR2STRPAIR` `typedef` which creates a pairing of two `STR2STR::iterators`.

These statements are logically followed by the instantiation of `phoneBook` and the creation of three iterators: `it`, `upperBound`, and `lowerBound`:

```
STR2STR phoneBook;
STR2STR::iterator it, upperBound, lowerBound;
```

The actual `phoneBook` entries are added using the `insert()` method:

```
// Inserting five pairs
  phoneBook.insert(STR2STR::value_type("111-111-1111",
                                       "Adam Smith"));
  phoneBook.insert(STR2STR::value_type("555-555-5555",
                                       "Tina Smith"));
  phoneBook.insert(STR2STR::value_type("222-222-2222",
                                       "Fred Smith"));
  phoneBook.insert(STR2STR::value_type("444-444-4444",
                                       "John Smith"));
  phoneBook.insert(STR2STR::value_type("333-333-3333",
                                       "Jane Smith"));
```

Using a now familiar iterator controlled `for` loop, `map.cpp` outputs the current container's contents:

```
// Print phoneBook
  cout << "phoneBook now contains:\n";
  for(it = phoneBook.begin(); it != phoneBook.end(); it++)
    cout << it->first << " " << it->second << endl;
```

The calls to `begin()` and `end()` are all old news. The question is why `it` is not tested with `<` and appropriately tested using `!=` (you do not know any relationship to container addresses so testing against a pointer <, >, <=, or >= makes no sense). Let's investigate the `cout` statement.

Since `map` elements are `pairs`, you can access their individual components using their respective data member names `first` and `second`. Most frequently, when accessing container elements with an iterator, *it* only requires the use of the dereference operator, as in:

```
*it
```

However, in this situtation, `it` points to more complex data type. You could actually write the syntax out in longhand, as in:

```
*it.first
*it.second
```

But this syntax presents an operator precedence-level nightmare since the period member-operator, `.`, binds or has a higher-precedence than the dereference operator, `*`. A knowledgeable and syntactically legal fix uses a set of parenthesis to raise the priority of the dereference operator, as in:

```
(*it).first
(*it).second
```

One way to eliminate this syntax nightmare is to use the arrow, or pointer-operator, `->`. This operator *requires* a pointer-type to its left, and `class` or `struct` member name to its right. The `for` loop's `cout` statement uses this syntactically cleaner style:

```
cout << it->first << "  " << it->second << endl;
```

The program then proceeds to demonstrate a method for determining the container's current number-of-entries with a call to the `size()` method:

```
// Print phoneBook's size
  cout << "\n\nphoneBook size = " << phoneBook.size();
```

Next, `map.cpp` demonstrates the necessary syntax and logic necessary to access a map container in reverse:

```
// Print phoneBook in reverse
  cout << "\n\nphoneBook in reverse order:\n";

  STR2STR::reverse_iterator rit;
  for(rit = phoneBook.rbegin(); rit != phoneBook.rend(); rit++)
    cout << rit->first << "  " << rit->second << endl;
```

First, a `reverse_iterator` is declared and immediately initialized to the address to the *last* container element with a call to `rbegin()`. Once again, the `for` loop test condition for continued iteration is not `it <`, but `it !=`. Contrary to what might be expected, the third statement in the `for` loop does not decrement `rit`, but instead increments the `reverse_iterator rit`! Just when you think you can outguess STL, it humbles you!

With `map.cpp` attempting to illustrate all of the common demands a program could put on a `map` container, the source code moves on to demonstrate how you would syntactically search a `map` container for a specific key using `find()`:

```
// Find key value "333-333-3333"
  cout << "\n\nName for phone number 333-333-3333 = ";
  it = phoneBook.find("333-333-3333");
  cout << it->second << endl;
```

The `cout` statement in this case does not print the key, but instead only the associated value.

Remembering that the map containers are sorted by the specified key makes it very easy to scan for subranges. This next code segment does exactly that by searching for all pairs with keys >= "222-222-2222" and <= "444-444-4444", using calls to `lower_bound()` and `upper_bound()`:

```
// Find subrange of key_values
  cout << "\n\nPairs between 222-222-222 and 444-444-444:\n";
  lowerBound = phoneBook.lower_bound("222-222-2222");
  upperBound = phoneBook.upper_bound("444-444-4444");
  for(it = lowerBound; it!= upperBound; it++)
    cout << it->first << it->second << endl;
```

While `map` containers by definition have unique `key` values, `multimap` containers may contain duplicate keys. The following code segment uses the `equal_range()` to locate, in the case of `map` containers, a single matching pair, but could be used by `multimap` containers to locate key subranges. Notice the use of the `typedef STR2STRPAIR` to declare the variable `itPair`, which is `equal_range()`'s return type for this application:

```
// Declare iterator pair
  STR2STRPAIR itPair;
  itPair = phoneBook.equal_range("444-444-4444");

  // Print one equal_range() value
  cout << "\n\nequal_range() = ";
  for(it = itPair.first; it != itPair.second; it++)
    cout << it->first << endl;
```

`itPair`'s two iterators are referenced using the data member names `first` and `second`, and proceeded by the variable's name, `itPair`, and the period member operator, (.).

An application using `map` containers may want to change a key's paired value, so this next code segment uses a call to the `find()` method to first locate the key and then uses the returned iterator's address to point to the value member, `second`, to update the name associated with the key phone number:

```
// Find key value "333-333-3333" again
  it = phoneBook.find("333-333-3333");
  it->second = "New Name";
  cout << "\n\n333-333-3333 with new paired name: ";
  cout << it->second << endl;
```

The `count()` method is used with both `map` and `multimap` containers and returns the number of container pairs that have a key (`map`) or keys (`multimap`) that match the search key:

```
// Counting key values matching "555-555-5555"
  cout << "\n\nNumber of 555-555-5555s = "
       << phoneBook.count("555-555-5555");
```

The `map.cpp` application next moves on to the syntax necessary to locate and then entirely delete an element pair with a call to `erase()` using only one actual argument, the key to delete:

```
// Erasing key value pair "111-111-1111"
  cout << "\n\nphoneBook minus 111-111-1111:\n";
  phoneBook.erase("111-111-1111");
  for(it = phoneBook.begin(); it != phoneBook.end(); it++)
    cout << it->first << " " << it->second << endl;
```

Finally, we achieve the professional and clean removal of the container from memory. Here again a call is made to `erase()`. This time the overloaded method is passed to two actual iterator arguments returned by `begin()` and `end()`:

```
// Erasing entire phoneBook
  phoneBook.erase(phoneBook.begin(),phoneBook.end());
  if(phoneBook.empty())
    cout << "\n\nThe phoneBook is empty!";
```

The output from the program looks like:

```
phoneBook now contains:
111-111-1111 Adam Smith
222-222-2222 Fred Smith
333-333-3333 Jane Smith
444-444-4444 John Smith
555-555-5555 Tina Smith


phoneBook size = 5

phoneBook in reverse order:
555-555-5555 Tina Smith
444-444-4444 John Smith
333-333-3333 Jane Smith
222-222-2222 Fred Smith
111-111-1111 Adam Smith


Name for phone number 333-333-3333 = Jane Smith


Pairs between 222-222-222 and 444-444-444:
222-222-2222Fred Smith
333-333-3333Jane Smith
444-444-4444John Smith
```

```
equal_range() = 444-444-4444


333-333-3333 with new paired name: New Name


Number of 555-555-5555s = 1

phoneBook minus 111-111-1111:
222-222-2222 Fred Smith
333-333-3333 New Name
444-444-4444 John Smith
555-555-5555 Tina Smith


The phoneBook is empty!
```

A <muitimap> Application

The following listing is a simple multimap application that inserts four names and phone numbers into a multimap using `insert()`. The application then determines how many elements are contained in the multiset using `size()` and locates the number of times a specific element occurs using `count()`.

```
// multimap.cpp
// Testing <multimap>
// insert(), count(), size(), value_type()
// Chris H. Pappas and William H. Murray, 2000

#pragma warning(disable:4786)
// "Microsoft has confirmed this to be a bug in the Microsoft
// products listed at the beginning of this article. We are
// researching this bug and will post new information here in
// the Microsoft Knowledge Base as it becomes available."

#include <map>
#include <string>
#include <iostream>

using namespace std;

typedef multimap<char*, char*> multimap_type;

void main( void )
{
    multimap_type item;
```

```
    item.insert(multimap_type::value_type("Adam Smith",
                                          "111-111-1111"));
    item.insert(multimap_type::value_type("Tina Smith",
                                          "222-222-2222"));
    item.insert(multimap_type::value_type("Fred Smith",
                                          "444-444-4444"));
    item.insert(multimap_type::value_type("Jane Smith",
                                          "333-333-3333"));

   cout << endl << "This multiset contains " << item.size()
      << " elements." << endl;

    cout << endl << "How many Adam Smith's in multiset: " <<
         item.count("Adam Smith") << endl << endl;
}
```

The output from this application is:

```
This multiset contains 4 elements.

How many Adam Smith's in multiset: 1
```

While this example is very similar to the `map.cpp` application in the previous section, you might have noticed a syntactical difference. The syntax for performing an insert is different for multimaps than for maps. This is because the `<multimap>` template does not provide a subscripting operator.

Summary

In this chapter you discovered that maps and multimaps are like a vector except that they have a user-defined key field and an associated data value(s), or pair. Unlike a vector, the index key can be any ordered type, and the paired data member can be *any* data type. You also learned that like vectors, methods such as `find()`, `begin()`, `end()`, and `size()` are used to give iterators legal starting, current, or ending pointer values to access container elements instead of the usual `array[subscript]` notation.

You are also aware that while `array[subscript]` notation is a legal syntax for `map` and `multimap` containers, there is a less error-prone syntax provided by STL.

CHAPTER 10

Hash Tables and the STL

In Chapter 6, we discussed the importance of the binary search tree for storing and retrieving information. You learned that the index into the tree was usually implemented as the index into a collection of elements. As fast as some of the techniques discussed then are, there are other ways to deal with collections of elements.

In this chapter we'll continue to examine storing and retrieving information, with the emphasis on cases where the key to the stored information is not a simple index value into a collection of elements.

For example, Table 10.1 shows a hypothetical key, array index, and elements for a simple collection of elements.

Table 10.1 Hash Table Key Values

Key	*Array Index*	*Element*
91	10	January
42	1	February
54	6	March
32	3	April
76	9	May
88	5	June
21	2	July
10	7	August
13	8	September
11	4	October
64	0	November
70	11	December

The point of using a hash table is that the key is tied directly to the element whereas the array index value is not. For example, the key value of 70 always means "December" in this example. However, if the above collection was sorted, the index values for the elements would change. To find "December" would require a search of the collection.

Finding an element in a collection with a key merely requires knowing the key, whereas finding an element in a collection with an array index requires a search.

How easily a hash implementation can be achieved forms the topic of this chapter.

The STL and Hashing

Unfortunately, at the time of this writing, the STL does not provide hash-based containers. In the future we might see associative containers, such as `hash_set<>` and `hash_map<>`, but until they are adopted, coding will have to progress along traditional C++ lines.

This does not mean that various STL techniques cannot be applied to hashing; it is just that at this point the specialized containers are not available.

Hashing Function

The success of hashing pivots upon the hashing function. The hashing function, in turn, must be easy to generate and should distribute the elements uniformly through the hash table. There should be a one-to-one mapping of a hash key value to a table element.

The question becomes, "How do we easily create unique hash key values that will be evenly distributed across the range of elements in a collection?" We'll examine several approaches in the following sections.

The Hash Key

Several techniques will be examined in this section for generating successful hash key values. Recall from the previous section that a hash key should be simple to generate, unique, and evenly distributed throughout the collection of elements.

Special Characters or Digits

Suppose that you are working with a rather small collection of elements, such as the names of several companies, and wish to generate key values that can be used to create a hash table.

We'll work with the first letter in each of the following names, as shown in Table 10.2, assigning a numeric value to them. We'll let a = 0, b = 1, and so on. This technique is also known as truncation because only part of the string or numeric digits are used to generate the key.

Table 10.2 Simple Key Values For a List of Companies

Company Name	*Value*
Camel Water Works	2
ABC Products	0
Electro-Electric Coop.	4
Barson Industries	1
Dawson Electric	3
Franklin Glasses	5

Well, initially, this seems to work. The key values are unique, easy to generate, and evenly distributed across the set. However, without much imagination, you can anticipate problems. What happens if the Alberta Boat Company and the Zimmer Dump Truck Company are added to the group? With the first entry, there will be a collision with ABC Products since both will generate a zero key. When Zimmer Dump Truck Company is added, the even distribution of key values will be gone.

Picking a special character or digit from the data often works for simple cases, but you'll see that a slight modification to the approach yields better results, as shown in the next section.

Folding

Imagine that your data consisted of a series of social security numbers, such as 123-45-6789. Using the folding method, the social security could be divided into groups of numeric digits, such as 123, 45, 6789. Then a sum could be formed by adding 123 + 45 + 6789 = 6957. The value 6957 could then be truncated, if necessary, to 957 to put it in the proper range of values, say 0 to 1000, if needed.

Unlike special characters or digits, the folding technique uses all of the information contained in the original data to form the keys.

Modulo Arithmetic

Another technique for forming key values is the use of modulo arithmetic. Let's use the last four digits of a person's social security number to illustrate this technique. So, instead of using 123-45-6789, we'll use 6789.

If we need three digit keys, or index values, we can perform modulo arithmetic on the original data to obtain the key.

The key can be generated by using this equation:

```
key value = original number mod (prime number)
```

Here, `mod` represents the modulo operation, which in C++ is achieved with `%`. A prime number should be selected close to but not greater than the maximum size for the three digit range. For example, if three digit keys are desired, then a number such as 911 might be used since 999 is the largest possible three digit number. First, the value would have to be tested as a prime. A true prime number is one that can only be divided evenly by one or itself. If 911 is a prime number, then the modulo operation on the original data would be:

```
key value = 6789 mod 911
```

This operation yields 412 for the key value. Table 10.3 shows a few numbers in the range of the sample number along with their three digit keys.

Table 10.3 Results of Modulo Arithmetic on Test Data

Original number	*Key value*
6780	403
6781	404
6782	405
6783	406
6784	407
6785	408
6786	409
6787	410
6788	411
6789	412
6790	413

While the operation appears to generate good key values, there is a problem. Initially, it appears as though the values are easy to calculate, evenly distributed, and unique (one-on-one mapping of data to the key). However, one-on-one mapping does not occur for all possible values. For values of 8611 and 9522, for example, the key returned will also be 412. This is the key value for 6789! When identical keys, or indices, are returned for different data, a collision is said to have occurred. There are techniques to handle collisions, as you will learn later in this chapter. Collisions can be eliminated entirely by using key values in the range of 0 to 999999 for this example, but that is considered inefficient when only a small number of elements are actually being considered in a set.

Generating Key Values—A Simple Hashing Function

Let's consider a simple hashing function and see what problems might arise in its implementation.

The hashing function we're about to create will require relatively small prime numbers. That means we need either a list of prime numbers or a small program that can test a prime number candidate. Prime numbers are numbers that can be divided evenly by one or themselves. Numbers such as 1, 2, 3, 5, and 7 are considered prime numbers. The number 2 is the only even number considered a prime. While the odd numbers 1, 3, 5, and 7 are primes, the number 15 is not because it is evenly divisible by both 3 and 5.

A simple prime number checker can be written that will simply divide the prime number candidate by all odd numbers from 3 up to the prime number candidate itself. This brute force attack can be shortened slightly by dividing the prime number candidate by all odd numbers from 3 to (prime number candidate / 2). This approach will work well with fast computers and with prime number candidates less than 10,000.

Here is a short C++ program that will test a prime number candidate to see if it is a prime. The number we're checking is 911.

```
// prime.cpp
// Simple tester for small prime numbers
// efficient in the range ( 3 <= range <= 10001 )
// Chris H. Pappas and William H. Murray, 2000

#include <iostream>

using namespace std;

void main( void )
{
    // prime = number to be tested
    int prime = 911;
    int flag = 0;

    for (int i = 3; i < prime / 2; i += 2) {
        if (prime % i == 0) {
            flag = 1;
        }
    }

    if (flag != 0) {
        cout << "Not a prime!" << endl  << endl;
    }
    else {
        cout << "Is a prime!" << endl << endl;
    }
}
```

The number proves to be a prime number and can be used in our hashing application that will be developed next.

The hashing function that will be developed will take advantage of modular arithmetic and use the prime number found in the previous example. The data to be hashed consists of the last four digits of a person's social security number and a unique integer value. Table 10.4 shows the original data for this example:

Table 10.4 Original Data For the Hashing Function

Social Security	*Data*
222-28-4567	14
232-15-5678	24
143-44-6789	34
111-33-7890	44
786-11-8901	54

The hashing application, `hashing.cpp`, will create a `vector<>` of `pairs<>`. The first element in the original pair will be an integer value created from the last four digits of the social security number, and the second element in the pair from the unique integer data value.

Examine the following STL implementation:

```
// hashing.cpp
// Simple hash table example
// Chris H. Pappas and William H. Murray, 2000

#include <iostream>
#include <vector>

using namespace std;

typedef struct pair<int,int> ic_PAIR;
typedef vector<ic_PAIR> pairVector;

unsigned int ssHash(int ss) {
    int temp = ss % 911;
    return temp;
}

void main( void )
{

    ic_PAIR pairofints;
    pairVector pv;
```

```
    pv.push_back(make_pair(ssHash(4567),14));
    pv.push_back(make_pair(ssHash(5678),24));
    pv.push_back(make_pair(ssHash(6789),34));
    pv.push_back(make_pair(ssHash(7890),44));
    pv.push_back(make_pair(ssHash(8901),54));

    vector<ic_PAIR>::iterator p = pv.begin();
    while(p != pv.end()) {
        cout << p->first << "\t" << p->second << endl;
        p++;
    }
    cout << endl;
}
```

When executed, this application returns:

```
12      14
212     24
412     34
602     44
702     54
```

The hashing key values are represented by the first column with the unique data value for each entry in the second column.

The key to this simple implementation is the hashing function itself.

```
unsigned int ssHash(int ss) {
    int temp = ss % 911;
    return temp;
}
```

The last four digits of the social security number are sent to the `ssHash()` function. There, a `modulo` operation is performed with the four digits of the social security number and a prime number. In this case, 911 has already been tested as a prime number. The resulting value replaces the first element in the `pair<int, int>` for each `vector< pair<int, int>>`.

The application works for the social security numbers supplied. However, if the last four digits of a social security number are 8611 and 9522, and the first two entries in the table are replaced, the following results are returned:

```
412     14
412     24
412     34
602     44
702     54
```

Since the `modulo` operation returns 412 for the social security numbers ending with 6789, 8611, and 9522, collisions have occurred. You will learn how collisions are handled in the next section.

Collision Resolution

As you have seen in the previous section, collisions between key values generated by hashing functions can occur for even small numbers of elements. One technique used to avoid collisions is to simply ensure that a unique key value exists for every element. If there is the possibility of 100 elements, then 100 key values are used. This approach is neither efficient or fast, especially when the number of actual elements is small.

This section will consider the problem of collisions and examine several techniques for handling them.

The Birthday Party

A catering firm caters birthday parties for various size companies. How many people would a company have to employ so that there is a good likelihood that two employees would have a birthday on the same day?

This probability problem actually demonstrates the likelihood of a collision for a relatively small sample of employees. When making an uninformed guess as to the answer, most people guess that the number is relatively high. Actually, the number is fairly low.

In a two-person company, the probability that person two has the same birthday as person one is:

```
1 - ((365 - 1) / 365) = 0.00273973
```

In a three-person company, the probability that at least two of the three employees have similar birthdays is:

```
1 - ((365 - 1) / 365 x (365 - 2) / 365) = 0.00820417
```

As the number of employees increases, the probability of similar birthdays increases. When the probability is 0.5 or greater, there is a very strong likelihood that at least two employees will have birthdays on the same day.

It is a simple process to write a C++ program to create a table showing employee numbers versus probability.

```
// birthday.cpp
// Testing for collisions
// Chris H. Pappas and William H. Murray, 2000

#include <iostream>

using namespace std;

void main( void )
{
    double probability = 1.0;

    cout << "Calculating probability of similar birthdays" << endl;

    cout << "# of employees" << "\t" << "probability" << endl;

    for (int i = 1; i<=25; i++) {
        probability *= (365.0 - i) / 365.0;
        cout << i << "\t" << 1.0 - probability << "\n";
    }
}
```

The tabular output from the `birthday.cpp` application is shown next. What can you discern from this information?

```
Calculating probability of similar birthdays
# of employees    probability
1                 0.00273973
2                 0.00820417
3                 0.0163559
4                 0.0271356
5                 0.0404625
6                 0.0562357
7                 0.0743353
8                 0.0946238
9                 0.116948
10                0.141141
11                0.167025
12                0.19441
13                0.223103
14                0.252901
15                0.283604
16                0.315008
17                0.346911
18                0.379119
19                0.411438
20                0.443688
```

```
21                    0.475695
22                    0.507297
23                    0.538344
24                    0.5687
25                    0.598241
```

Once the probability is greater than 0.5, there will be a greater than even chance that two employees will have the same birthday. You can see from the calculations that this value is achieved with as few as 22 employees.

The point? Collisions, or duplications, can occur for even a small number of elements under the right circumstances. The problems this presents for developing good hashing functions can be severe if not handled properly.

Open Addressing

This approach is used when an attempt is made by the hashing function to insert an element into an already occupied location. Open addressing usually employs some form of probing technique. The probing technique looks for another location to place the new data. The way in which the probing is done is called the probing sequence.

When probing techniques are used to insert elements in non-expected locations, because the calculated locations are full, it is critical that the probing sequence can be re-established in order to extract the data.

Linear Probing

Linear probing is perhaps the most straightforward of all of the probing techniques. Linear probing starts with the location where the collision occurs and starts searching for an empty location, in a linear fashion, that is not occupied.

In the example where the hashing function returned three identical key values, linear probing might yield the results as shown in Table 10.5.

Table 10.5 Collision Resolution with Linear Probing

Original	*Data*	*Linear Probing*	*Data*
412	14	412	14
412	24	413	24
412	34	414	34
602	44	602	44
702	54	702	54

If the linear probing reaches the end of the sequence, it should then go to the start of the sequence and continue probing. By doing this, any empty locations that existed before the collision occurred will also be considered.

The `hashing.cpp` application from an earlier section will be modified to include simple linear probing. Examine the following listing and note the code changes, shown in a bold font, from the earlier `hashing.cpp` application.

```
// linear.cpp
// Simple hash table example with linear probing
// Chris H. Pappas and William H. Murray, 2000

#include <iostream>
#include <vector>

using namespace std;

typedef struct pair<int,int> ic_PAIR;
typedef vector<ic_PAIR> pairVector;
typedef vector<int> usedKeys;

unsigned int ssHash(int ss) {

    static usedKeys uk;

    int temp = ss % 911;

    vector<int>::iterator p = uk.begin();
    while (p != uk.end()) {
        if (*p == temp) {
            temp++;
            p = uk.begin();
        }
        else {
            p++;
        }
    }
    uk.push_back(temp);

    return temp;
}

void main( void )
{
    pairVector pv;
```

```
    pv.push_back(make_pair(ssHash(8611),14));
    pv.push_back(make_pair(ssHash(9522),24));
    pv.push_back(make_pair(ssHash(6789),34));
    pv.push_back(make_pair(ssHash(7890),44));
    pv.push_back(make_pair(ssHash(8901),54));

    vector<ic_PAIR>::iterator p = pv.begin();
    while(p != pv.end()) {
        cout << p->first << "\t" << p->second << endl;
        p++;
    }
    cout << endl;
}
```

In order to succeed with linear probing, it will be necessary to keep track of which keys have already been used. The technique used in this application will be to generate a key using the following equation:

```
int temp = ss % 911;
```

The key that is generated and saved in the `temp` variable is then checked against all other generated keys to see if it is a duplicate. Previously generated keys are saved in the `static` vector named `uk`. Note that since the `static` qualifier is used, each vector element is preserved between calls to the function.

```
vector<int>::iterator p = uk.begin();
while (p != uk.end()) {
    if (*p == temp) {
        temp++;
        p = uk.begin();
    }
    else {
        p++;
    }
}
uk.push_back(temp);
```

The plan is to traverse the vector from the start until the end. During this traversal, each previously generated key is compared with the new key in the variable `temp`. If the new value in the variable `temp` is not in the vector, the iterator will be incremented. Finally, the value in the variable `temp` will be saved to the vector. This will extend the vector by one key value by using `uk.push_back()`.

If the new value in the variable `temp` is in the vector, the value in `temp` will be incremented by one. The value in the iterator will be set back to the start of the vector so that the whole vector will be traversed again. If the new value in the variable `temp` (that is, the original `temp` value + `1`) is not found in the vector, then the iterator is incremented and the new value is saved at the end of the vector using `uk.push_back()`. If the new value in the variable `temp` is found in the vector also, then the whole process of incrementing the variable is repeated until a value is found that is not currently in the vector.

The output for the `linear.cpp` application is shown next.

```
412     14
413     24
414     34
602     44
702     54
```

If you examine Table 10.5 again, or the output from this application, you might be able to discern the downside to linear probing. The downside is the problem of clustering. Notice that 412, 413, and 414 are values that are packed close together, whereas 602 and 702 are well distributed across the range of key values. With linear probing, the more frequently collisions occur, the greater the likelihood of clustering problems.

Just as a matter of interest, if you had wished to code the previous algorithm using traditional arrays, the coding would have taken on the following form:

```
int i = 0;
while (usedKeys[i] != 0)
    if (usedKeys[i] == temp) {
        temp++;
        i = 0;
    }
    else {
        i++;
}
usedKeys[i] = temp;
```

The `usedKeys[]` array would be initialized to a certain size and would use the `static` qualifier. Structurally, this code is very similar in appearance to the code developed using a vector.

Quadratic Probing

In the previous section you learned the downside to using a linear probe is the problem of clustering. Since duplicate values are eliminated by incrementing each repeating value by one, there is a tendency for these new values to group around the originating key.

Quadratic probing can eliminate this primary problem of clustering by forcing the duplicate key values farther apart by applying the following algorithm for each repeating key value:

$$\text{new key} = \text{original key} + n^2$$

In this equation, the variable n represents the number of replications for the original key. In our example where the hashing function returned three identical key values, quadratic probing might yield the results shown in Table 10.6 for our modified algorithm.

Table 10.6 Cluster Elimination with Quadratic Probing

Original	*Data*	*Quadratic Probing*	*Data*
412	14	412	14
412	24	413	24
412	34	416	34
602	44	602	44
702	54	702	54

In the previous example, if there were five original key values of 412, quadratic probing would have calculated the new values to be:

```
412, (412 + 1²), (412 + 2²), (412 + 3²), (412 + 4²)
412, 413, 416, 421, 428
```

The quadratic probing algorithm can be implemented easily in the linear probing example of the previous section. The changes made to the previous example are shown in a bold font in the following listing:

```
// quadratic.cpp
// Simple hash table example with quadratic probing
// Chris H. Pappas and William H. Murray, 2000

#include <iostream>
#include <vector>

using namespace std;

typedef struct pair<int,int> ic_PAIR;
typedef vector<ic_PAIR> pairVector;
typedef vector<int> usedKeys;

unsigned int ssHash(int ss) {

    static usedKeys uk;
    static int n;

    int temp = ss % 911;
```

```
    vector<int>::iterator p = uk.begin();
    while (p != uk.end()) {
        if (*p == temp) {
            temp += n * n;
            n++;
            p = uk.begin();
        }
        else {
            p++;
        }
    }
    uk.push_back(temp);

    return temp;
}


void main( void )
{
    pairVector pv;

    pv.push_back(make_pair(ssHash(8611),14));
    pv.push_back(make_pair(ssHash(9522),24));
    pv.push_back(make_pair(ssHash(6789),34));
    pv.push_back(make_pair(ssHash(7890),44));
    pv.push_back(make_pair(ssHash(8901),54));

    vector<ic_PAIR>::iterator p = pv.begin();
    while(p != pv.end()) {
        cout << p->first << "\t" << p->second << endl;
        p++;
    }
    cout << endl;
}
```

The output from the quadratic probing application shows the anticipated results.

```
412     14
413     24
416     34
602     44
702     54
```

One of the problems often encountered with quadratic probing is a phenomenon called secondary clustering. Secondary clustering can result in quadratic probing because when two hash locations are identical, the same probing sequence can be employed for both.

Double Hashing

Another variation used to eliminate clustering is double hashing. For both linear and quadratic probing, the probing sequence is independent of the original key value. With double hashing, the probe sequence is dependent upon the original key value. In other words, once a duplicate key is found, the probing sequence is derived from some variation of that key.

For example, if:

```
original key = data % (primary prime number)
```

then,

```
new key = secondary prime number - ((last duplicate key replacement) *
                                      mod (secondary prime number))
```

For our example where the hashing function returned three identical key values using the primary prime number of 911, double hashing might yield the following results, shown in Table 10.7, for a secondary prime of 257.

Table 10.7 A Double Hash Probing Sequence

Original	*Data*	*Double Hash Probing*	*Data*
412	14	412	14
412	24	102	24
412	34	155	34
602	44	602	44
702	54	702	54

The double hash algorithm just described is implemented in the following application. Again, only slight modifications to the original `linear.cpp` application are necessary.

```
// doublehash.cpp
// Simple hash table example with double-hash probing
// Chris H. Pappas and William H. Murray, 2000

#include <iostream>
#include <vector>

using namespace std;

typedef struct pair<int,int> ic_PAIR;
typedef vector<ic_PAIR> pairVector;
typedef vector<int> usedKeys;

unsigned int ssHash(int ss) {
```

```
    static usedKeys uk;

    int temp = ss % 911;

     vector<int>::iterator p = uk.begin();
    while (p != uk.end()) {
        if (*p == temp) {
            // for double-hashing
            // chose a prime (257) smaller
            // than original prime (911)
            temp = 257 - (temp % 257);
            p = uk.begin();
        }
        else {
            p++;
        }
    }
    uk.push_back(temp);

    return temp;
}


void main( void )
{
    pairVector pv;

    pv.push_back(make_pair(ssHash(8611),14));
    pv.push_back(make_pair(ssHash(9522),24));
    pv.push_back(make_pair(ssHash(6789),34));
    pv.push_back(make_pair(ssHash(7890),44));
    pv.push_back(make_pair(ssHash(8901),54));

    vector<ic_PAIR>::iterator p = pv.begin();
    while(p != pv.end()) {
        cout << p->first << "\t" << p->second << endl;
        p++;
    }
    cout << endl;
}
```

The results of this double hash match the predicted results.

```
412    14
102    24
155    34
602    44
702    54
```

Double hashing is also known as rehashing. Implementing successful rehashing algorithms can sometimes be difficult if every key location is to be accessed. The careful choice of both primary and secondary prime numbers plays a key role in the successful implementation of double hashing functions.

Buckets and Chains

A different approach (from those described in the open addressing section) for collision resolution is to change the form of the hash table itself. When a hash table's form is changed, it can accommodate more than one element at a given location.

Two techniques are popular: buckets and separate chaining. Both concepts will be described in the following sections.

Buckets

The principle underlying the use of buckets is to divide the elements in a collection and place them in different locations, or buckets. Buckets are designed to hold multiple elements and so, by their nature, tend to eliminate collisions. Traditionally, buckets resolve collision problems by using separate and unique arrays. With STL, the data structure is typically a `<multiset>`, `<list>`, or `<vector>`.

Let's develop a simple application that will make use of ten buckets. The last four digits of a social security number will be divided among the buckets, as shown in Table 10.8.

Table 10.8 Bucket IDs and Integer Ranges

Bucket ID	*Integer Range*
a	0 to 999
b	1000 to 1999
c	2000 to 2999
d	3000 to 3999
e	4000 to 4999
f	5000 to 5999
g	6000 to 6999
h	7000 to 7999
i	8000 to 8999
j	9000 to 9999

The application must calculate the hashing key and place it in the proper bucket. The path to the bucket must be traceable for retrieving elements, so another `<pair>` is created keeping track of the bucket ID and the hashing key.

```
typedef struct pair<char,int> id_PAIR;
```

The following listing shows the code for this simple bucket application.

```
// bucket.cpp
// Simple hash table example with 10 buckets
// Chris H. Pappas and William H. Murray, 2000

#include <iostream>
#include <vector>

using namespace std;

typedef struct pair<int,int> ic_PAIR;
typedef struct pair<char,int> id_PAIR;
typedef vector<ic_PAIR> pairVector;
typedef vector<id_PAIR> bucketVector;

unsigned int ssHash(int ss) {

    int temp = ss % 911;

    bucketVector bv;

    if ((ss >= 0) & (ss < 1000))
        bv.push_back(make_pair('a', temp));
    else if (ss < 2000)
        bv.push_back(make_pair('b', temp));
    else if (ss < 3000)
        bv.push_back(make_pair('c', temp));
    else if (ss < 4000)
        bv.push_back(make_pair('d', temp));
    else if (ss < 5000)
        bv.push_back(make_pair('e', temp));
    else if (ss < 6000)
        bv.push_back(make_pair('f', temp));
    else if (ss < 7000)
        bv.push_back(make_pair('g', temp));
    else if (ss < 8000)
        bv.push_back(make_pair('h', temp));
    else if (ss < 9000)
        bv.push_back(make_pair('i', temp));
    else bv.push_back(make_pair('j', temp));

    return temp;
}
```

```
void main( void )
{
    pairVector pv;

    pv.push_back(make_pair(ssHash(8611),14));
    pv.push_back(make_pair(ssHash(9522),24));
    pv.push_back(make_pair(ssHash(6789),34));
    pv.push_back(make_pair(ssHash(7890),44));
    pv.push_back(make_pair(ssHash(8901),54));

    vector<ic_PAIR>::iterator p = pv.begin();
    while(p != pv.end()) {
        cout << p->first << "\t" << p->second << endl;
        p++;
    }
    cout << endl;
}
```

Upon execution, this application yields the following results:

```
412    14
412    24
412    34
602    44
702    54
```

Initially, it appears that using buckets has been a failure. However, what is not shown in this output is the actual division of data among the buckets. Table 10.9 shows the internal division of elements and keys.

Table 10.9 Bucket IDs and Generated Hash Keys

Bucket ID	*Generated Key*
a	
b	
c	
d	
e	
f	
g	412
h	602
I	412, 702
j	412

You can see from Table 10.9 that even though our hashing function generated three keys with a value of 412, a collision did not occur because each was placed in a separate bucket. The same algorithm can be used for data retrieval.

Because of the simplicity of this example, the use of a data structure to hold each bucket's contents was not necessary. As an exercise, you may want to create an array for each bucket's key and element or build upon the code shown first in the linear probing example earlier in this chapter.

As the number of buckets increases, the likelihood of a collision decreases. However, as the number of buckets increases, so does the likelihood of using more and more of the computer's memory resources. In order to reduce the amount of system resources frequently allocated with the use of buckets, another approach is often used—the linked list. This approach will be discussed in the next section.

Separate Chaining

The use of linked lists, for collision prevention during hashing, is often referred to as separate chaining. With separate chaining, each entry in a hash table points to a separate and unique linked list. This is a modification to the bucket approach and eliminates the problem of preallocated system resources since linked lists grow dynamically. Separate chaining can be achieved in several ways. Traditionally, an array of linked lists or a doubly linked list is used. The advantage of linked lists over buckets is that the individual linked lists can be as long as necessary in order to resolve collision problems. The disadvantage to this approach is that retrieving or deleting information increases in proportion to the size of the linked lists.

The following listing shows how chaining can be implemented in traditional C++ code:

```
// chain.cpp
// C++ implementation of chaining algorithm
// using linked lists
// Chris H. Pappas and William H. Murray, 2000

#include <iostream>

using namespace std;

// node to hold matching hash key value
typedef struct matchingKeyNode {
    int DataValue;
    matchingKeyNode *NextMatchingKey;
} MATCHINGKEYNODE;
```

```
// node to hold unique hash key and associated value
typedef struct chainNode {
    int KeyValue;
    int DataValue;
    chainNode *NextChainNode;
    MATCHINGKEYNODE *MatchingKeyList;
} CHAINNODE;

class CHAIN {
private:
    // pointer to first CHAINNODE
    CHAINNODE *Chain;
public:
    // constructor initializes list to empty
    CHAIN() { Chain = NULL; };
    void InsertNewKey(int NewKey,int NewValue);
    void InsertMatchingKeyValue(chainNode *HeadNode,
                                int NewValue);
    void PrintChainKeys(void);
};

void CHAIN::InsertNewKey(int NewKey, int NewValue)
{
    bool NoMatchingKey = true;
    CHAINNODE *NodeBehind, *CurrentNode;

    // initialize pointers to first CHAINNODE
    NodeBehind = CurrentNode = Chain;

    // while there are nodes and no matching key
    while( CurrentNode && NoMatchingKey )
        if( CurrentNode->KeyValue == NewKey )
            // found a matching KeyValue
            NoMatchingKey = false;
        else {
            // move pointers to examine next CHAINNODE
            NodeBehind = CurrentNode;
            CurrentNode = CurrentNode->NextChainNode;
        }
    if( NoMatchingKey ) {
        // create new CHAINNODE, fill with data
        CurrentNode = new CHAINNODE;
        CurrentNode->KeyValue = NewKey;
        CurrentNode->DataValue = NewValue;
        CurrentNode->NextChainNode = NULL;
        CurrentNode->MatchingKeyList= NULL;
        if( !Chain )
```

```
            // make new CHAINNODE front of list
            Chain = CurrentNode;
        else
            // link new CHAINNODE to end of existing list
            NodeBehind->NextChainNode = CurrentNode;
    }
    // KeyValue not unique, create/add MATCHINGKEYNODE
    else InsertMatchingKeyValue(CurrentNode,NewValue);
};

void CHAIN::InsertMatchingKeyValue(chainNode *HeadNode,
                                   int NewValue)
{
    MATCHINGKEYNODE *DuplicateKeyNode, *NewDuplicateKeyNode;

    // DuplicateKeyNode set to addr of first MATCHINGKEYNODE
    DuplicateKeyNode = HeadNode->MatchingKeyList;

    // create new MATCHINGKEYNODE fill with data
    NewDuplicateKeyNode = new MATCHINGKEYNODE;
    NewDuplicateKeyNode->DataValue = NewValue;
    NewDuplicateKeyNode->NextMatchingKey = NULL;

    if( !DuplicateKeyNode )
        // if no MATCHINGKEYNODEs make this one front of list
        HeadNode->MatchingKeyList = NewDuplicateKeyNode;
    else {
        // dup key nodes exist, get end of MATCHINGKEYNODEs
        while( DuplicateKeyNode->NextMatchingKey != NULL )
            DuplicateKeyNode = DuplicateKeyNode->NextMatchingKey;
        DuplicateKeyNode->NextMatchingKey = NewDuplicateKeyNode;
    }
};

void CHAIN::PrintChainKeys(void)
{
    CHAINNODE *CurrentNode = Chain;
    MATCHINGKEYNODE *CurrentMatchingKeyNode;

    // while there are nodes
    while( CurrentNode ) {
        // print CHAINNODE KeyValue and DataValue
        cout << CurrentNode->KeyValue  << '\t'
             << CurrentNode->DataValue << endl;
        CurrentMatchingKeyNode = CurrentNode->MatchingKeyList;
```

```
        // if CHAINNODE has MATCHINGKEYNODEs print DataValues
        if( CurrentMatchingKeyNode ) {
            cout << '\t' << CurrentMatchingKeyNode->DataValue
                 << endl;
            CurrentMatchingKeyNode = CurrentMatchingKeyNode \
                                       ->NextMatchingKey;
        }
        // move to next CHAINNODE
        CurrentNode = CurrentNode->NextChainNode;
    }
}


void main(void)
{
  CHAIN chain;

  // attempt to insert unique keys
  chain.InsertNewKey(412,10);
  chain.InsertNewKey(413,20);
  chain.InsertNewKey(602,30);

  // attemp to insert duplicate keys
  chain.InsertNewKey(602,40);
  chain.InsertNewKey(412,50);
  chain.InsertNewKey(413,60);
  chain.PrintChainKeys();
}
```

This application, `chain.cpp`, begins with two typedefs, `matchingKeyNode` and `chainNode`:

```
// node to hold matching hash key value
typedef struct matchingKeyNode {
    int DataValue;
    matchingKeyNode *NextMatchingKey;
} MATCHINGKEYNODE;

// node to hold unique hash key and associated value
typedef struct chainNode {
    int KeyValue;
    int DataValue;
    chainNode *NextChainNode;
    MATCHINGKEYNODE *MatchingKeyList;
} CHAINNODE;
```

Since MatchingKeyNode is used to hold those DataValues that hash to the same KeyValue, the node doesn't need to store a KeyValue as does ChainNode. Also, since matchingKeyNodes are a different type than ChainNodes, the NextMatchingKey pointer is a different pointer type (matchingKeyNode *) than chainnode's NextChainNode (chainNode *). Finally, ChainNode has two pointers, one to the NextChainNode, and the second, MatchingKeyList, which points to any unique DataValues hashing to the same KeyValue.

Note: In the previous paragraph, did you notice that both pointer types, NextMatchingKey and NextChainNode, were defined with the mixed case tag field names matchingKeyNode and chainNode instead of matchingkeynode and chainnode. Do you know why? Remember, the C/C++ compilers cannot use an identifier until the compilers have seen their formal definition. The typedef names, matchingkeynode and chainnode, come after the definitions for the members, NextMatchingKey and NextChainNode. Programmers are often confused why typedefs for structures sometimes need the optional tag field name when the typedef syntax demands a name for the type. Initially, this duplicate identifier naming convention seems redundant. These two typedefed structures prove why you must at times include the optional tag field name. Finally, MatchingKeyList did use the identifier matchingkeynode because at this point the compiler has seen its definition.

The chain.cpp chain class does all the linked list manipulation for the chaining algorithm.

```
class CHAIN {
private:
    // pointer to first CHAINNODE
    CHAINNODE *Chain;
public:
    // constructor initializes list to empty
    CHAIN() { Chain = NULL; };
    void InsertNewKey(int NewKey,int NewValue);
    void InsertMatchingKeyValue(chainNode *HeadNode,
                                int NewValue);
    void PrintChainKeys(void);
};
```

The private pointer, Chain, is responsible for tracking the entire list of unique key values and their associated values. The Chain() constructor initializes this pointer to null. Remember from previous chapters that a linked list program *cannot* ask if a pointer address is valid. However, the program can ask the logical question: Is the pointer initialized and telling me that it officially points nowhere? That is the purpose of the ANSI C/C++ agreed upon symbolic constant null.

Note: NULL is an architecture-specific value. Do *not* use any numeric representation for NULL; always use the portable ANSI C/C++ symbolic constant NULL.

The Chain method, InsertNewKey(), is responsible for starting the insertion of a key and data value, both of which are passed in the method's call statements. The method also recognizes a non-unique key and appropriately calls the Chain method, InsertMatchingKeyValue(), which only needs the address of the matching key's CHAINNODE called HeadNode and the unique NewValue. The Chain method, PrintChainKeys(), displays the list of unique KeyValues and associated DataValues.

The main() program begins by first instantiating the CHAIN class:

```
CHAIN chain;
```

In previous chapters you learned how the proper use of upper and lower case identifiers helps to minimize the identifier burden placed on C/C++ programmers. Here, because the class name CHAIN is all upper case, the instance identifier chain can use the same letters and yet keep the compiler happy since it actually sees two totally different identifiers. Also remember that header files are the proper location for application-specific definitions and, in the C++ programming community, are always declared in all caps. Mixed case identifiers are reserved for actual variables or object instances.

The main program then moves on to three calls to the method, InsertNewKey(), using uniquely hashed key data:

```
// insert unique keys
chain.InsertNewKey(412,10);
chain.InsertNewKey(413,20);
chain.InsertNewKey(602,30);
```

The main program terminates by indirectly testing the InsertMatchingKeyValue() method with the non-unique key data seen below:

```
// insert duplicate keys
chain.InsertNewKey(602,40);
chain.InsertNewKey(412,50);
chain.InsertNewKey(413,60);
chain.PrintChainKeys();
```

The main program either passes a unique or duplicate key value, called NewKey, and a unique data value for storage, called NewValue:

```
void CHAIN::InsertNewKey(int NewKey, int NewValue)
```

The declaration for the Boolean variable NoMatchingKey sets an initial value of true, and is used to traverse the list of KeyValues until the list is either exhausted or a matching KeyValue is found.

The pointer variable, CurrentNode, is used to point to the CHAINNODE being examined for NewKey equal to KeyValue. The pointer, NodeBehind, trails behind the pointer,

CurrentNode, and is used to remember the last valid CHAINNODE address whenever CurrentNode goes to NULL (end-of-list).

```
{
    bool NoMatchingKey = true;
    CHAINNODE *NodeBehind, *CurrentNode;
```

Both pointers are initially set to the address of the front of the Chain, which could either be null if the list is empty or a valid front CHAINNODE address:

```
    // initialize pointers to first CHAINNODE
    NodeBehind = CurrentNode = Chain;
```

Notice how the following while loop uses the contents of the pointer variable CurrentNode as a Boolean value. Remember, in C++, any non-zero value is interpreted as true and any zero value as false. When the list is empty, CurrentNode is null or false and immediately stops the list traversal loop:

```
    // while there are nodes and no matching key
    while( CurrentNode && NoMatchingKey )
```

The nested if statement either detects a matching KeyValue setting NoMatchingKey to true, thereby terminating the loop, or updates the pointers NodeBehind and CurrentNode:

```
        if( CurrentNode->KeyValue == NewKey )
            // found a matching KeyValue
            NoMatchingKey = false;
        else {
            // move pointers to examine next CHAINNODE
            NodeBehind = CurrentNode;
            CurrentNode = CurrentNode->NextChainNode;
        }
```

The previous while loop terminates for either one of two reasons: either there was no matching KeyValue in the Chain or there was a matching value. This situation is detected by the next if..else statement. If there is NoMatchingKey, the true-part of the if statement dynamically allocates the storage for a new CHAINNODE, storing the address in CurrentNode. The new KeyValue and NewValue are stored in the new node, along with the two pointers being initialized to NULL, indicating that the new node is at the end of the Chain list with no MatchingKeyList:

```
    if( NoMatchingKey ) {
        // create new CHAINNODE, fill with data
        CurrentNode = new CHAINNODE;
        CurrentNode->KeyValue = NewKey;
        CurrentNode->DataValue = NewValue;
        CurrentNode->NextChainNode = NULL;
        CurrentNode->MatchingKeyList= NULL;
```

With the new node built and initialized, the algorithm goes on to decipher if the new node is the only, and first, node in the Chain—if so, assigning the address of the new node to the pointer, Chain. Otherwise, the new node is going to be inserted at the end of an existing list. Remember, NodeBehind holds on to the address of the previous node examined for a KeyValue match. In the case of the else, NodeBehind is holding on to the address of the last node in the Chain since CurrentNode's address now holds the address of the new node.

The algorithm could have declared an additional local pointer called NewChainNode to hold the address of the newly created CHAINNODE; however, this would have added an additional variable declaration. Instead, the algorithm recognizes at this point that CurrentNode is no longer needed to traverse the Chain and is reused to hold the address of the new node.

```
        if( !Chain )
            // make new CHAINNODE front of list
            Chain = CurrentNode;
        else
            // link new CHAINNODE to end of existing list
            NodeBehind->NextChainNode = CurrentNode;
    }
```

When a matching KeyValue is detected, the algorithm calls the method, InsertMatchingKeyValue(), and sends over the address of the Chain node containing the matching KeyValue, and the NewValue to be stored:

```
    // KeyValue not unique, create/add MATCHINGKEYNODE
    else InsertMatchingKeyValue(CurrentNode,NewValue);
};
```

Next, the method, InsertMatchingKeyValue(), receives CurrentNode as HeadNode—logically representing the position of this node's address. HeadNode is the CHAINNODE containing the matching KeyValue and owns the pointer to the MatchingKeyList which InsertMatchingKeyValue() is about to update:

```
void CHAIN::InsertMatchingKeyValue(chainNode *HeadNode,
                                   int NewValue)
{
```

The method declares two local pointers used to traverse any existing MATCHINGKEYNODES and inserts the new MATCHINGKEYNODE:

```
    MATCHINGKEYNODE *DuplicateKeyNode, *NewDuplicateKeyNode;
```

Next, DuplicateKeyNode is set equal to the address of the first MATCHINGKEYNODE. This could be null if this is the first MATCHINGKEYNODE to be added, otherwise it is pointing to a previously inserted MATCHINGKEYNODE:

```
    // DuplicateKeyNode set to address of first MATCHINGKEYNODE
    DuplicateKeyNode = HeadNode->MatchingKeyList;
```

Whether or not there is an exisiting `MatchingKeyList`, a new `MATCHINGKEYNODE` needs to be built and initialized with just the `NewValue`:

```
    // create new MATCHINGKEYNODE fill with data
    NewDuplicateKeyNode = new MATCHINGKEYNODE;
    NewDuplicateKeyNode->DataValue = NewValue;
    NewDuplicateKeyNode->NextMatchingKey = NULL;
```

At this point, the algorithm needs to determine if the `NewDuplicateKeyNode` is the first and only node in the `MatchingKeyList` or not. This is accomplished with a test of `DuplicateKeyNode`'s contents. Remember, `NULL` is viewed as a logical `false`; any valid address is viewed as a logical `true`.

If there is no `MatchingKeyList`, the `if` part of the `if..else` kicks in, assigning the `HeadNode`'s `MatchingKeyList` equal to the address of the `NewDuplicateKeyNode`. Otherwise, the `else` statement kicks in the `while` loop:

```
    if( !DuplicateKeyNode )
        // there are no MATCHINGKEYNODEs make this one front
        HeadNode->MatchingKeyList = NewDuplicateKeyNode;
    else {
        // dup key nodes exist - find end of MATCHINGKEYNODEs
        while( DuplicateKeyNode->NextMatchingKey != NULL )
            DuplicateKeyNode = DuplicateKeyNode->NextMatchingKey;
        DuplicateKeyNode->NextMatchingKey = NewDuplicateKeyNode;
    }
};
```

The `while` loop traverses an existing `MatchingKeyList` until `DuplicateKeyNode`'s `NextMatchingKey` is equal to `NULL`, indicating that `DuplicateKeyNode` is pointing to the last `MATCHINGKEYNODE` in the list. For review purposes, the `while` loop test condition uses the look ahead, or look through, logic and syntax:

```
DuplicateKeyNode->NextMatchingKey != NULL
```

With this syntax, when `DuplicateKeyNode` is holding the address to the last `MATCHINGKEYNODE`, the `while` loop recognizes this and terminates, leaving the pointer, `DuplicateKeyNode`, holding the necessary address to connect the `NewDuplicateKeyNode` to the end of the `MatchingKeyList`!

The `PrintChainKeys()` method contains two list traversal loops. The first, or outer loop, traverses the `Chain` list:

```
void CHAIN::PrintChainKeys(void)
{
    CHAINNODE *CurrentNode = Chain;
    MATCHINGKEYNODE *CurrentMatchingKeyNode;

    // while there are nodes
    while( CurrentNode ) {
        // print CHAINNODE KeyValue and DataValue
        cout << CurrentNode->KeyValue  << '\t'
             << CurrentNode->DataValue << endl;
        CurrentMatchingKeyNode = CurrentNode->MatchingKeyList;
         .
         .
         .
        // move to next CHAINNODE
        CurrentNode = CurrentNode->NextChainNode;
    }
```

Notice that the inner loop traverses any `CHAINNODEs` with a `MatchingKeyList`:

```
    // if CHAINNODE has MATCHINGKEYNODEs print DataValues only
        if( CurrentMatchingKeyNode ) {
            cout << '\t' << CurrentMatchingKeyNode->DataValue << endl;
            CurrentMatchingKeyNode = CurrentMatchingKeyNode-
>NextMatchingKey;
        }
```

At this point, all that remains is to update the `CHAIN` class incorporating the previously discussed hashing algorithm.

The output from this application shows the action of chaining.

```
412     10
        50
413     20
        60
602     30
        40
```

The fact that the same key value has multiple entries indicates that the chaining application is working as expected.

Summary

In this chapter you have learned various techniques for developing robust hashing applications. As you worked through multiple applications, you have learned the advantages and disadvantages of these techniques.

CHAPTER 11

Matrices and the STL

As a college student you have probably taken several calculus courses followed by a course in discrete mathematics and one in linear algebra. It was probably in your linear algebra course that you first appreciated the powerful mathematics that could be used with matrices. However, linear algebra was not your first intro duction to matrices—it was most likely your first programming course! The most frequently encountered matrix, in programming, is a two-dimensional data array. These two-dimensional data arrays are used to hold integers, floats, characters, and strings.

The power of matrix manipulations forms the backbone of computer gaming and other areas of computer science where two-dimensional information is stored and retrieved. It is rightly considered essential in any study of data structures.

A matrix is not a data abstraction in C++ or one provided by the STL. However, the STL can provide powerful programming abilities as it did for hash tables in the previous chapter. In this chapter, we'll consider many aspects of the matrix, as it applies to programming, and provide programming implementations in both traditional C++ and with the STL.

If you find some of the examples in this chapter simple or redundant, be patient. This chapter gradually builds in complexity and those simple and redundant examples make sure you understand all aspects of matrix manipulations using STL vectors.

One-Dimensional Arrays and Vectors

By this point you are very familiar with the relationship that exists between traditional C++ one-dimensional arrays and STL vectors. In order to prepare for a unique look at two-dimensional arrays and the STL equivalent, this section will review the basic fundamentals of both arrays and vectors.

Using Traditional C++ Implementation: Arrays

In C++ we treat `arrays`, in general, as variables containing several homogeneous data types. Each data item or element in an array can be accessed by using a subscript, or index, into the variable. In C++, an array is not a standard data type; instead, it is an aggregate type made up of any other type of data. For example, it is possible to have an array of characters, integers, floats, doubles, arrays, pointers, structures, and so on.

Let's review the four basic properties of an array:

- The individual data items in the array are called *elements*.
- All elements must be of the same data type.
- All elements are stored contiguously in the computer's memory, and the subscript (or index) of the first element is zero.
- The name of the array is a constant value that represents the address of the first element in the array.

Since all elements of an array are assumed to be the same size, arrays cannot be defined by using mixed data types. Without this assumption, it would be very difficult to determine where any given element was stored. Since the elements are all the same size and since that fact is used to help determine how to locate a given element, it follows that the elements are stored contiguously in the computer's memory (with the lowest address corresponding to the first element; the highest address to the last element). This means that there is no filler space between elements and that they are physically adjacent in the computer.

It is possible to have arrays within arrays, that is, multidimensional arrays.

Note: If an array element is a structure, then mixed data types can exist in the array by existing inside the structure member.

The name of an array represents a constant value that cannot change during the execution of the program. For this reason, arrays can never be used as `lvalues`. `lvalues` represent storage locations that can have their contents altered by the program; they frequently appear to the left of assignment statements. If array names were legal `lvalues`, your program could change their contents. The effect would be to change the starting address of the array itself. This may seem like a small thing, but some forms of expressions that might appear valid on the surface are not allowed. All programmers eventually learn these subtleties, but it helps if you understand why these differences exist.

The following are examples of array declarations:

```
int  intarray[12];  // an array of twelve integers
char charray[20];   // an array of twenty characters
```

As is true with all data declarations, an array's declaration begins with its data type, followed by a valid array name and a pair of matching square brackets enclosing a constant expression. The constant expression defines the size of the array. It is illegal to use a variable name inside the square brackets. For this reason it is not possible to avoid specifying the array size until the program executes. The expression must reduce to a constant value so that the compiler knows exactly how much storage space to reserve for the array.

It is best to use defined constants to specify the size of the array:

```
#define intARRAY_MAX 20
#define fltARRAY_MAX 15

int intarray[intARRAY_MAX];
float fltarray[fltARRAY_MAX];
```

Use of defined constants guarantees that subsequent references to the array will not exceed the defined array size. For example, it is very common to use a `for` loop to access array elements:

```
#include <iostream.h>

#define intARRAY_MAX 20

int intarray[intARRAY_MAX];

main()
{
  int i;
  for(i = 0; i < intARRAY_MAX; i++) {
  .
  .
  .
  }
  return(0);
}
```

In the next section we'll see how arrays are actually initialized in C++.

Initializing Arrays

Arrays are initialized by one of the following three techniques:

- By default when they are created (global and static arrays only).
- During program execution (when data is copied into the array).
- Explicitly when they are created (by supplying constant initializing data).

You can only use constant data to initialize an array when it is created. If the array elements must receive their values from variables, you must initialize the array by writing explicit statements as part of the program code.

Default Initialization: The ANSI C standard states that arrays are either global (defined outside of `main()` and any other function) or static automatic (static, but defined after any opening brace) and will always be initialized to binary zero if no other initialization data is supplied. C++ initializes numeric arrays to zero. Pointer arrays, on the other hand, are initialized to null. The first subscript for all arrays in C++ is zero. If you are wondering why, remember that one of C++'s strengths is its close link to assembly language. In assembly language, the first element in a table is always at the zeroth offset.

Explicit Initialization: Just as you can define and initialize variables of type `int`, `char`, `float`, `double`, and so on, you can also initialize arrays. The ANSI C standard lets you supply initialization values for any array, global or otherwise, defined anywhere in a program. The following code segment illustrates how to define and initialize two arrays:

```
int intarray[3] = {-1,0,1};
static float fltpercent[4] = {1.141579,0.75,55E0,-.33E1};
```

The first line of code declares the `intarray` array to be three integers and provides the values of the elements in curly braces, separated by commas. As usual, a semicolon ends the statement. The effect of this is that after the compiled program loads into the memory of the computer, the reserved space for the `intarray` array will already contain the initial values, so they won't need assignments when the program executes. It is important to realize that this is more than just a convenience—it happens at a different time. If the program goes on to change the values of the `intarray` array, they stay changed. Many compilers permit you to initialize arrays only if they are global or static, as in the second line of code. This statement initializes the array, `fltpercent`, when the entire program loads.

Unsized Initialization: You can provide the size of the array or the list of actual array values. It usually doesn't matter for most compilers, as long as you provide at least one of them. For example, a program will frequently want to define its own set of error messages. This can be done two ways. Here is the first method:

```
char szInput_Error[37] = "Please enter a value between 0 - 9:\n";
```

This method requires you to count the number of characters in the string, remembering to add `1` to the count for the unseen null-string terminator `\0`. This can become a very tedious approach at best, straining the eyes as you count the number of characters, and very error prone. The second method allows C++ to automatically dimension the arrays through the use of unsized arrays, as shown here:

```
char szInput_Error[] = "Please enter a value between 0 - 9:\n";
```

When an array initialization statement is encountered and the array size is not specified, the compiler automatically creates an array big enough to hold all of the specified data.

Unsized array initializations are not restricted to one-dimensional arrays. For two-dimensional arrays, or matrices, you must specify all but the leftmost dimension for C++ to properly index the array. With this approach, tables can be created of varying lengths, with the C++ compiler automatically allocating enough storage.

Accessing Array Elements

A variable declaration usually reserves one or more cells in internal memory and, through a lookup table, associates a name with the cell or cells that you can use to access them. For example, the following definition reserves only one integer-sized cell in internal memory and associates the name `ivideo_tapes` with that cell.

```
int ivideo_tapes;
```

On the other hand, the next definition reserves seven contiguous cells in internal memory and associates the name `ivideo_library` with the seven cells.

```
int ivideo_library[7];
```

Since all array elements must be of the same data type, each of the seven cells in the array `ivideo_library` can hold one integer.

Consider the difference between accessing the single cell associated with the variable `ivideo_tapes` and the seven cells associated with the array `ivideo_library`. To access the cell associated with the variable `ivideo_tapes`, simply use the name `ivideo_tapes`. For the array `ivideo_library`, you must specify an `index` to indicate exactly which cell among the seven you wish to access. The following statements designate the first cell, the second cell, the third cell, and so on, up to the last cell of the array:

```
ivideo_library[0];
ivideo_library[1];
ivideo_library[2];
ivideo_library[3];
    .
    .
    .
ivideo_library[6];
```

When accessing an array element, the integer enclosed in the square brackets is the index, which indicates the `offset`, or the distance between the cell to be accessed and the first cell.

Finding Array Dimensions

The `sizeof()` operator returns the physical size, in bytes, of the data object to which it is applied. This operator can be used with any type of data object except bit-fields. A frequent use of `sizeof()` is to determine the physical size of a variable when the size of the variable's data type can vary from machine to machine.

This concept becomes essential when the program must be portable and independent of any particular hardware.

Note: There is an `int` type cast on the result returned by `sizeof()` in the ANSI C standard. Here, `sizeof()` does not return an `int` type. Instead, `sizeof()` returns a data type, `size_t`, that is large enough to hold the return value. The ANSI C standard added this to C++ because on certain computers an integer is not big enough to represent the size of all data items.

In the next sections, we'll examine a few simple traditional C++ and STL applications that will prepare us for matrix work.

Summing Elements in a One-Dimensional Array

The following application, `Add1Ary.cpp`, illustrates the traditional C++ approach for adding a collection of elements together in an array.

```
//  Add1Ary.cpp
//  Program demonstrates how to sum the elements in
//  a one-dimensional array
//  Chris H. Pappas and William H. Murray, 2000

#include <iostream>

using namespace std;

#define iELEMENTS 5

main()
{

    int iadd[iELEMENTS] = {10, 21, 12, 43, 46};
    int sum = 0;

    cout << "For the array elements:" << endl << endl;

    for(int i = 0; i < iELEMENTS; i++) {
        cout << iadd[i] << endl;
        sum += iadd[i];
    }

    cout << endl << "The sum is: " << sum << endl << endl;


  return(0);
}
```

The application uses a single `for` loop with the variable `i` as the index into the traditional C++ array. The sum is formed in the variable `sum` during each pass through the loop.

Multiplying Elements in a One-Dimensional Array

The previous application can be modified easily to form the product of array elements. This application is named `Mul1Ary.cpp`.

```
//  Mul1Ary.cpp
//  Program demonstrates how to multiply the elements in
//  a one-dimensional array
//  Chris H. Pappas and William H. Murray, 2000

#include <iostream>

using namespace std;

#define iELEMENTS 5

main()
{

    int iproduct[iELEMENTS] = {10, 21, 12, 43, 46};
    int product = 1;

    cout << "For the array elements:" << endl << endl;

    for(int i = 0; i < iELEMENTS; i++) {
        cout << iproduct[i] << endl;
        product *= iproduct[i];
    }

    cout << endl << "The product is: " << product << endl << endl;


  return(0);
}
```

The product is saved in the variable `product`. In this and the previous application you have seen how easy it is to work with the elements in one-dimensional arrays. In the next sections you'll be reminded again that the STL approach is just as straightforward.

Using an STL Implementation: `<vector>`

If `<vector>` containers are arrays, then are arrays `<vector>` containers? This question has been posed several times. The answer is no! Using `<vector>` containers is logically and syntactically very similar to using simple C++ arrays. However, unlike statically allocated arrays, <vector> containers are dynamic. Dynamic in the sense of linked-list technology, meaning that the <vector> container can grow and shrink its size to maximize the use of computer system resources.

The term *vector* is commonly used to mean an indexed collection of similarly typed values. In C++, this abstract concept can be represented as a one-dimensional array. Recall, from the previous section, that an array is a fixed-size collection of values of homogeneous data types, indexed by integer keys.

Legal array index values range from zero to one less than the size of the collection. Values are accessed using the subscript operator. A programmer can think of the elements of an array as being placed end to end in memory. The underlying C++ language provides only a primitive mechanism for the support of one-dimensional arrays, and this mechanism provides few safeguards. Most importantly, index values are *not* checked against declared bounds at run time.

The problem is compounded by the fact that there is no way to determine from the value of a simple C++ array the extent, or number of elements, it should contain. Furthermore, there are even fewer high-level operations defined for the array type than there are for character strings. By adding a new abstraction layer on top of the basic language framework, we can correct many of these deficiencies.

A templatized vector, viewed as a data abstraction, is different in one very important respect from the data types we have previously investigated. As an abstract concept, the idea of a vector describes an incomplete data type. The solution of any particular problem might require a vector of integers, a vector of floating-point values, or even a vector of strings. In order to abstract the concept of a vector out of these more concrete realizations, we need a facility to parameterize a type description with another type. That is, we need some way to describe the idea of a vector of type `T`, where `T` represents an unknown type.

Within a vector class description the unknown parameter type `T` can be used in any situation requiring the use of a type name. This allows you to declare an instance variable as a pointer to `T`, and we can declare an operator as returning a `T` reference. In the `copy` constructor, we need to refer to an object of the same type as the receiver. Although only the keyword `vector` is used, it is implicitly assumed to mean vector of `T`.

In order to use a template class as a type, bindings must be provided for the unknown argument types. This is accomplished by providing the element type in a list, again surrounded by angle brackets. For example, the following listing declares a vector of five integer values, each entry initialized to `0`, next a vector consisting of 20 un-initialized, float-precision values, and finally a vector of ten strings, all initialized to the string "xyz."

```
// overloaded <vector> constructors
vector<int> iVector(5,0);
vector<float> fVector(20);
vector<string> szVector(10,"xyz");
```

Accessing an individual <vector> element is no more difficult than accessing a simple array element. The syntax looks identical:

```
standardArrayElementReference[1];
myVectorInstanceElementReference[1];
```

The syntax changes slightly when traversing an entire <vector> versus an array. An array is traversed with the following `for` loop syntax:

```
// traversing a simple array
for( int offset = 0; offset < MAX_ELEMENTS; offset++)...
```

To traverse a <vector>, the following `for` loop syntax is used coupled with the use of an iterator.

```
// traversing a <vector> instance
vector<int>::iterator iteratorOffset;
for( iteratorOffset = myVector.front(); iteratorOffset !=
myVector.end();
     iteratorOffset++)...
```

The <vector> template contains a type definition for the name iterator. This permits an iterator to be easily declared for any particular type of vector value. The template functions `begin()` and `end()` yield random access iterators for the vector. Again, note that the iterators yielded by these operations can become invalidated after insertion or removal of elements.

Summing Elements in an STL <vector>

The following application, `Add1Vec.cpp`, illustrates the STL approach for adding a collection of elements together using a <vector>.

```
//  Add1Vec.cpp
//  Program demonstrates how to sum the elements in
//  a <vector>
//  Chris H. Pappas and William H. Murray, 2000

#include <iostream>
#include <vector>

using namespace std;

typedef vector<int> iVector;

main()
{
    iVector iVectorInst;
```

```
    iVectorInst.push_back(10);
    iVectorInst.push_back(21);
    iVectorInst.push_back(12);
    iVectorInst.push_back(43);
    iVectorInst.push_back(46);

    int sum = 0;

    cout << "For the array elements:" << endl << endl;

    vector<int>::iterator p = iVectorInst.begin();
    while( p!= iVectorInst.end()) {
        cout << *p << endl;
        sum += *p;
        p++;
    }

    cout << endl << "The sum is: " << sum
         << endl << endl;


  return(0);
}
```

The application uses a single `while` loop with the iterator `p` used to access individual `<vector>` elements. The sum is formed in the variable `sum` during each pass through the `while` loop. The iterator is a simple pointer that allows us to access each element in the vector.

Multiplying Elements in an STL `<vector>`

The previous application can be modified to calculate the product of `<vector>` elements. This application is named `Mul1Vec.cpp`.

```
//  Mul1Vec.cpp
//  Program demonstrates how to multiply the elements in
//  a <vector>
//  Chris H. Pappas and William H. Murray, 2000

#include <iostream>
#include <vector>

using namespace std;

typedef vector<int> iVector;

main()
{
    iVector iVectorInst;
```

```
    iVectorInst.push_back(10);
    iVectorInst.push_back(21);
    iVectorInst.push_back(12);
    iVectorInst.push_back(43);
    iVectorInst.push_back(46);

    int product = 1;

    cout << "For the array elements:" << endl << endl;

    vector<int>::iterator p = iVectorInst.begin();
    while( p!= iVectorInst.end()) {
       cout << *p << endl;
       product *= *p;
       p++;
    }

    cout << endl << "The product is: " << product
        << endl << endl;


  return(0);
}
```

The product is saved in the variable `product`. So far, this has just been simple programming with STL capabilities. Keep in mind that the use of STL `<vector>` containers is dynamic, while that of traditional C++ arrays is static.

Matrices

In this section you'll see traditional C++ array manipulation in the form of matrices and an STL approach to the problem. You will see that two-dimensional arrays use a simple extension of the one-dimensional array syntax while the STL approach will be quite novel.

Using Traditional C++ Implementation: Arrays

A matrix is a two-dimensional collection of elements that can be easily manipulated with traditional C++ array syntax. Syntactically, a matrix might be represented in the following manner:

```
int iadd[iROWS][iCOLUMNS] = {1, 3, 5, 7,
                              2, 4, 6, 8,
                              1, 2, 3, 4};
```

Here, the matrix contains 12 integer elements. The elements are actually stored in 12 consecutive memory locations, but were divided by the programmer to appear as two-dimensional.

Elements in any of the three rows can be accessed by indexing the rows index value from `0` to `2`. Elements in any of the four columns can be accessed by indexing the columns index value from `0` to `3`.

Manipulating matrix values, using C++ arrays, usually entails the use of two `for` loops in order to control both index values.

The following examples expand the one-dimensional array example of the previous section.

Summing Elements in a Two-Dimensional Array (Matrix)

The following application, `Add2aAry`, illustrates the traditional C++ approach for adding a collection of matrix elements together using array syntax.

```
//  Add2Ary.cpp
//  Program demonstrates summing elements in a
//  two-dimensional array
//  Chris H. Pappas and William H. Murray, 2000

#include <iostream>

using namespace std;

#define iROWS 3
#define iCOLUMNS 4

main()
{
    int iadd[iROWS][iCOLUMNS] = {1, 3, 5, 7,
                                 2, 4, 6, 8,
                                 1, 2, 3, 4};
    int sum = 0;

    cout << "For the array elements:" << endl << endl;

    for(int i = 0; i < iROWS; i++) {
        cout << endl;
        for(int j = 0; j < iCOLUMNS; j++) {
            cout << iadd[i][j] << "\t";
            sum += iadd[i][j];
        }
        cout << endl;
    }

    cout << endl << "The sum is: " << sum
         << endl << endl;

  return(0);
}
```

In this example, the elements are added by going down columns. So the sum is formed by adding `1 + 2 + 1`, then the row is incremented, and then `3 + 4 + 2`..., and so on. A little formatting on the output makes the appearance neater.

The output from this example takes the following form:

```
For the array elements:


1   3   5   7

2   4   6   8

1   2   3   4

The sum is: 46
```

It will only require minor changes to convert the matrix addition example to one that will multiply all of the elements in a matrix together.

Multiplying Elements in a Two-Dimensional Array (Matrix)

In the previous example, each of the matrix elements in the C++ array were accessed and used to form a sum. In the `Mul2Ary.cpp` application, each element will be accessed in a similar manner, except that this time a product will be formed from all of the matrix elements.

```
//  Mul2Ary.cpp
//  Program demonstrates multiplying elements in a
//  two-dimensional array
//  Chris H. Pappas and William H. Murray, 2000

#include <iostream>

using namespace std;

#define iROWS 3
#define iCOLUMNS 4

main()
{
    int imul[iROWS][iCOLUMNS] = {2, 4, 6, 8,
                                 1, 3, 5, 7,
                                 1, 2, 3, 4};
    int product = 1;

    cout << "For the array elements:" << endl << endl;
```

```
    for(int i = 0; i < iROWS; i++) {
        cout << endl;
        for(int j = 0; j < iCOLUMNS; j++) {
            cout << imul[i][j] << "\t";
            product *= imul[i][j];
        }
        cout << endl;
    }

    cout << endl << "The product is: " << product
         << endl << endl;

  return(0);
}
```

In this application, the elements are multiplied by going down columns. So the product is formed by multiplying `1 * 2 * 1`, then the row is incremented, and then `3 * 4 * 2...`, and so on.

The output from this example is as anticipated:

```
For the array elements:


2    4    6    8

1    3    5    7

1    2    3    4

The product is: 967680
```

The syntax used in this example and the previous application is just an extension of the syntax used to access one-dimensional arrays. In the next section, you'll see that a unique approach is required if we are going to continue our work with `<vector>` containers.

Using an STL Implementation: Vector of Vectors

A vector, by nature, is one-dimensional. We can, however, create a vector of vectors using the following syntax:

```
vector < vector<int> >
```

This gives us the two dimensions required for matrix operations. In the next sections, you'll see several complete applications that illustrate matrix operations using vector or vectors. You will also learn two unique approaches to accessing elements within the vector of vectors.

Summing Elements in a Vector of Vectors (Matrix)

The following application, `Add2Vec`, illustrates an STL approach to adding a collection of matrix elements together using a vector of vectors.

```
//  Add2Vec.cpp
//  Program demonstrates how to sum the elements in
//  a matrix using a vector of vectors.
//  Chris H. Pappas and William H. Murray, 2000

#include <iostream>
#include <vector>

using namespace std;

typedef vector<int> v;

main()
{
    v v1, v2, v3, v4, temp;

    // create four vectors with three elements each
    v1.push_back(10); v1.push_back(21); v1.push_back(5);
    v2.push_back(12); v2.push_back(43); v2.push_back(73);
    v3.push_back(46); v3.push_back(17); v3.push_back(33);
    v4.push_back(54); v4.push_back(67); v4.push_back(3);

    vector< vector<int> > iVector;

    // put the four vectors into vector< vector<> >
    iVector.push_back(v4);
    iVector.push_back(v3);
    iVector.push_back(v2);
    iVector.push_back(v1);

    // prepare to sum elements
    int sum = 0;
    cout << "For the vector< vector<> > elements:"
         << endl << endl;

    // iterator for vector< vector<> >
    vector<vector<int> >::iterator p = iVector.begin();

    // use two while loops to retrieve individual
    // elements for summing
    while ( p!= iVector.end()) {
        temp = iVector.back();
```

```
        // iterator for vector<int>
        // each time a vector<int> is returned
        // from vector vector<> >, temp will
        // point to begin() of that vector.
        vector<int>::iterator q = temp.begin();
            while( q != temp.end()) {
                cout << *q << "\t";
                sum += *q;
                q++;
            }
        iVector.pop_back();
        cout << endl << endl;
    }

    cout << endl << "The sum is: " << sum << endl << endl;

  return(0);
}
```

In this application a vector of vectors is created by first forming four individual vectors of type `vector<int>`. This is achieved with the following syntax:

```
v v1, v2, v3, v4, temp;
```

The vector, temp, is also of type `vector<int>` and will be used as a temporary storage location.

Integer values are then placed in each vector.

```
// create four vectors with three elements each
v1.push_back(10); v1.push_back(21); v1.push_back(5);
v2.push_back(12); v2.push_back(43); v2.push_back(73);
v3.push_back(46); v3.push_back(17); v3.push_back(33);
v4.push_back(54); v4.push_back(67); v4.push_back(3);
```

Thus, four vectors are created with three elements each. Each vector is one-dimensional, as shown in Table 11.1.

Table 11.1 Individual Vectors and Vector Elements

vector	*element a*	*element b*	*element c*
v1	10	21	5
v2	12	43	73
v3	46	17	33
v4	54	67	3

A two-dimensional matrix can be formed by creating a vector of vectors. Syntactically, this is done with the following code:

```
vector< vector<int> > iVector;
```

Now, the individual vectors, `v4` through `v1`, are placed in the vector of vectors, `iVector`.

```
// put the four vectors into vector< vector<> >
iVector.push_back(v4);
iVector.push_back(v3);
iVector.push_back(v2);
iVector.push_back(v1);
```

In order to index through the individual elements of `iVector`, we'll need an iterator that will allow us to move up and down the previously stored vectors `v4` through `v1`.

```
// iterator for vector< vector<> >
vector<vector<int> >::iterator p = iVector.begin();\
```

Again, the iterator `p` will serve as a pointer to the row data, shown earlier in Table 11.1.

Another iterator, `q`, will be used to point to individual elements within a row.

```
vector<int>::iterator q = temp.begin();
```

This iterator acts as a pointer to the column data shown in Table 11.1. Retrieving individual elements and forming a sum requires two loops. Since every element will be used, two `while` loops are used in this application.

```
while ( p!= iVector.end()) {
     temp = iVector.back();
     vector<int>::iterator q = temp.begin();
          while( q != temp.end()) {
               cout << *q << "\t";
               sum += *q;
               q++;
          }
     iVector.pop_back();
     cout << endl << endl;
}
```

The `temp` vector is used to retrieve the vector at the end of `iVector` in the outer `while` loop. Then the `q` iterator is used to sum the individual elements within that temporary vector. Next, `iVector.pop_back()` removes the vector from the end of `iVector` and the process is repeated until `iVector` no longer contains any vectors. The sum is accumulated and eventually printed to the screen.

An alternative technique for accessing matrix elements will be illustrated later in this chapter when the dot product of two matrices is calculated.

The output for this application is:

```
For the vector< vector<> > elements:

10    21     5

12    43    73

46    17    33

54    67     3


The sum is: 384
```

In the next section, you'll see that this application can be modified to calculate the product of the matrices individual elements.

Multiplying Elements in a Vector of Vectors (Matrix)

The following application, `Mul2Vec`, illustrates an STL approach for multiplying a collection of matrix elements together using a vector of vectors.

```
//  Mul2Vec.cpp
//  Program demonstrates how to multiply the elements in
//  a matrix using a vector of vectors.
//  Chris H. Pappas and William H. Murray, 2000

#include <iostream>
#include <vector>

using namespace std;

typedef vector<int> v;

main()
{
    v v1, v2, v3, v4, temp;

    // create four vectors with three elements each
    v1.push_back(2); v1.push_back(4); v1.push_back(6);
    v2.push_back(1); v2.push_back(3); v2.push_back(5);
    v3.push_back(4); v3.push_back(4); v3.push_back(4);
    v4.push_back(3); v4.push_back(2); v4.push_back(1);
```

```
    vector< vector<int> > iVector;

    // put the four vectors into vector< vector<> >
    iVector.push_back(v4);
    iVector.push_back(v3);
    iVector.push_back(v2);
    iVector.push_back(v1);

    // prepare to sum elements
    int product = 1;
    cout << "For the vector< vector<> > elements:"
        << endl << endl;

    // iterator for vector< vector<> >
    vector<vector<int> >::iterator p = iVector.begin();

    // use two while loops to retrieve individual
    // elements for summing
    while ( p!= iVector.end()) {
        temp = iVector.back();
        // iterator for vector<int>
        // each time a vector<int> is returned
        // from vector vector<> >, temp will
        // point to begin() of that vector.
        vector<int>::iterator q = temp.begin();
            while( q != temp.end()) {
                cout << *q << "\t";
                product *= *q;
                q++;
            }
        iVector.pop_back();
        cout << endl << endl;
    }

    cout << endl << "The product is: " << product
        << endl << endl;

  return(0);
}
```

This application is a modification of the previous Add2Vec.cpp application. The output from this application is:

```
For the vector< vector<> > elements:

2     4     6

1     3     5

4     4     4

3     2     1


The product is: 276480
```

Since only minor changes were made to the previous example, no additional code explanation is needed.

Of course, now might be a good time to experiment and modify the program to accept `floats`!

Scalar Multiplication of a Matrix Using Vector of Vectors

The multiplication of a matrix by a scalar value can be found by multiplying each individual element in the matrix by that value.

In the following application, `ScalarxVec`, a four-by-four matrix will be multiplied by the scalar value of three.

```
//  ScalarxVec.cpp
//  Program demonstrates how to multiply a matrix
//  by a scalar value.
//  Chris H. Pappas and William H. Murray, 2000

#include <iostream>
#include <vector>

using namespace std;

typedef vector<int> v;

main()
{
    v v1, v2, v3, v4, temp;

    // create four vectors with three elements each
    v1.push_back(2); v1.push_back(4); v1.push_back(6);
    v2.push_back(1); v2.push_back(3); v2.push_back(5);
    v3.push_back(4); v3.push_back(4); v3.push_back(4);
    v4.push_back(3); v4.push_back(2); v4.push_back(1);
```

```
    vector< vector<int> > iVector;

    // put the four vectors into vector< vector<> >
    iVector.push_back(v4);
    iVector.push_back(v3);
    iVector.push_back(v2);
    iVector.push_back(v1);

    // prepare to sum elements
    int product = 1;
    cout << "The original matrix multiplied by a scalar:"
         << endl << endl;

    // iterator for vector< vector<> >
    vector<vector<int> >::iterator p = iVector.begin();

    // use two while loops to retrieve individual
    // elements for summing
    while ( p!= iVector.end()) {
        temp = iVector.back();
        // iterator for vector<int>
        // each time a vector<int> is returned
        // from vector vector<> >, temp will
        // point to begin() of that vector.
        vector<int>::iterator q = temp.begin();
            while( q != temp.end()) {
                // multiply matrix by 3
                product = *q * 3;
                cout << product << "\t";
                q++;
            }
        iVector.pop_back();
        cout << endl << endl;
    }

    cout << endl << endl;

  return(0);
}
```

This application modifies the `Mul2Vec.cpp` application, slightly, to output each matrix element multiplied by the scalar value of three.

```
The original matrix multiplied by a scalar:

6    12    18

3     9    15

12   12    12

9     6     3
```

Refer to the application's code and note, again, the use of two `while` loops and two iterators.

There is another type of matrix multiplication that is frequently encountered. The other form of matrix multiplication involves the multiplication of two matrices and is achieved by calculating the dot product. An example of this type of matrix multiplication will be included later in this chapter.

Adding Two Matrices Using Vector of Vectors

The technique for accessing elements in the `iVector` vector of vectors has been working well in the previous applications, since each element is accessed in order. This technique can be extended to allow us to calculate the sum of two matrices. When two matrices are added the sum is formed by adding the elements, in similar matrix positions, together.

For example:

```
1  2  3       0  2  0        1  4   3
4  5  6   +   0  0  5   =    4  5  11
7  8  9       7  0  0       14  8   9
```

Here is an application that achieves those results.

```
//  Matrix+Matrix.cpp
//  Program demonstrates how to add two matrices
//  together using a vector of vectors.
//  Chris H. Pappas and William H. Murray, 2000

#include <iostream>
#include <vector>

using namespace std;

typedef vector<int> va, vb;

main()
{
```

```
va va1, va2, va3, va4, tempa;
vb vb1, vb2, vb3, vb4, tempb;

// create four vectors with three elements each
va1.push_back(10); va1.push_back(21); va1.push_back(5);
va2.push_back(12); va2.push_back(43); va2.push_back(73);
va3.push_back(46); va3.push_back(17); va3.push_back(33);
va4.push_back(54); va4.push_back(67); va4.push_back(3);

// create another four vectors with three elements each
vb1.push_back(20); vb1.push_back(11); vb1.push_back(15);
vb2.push_back(2);  vb2.push_back(50); vb2.push_back(19);
vb3.push_back(6);  vb3.push_back(71); vb3.push_back(43);
vb4.push_back(11); vb4.push_back(5);  vb4.push_back(40);

vector< vector<int> > iVectora, iVectorb;

// put the four va vectors into iVectora
// to form the iVectora matrix
iVectora.push_back(va4);
iVectora.push_back(va3);
iVectora.push_back(va2);
iVectora.push_back(va1);

// put the four vb vectors into iVectorb
// to form the iVectorb matrix
iVectorb.push_back(vb4);
iVectorb.push_back(vb3);
iVectorb.push_back(vb2);
iVectorb.push_back(vb1);

// prepare to add the matrices
int sum = 0;
cout << "The sum of the two matrices is:"
     << endl << endl;

// iterators for two matrices
vector<vector<int> >::iterator p = iVectora.begin();
vector<vector<int> >::iterator q = iVectorb.begin();

// use two while loops to retrieve individual
// elements during addition of two matrices
while ((p != iVectora.end()) && (q != iVectorb.end())) {
    tempa = iVectora.back();
    tempb = iVectorb.back();
    // iterator for vector<int>
    // each time a vector<int> is returned
```

```
        // from a matrix, tempa or tempb will
        // point to begin() of that vector.
        vector<int>::iterator r = tempa.begin();
        vector<int>::iterator s = tempb.begin();
            while(( r != tempa.end()) && (s != tempb.end())) {
                sum = *r + *s;
                cout << sum << "\t";
                r++;
                s++;
            }
        iVectora.pop_back();
        iVectorb.pop_back();
        cout << endl << endl;
    }

    cout << endl << endl;

  return(0);
}
```

The results of this application are easy to check.

```
The sum of the two matrices is:

30    32    20

14    93    92

52    88    76

65    72    43
```

Well, as you can see from studying the listing, the code from the previous example was basically doubled. Two matrices are initialized, two iterators are used to track row positions, and two iterators are used to track column positions. Under what conditions could we have gotten by without two complete sets of redundant code?

```
while(( r != tempa.end()) && (s != tempb.end())) {
    sum = *r + *s;
    cout << sum << "\t";
    r++;
    s++;
```

The sum for a given element position is calculated from the elements of `tempa` and `tempb` using the iterators `r` and `s`.

In the next section, we'll show you how to access individual matrix elements in a slightly different fashion—one involving pointer arithmetic.

Multiplying Two Matrices (dot product) Using Vector of Vectors

The calculation of the dot product of two matrices is frequently encountered in engineering as well as mathematics. If you are an engineer, scientist, or mathematician, you have probably programmed a solution to matrix multiplication in C++ using array syntax. In this section, we'll examine the solution to the problem using a vector of vectors to form each matrix.

The dot product of two matrices is illustrated by using row and column subscripts for matrix elements:

$$\begin{matrix} a_{11} & a_{12} & a_{13} \\ a_{21} & a_{22} & a_{23} \\ a_{31} & a_{32} & a_{33} \end{matrix} \quad x \quad \begin{matrix} b_{11} & b_{12} & b_{13} \\ b_{21} & b_{22} & b_{23} \\ b_{31} & b_{32} & b_{33} \end{matrix} \quad = \quad \begin{matrix} c_{11} & c_{12} & c_{13} \\ c_{21} & c_{22} & c_{23} \\ c_{31} & c_{32} & c_{33} \end{matrix}$$

Matrix multiplication is achieved by multiplying a row in matrix `a` by a column in matrix `b`. The products are then summed to give the appropriate results in matrix `c`.

For example, if we wish to calculate c_{11}, the result is formed with the following calculation:

$$c_{11} = (a_{11} \text{ x } b_{11}) + (a_{12} \text{ x } b_{21}) + (a_{13} \text{ x } b_{31})$$

For the application that follows, those individual values would be:

$$c_{11} = (1 \text{ x } 10) + (2 \text{ x } 13) + (3 \text{ x } 16) = 10 + 26 +48$$
$$= 84$$

You might want to try a calculation for c_{21} or c_{32} just to be sure you know how this works.

Now the implementation is a little trickier, but as we mentioned, this is a classical programming problem, so the solution is quite common in most advanced programming books. Generally, three `for` loops are used to calculate the individual cell products and they then form a sum.

```
//  MatrixXMatrix.cpp
//  Program demonstrates how to multiply two matrices
//  together using a vector of vectors (dot product).
//  Chris H. Pappas and William H. Murray, 2000

#include <iostream>
#include <vector>

using namespace std;
```

```
typedef vector<int> va, vb;

main()
{
    va va1, va2, va3, tempa;
    vb vb1, vb2, vb3, tempb;

    // create three vectors with three elements each
    va1.push_back(1); va1.push_back(2); va1.push_back(3);
    va2.push_back(4); va2.push_back(5); va2.push_back(6);
    va3.push_back(7); va3.push_back(8); va3.push_back(9);

    // create another three vectors with three elements each
    vb1.push_back(10); vb1.push_back(11); vb1.push_back(12);
    vb2.push_back(13); vb2.push_back(14); vb2.push_back(15);
    vb3.push_back(16); vb3.push_back(17); vb3.push_back(18);

    vector< vector<int> > iVectora, iVectorb;

    // put the three va vectors into iVectora
    // to form the iVectora matrix
    iVectora.push_back(va1);
    iVectora.push_back(va2);
    iVectora.push_back(va3);

    // put the three vb vectors into iVectorb
    // to form the iVectorb matrix
    iVectorb.push_back(vb1);
    iVectorb.push_back(vb2);
    iVectorb.push_back(vb3);

    // iterators for two matrices
    vector<vector<int> >::iterator p = iVectora.begin();
    vector<vector<int> >::iterator q = iVectorb.begin();

    // prepare to multiply matrixa x matrixb
    cout << "The dot product of the two matrices is:"
         << endl << endl;

    // calculate and print the dot product
    for (int r = 0; r < 3; r++) {
        for (int c = 0; c < 3; c++) {
            int sum = 0;
            for (int i = 0; i < 3; i++) {
                sum+=((*(p + r))[i] * (*(q + i))[c]);
            }
            cout << sum << "\t";
```

```
        }
        cout << endl << endl;
    }

    cout << endl << endl;

  return(0);
}
```

The row and column values for the matrix are controlled with the two outer `for` loops by incrementing integers `r` and `c`. Using the elements pointed to by these values yields three separate products that are summed together within the inner `for` loop. That accumulated sum represents the cell value for the dot product.

```
    // calculate and print the dot product
    for (int r = 0; r < 3; r++) {
        for (int c = 0; c < 3; c++) {
            int sum = 0;
            for (int i = 0; i < 3; i++) {
                sum+=((*(p + r))[i] * (*(q + i))[c]);
            }
            cout << sum << "\t";
        }
        cout << endl << endl;
    }
```

The most interesting line of code in the previous partial listing is the line that allows us to access matrix elements.

```
sum+=((*(p + r))[i] * (*(q + i))[c]);
```

You might recognize the various elements of pointer arithmetic in this line of code. For the first matrix, the iterator `p` is used to access row information.

The iterator `p` is initialized to point to row zero.

*p

To point to row two, we can use:

```
*(p + 1)
```

Then for row three:

```
*(p + 2)
```

This indexing is done automatically with the use of a `for` loop and indexing the row, `r`, value.

Now, for any individual row, a column value can be specified as follows. For the element in the matrix, row one, column one:

```
*p[0]
```

For the same row, column two:

```
*p[1]
```

Or, for row three, column three:

```
*(p + 2)[2]
```

The column values are indexed with the integer `c` using the second `for` loop. This application's dot product results are shown next.

```
The dot product of the two matrices is:

84       90      96

201     216     231

318     342     366
```

This matrix multiplication is written to solve a 3×3 matrix multiplication. What code modifications would be needed to calculate the dot product of two 4×4 matrices?

Sparse Arrays (Matrices)

A sparse array is an array with a large number of array values equal to a default value, such as `-1` or `0`. For example, the following matrix qualifies as a sparse array.

```
0  0  1  0  0  0  0
0  0  0  0  0  0  0
0  0  0  0  3  0  0
0  0  0  0  0  0  0
0  0  0  0  0  0  0
0  0  0  0  0  0  2
0  0  0  0  0  5  0
```

With traditional C++ implementations, the problem with sparse arrays is the large amount of memory allocation needed for a relatively small number of true data values. This problem might sound reminiscent of the problems encountered in Chapter 10 when dealing with hashing functions—and it is.

The approach to handling sparse arrays with the STL is to identify the default value, such as `-1` or `0`, and then only retain true data values. Most frequently maps are used for this purpose. The advantages of maps and multimaps were discussed earlier in Chapter 9.

Summary

In this chapter you have learned how matrices can be manipulated in terms of data storage and retrieval. You have seen examples that have used array syntax, pointers, and pointer arithmetic to access individual matrix elements in both traditional C++ examples and examples using the STL. The examples have included programs that add and multiply one and two-dimensional array elements, add two matrices, and multiply two matrices. The topic of matrices is an integral part of data structures. In the next chapter, we'll put this information to good use as we look at graphs.

CHAPTER 12

Graphs and the STL

In the previous chapter you learned that matrices could be treated as ADTs (Abstract Data Types). Matrices are discussed in detail in college Linear Algebra courses, but are often first used in introductory programming courses teaching one- and two-dimensional array concepts.

Students will recognize a similar encounter with graphs. In our earliest computing work, we have used graphs to plot data. The data plotted is typically stored in one-, two-, or three-dimensional arrays, vectors, lists, and so on. The graphs plotted take the form of line, pie, and bar charts.

Graphing theory, as you are about to learn, goes far beyond those simple experiences. Yet it is our familiarities with graphing at this fundamental level that will help us understand the more advanced concepts of this interesting topic.

By the end of this chapter, you should agree that graphs too hold a rightful place as ADTs.

Graph Definitions and Terminology

The graphic applications that we are most familiar with allow us to portray data in unique manners. For example, there might be a relationship between the months in a year and bathing suit sales. Table 12.1 illustrates a hypothetical relationship.

Table 12.1 Swim Suit Sales

Month	*Sales*
1	2
2	4
3	3
4	10
5	33
6	65
7	72
8	52
9	47
10	29
11	14
12	7

Instead of viewing this data as a mere table, you have learned that it can be represented as a bar chart, as shown in Figure 12.1.

Of course, the very same data could be represented as a line chart if the bar chart representation was not satisfactory. A line chart of the same data is shown in Figure 12.2.

These two charts represent very useful graphic applications that allow us to present data in several different forms.

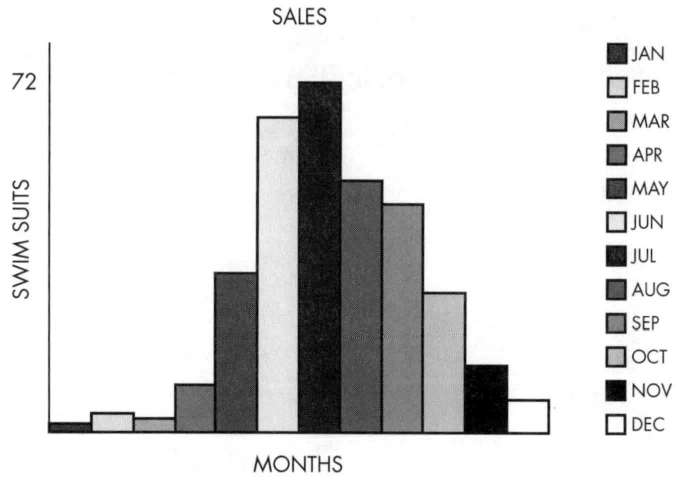

Figure 12.1
A bar chart of swim suit sales versus month.

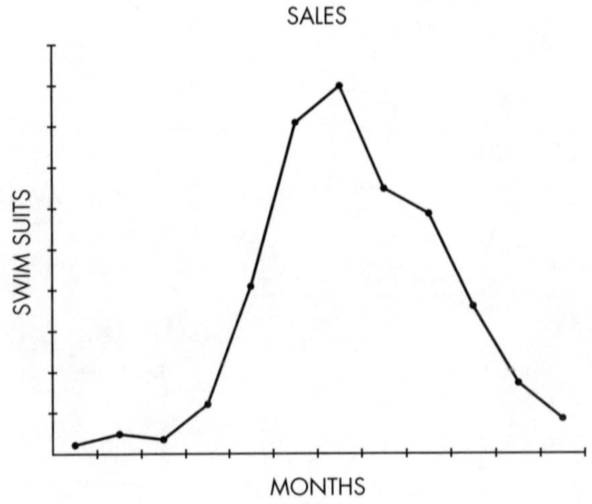

Figure 12.2
A line chart of swim suit sales versus month.

Graph theory allows us to go beyond simple data presentations and allows us to examine the relationships that exist between the data elements themselves. The remainder of this chapter will focus on that aspect of graph theory.

What Is a Graph?

A graph can obviously be more complex than simply representing data elements, as illustrated in the previous section.

For example, a two-dimensional graph can be viewed as containing two collections of elements. One collection forms the graph's vertices or nodes. The other collection forms the graph's edges that connect the vertices or nodes.

To broaden our concept of a graph, consider the Ocean Lakes Family Campground located in Myrtle Beach, SC. The campground provides several related, but distinct, services for the camper. Upon entering the campground, the administration and registration buildings allow campers to register and secure camp site information. To the south of these buildings are the campground's golf cart rental building, trailer sales building, security building, property rental building, and maintenance buildings. At other locations throughout the property are the campground store, snack bar, and numerous bathhouses, as illustrated in Figure 12.3.

The question is, how does this layout apply to our definition of a graph?

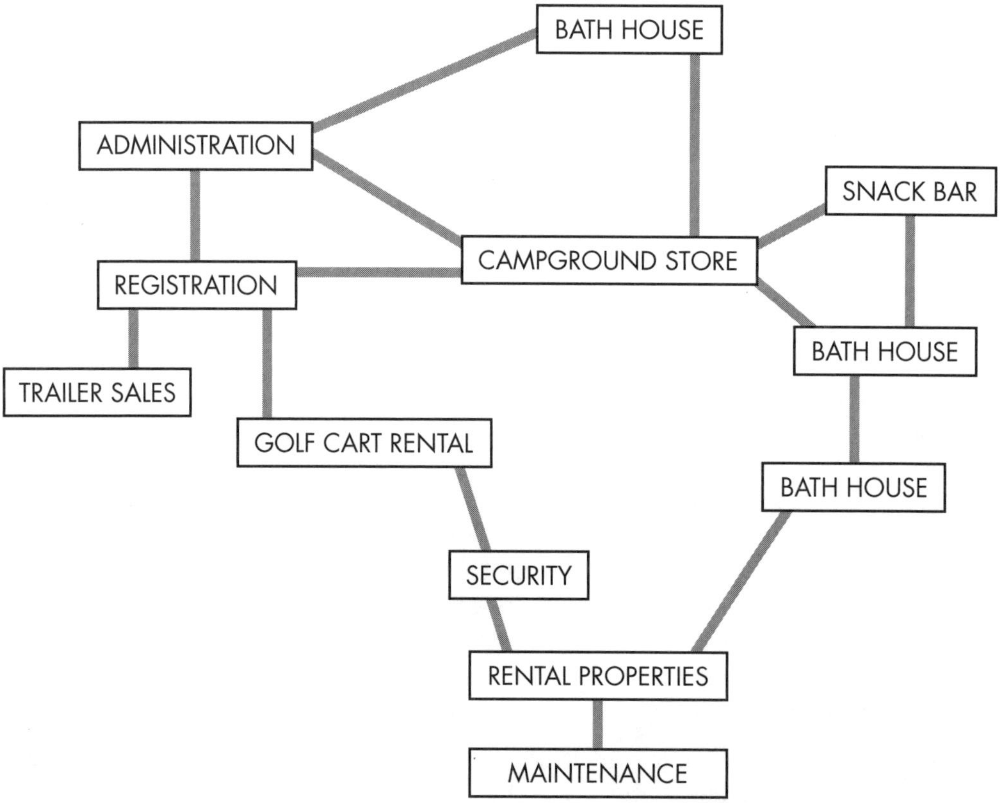

Figure 12.3 A graph of vertices and edges for the Ocean Lakes Family Campground.

Vertices, Nodes, and Edges

In our previous description of the Ocean Lakes Family Campground, the various buildings form the vertices or nodes of our graph. The interconnecting paved roads form the edges to the graph.

If we return to the line chart of swim suit sales, the monthly sales figures would represent the vertices or nodes and the interconnecting lines would represent the graph's edges.

Subgraphs

A subgraph consists of a subset of the graphs vertices and edges. For example, the administration, security, and maintenance buildings of the Ocean Lakes Family Campground might not be important for most campers. However, in terms of day-to-day campground operations they are very important. An operation's subgraph might consist of just the administration, security, and maintenance buildings, as shown in Figure 12.4.

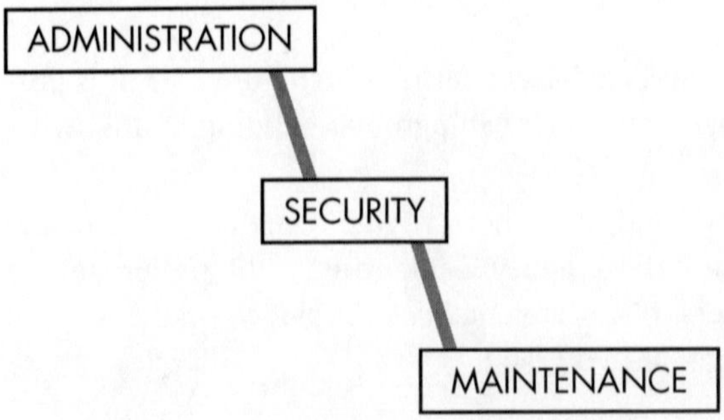

Figure 12.4
A subgraph of the Ocean Lakes Family Campground.

This subgraph consists of three vertices or nodes and two edges.

Adjacency

Vertices or nodes are considered as being adjacent when they are connected by an edge. In Figure 12.4, the administration and security buildings are considered as being adjacent. Likewise, the security and maintenance buildings are considered as being adjacent. However, the administration and maintenance buildings are not considered adjacent since an edge does not directly connect them. For the Ocean Lakes Family Campground, this would mean that you could not reach the maintenance building on a paved road from the administration building without passing the security building.

Paths

Paths are considered as a sequence of edges starting at one vertex and ending at another. If you refer to Figure 12.3, shown earlier, there is a path leading from the administration building to a bath house, to the campground store to the snack bar, to another bath house, and back to the campground store. By definition, a path can use the same vertex or node more than once. By contrast, a simple path may not use a vertex or node more than once.

In Figure 12.3, the path from the administration building to the bath house to the campus store is a simple path.

Cycle

A cycle is a path that begins and ends at the same vertex. A simple cycle is one that does not use the same vertex (other than the starting vertex) or edges more than once. In Figure 12.3, a simple cycle would consist of the path from the administration building to the registration building to the campground store and back to the administration building.

A cycle that would not be considered simple would be a path from the administration building to the registration building to the trailer sales building to the campground store and back to the administration building. This is because the registration vertex would have to be visited twice—once upon leaving for the trailer sales building and once upon returning.

Connected and Disconnected

A connected graph provides a path between adjacent vertices. In Figure 12.3, it is possible to get from any campground building to any other campground building by following a path (paved road).

A disconnected graph, on the other hand, does not provide a path to each of the graph's vertices. In the case of the Ocean Lakes Family Campground, the trailer storage area (not shown) is not available to campers. If this area had been provided on the original graph, it would have made the graph a disconnected graph.

Completed

A completed, connected graph provides an edge between each pair of vertices or nodes. For example, if the Ocean Lakes Family Campground consisted of just the administration, registration, and campground store vertices, as shown earlier in Figure 12.3, the graph would have been considered a completed graph. That is because it is possible to get to any other vertex or node using a single edge from any vertex or node.

When the whole campground graph is considered, it is obvious that you cannot get from the security building to the administration building without using multiple edges. Those edges take you through the golf cart rental and registration vertices.

Weighted

A graph is considered weighted if values are assigned to the edges of the graph. Very commonly, edge values are used to represent distances. In our earlier example, edge values might represent the distances, measured in feet, yards, or miles, from one Ocean Lakes Family Campground building to another.

Directed and Undirected

A directed graph or digraph is a graph where the edges represent a direction. The Ocean Lakes Family Campground is an undirected graph because there is no direction associated with the edges.

One-way streets often create digraphs, as illustrated in Figure 12.5.

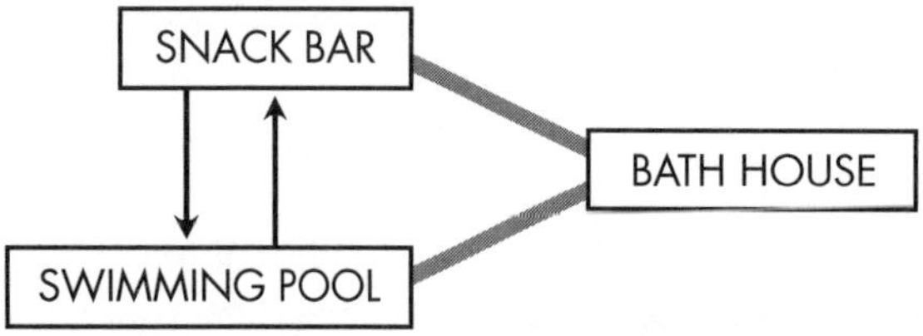

Figure 12.5
A directed graph or digraph.

Note: A directed graph or digraph that is completed (see earlier definition) is considered strongly connected. If the graph is undirected and completed, it is considered weakly connected.

Free Tree

Refer to Figure 12.3 and consider just the vertices registration, golf cart rental, security, and rental properties as making up a subgraph. This subgraph forms a tree, but since the vertices are connected, without a cycle, it also forms a unique type of tree called a free tree.

Notice, in Figure 12.5, that two of the vertices are connected by two edges. If the edges are part of a weighted graph, they do not have to be the same value.

Operations

Insertion and deletion operations are required of most ADTs. In addition to these operations, for a graph it is often necessary to be able to find the number of vertices (nodes) and edges.

Additional operations might include the insertion of a vertex or edge in a graph. These operations are achieved using the skills we have developed in the previous eleven chapters. The next section will describe operations that are unique to graphs.

Graph Implementation

There are many ways to represent a graph. The two most common ways are the adjacency matrix and adjacency list. In the following sections we'll examine each representation and consider practical examples using the Ocean Lakes Family Campground (OLFC) discussed earlier.

Adjacency Matrix

In order to discuss the creation of an adjacency matrix, we'll modify the graph of the OLFC, shown earlier in Figure 12.3, to use the numeric values for the vertices as shown in Figure 12.6.

Traditionally, an adjacency matrix is held in a two-dimensional array in C++. We'll consider that case first. To form an adjacency matrix for a graph, we'll need an array with dimensions `0...n - 1`, where `n` represents the number of vertices or nodes in the graph. For our example, there are twelve nodes. The nodes are numbered from `0` to `11`. Thus, the matrix information can be held in an array whose dimensions are `(0...11)(0...11)`.

For a graph that is not weighted, a Boolean value of one is usually used to represent the presence of an edge between vertices. For weighted graphs, the actual weight is often used in place of the Boolean one. When an edge does not exist between vertices, a Boolean value of zero is used. A vertex or node is always considered as connected to itself, so for these situations a Boolean value of one is also used.

Using the rules just discussed, an adjacency matrix is formed from the OLFC information provided in Figure 12.6 to create Table 12.2.

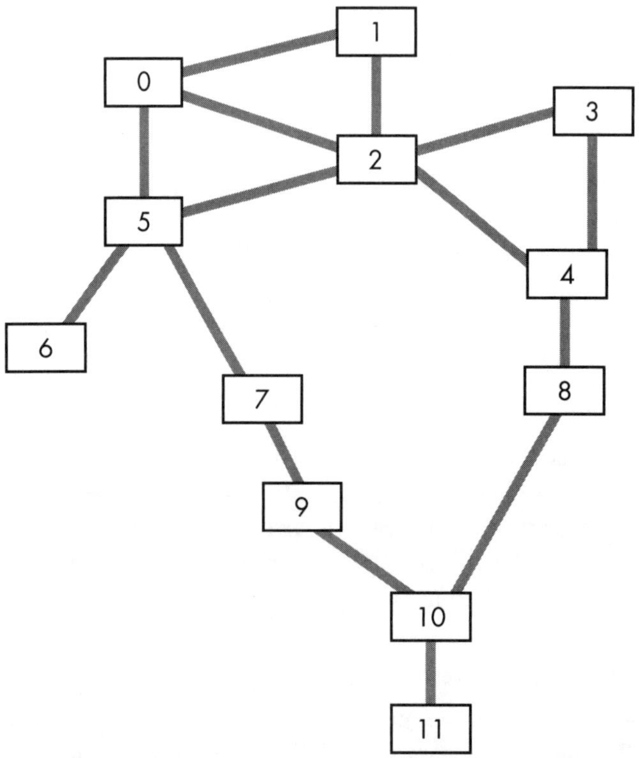

Figure 12.6
A symbolic graph of the Ocean Lakes Family Campground.

Table 12.2 An Adjacency Matrix for the OLFC Graph

	0	1	2	3	4	5	6	7	8	9	10	11
0	1	1	1	0	0	1	0	0	0	0	0	0
1	1	1	1	0	0	0	0	0	0	0	0	0
2	1	1	1	1	1	1	0	0	0	0	0	0
3	0	0	1	1	1	0	0	0	0	0	0	0
4	0	0	1	1	1	0	0	0	1	0	0	0
5	1	0	1	0	0	1	1	1	0	0	0	0
6	0	0	0	0	0	1	1	0	0	0	0	0
7	0	0	0	0	0	1	0	1	0	1	0	0
8	0	0	0	0	1	0	0	0	1	0	1	0
9	0	0	0	0	0	0	0	1	0	1	1	0
10	0	0	0	0	0	0	0	0	1	1	1	1
11	0	0	0	0	0	0	0	0	0	0	1	1

For example, using Table 12.2, note that vertex (node) 2 can be reached from vertices 0, 1, 2, 3, 4, and 5. In other words, there is an edge connecting each of these vertices.

Converting this matrix of information into a two-dimensional C++ array is straightforward.

```
int OLFC[12][12] = {{1, 1, 1, 0, 0, 1, 0, 0, 0, 0, 0, 0},
                    {1, 1, 1, 0, 0, 0, 0, 0, 0, 0, 0, 0},
                    {1, 1, 1, 1, 1, 1, 0, 0, 0, 0, 0, 0},
                    {0, 0, 1, 1, 1, 0, 0, 0, 0, 0, 0, 0},
                    {0, 0, 1, 1, 1, 0, 0, 0, 1, 0, 0, 0},
                    {1, 0, 1, 0, 0, 1, 1, 1, 0, 0, 0, 0},
                    {0, 0, 0, 0, 0, 1, 1, 0, 0, 0, 0, 0},
                    {0, 0, 0, 0, 0, 1, 0, 1, 0, 1, 0, 0},
                    {0, 0, 0, 0, 1, 0, 0, 0, 1, 0, 1, 0},
                    {0, 0, 0, 0, 0, 0, 0, 1, 0, 1, 1, 0},
                    {0, 0, 0, 0, 0, 0, 0, 0, 1, 1, 1, 1},
                    {0, 0, 0, 0, 0, 0, 0, 0, 0, 0, 1, 1}};
```

You learned in Chapter 11 how to overcome some of the limitations of C++ arrays by using the STL, and you saw that this same information could be stored in a vector of vectors. The following portion of code illustrates how this might be achieved:

```
#include <iostream>
#include <vector>
    .
    .
    .
typedef vector<int> va;

va va1, va2, va3, va4, va5, va6,
   va7, va8,va9, va10, va11, va12;

vector< vector<int> > iVectora;

// iterator for adjacency matrix
vector<vector<int> >::iterator p;

main()
{
     // create twelve vectors with twelve elements each
     va1.push_back(1); va1.push_back(1); va1.push_back(1);
     va1.push_back(0); va1.push_back(0); va1.push_back(1);
     va1.push_back(0); va1.push_back(0); va1.push_back(0);
     va1.push_back(0); va1.push_back(0); va1.push_back(0);

     va2.push_back(1); va2.push_back(1); va2.push_back(1);
     va2.push_back(0); va2.push_back(0); va2.push_back(0);
```

```
va2.push_back(0); va2.push_back(0); va2.push_back(0);
va2.push_back(0); va2.push_back(0); va2.push_back(0);

va3.push_back(1); va3.push_back(1); va3.push_back(1);
va3.push_back(1); va3.push_back(1); va3.push_back(1);
va3.push_back(0); va3.push_back(0); va3.push_back(0);
va3.push_back(0); va3.push_back(0); va3.push_back(0);
 .
 .
 .
va12.push_back(0); va12.push_back(0); va12.push_back(0);
va12.push_back(0); va12.push_back(0); va12.push_back(0);
va12.push_back(0); va12.push_back(0); va12.push_back(0);
va12.push_back(0); va12.push_back(1); va12.push_back(1);

// put the twelve va vectors into iVectora
// to form the iVectora adjacency matrix
iVectora.push_back(va1);
iVectora.push_back(va2);
iVectora.push_back(va3);
iVectora.push_back(va4);
iVectora.push_back(va5);
iVectora.push_back(va6);
iVectora.push_back(va7);
iVectora.push_back(va8);
iVectora.push_back(va9);
iVectora.push_back(va10);
iVectora.push_back(va11);
iVectora.push_back(va12);

p = iVectora.begin();
```

If there is a need to associate a value with a vertex, an additional one-dimensional array or vector can be used.

The adjacency matrix is very efficient when it comes to determining if an edge exists between vertices. For example, is there an edge between vertex 2 and vertex 3? The answer will be yes if the Boolean value of OLFC[2][3] is a one when using an array.

You will probably agree that it is very easy to represent an adjacency matrix as an array or an STL vector of vectors. In the next section, you will learn of yet another way to hold graph information: the adjacency list.

Adjacency List

Graph information stored in an adjacency list is really stored in a number of linked lists.

A linked list exists from one vertex to another vertex when there also exists an edge between the two vertices.

From Table 12.2, shown earlier, the following links can be established for the undirected OLFC graph:

```
[0] -> [1][.] -> [2][.] -> [5][x]
[1] -> [0][.] -> [2[x]
[2] -> [0][.] -> [1][.] - [3][.] -> [4][.] -> [5][x]
[3] -> [2][.] -> [4][x]
[4] -> [2][.] -> [3][.] -> [8][x]
[5] -> [0][.] -> [2][.] -> [6][.] -> [7][x]
[6] -> [5][x]
[7] -> [5][.] -> [9][x]
[8] -> [4][.] -> [10][x]
[9] -> [7][.] -> [10][x]
[10] -> [8][.] -> [9][.] -> [11][x]
[11] -> [10][x]
```

If the graph is weighted, then a weight value for each edge can be provided with each link. For example, if a distance of three miles existed between vertices 4 and 8 and a distance of five miles between vertices 8 and 10, we could write:

```
[8] -> [4][3][.] -> [10][5][x]
```

The adjacency list is very efficient if you want to find which vertices are adjacent to a particular vertex. For example, using Table 12.2, the vertices adjacent to vertex 5 are 0, 2, 6, and 7.

We'll examine the topic of graph traversals in the next section.

Graph Traversals

In this section, two popular techniques for graph traversal are examined. First, the depth-first search technique is discussed followed by the breadth-first search technique.

Full coded examples complete this section and provide you with concrete examples that can be expanded to other areas of graph theory.

Depth-First Search

In a depth-first graph traversal search the traversal goes from the indicated vertex as far (as deep) into the graph as possible. If your graph is described with an adjacency matrix, you would be moving down rows in the matrix. When the maximum depth has been found, the depth-first algorithm will back up and attempt to locate an adjacent vertex at the same depth.

To illustrate this concept, consider the following sample graph (Figure 12.7):

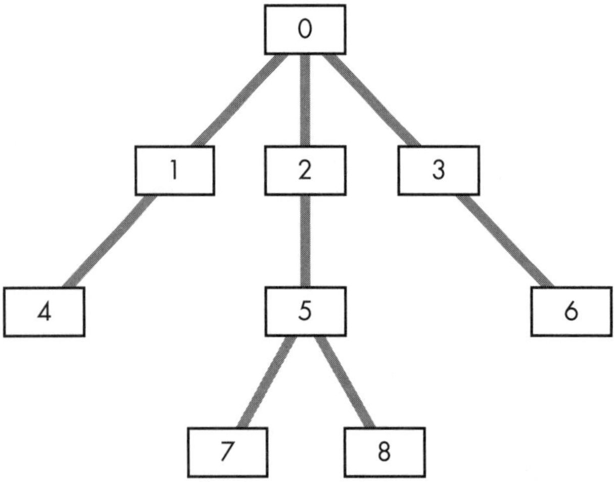

Figure 12.7
A sample graph used to investigate depth-first traversal.

From this sample graph an adjacency matrix can be created, as shown in Table 12.3.

Table 12.3 An Adjacency Matrix For the Sample Graph

	0	1	2	3	4	5	6	7	8
0	1	1	1	1	0	0	0	0	0
1	1	1	0	0	1	0	0	0	0
2	1	0	1	0	0	1	0	0	0
3	1	0	0	0	0	0	0	0	1
4	1	0	0	0	1	0	0	0	0
5	0	0	1	0	0	1	1	1	0
6	0	0	0	0	0	1	1	0	0
7	0	0	0	0	0	1	0	1	0
8	0	0	0	1	0	0	0	0	1

Using Figure 12.7 as a guide, we would anticipate a depth-first search to yield the following results if we start at vertex `0`:

`0` ➛ `1` ➛ `4`, then back up and track `2` ➛ `5` ➛ `7` ➛ `8`, then back up again and produce `3` ➛ `6`.

In the following sections, we'll implement this algorithm with traditional C++ arrays and then use an STL vector of vectors (`vector< vector<int> >`).

A Traditional C++ Implementation of Depth-First Search

An algorithm for a depth-first search will have a recursive form. Consider the following implementation, using a traditional C++ approach with arrays:

```
//  ArrayDepth.cpp
//  Program demonstrates how to do a
//  Depth-First search on an adjacency
//  matrix.
//  Chris H. Pappas and William H. Murray, 2000

#include <iostream>

using namespace std;

void WalkPath(int);

#define AryDim 9

int BeenHere[AryDim];

int MATRIX[AryDim][AryDim] = {{1, 1, 1, 1, 0, 0, 0, 0, 0},
                              {1, 1, 0, 0, 1, 0, 0, 0, 0},
                              {1, 0, 1, 0, 0, 1, 0, 0, 0},
                              {1, 0, 0, 1, 0, 0, 1, 0, 1},
                              {0, 1, 0, 0, 1, 0, 0, 0, 0},
                              {0, 0, 1, 0, 0, 1, 0, 1, 1},
                              {0, 0, 0, 1, 0, 0, 1, 0, 0},
                              {0, 0, 0, 0, 0, 1, 0, 1, 0},
                              {0, 0, 0, 0, 0, 1, 0, 0, 1}};


main()
{
  for (int row = 0; row < AryDim; row++) {
      if (!BeenHere[row])
          WalkPath(row);
  }
  cout << endl << endl;

  return(0);
}

void WalkPath(int row)
{
    cout << row << endl;
    BeenHere[row] = 1;
    for (int column = 0; column < AryDim; column++) {
        if ((MATRIX[row][column] == 1) && (!BeenHere[column]))
            WalkPath(column);
    }
}
```

The adjacency matrix, `MATRIX`, is a two-dimensional array with rows and columns. In a depth-first search, we'll start on a row with the chosen vertex (`0` in this example). A simple `for` loop in `main()` will do the job.

```
for (int row = 0; row < AryDim; row++) {
     if (!BeenHere[row])
          WalkPath(row);
}
```

If the algorithm has not been to this vertex, then we will proceed with a call to the recursive `WalkPath()` function. Note that since the `BeenHere[]` array is global, all positions are initialized to zero. In other words, the algorithm assumes that no vertices have to be accessed at this point.

```
void WalkPath(int row)
{
     cout << row << endl;
     BeenHere[row] = 1;
     for (int column = 0; column < AryDim; column++) {
          if ((MATRIX[row][column] == 1) && (!BeenHere[column]))
               WalkPath(column);
     }
}
```

If the algorithm calls the `WalkPath()` function, then the row location for the `MATRIX[]` array is marked to indicate that the algorithm has been to that location. The information is saved in a one-dimensional array, named `BeenHere[]`.

The search will be continued, column by column, moving ever deeper into the adjacency matrix. A `for` loop handles this traversal.

For all cases where there is a one at `MATRIX[row][column]` and where `BeenHere[column]` is not a one (indicating that the algorithm has never been to this vertex), the function, `WalkPath()`, will be called recursively.

The output for the sample graph is:

```
0
1
4
2
5
7
8
3
6
```

These are, of course, the anticipated results.

Since the code listing is fairly short, let's modify the code listing to perform a depth-first search on the adjacency matrix for the Ocean Lakes Family Campground. Use Figure 12.6 and Table 12.2, shown earlier, to construct the matrix shown in the following listing.

```
//  ArrayDepth.cpp
//  Program demonstrates how to do a
//  Depth-First search on an adjacency
//  matrix.
//  Chris H. Pappas and William H. Murray, 2000

#include <iostream>

using namespace std;

void WalkPath(int);

#define AryDim 12

int BeenHere[AryDim];

int OLFC[AryDim][AryDim] = {{1, 1, 1, 0, 0, 1, 0, 0, 0, 0, 0, 0},
                            {1, 1, 1, 0, 0, 0, 0, 0, 0, 0, 0, 0},
                            {1, 1, 1, 1, 1, 1, 0, 0, 0, 0, 0, 0},
                            {0, 0, 1, 1, 1, 0, 0, 0, 0, 0, 0, 0},
                            {0, 0, 1, 1, 1, 0, 0, 0, 1, 0, 0, 0},
                            {1, 0, 1, 0, 0, 1, 1, 1, 0, 0, 0, 0},
                            {0, 0, 0, 0, 0, 1, 1, 0, 0, 0, 0, 0},
                            {0, 0, 0, 0, 0, 1, 0, 1, 0, 1, 0, 0},
                            {0, 0, 0, 0, 1, 0, 0, 0, 1, 0, 1, 0},
                            {0, 0, 0, 0, 0, 0, 0, 1, 0, 1, 1, 0},
                            {0, 0, 0, 0, 0, 0, 0, 0, 1, 1, 1, 1},
                            {0, 0, 0, 0, 0, 0, 0, 0, 0, 0, 1, 1}};

main()
{
  for (int row = 0; row < AryDim; row++) {
      if (!BeenHere[row])
          WalkPath(row);
  }
  cout << endl << endl;

  return(0);
}

void WalkPath(int row)
{
    cout << row << endl;
    BeenHere[row] = 1;
    for (int column = 0; column < AryDim; column++) {
        if ((OLFC[row][column] == 1) && (!BeenHere[column]))
            WalkPath(column);
    }
}
```

The results provided by this application for a depth-first search of the OLFC adjacency matrix are:

```
0
1
2
3
4
8
10
9
7
5
6
11
```

We'll leave the verification of the results up to you. You should take the time to trace, with paper and pencil, through the adjacency matrix and see if you agree with the results.

An STL Implementation of Depth-First Search

The implementation of an STL depth-first algorithm requires the use of a vector of vectors. The concept of using a `vector< vector<int> >` was first discussed in Chapter 11. Structurally, the STL code will be very similar to the depth-first application implemented with arrays.

The following listing is for the complete STL implementation of a depth-first search on the OLFC adjacency matrix.

```
//  STLDepth.cpp
//  Program demonstrates how to do a depth-first
//  on an adjacency matrix using an STL
//  vector < vector<> >.
//  Chris H. Pappas and William H. Murray, 2000

#include <iostream>
#include <vector>

using namespace std;

void WalkPath(int);

#define VecDim 12

typedef vector<int> va, bh;
vector< vector<int> > iVect;
```

```
va va1, va2, va3, va4, va5, va6,
   va7, va8,va9, va10, va11, va12;
bh iBeenHere;

// iterator for adjacency matrix
vector<vector<int> >::iterator p;
// iterator for iBeenHere vector
vector<int>::iterator q;

main()
{
    // create twelve vectors with twelve elements each
    va1.push_back(1); va1.push_back(1); va1.push_back(1);
    va1.push_back(0); va1.push_back(0); va1.push_back(1);
    va1.push_back(0); va1.push_back(0); va1.push_back(0);
    va1.push_back(0); va1.push_back(0); va1.push_back(0);

    va2.push_back(1); va2.push_back(1); va2.push_back(1);
    va2.push_back(0); va2.push_back(0); va2.push_back(0);
    va2.push_back(0); va2.push_back(0); va2.push_back(0);
    va2.push_back(0); va2.push_back(0); va2.push_back(0);

    va3.push_back(1); va3.push_back(1); va3.push_back(1);
    va3.push_back(1); va3.push_back(1); va3.push_back(1);
    va3.push_back(0); va3.push_back(0); va3.push_back(0);
    va3.push_back(0); va3.push_back(0); va3.push_back(0);

    va4.push_back(0); va4.push_back(0); va4.push_back(1);
    va4.push_back(1); va4.push_back(1); va4.push_back(0);
    va4.push_back(0); va4.push_back(0); va4.push_back(0);
    va4.push_back(0); va4.push_back(0); va4.push_back(0);

    va5.push_back(0); va5.push_back(0); va5.push_back(1);
    va5.push_back(1); va5.push_back(1); va5.push_back(0);
    va5.push_back(0); va5.push_back(0); va5.push_back(1);
    va5.push_back(0); va5.push_back(0); va5.push_back(0);

    va6.push_back(1); va6.push_back(0); va6.push_back(1);
    va6.push_back(0); va6.push_back(0); va6.push_back(1);
    va6.push_back(1); va6.push_back(1); va6.push_back(0);
    va6.push_back(0); va6.push_back(0); va6.push_back(0);

    va7.push_back(0); va7.push_back(0); va7.push_back(0);
    va7.push_back(0); va7.push_back(0); va7.push_back(1);
    va7.push_back(1); va7.push_back(0); va7.push_back(0);
    va7.push_back(0); va7.push_back(0); va7.push_back(0);
```

```
va8.push_back(0); va8.push_back(0); va8.push_back(0);
va8.push_back(0); va8.push_back(0); va8.push_back(1);
va8.push_back(0); va8.push_back(1); va8.push_back(0);
va8.push_back(1); va8.push_back(0); va8.push_back(0);

va9.push_back(0); va9.push_back(0); va9.push_back(0);
va9.push_back(0); va9.push_back(1); va9.push_back(0);
va9.push_back(0); va9.push_back(0); va9.push_back(1);
va9.push_back(0); va9.push_back(1); va9.push_back(0);

va10.push_back(0); va10.push_back(0); va10.push_back(0);
va10.push_back(0); va10.push_back(0); va10.push_back(0);
va10.push_back(0); va10.push_back(1); va10.push_back(0);
va10.push_back(1); va10.push_back(1); va10.push_back(0);

va11.push_back(0); va11.push_back(0); va11.push_back(0);
va11.push_back(0); va11.push_back(0); va11.push_back(0);
va11.push_back(0); va11.push_back(0); va11.push_back(1);
va11.push_back(1); va11.push_back(1); va11.push_back(1);

va12.push_back(0); va12.push_back(0); va12.push_back(0);
va12.push_back(0); va12.push_back(0); va12.push_back(0);
va12.push_back(0); va12.push_back(0); va12.push_back(0);
va12.push_back(0); va12.push_back(1); va12.push_back(1);

// put the twelve va vectors into iVect
// to form the iVect adjacency matrix
iVect.push_back(va1);
iVect.push_back(va2);
iVect.push_back(va3);
iVect.push_back(va4);
iVect.push_back(va5);
iVect.push_back(va6);
iVect.push_back(va7);
iVect.push_back(va8);
iVect.push_back(va9);
iVect.push_back(va10);
iVect.push_back(va11);
iVect.push_back(va12);

// initialize all iBeenHere vector
// values to 0 (or any other value)
for(int i = 0; i < VecDim ; i++)
    iBeenHere.push_back(0);

// use iterators to point to start of
// vectors
```

```
    p = iVect.begin();
    q = iBeenHere.begin();

    for (int row = 0; row < VecDim; row++) {
        if (!(*(q + row)))
            WalkPath(row);
    }
    cout << endl << endl;

  return(0);
}

void WalkPath(int row)
{
    (*(q + row)) = 1;

    cout << row << endl;

    for (int column = 0; column < VecDim; column++) {
        if (((*(p + row))[column] == 1) && (!(*(q + column))))
            WalkPath(column);
    }
}
```

In this code implementation 12 vectors are created (va1 to va12). Each vector will be used to hold a row from the adjacency matrix. The iVect vector is actually a vector< vector<int> >. Here, iVect will eventually hold the 12 vectors (va1 to va12).

Another vector, iBeenHere, will be used to log locations that have already been accessed at least once.

The iterators for both iVect and iBeenHere are created at this time, as you can see in the following partial code listing:

```
typedef vector<int> va, bh;
vector< vector<int> > iVect;

va va1, va2, va3, va4, va5, va6,
   va7, va8,va9, va10, va11, va12;
bh iBeenHere;

// iterator for adjacency matrix
vector<vector<int> >::iterator p;
// iterator for iBeenHere vector
vector<int>::iterator q;
```

Each of the 12 vectors (va1 to va12) is initialized with the respective data from Table 12.2, shown earlier. The vector::push_back() member function is used for this purpose.

```
// create twelve vectors with twelve elements each
va1.push_back(1); va1.push_back(1); va1.push_back(1);
va1.push_back(0); va1.push_back(0); va1.push_back(1);
va1.push_back(0); va1.push_back(0); va1.push_back(0);
va1.push_back(0); va1.push_back(0); va1.push_back(0);

va2.push_back(1); va2.push_back(1); va2.push_back(1);
va2.push_back(0); va2.push_back(0); va2.push_back(0);
va2.push_back(0); va2.push_back(0); va2.push_back(0);
va2.push_back(0); va2.push_back(0); va2.push_back(0);
 .


  .
  .
va12.push_back(0); va12.push_back(0); va12.push_back(0);
va12.push_back(0); va12.push_back(0); va12.push_back(0);
va12.push_back(0); va12.push_back(0); va12.push_back(0);
va12.push_back(0); va12.push_back(1); va12.push_back(1);
```

The individual vectors are then placed in `iVect`, forming a two-dimensional array or matrix.

```
iVect.push_back(va1);
  .
  .
  .
iVect.push_back(va12);
```

Next, a simple `for` loop is used to initialize all of the `iBeenHere` vector elements to zero. A zero will be used to indicate that the vertex has not yet been visited.

```
// initialize all iBeenHere vector
// values to 0 (or any other value)
for(int i = 0; i < VecDim ; i++)
    iBeenHere.push_back(0);
```

The next portion of code uses pointer arithmetic to examine row locations in the adjacency matrix. The iterator, `q`, points to the beginning of the `iBeenHere` vector.

```
for (int row = 0; row < VecDim; row++) {
    if (!(*(q + row)))
        WalkPath(row);
}
```

The elements in the `iBeenHere` vector are examined by indexing across the variable using `(*(q + row))`. If the element value returned for any pointer position is a zero, then `WalkPath()` is called.

`WalkPath()` is called recursively. A row position is passed to this function. The corresponding `iBeenHere` element is then set to a one, again using pointer arithmetic. At this point, the row position is printed using the variable `row`.

```
void WalkPath(int row)
{
    (*(q + row)) = 1;

    cout << row << endl;

    for (int column = 0; column < VecDim; column++) {
        if (((*(p + row))[column] == 1) && (!(*(q + column))))
            WalkPath(column);
    }
}
```

The adjacency matrix is examined by manipulating both the row and column of the matrix using pointer arithmetic, `(*(p + row)[column])`. As the search is continued, column by column, we move ever deeper into the adjacency matrix. A `for` loop handles this traversal by incrementing the column position of the matrix.

Notice that the `WalkPath()` function is initially passed a row value. However, when this function is called recursively, it is subsequently passed a column value. This is the mechanism required to move down (deeper) into the adjacency matrix.

In the next section, a breadth-first search will be implemented. You'll see that it is very similar in form to the depth-first search.

Breadth-First Search

In a breadth-first graph traversal search, the traversal goes from the indicated vertex to as many vertices as possible at the same depth. If the graph is described with an adjacency matrix, the movement would be across columns in the matrix. When the maximum breadth has been found, the breadth-first algorithm will back up and attempt to locate an adjacent vertex at the next depth.

To illustrate this concept, let's revisit the graph used earlier in the depth-first search example (Figure 12.8).

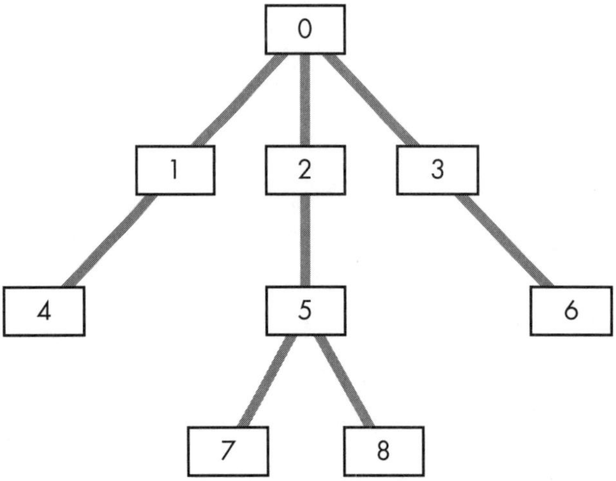

Figure 12.8
A sample graph used to investigate breadth-first traversal.

From this graph, the adjacency matrix, illustrated in Table 12.4, can be created.

Table 12.4 An Adjacency Matrix for the Sample Graph

	0	1	2	3	4	5	6	7	8
0	1	1	1	1	0	0	0	0	0
1	1	1	0	0	1	0	0	0	0
2	1	0	1	0	0	1	0	0	0
3	1	0	0	0	0	0	0	0	1
4	1	0	0	0	1	0	0	0	0
5	0	0	1	0	0	1	1	1	0
6	0	0	0	0	0	1	1	0	0
7	0	0	0	0	0	1	0	1	0
8	0	0	0	1	0	0	0	0	1

Using Figure 12.8 as a guide, we would anticipate a breadth-first search to yield the following results if we start at vertex `0`:

A `0` first, then down a row to yield `1` → `2` → `3`, then down another row for `4` → `5` → `6`, then down the last row to `7` → `8`.

As we did in the depth-first section, we'll implement this breadth-first algorithm with traditional C++ arrays and then use an STL vector or vectors (`vector< vector<int> >`).

A Traditional C++ Implementation of a Breadth-First Search

An algorithm for a breadth-first search will also have a recursive form. Here is the implementation using a traditional C++ approach with arrays. Notice the similarity of this program with the depth-search program listed earlier.

```
//   ArrayBreadth.cpp
//   Program demonstrates how to do a
//   Breadth-First search on an adjacency
//   matrix.
//   Chris H. Pappas and William H. Murray, 2000

#include <iostream>

using namespace std;

void WalkPath(int);

#define AryDim 9

int BeenHere[AryDim];

int MATRIX[AryDim][AryDim] = {{1, 1, 1, 1, 0, 0, 0, 0, 0},
                              {1, 1, 0, 0, 1, 0, 0, 0, 0},
                              {1, 0, 1, 0, 0, 1, 0, 0, 0},
                              {1, 0, 0, 1, 0, 0, 1, 0, 1},
                              {0, 1, 0, 0, 1, 0, 0, 0, 0},
                              {0, 0, 1, 0, 0, 1, 0, 1, 1},
                              {0, 0, 0, 1, 0, 0, 1, 0, 0},
                              {0, 0, 0, 0, 0, 1, 0, 1, 0},
                              {0, 0, 0, 0, 0, 1, 0, 0, 1}};


main()
{
  for (int column = 0; column < AryDim; column++) {
      if (!BeenHere[column])
          WalkPath(column);
  }
  cout << endl << endl;

  return(0);
}

void WalkPath(int column)
{
    cout << column << endl;
    BeenHere[column] = 1;
    for (int row = 0; row < AryDim; row++) {
        if ((MATRIX[column][row] == 1) && (!BeenHere[column]))
            WalkPath(column);
    }
}
```

The adjacency matrix, `MATRIX`, is a two-dimensional array with rows and columns. In a breadth-first search, we'll start on a column with the chosen vertex (`0` in this example). Again, a simple `for` loop in `main()` will do the job.

```
for (int column = 0; column < AryDim; column++) {
    if (!BeenHere[column])
        WalkPath(column);
}
```

If the algorithm has not been to this vertex, then we will proceed with the recursive `WalkPath()` function. Here again, the `BeenHere[]` array is global so all positions are initialized to zero. This means that the algorithm has not yet been to any vertices.

```
void WalkPath(int column)
{
    cout << column << endl;
    BeenHere[column] = 1;

    for (int row = 0; row < AryDim; row++) {
        if ((MATRIX[column][row] == 1) && (!BeenHere[column]))
            WalkPath(column);
    }
}
```

When the `WalkPath()` function is called, the row location for the `MATRIX[]` array is marked to indicate that the algorithm has been to that location. The information is saved in a one-dimensional array, named `BeenHere[]`.

We now want to continue our search, row by row, moving across the adjacency matrix. A `for` loop handles this traversal.

For all cases where there is a one at `MATRIX[column][row]` and where `BeenHere[column]` is not a one (indicating that the algorithm has never been to this vertex), the function will be called recursively.

The output for the sample graph is:

```
0
1
2
3
4
5
6
7
8
```

These are, of course, the anticipated results. Since the code listing is fairly short, let's see the results of a breadth-first search on the adjacency matrix for the Ocean Lakes Family Campground. Use Figure 12.6 and Table 12.2, shown earlier, to construct the matrix shown in the following listing:

```
//  ArrayBreadth.cpp
//  Program demonstrates how to do a
//  Breadth-First search on an adjacency
//  matrix.
//  Chris H. Pappas and William H. Murray, 2000

#include <iostream>

using namespace std;

void WalkPath(int);

#define AryDim 12

int BeenHere[AryDim];

int OLFC[AryDim][AryDim] = {{1, 1, 1, 0, 0, 1, 0, 0, 0, 0, 0, 0},
                            {1, 1, 1, 0, 0, 0, 0, 0, 0, 0, 0, 0},
                            {1, 1, 1, 1, 1, 1, 0, 0, 0, 0, 0, 0},
                            {0, 0, 1, 1, 1, 0, 0, 0, 0, 0, 0, 0},
                            {0, 0, 1, 1, 1, 0, 0, 0, 1, 0, 0, 0},
                            {1, 0, 1, 0, 0, 1, 1, 1, 0, 0, 0, 0},
                            {0, 0, 0, 0, 0, 1, 1, 0, 0, 0, 0, 0},
                            {0, 0, 0, 0, 0, 1, 0, 1, 0, 1, 0, 0},
                            {0, 0, 0, 0, 1, 0, 0, 0, 1, 0, 1, 0},
                            {0, 0, 0, 0, 0, 0, 0, 1, 0, 1, 1, 0},
                            {0, 0, 0, 0, 0, 0, 0, 0, 1, 1, 1, 1},
                            {0, 0, 0, 0, 0, 0, 0, 0, 0, 0, 1, 1}};

main()
{
  for (int column = 0; column < AryDim; column++) {
      if (!BeenHere[column])
          WalkPath(column);
  }
  cout << endl << endl;

  return(0);
}

void WalkPath(int column)
{
```

```
    cout << column << endl;
    BeenHere[column] = 1;
    for (int row = 0; row < AryDim; row++) {
        if ((OLFC[column][row] == 1) && (!BeenHere[column]))
            WalkPath(column);
    }
}
```

The results provided by this application for a breadth-first search of the OLFC adjacency matrix are:

```
0
1
2
3
4
5
6
7
8
9
10
11
```

Again, we'll leave the verification of the results up to you. You might want to trace through the adjacency matrix and see if you agree with the results.

An STL Implementation of a Breadth-First Search

The implementation of an STL breadth-first algorithm also requires the use of a vector of vectors. Structurally, this will be very similar to the depth-first STL application implemented in an earlier section.

The following listing is for the complete STL implementation of a breadth-first search on the adjacency matrix:

```
//  STLBreadth.cpp
//  Program demonstrates how to do a breadth-first
//  on an adjacency matrix using an STL
//  vector < vector<> >.
//  Chris H. Pappas and William H. Murray, 2000

#include <iostream>s
#include <vector>

using namespace std;

void WalkPath(int);
```

```
#define VecDim 12

typedef vector<int> va, bh;
vector< vector<int> > iVect;

va va1, va2, va3, va4, va5, va6,
   va7, va8,va9, va10, va11, va12;
bh iBeenHere;

// iterator for adjacency matrix
vector<vector<int> >::iterator p;
// iterator for iBeenHere vector
vector<int>::iterator q;

main()
{
    // create twelve vectors with twelve elements each
    va1.push_back(1); va1.push_back(1); va1.push_back(1);
    va1.push_back(0); va1.push_back(0); va1.push_back(1);
    va1.push_back(0); va1.push_back(0); va1.push_back(0);
    va1.push_back(0); va1.push_back(0); va1.push_back(0);

    va2.push_back(1); va2.push_back(1); va2.push_back(1);
    va2.push_back(0); va2.push_back(0); va2.push_back(0);
    va2.push_back(0); va2.push_back(0); va2.push_back(0);
    va2.push_back(0); va2.push_back(0); va2.push_back(0);

    va3.push_back(1); va3.push_back(1); va3.push_back(1);
    va3.push_back(1); va3.push_back(1); va3.push_back(1);
    va3.push_back(0); va3.push_back(0); va3.push_back(0);
    va3.push_back(0); va3.push_back(0); va3.push_back(0);

    va4.push_back(0); va4.push_back(0); va4.push_back(1);
    va4.push_back(1); va4.push_back(1); va4.push_back(0);
    va4.push_back(0); va4.push_back(0); va4.push_back(0);
    va4.push_back(0); va4.push_back(0); va4.push_back(0);

    va5.push_back(0); va5.push_back(0); va5.push_back(1);
    va5.push_back(1); va5.push_back(1); va5.push_back(0);
    va5.push_back(0); va5.push_back(0); va5.push_back(1);
    va5.push_back(0); va5.push_back(0); va5.push_back(0);

    va6.push_back(1); va6.push_back(0); va6.push_back(1);
    va6.push_back(0); va6.push_back(0); va6.push_back(1);
    va6.push_back(1); va6.push_back(1); va6.push_back(0);
    va6.push_back(0); va6.push_back(0); va6.push_back(0);
```

```
va7.push_back(0); va7.push_back(0); va7.push_back(0);
va7.push_back(0); va7.push_back(0); va7.push_back(1);
va7.push_back(1); va7.push_back(0); va7.push_back(0);
va7.push_back(0); va7.push_back(0); va7.push_back(0);

va8.push_back(0); va8.push_back(0); va8.push_back(0);
va8.push_back(0); va8.push_back(0); va8.push_back(1);
va8.push_back(0); va8.push_back(1); va8.push_back(0);
va8.push_back(1); va8.push_back(0); va8.push_back(0);

va9.push_back(0); va9.push_back(0); va9.push_back(0);
va9.push_back(0); va9.push_back(1); va9.push_back(0);
va9.push_back(0); va9.push_back(0); va9.push_back(1);
va9.push_back(0); va9.push_back(1); va9.push_back(0);

va10.push_back(0); va10.push_back(0); va10.push_back(0);
va10.push_back(0); va10.push_back(0); va10.push_back(0);
va10.push_back(0); va10.push_back(1); va10.push_back(0);
va10.push_back(1); va10.push_back(1); va10.push_back(0);

va11.push_back(0); va11.push_back(0); va11.push_back(0);
va11.push_back(0); va11.push_back(0); va11.push_back(0);
va11.push_back(0); va11.push_back(0); va11.push_back(1);
va11.push_back(1); va11.push_back(1); va11.push_back(1);

va12.push_back(0); va12.push_back(0); va12.push_back(0);
va12.push_back(0); va12.push_back(0); va12.push_back(0);
va12.push_back(0); va12.push_back(0); va12.push_back(0);
va12.push_back(0); va12.push_back(1); va12.push_back(1);

// put the twelve va vectors into iVect
// to form the iVect adjacency matrix
iVect.push_back(va1);
iVect.push_back(va2);
iVect.push_back(va3);
iVect.push_back(va4);
iVect.push_back(va5);
iVect.push_back(va6);
iVect.push_back(va7);
iVect.push_back(va8);
iVect.push_back(va9);
iVect.push_back(va10);
iVect.push_back(va11);
iVect.push_back(va12);

// initialize all iBeenHere vector
// values to 0 (or any other value)
```

```
    for(int i = 0; i < VecDim ; i++)
        iBeenHere.push_back(0);

    // use iterators to point to start of
    // vectors
    p = iVect.begin();
    q = iBeenHere.begin();

    for (int column = 0; column < VecDim; column++) {
        if (!(*(q + column)))
            WalkPath(column);
    }
    cout << endl << endl;

  return(0);
}

void WalkPath(int column)
{
    (*(q + column)) = 1;

    cout << column << endl;

    for (int row = 0; row < VecDim; row++) {
        if (((*(p + column))[row] == 1) && (!(*(q + column))))
            WalkPath(column);
    }
}
```

In this code implementation, 12 vectors are created (`va1` to `va12`), just as they were in the STL depth-first application. Each vector is used to hold a row from the adjacency matrix. The `iVect` vector is a `vector< vector<int> >` that will eventually hold the 12 vectors (`va1` to `va12`).

The vector, `iBeenHere`, is used to log locations that have already been accessed at least once.

The individual vector elements are initialized, as they were in the depth-first application, and then used to form the `vector< vector<int> >` matrix.

Pointer arithmetic is used to examine column locations in the adjacency matrix. The iterator, `q`, points to the beginning of the `iBeenHere` vector.

```
    for (int column = 0; column < VecDim; column++) {
        if (!(*(q + column)))
            WalkPath(column);
    }
```

The elements in the `iBeenHere` vector are examined by indexing across the variable using `(*(q + column))`. If the element value returned for any pointer position is a zero, then the `WalkPath()` function is called.

The `WalkPath()` function is called recursively, as it was in the depth-first search application. A column position is now passed to this function. The corresponding `iBeenHere` element is then set to a one, again using pointer arithmetic. At this point, the column position is printed using the variable `column`.

```
void WalkPath(int column)
{
    (*(q + column)) = 1;

    cout << column << endl;

    for (int row = 0; row < VecDim; row++) {
        if (((*(p + column))[row] == 1) && (!(*(q + column))))
            WalkPath(column);
    }
}
```

The adjacency matrix is examined by manipulating both the column and the row. In this application, the search is continued, row by row. The movement is across the adjacency matrix, as far as possible. Here a `for` loop is used for this traversal by incrementing the row position of the matrix.

The `WalkPath()` function is initially passed a column value. However, when this function is called recursively, it is subsequently passed a row value. This is the mechanism required to traverse the adjacency matrix.

Graph Application

In addition to vertices, weighted graphs contain information on the weight or value of the edge used to connect vertices. This information is very useful in determining, for example, the minimum distance between a given pair of vertices. The weight value, in reality, does not have to be a distance. The weight can be used to represent almost anything, such as distance, cost, time to perform a task, and so on.

In this section, we'll examine the implementation of Floyd's algorithm. Floyd's algorithm is most frequently used to find minimum values between vertices. However, with just a few minor changes, it could also be used to find maximum values. Dijkstra's shortest path algorithm is an alternate means of determining the same information.

For this section, we'll use the information developed for the Ocean Lakes Family Campground created earlier in this chapter. Using the information provided in Figure 12.6, shown earlier, let's create a table of vertices and edge values that will represent OCFC buildings and the distances between them. This information is shown in Table 12.5.

Table 12.5 Vertices and Edge Values For the OLFC

Building to Building (vertex to vertex)	*Distance (edge weight)*
0 to 1	2
0 to 2	2
0 to 5	1
1 to 2	1
2 to 3	2
2 to 4	2
3 to 4	1
4 to 8	1
5 to 6	1
5 to 7	2
7 to 9	1
8 to 10	3
9 to 10	1
10 to 11	1

The distance values given in Table 12.5 do not have units. The values could be feet, miles, meters, or kilometers. From Table 12.5, the vertex and distance information is added to a table that can easily be translated to an adjacency matrix. Table 12.6 is actually a modified version of Table 12.2 developed earlier in this chapter.

Table 12.6 The OLFC Adjacency Matrix with Distances Added Between Vertices

	0	1	2	3	4	5	6	7	8	9	10	11
0	1/0	1/2	1/2	0	0	1/1	0	0	0	0	0	0
1	1/2	1/0	1/1	0	0	0	0	0	0	0	0	0
2	1/2	1/1	1/0	1/2	1/2	1/2	0	0	0	0	0	0
3	0	0	1/2	1/0	1/1	0	0	0	0	0	0	0
4	0	0	1/2	1/1	1/0	0	0	0	1/1	0	0	0
5	1/1	0	1/2	0	0	1/0	1/1	1/2	0	0	0	0
6	0	0	0	0	0	1/1	1/0	0	0	0	0	0
7	0	0	0	0	0	1/2	0	1/0	0	1/1	0	0
8	0	0	0	0	1/1	0	0	0	1/0	0	1/3	0
9	0	0	0	0	0	0	0	1/1	0	1/0	1/1	0
10	0	0	0	0	0	0	0	0	1/3	1/1	1/0	1/1
11	0	0	0	0	0	0	0	0	0	0	1/1	1/0

Note that the vertex information is given as the first integer, followed by a slash and a second integer. The vertex information is used to indicate that a direct path exists from one vertex to another. The second integer is the weight or edge value between vertices.

In the next section, you'll see how Floyd's algorithm can be implemented for this adjacency matrix. With the algorithm in place, it will be possible to find the shortest distance between any two connected vertices.

Floyd's Algorithm Implementation with Arrays

The implementation of Floyd's algorithm is usually achieved with three `for` loops. The `for` loops allow the adjacency array to be traversed in such a manner that all reachable vertices will be considered.

```
for (i = 0; i < AryDim; i++)
    for (j = 0; j < AryDim; j++)
        for (k = 0; k < AryDim; k++)
            if (OLFC[j][k] >= (OLFC[j][i] + OLFC[i][k]))
                OLFC[j][k] = OLFC[j][i] + OLFC[i][k];
```

The `if` statement is included in the Floyd algorithm in order that the smallest of two values will be selected—`OLFC[j][k]` or `(OLFC[j][i] + OLFC[i][k])`—during the traversal of the `for` loops. We'll investigate this operation in a little more detail in the next section.

In order to prepare Table 12.6 for inclusion in a matrix, two special conditions must be considered. First, the distance from a vertex to itself is zero. Second, if the finishing vertex is not reachable directly from the starting vertex, a special value is needed (i.e., no distance value is included in a table's cell). A zero cannot be used because that would represent a minimal distance. Infinity cannot be used because that value cannot be represented as an integer number. The solution is to use a carefully selected large integer value. The value selected must be outside the range of values used by the graph.

Satisfy yourself that the `OLFC[AryDim][AryDim]` array used in the program listing meets these requirements. An integer value of 100 is used as the large integer value. Note also that this array only includes the weighted values shown in Table 12.6.

```
//  ArrayFloyd.cpp
//  Program finds the minimum distances
//  between vertices in a weighted adjacency matrix
//  using Floyd's algorithm.
//  Chris H. Pappas and William H. Murray, 2000

#include <iostream>

using namespace std;

#define AryDim 12
```

```
int OLFC[AryDim][AryDim] = {{0, 2, 2, 100, 100, 1,
                              100, 100, 100, 100, 100, 100},
                             {2, 0, 1, 100, 100, 100,
                              100, 100, 100, 100, 100, 100},
                             {2, 1, 0, 2, 2, 2,
                              100, 100, 100, 100, 100, 100},
                             {100, 100, 2, 0, 1, 100, 100,
                              100,100, 100, 100, 100},
                             {100, 100, 2, 1, 0, 100, 100,
                              100, 1, 100, 100, 100},
                             {1, 100, 2, 100, 100, 0,
                              1, 2, 100, 100, 100, 100},
                             {100, 100, 100, 100, 100, 1,
                              0, 100, 100, 100, 100, 100},
                             {100, 100, 100, 100, 100, 2,
                              100, 0, 100, 1, 100, 100},
                             {100, 100, 100, 100, 1, 100,
                              100, 100, 0, 100, 3, 100},
                             {100, 100, 100, 100, 100, 100,
                              100, 1, 100, 0, 1, 100},
                             {100, 100, 100, 100, 100, 100,
                              100, 100, 3, 1, 0, 1},
                             {100, 100, 100, 100, 100, 100,
                              100, 100, 100, 100, 1, 0}};

main()
{
    int i, j, k;

    // determine minimum distance between vertices
    // using Floyd's algorithm
    for (i = 0; i < AryDim; i++)
        for (j = 0; j < AryDim; j++)
            for (k = 0; k < AryDim; k++)
                if (OLFC[j][k] >= (OLFC[j][i] + OLFC[i][k]))
                   OLFC[j][k] = OLFC[j][i] + OLFC[i][k];

    // print distance information to the screen
    for (j = 0; j < AryDim; j++)  {
        for (k = 0; k < AryDim; k++) {
             if ((OLFC[j][k] != 100) && (OLFC[j][k] != 0))
                cout << "From vertex " << j
                     << " to vertex " << k
                     << " the minimum distance is: "
                     << OLFC[j][k] << endl;
        }
        cout << endl;
    }
    cout << endl << endl;

    return(0);
}
```

The conditional statement,

```
if ((OLFC[j][k] != 100) && (OLFC[j][k] != 0))
```

is used to eliminate the unreachable possibilities and the cases where movement is from and to the same vertex.

A partial listing of the output from this application is shown in the following listing:

```
From vertex 0 to vertex 1 the minimum distance is: 2
From vertex 0 to vertex 2 the minimum distance is: 2
From vertex 0 to vertex 3 the minimum distance is: 4
From vertex 0 to vertex 4 the minimum distance is: 4
From vertex 0 to vertex 5 the minimum distance is: 1
From vertex 0 to vertex 6 the minimum distance is: 2
From vertex 0 to vertex 7 the minimum distance is: 3
From vertex 0 to vertex 8 the minimum distance is: 5
From vertex 0 to vertex 9 the minimum distance is: 4
From vertex 0 to vertex 10 the minimum distance is: 5
From vertex 0 to vertex 11 the minimum distance is: 6

From vertex 1 to vertex 0 the minimum distance is: 2
From vertex 1 to vertex 2 the minimum distance is: 1
From vertex 1 to vertex 3 the minimum distance is: 3
From vertex 1 to vertex 4 the minimum distance is: 3
From vertex 1 to vertex 5 the minimum distance is: 3
From vertex 1 to vertex 6 the minimum distance is: 4
From vertex 1 to vertex 7 the minimum distance is: 5
From vertex 1 to vertex 8 the minimum distance is: 4
From vertex 1 to vertex 9 the minimum distance is: 6
From vertex 1 to vertex 10 the minimum distance is: 7
From vertex 1 to vertex 11 the minimum distance is: 8
        .
        .
        .
From vertex 10 to vertex 0 the minimum distance is: 5
From vertex 10 to vertex 1 the minimum distance is: 7
From vertex 10 to vertex 2 the minimum distance is: 6
From vertex 10 to vertex 3 the minimum distance is: 5
From vertex 10 to vertex 4 the minimum distance is: 4
From vertex 10 to vertex 5 the minimum distance is: 4
From vertex 10 to vertex 6 the minimum distance is: 5
From vertex 10 to vertex 7 the minimum distance is: 2
From vertex 10 to vertex 8 the minimum distance is: 3
From vertex 10 to vertex 9 the minimum distance is: 1
From vertex 10 to vertex 11 the minimum distance is: 1
```

```
From vertex 11 to vertex 0 the minimum distance is: 6
From vertex 11 to vertex 1 the minimum distance is: 8
From vertex 11 to vertex 2 the minimum distance is: 7
From vertex 11 to vertex 3 the minimum distance is: 6
From vertex 11 to vertex 4 the minimum distance is: 5
From vertex 11 to vertex 5 the minimum distance is: 5
From vertex 11 to vertex 6 the minimum distance is: 6
From vertex 11 to vertex 7 the minimum distance is: 3
From vertex 11 to vertex 8 the minimum distance is: 4
From vertex 11 to vertex 9 the minimum distance is: 2
From vertex 11 to vertex 10 the minimum distance is: 1
```

As an exercise, you might want to trace a path through the three `for` loops and confirm the operation of the algorithm. The shortest paths are easy to check using Figure 12.6 and the information provided in Table 12.5.

Floyd's Algorithm Details

Floyd's algorithm uses three `for` loops. In order to study how the process of determining the shortest path between vertices is calculated and stored, we should be able to track the changes to the array during each pass through the `for` loops.

Modify the original program listing to include the following code. You can eliminate the portion of code from the original listing that printed the output from the application.

```
// determine minimum distance between vertices
// using Floyd's algorithm
for (i = 0; i < AryDim; i++) {
     cout << endl << "when i = " << i << endl;
     for (j = 0; j < AryDim; j++) {
          for (k = 0; k < AryDim; k++) {
               if (OLFC[j][k] >= (OLFC[j][i] + OLFC[i][k]))
                  OLFC[j][k] = OLFC[j][i] + OLFC[i][k];
               if (OLFC[j][k] == 100)
                   cout << "-   ";
               else
                   cout << OLFC[j][k] << "    ";
          }
     cout << endl;
     }
}
```

The formatted output from this operation allows us to view the contents of the array. Here is a partial listing of the output for the OLFC when the previous modification is made to the code. Notice that in this output, the large integer values used to indicate that there is no direct path between specific vertices have been replaced with dashes.

```
when i = 0
0  2  2  -  -  1  -  -  -  -  -  -
2  0  1  -  -  3  -  -  -  -  -  -
2  1  0  2  2  2  -  -  -  -  -  -
-  -  2  0  1  -  -  -  -  -  -  -
-  -  2  1  0  -  -  -  1  -  -  -
1  3  2  -  -  0  1  2  -  -  -  -
-  -  -  -  -  1  0  -  -  -  -  -
-  -  -  -  -  2  -  0  -  1  -  -
-  -  -  -  1  -  -  -  0  -  3  -
-  -  -  -  -  -  -  1  -  0  1  -
-  -  -  -  -  -  -  -  3  1  0  1
-  -  -  -  -  -  -  -  -  -  1  0

when i = 1
0  2  2  -  -  1  -  -  -  -  -  -
2  0  1  -  -  3  -  -  -  -  -  -
2  1  0  2  2  2  -  -  -  -  -  -
-  -  2  0  1  -  -  -  -  -  -  -
-  -  2  1  0  -  -  -  1  -  -  -
1  3  2  -  -  0  1  2  -  -  -  -
-  -  -  -  -  1  0  -  -  -  -  -
-  -  -  -  -  2  -  0  -  1  -  -
-  -  -  -  1  -  -  -  0  -  3  -
-  -  -  -  -  -  -  1  -  0  1  -
-  -  -  -  -  -  -  -  3  1  0  1
-  -  -  -  -  -  -  -  -  -  1  0

when i = 2
0  2  2  4  4  1  -  -  -  -  -  -
2  0  1  3  3  3  -  -  -  -  -  -
2  1  0  2  2  2  -  -  -  -  -  -
4  3  2  0  1  4  -  -  -  -  -  -
4  3  2  1  0  4  -  -  1  -  -  -
1  3  2  4  4  0  1  2  -  -  -  -
-  -  -  -  -  1  0  -  -  -  -  -
-  -  -  -  -  2  -  0  -  1  -  -
-  -  -  -  1  -  -  -  0  -  3  -
-  -  -  -  -  -  -  1  -  0  1  -
-  -  -  -  -  -  -  -  3  1  0  1
-  -  -  -  -  -  -  -  -  -  1  0
```

.

.

.

```
when i = 11
0  2  2  4  4  1  2  3  5  4  5  6
2  0  1  3  3  3  4  5  4  6  7  8
2  1  0  2  2  2  3  4  3  5  6  7
4  3  2  0  1  4  5  6  2  6  5  6
4  3  2  1  0  4  5  6  1  5  4  5
1  3  2  4  4  0  1  2  5  3  4  5
2  4  3  5  5  1  0  3  6  4  5  6
3  5  4  6  6  2  3  0  5  1  2  3
5  4  3  2  1  5  6  5  0  4  3  4
4  6  5  6  5  3  4  1  4  0  1  2
5  7  6  5  4  4  5  2  3  1  0  1
6  8  7  6  5  5  6  3  4  2  1  0
```

Recall that the game plan is to examine all possible paths between vertices and retain only the shortest path. This is achieved with the following conditional statement, but watch out for the array indices manipulations!

```
if (OLFC[j][k] >= (OLFC[j][i] + OLFC[i][k]))
    OLFC[j][k] = OLFC[j][i] + OLFC[i][k];
```

As an example, return to the partial listing of the output and examine the element at column position three and row zero when the variable `i` is equal to one (a value of "-" or 100). Notice that when the variable `i` changes to two, this element has been changed to a four. Let's see how this happens.

For the following conditional statement, where `i = 2`, `j = 0`, and `k = 3`:

```
if (OLFC[j][k] >= (OLFC[j][i] + OLFC[i][k]))

OLFC[j][k] = OLFC[0][3] = 100
OLFC[j][i] = OLFC[0][2] = 2
OLFC[i][k] = OLFC[2][3] = 2
```

since `100 >= 2 + 2`, the conditional statement is true and the value held at cell location `OLFC[0][3]` will be changed from `100` to a `4`.

The process continues until the outer loop has been processed 12 times, arriving at the values shown for `i = 11` in the earlier partial listing.

The values in the array, at this point, represent the shortest paths from a given vertex to another. For example, the first row represents vertex `0`. Each column represents another vertex from `0` to `11`. So, the shortest distance from vertex `0` to vertex `11` is a value of `6`.

Floyd's Algorithm Implementation with STL Vectors

In the previous example you may have noticed that the array used in the program only included the weight or edge information from Table 12.6. There is no easy way to create a single array that would contain both the vertex and edge information. However, we can create a vector of pairs with STL. The matrix can then be held in a vector of vector pairs, with the first element in the pair representing the vertex information and the second element in the pair representing the edge information.

Examine the following STL implementation of Floyd's algorithm. As you look at the listing, notice how the information from Table 12.6 is first saved as a pair in the vector. Then, as we have done before, that information is used to create a vector of vector pairs.

```
//   STLFloyd.cpp
//   Program demonstrates how to implement
//   the Floyd minimum distance algorithm
//   using an STL
//   Chris H. Pappas and William H. Murray, 2000

#pragma warning(disable:4786)

#include <iostream>
#include <vector>

using namespace std;

#define VecDim 12

typedef struct pair<int, int> ic_PAIR;
typedef vector<ic_PAIR> va;
vector< vector<ic_PAIR> > iVect;

va va1, va2, va3, va4, va5, va6,
   va7, va8,va9, va10, va11, va12;

// iterator for adjacency matrix
vector<vector<ic_PAIR> >::iterator p;

main()
{
    // create twelve vectors with twelve elements each
    va1.push_back(make_pair(1, 0));
    va1.push_back(make_pair(1, 2));
    va1.push_back(make_pair(1, 2));
    va1.push_back(make_pair(0, 100));
    va1.push_back(make_pair(0, 100));
    va1.push_back(make_pair(1, 1));
    va1.push_back(make_pair(0, 100));
    va1.push_back(make_pair(0, 100));
    va1.push_back(make_pair(0, 100));
    va1.push_back(make_pair(0, 100));
    va1.push_back(make_pair(0, 100));
    va1.push_back(make_pair(0, 100));
```

```
va2.push_back(make_pair(1, 2));
va2.push_back(make_pair(1, 0));
va2.push_back(make_pair(1, 1));
va2.push_back(make_pair(0, 100));
va2.push_back(make_pair(0, 100));
va2.push_back(make_pair(0, 100));
va2.push_back(make_pair(0, 100));
va2.push_back(make_pair(0, 100));
va2.push_back(make_pair(0, 100));
va2.push_back(make_pair(0, 100));
va2.push_back(make_pair(0, 100));
va2.push_back(make_pair(0, 100));

va3.push_back(make_pair(1, 2));
va3.push_back(make_pair(1, 1));
va3.push_back(make_pair(1, 0));
va3.push_back(make_pair(1, 2));
va3.push_back(make_pair(1, 2));
va3.push_back(make_pair(1, 2));
va3.push_back(make_pair(0, 100));
va3.push_back(make_pair(0, 100));
va3.push_back(make_pair(0, 100));
va3.push_back(make_pair(0, 100));
va3.push_back(make_pair(0, 100));
va3.push_back(make_pair(0, 100));

va4.push_back(make_pair(0, 100));
va4.push_back(make_pair(0, 100));
va4.push_back(make_pair(1, 2));
va4.push_back(make_pair(1, 0));
va4.push_back(make_pair(1, 1));
va4.push_back(make_pair(0, 100));
va4.push_back(make_pair(0, 100));
va4.push_back(make_pair(0, 100));
va4.push_back(make_pair(0, 100));
va4.push_back(make_pair(0, 100));
va4.push_back(make_pair(0, 100));
va4.push_back(make_pair(0, 100));

va5.push_back(make_pair(0, 100));
va5.push_back(make_pair(0, 100));
va5.push_back(make_pair(1, 2));
va5.push_back(make_pair(1, 1));
va5.push_back(make_pair(1, 0));
va5.push_back(make_pair(0, 100));
va5.push_back(make_pair(0, 100));
va5.push_back(make_pair(0, 100));
va5.push_back(make_pair(1, 1));
```

```
va5.push_back(make_pair(0, 100));
va5.push_back(make_pair(0, 100));
va5.push_back(make_pair(0, 100));

va6.push_back(make_pair(1, 1));
va6.push_back(make_pair(0, 100));
va6.push_back(make_pair(1, 2));
va6.push_back(make_pair(0, 100));
va6.push_back(make_pair(0, 100));
va6.push_back(make_pair(1, 0));
va6.push_back(make_pair(1, 1));
va6.push_back(make_pair(1, 2));
va6.push_back(make_pair(0, 100));
va6.push_back(make_pair(0, 100));
va6.push_back(make_pair(0, 100));
va6.push_back(make_pair(0, 100));

va7.push_back(make_pair(0, 100));
va7.push_back(make_pair(0, 100));
va7.push_back(make_pair(0, 100));
va7.push_back(make_pair(0, 100));
va7.push_back(make_pair(0, 100));
va7.push_back(make_pair(1, 1));
va7.push_back(make_pair(1, 0));
va7.push_back(make_pair(0, 100));
va7.push_back(make_pair(0, 100));
va7.push_back(make_pair(0, 100));
va7.push_back(make_pair(0, 100));
va7.push_back(make_pair(0, 100));

va8.push_back(make_pair(0, 100));
va8.push_back(make_pair(0, 100));
va8.push_back(make_pair(0, 100));
va8.push_back(make_pair(0, 100));
va8.push_back(make_pair(0, 100));
va8.push_back(make_pair(1, 2));
va8.push_back(make_pair(0, 100));
va8.push_back(make_pair(1, 0));
va8.push_back(make_pair(0, 100));
va8.push_back(make_pair(1, 1));
va8.push_back(make_pair(0, 100));
va8.push_back(make_pair(0, 100));

va9.push_back(make_pair(0, 100));
va9.push_back(make_pair(0, 100));
va9.push_back(make_pair(0, 100));
va9.push_back(make_pair(0, 100));
va9.push_back(make_pair(1, 1));
```

```
va9.push_back(make_pair(0, 100));
va9.push_back(make_pair(0, 100));
va9.push_back(make_pair(0, 100));
va9.push_back(make_pair(1, 0));
va9.push_back(make_pair(0, 100));
va9.push_back(make_pair(1, 3));
va9.push_back(make_pair(0, 100));

va10.push_back(make_pair(0, 100));
va10.push_back(make_pair(0, 100));
va10.push_back(make_pair(0, 100));
va10.push_back(make_pair(0, 100));
va10.push_back(make_pair(0, 100));
va10.push_back(make_pair(0, 100));
va10.push_back(make_pair(0, 100));
va10.push_back(make_pair(1, 1));
va10.push_back(make_pair(0, 100));
va10.push_back(make_pair(1, 0));
va10.push_back(make_pair(1, 1));
va10.push_back(make_pair(0, 100));

va11.push_back(make_pair(0, 100));
va11.push_back(make_pair(0, 100));
va11.push_back(make_pair(0, 100));
va11.push_back(make_pair(0, 100));
va11.push_back(make_pair(0, 100));
va11.push_back(make_pair(0, 100));
va11.push_back(make_pair(0, 100));
va11.push_back(make_pair(0, 100));
va11.push_back(make_pair(1, 3));
va11.push_back(make_pair(1, 1));
va11.push_back(make_pair(1, 0));
va11.push_back(make_pair(1, 1));

va12.push_back(make_pair(0, 100));
va12.push_back(make_pair(0, 100));
va12.push_back(make_pair(0, 100));
va12.push_back(make_pair(0, 100));
va12.push_back(make_pair(0, 100));
va12.push_back(make_pair(0, 100));
va12.push_back(make_pair(0, 100));
va12.push_back(make_pair(0, 100));
va12.push_back(make_pair(0, 100));
va12.push_back(make_pair(0, 100));
va12.push_back(make_pair(1, 1));
va12.push_back(make_pair(1, 0));
```

```
    // put the twelve va vectors into iVect
    // to form the iVect adjacency matrix
    iVect.push_back(va1);
    iVect.push_back(va2);
    iVect.push_back(va3);
    iVect.push_back(va4);
    iVect.push_back(va5);
    iVect.push_back(va6);
    iVect.push_back(va7);
    iVect.push_back(va8);
    iVect.push_back(va9);
    iVect.push_back(va10);
    iVect.push_back(va11);
    iVect.push_back(va12);

    // use iterator to point to start of vectors
    p = iVect.begin();

    int i, j, k;

    // determine minimum distance between vertices
    // using Floyd's algorithm
    for (i = 0; i < VecDim; i++)
        for (j = 0; j < VecDim; j++)
            for (k = 0; k < VecDim; k++)
                 if ((*(p + j))[k].second >= ((*(p + j))[i].second
                                              + (*(p + i))[k].second))
                   (*(p + j))[k].second = (*(p + j))[i].second
                                              + (*(p + i))[k].second;

    // print distance information to the screen
    for (j = 0; j < VecDim; j++)  {
        for (k = 0; k < VecDim; k++) {
            if (((*(p + j))[k].second != 100) &&
                ((*(p + j))[k].second != 0))
                cout << "From vertex " << j
                     << " to vertex " << k
                     << " the minimum distance is: "
                     << (*(p + j))[k].second << endl;
        }
        cout << endl;
    }
    cout << endl << endl;

  return(0);
}
```

The heart of this STL implementation still revolves around the three `for` loops discussed earlier in this section.

```
// determine minimum distance between vertices
// using Floyd's algorithm
for (i = 0; i < VecDim; i++)
    for (j = 0; j < VecDim; j++)
        for (k = 0; k < VecDim; k++)
              if ((*(p + j))[k].second >= ((*(p + j))[i].second
                                          + (*(p + i))[k].second))
                (*(p + j))[k].second = (*(p + j))[i].second
                                          + (*(p + i))[k].second;
```

The key difference between this example and the array implementation discussed in the previous section is the use of pointer arithmetic for gaining access to vector information. This technique was used extensively in Chapter 11. This process is further complicated by the use of STL pairs. Recall that the information we need for this application is contained as the second element in a pair, hence, the syntax

```
(*(p + j))[k].second ...
```

The advantage of using a vector of vector pairs is that both the vertex and edge information is immediately available in the application. Perhaps you will want to create an application that will do a breadth-first search on the graph before using Floyd's algorithm to determine minimal distances.

The output from this application is identical to that shown for the Floyd algorithm implemented with an array.

Summary

In this chapter you learned a good deal of information about graph theory. You have also seen six complete coded examples for depth-first, breadth-first, and Floyd's algorithm implemented with traditional C++ arrays and STL vectors.

Once you have learned how to manipulate graph information, as we have discussed in this chapter, you will find that the implementation of other algorithms associated with graphs is not that difficult.

Index

A

J

K

L

M

N

Q

R

S

T

U

V

W

X

Y